JN
6518
D88

D1443404

# THE DYNAMICS
# OF SOVIET POLITICS

*Russian Research Center Studies, 76*

DOUGLAS COLLEGE LIBRARY

# THE
# DYNAMICS
# OF SOVIET
# POLITICS

EDITED BY

Paul Cocks

Robert V. Daniels

Nancy Whittier Heer

Harvard University Press

Cambridge, Massachusetts

and London, England 1976

DOUGLAS COLLEGE LIBRARY

Copyright © 1976 by the President and Fellows
of Harvard College

All rights reserved

Printed in the United States of America

*Library of Congress Cataloging in Publication Data*

The Dynamics of Soviet politics.

(Russian Research Center Studies ; 76)
Includes index.
1. Russia—Politics and government—1953–
—Addresses, essays, lectures. 2. Kommunisti-
cheskaia partiia Soveiskogo Soiuza—Addresses,
essays, lectures. 3. Decision-making in political
science—Addresses, essays, lectures. 4. Power
(Social sciences)—Addresses, essays, lectures.
I. Cocks, Paul, 1941–      II. Daniels, Robert
Vincent. III. Heer, Nancy Whittier. IV. Series:
Harvard University. Russian Research Center.
Studies ; 76.
JN6518.D88          320.9′47′085          76–21667
ISBN 0–674–21881–7

*To the*
*memory*
*of*
*Merle Fainsod*

# Contents

# PART ONE

Problems and Perspectives

# Do We Know All There Is to Know about the USSR?

## ADAM B. ULAM

1

Some would deem this question absurd and so it is. And yet our strategists of research, the foundations and academic institutions in this country, have for some time acted on the assumption that there is little new and exciting that we can learn through further study of those interrelated phenomena, Russia-the Soviet Union-Communism. So much money has been spent, we are told, on training experts, on filling up "gaps in our knowledge" concerning things Russian. Isn't it about time to direct our attention and resources to problems of greater urgency and relevance: the Third World, the urban problem, education? Some would argue that the original impetus toward Russian studies came with the Cold War. Now this war has been replaced by a lukewarm détente. Anyway, we have trained enough experts, thank God, and we don't need more.

And on another level this feeling is being echoed by the despairing would-be student of Soviet affairs. What is he going to work on? Tolstoy and Solzhenitsyn, the current dissidents, and nineteenth-century Populists, the Tsarist administrator, and the Party secretary—they all "have been done." Monographs and doctoral dissertations have proliferated, leaving seemingly but nooks and crannies to be explored. After more than thirty years the sense of excitement, the pioneering spirit appears to have departed from Soviet and Russian studies. What is ahead but the plodding effort to retrace the path already traveled by others, hoping against hope that here and there we shall be able to discover a shortcut, correct an occasional misstep?

And yet this very feeling is a good testimony of how far we are from having reached scholarly maturity concerning Russia and the Soviet Union. For in scholarship as in life it is a trait of adolescence if not indeed of childhood to have our interests directed by a passion for novelty and a search for thrills. And so this defeatism about the future of Soviet and Russian studies reflects a certain immaturity of American academic life in general and of our social sciences in particular: we tend to seek new and dazzling techniques of dubious validity and to forget that valuable innovations and breakthroughs are most often produced by the patient accumulation of "old" knowledge and experience. We strain at being "relevant" and forget how often a useful invention is a product of sheer intellectual curiosity. Yes, Virginia, there is a lot to be done in Soviet studies; it is those whose horizons have become filled by research grants and consultant fees who do not see it, for their hearts have become hardened and they are unable to experience the joy of sheer scholarship.

But even from the crassly utilitarian point of view, much remains to be done. Do we know enough about the ideology and society which have come to affect our own everyday lives? Do we understand them from the perspective of an intelligent layman, or can a specialist analyzing Soviet politics, economy, or society be confident that the already-existing body of literature yields enough data for a meticulous analysis? A cursory look at our press and our learned journals will provide enough to say "no" to both of these questions. We need to know more; and the knowledge we do have has to be constantly reappraised in view of new data.

Stereotypes and oversimplifications still abound. Some years ago Senator Humphrey, then up and coming among Democratic politicians, paid a call on Mr. Khrushchev, then still in power. The latter ruminated on his unhappiness with the Chinese Communists, and he observed that they neglected the need for material incentives in their economic policies (this was the period of the Great Leap Forward). Mr. Humphrey shared with his American readers his surprise: he had not known (and he used to be a practicing political scientist) that Marxism believed in material incentives.

We certainly need to know more about Marxism and about its vicissitudes in Russia and China. Marxism remains one of the most discussed and written-about subjects within the international intellectual establishment of the West. And yet even at its very summit the essential meaning of the doctrine is but dimly perceived. Mlle. De Beauvoir is not atypical but only more frank than many intellectuals of the Left when she writes in her autobiography: "I made no distinction between Marxism and any other philosophy to which I had become accustomed," and confesses the extent of her endeavor to find out what it was that she so fervently believed in: she was prevailed upon to read *Das Kapital,* and "A new day dawned upon my world at the instant that I saw labour as the source and substance of all values."

Yet if acquaintance with a person's childhood is important for the understanding of the adult, so a thorough familiarity with Marxism, and not merely with "young Marx" or "alienation," must precede a deciphering of the meaning of the Soviet or the Chinese Communist experiment. We do not make up for this deficiency by venturing on a study of contemporary Russia and China armed only with the latest theory of bureaucracy, of underdevelopment, or of postindustrial society. They all may help, to be sure, but the knowledge of the beliefs and passions in which those experiments were conceived remains indispensable. One may object and point out that it is at least doubtful that Brezhnev ever read much Marx, or that Mao remembers much of what he has read. But can we form an adequate picture of the present condition of Western civilization without understanding the Christian experience? And so with Marxism and current problems of Communism.

If we can still usefully and pleasurably study a subject like Marxism, in and on which more has been written than we can hope to read in our lifetime, what shall we say about other dimensions of Russian-Soviet studies? Well, the foundations and despairing would-be writers of doctoral dissertations notwithstanding, room still exists for good and interesting work in practically all directions. In fact, part of our optical illusion that further digging will bring but negligible yields arises precisely from various deficiencies of previous explorations. No one reading Gibbon's *Decline and Fall* when it first appeared could have concluded that, since there was now a "definitive work" on the subject, further study of the Eastern Empire would be both unprofitable and unexciting and one ought therefore turn to subjects of current relevance. It is a frequent characteristic of a first-rate work that it poses more interesting questions than it solves, challenges its readers to different interpretations, and most of all—by demonstrating the inherent fascination of the subject—invites further study.

But putting aside such homilies, we can see from even a cursory look at the existing literature that much interesting and important work remains to be done. The Soviets' secretive ways hamper the endeavors of the Western Sovietologist yet by the same token ought to make the latter's work more intriguing. It is not unscholarly but on the contrary challenging to scholarship of the highest kind to try to reconstruct the past or to portray the present on the basis of incomplete and imperfect data; it is only when we have no data and fail to label a speculation as such that we sin against the cardinal tenets of scholarship. But the Soviets' reluctance to provide us with facts or the tendency to color data with propaganda has never been as great an impediment to scholarship as is commonly assumed, has never set up an unbreachable barrier to research on several important topics of the past and the present. Occasionally, as between 1960 and 1965, the Communist Party archives release some of their secrets and provide us with the means, as yet not fully exploited, to rewrite and reinterpret many crucial periods of Soviet political and economic history. Since Khrushchev's fall his successors have tried to put the lid on the Pandora's box which he had opened, but in post-Stalin Russia such efforts can never be entirely successful. The exigencies of contemporary Soviet society make it imperative that the discussion of social and economic issues facing it must continue to be freer and hence more informative than before. In the last few years some illuminating Politburo or Central Committee minutes of Stalin's or even Khrushchev's time might well have been put through a shredder, but the Western sociologist and economist continues to benefit through his Soviet confrere's research and discussions. No, contemporary Russia is not an enigma wrapped up in a puzzle, it is a fascinating field of study, insufficiently unwrapped, alas, from deadening stereotypes and ideological preconceptions.

Since the essays that follow are by students of a man who was a political scientist and historian, they represent but one aspect of past and present Soviet reality, though perhaps the dominant one. (We cannot agree with our Marxist counterparts that politics is always or even mostly a handmaiden of economics.) Hopefully these essays point up how much can be learned by careful and intensive scholarship about the workings of a system that does not publicize its inner workings, where there are no licensed opposition, no prying congressional committees, no indiscreet newspapermen to dig out the facts. What is offered here are but samples illustrating their authors' major scholarly concerns. But they point up how much work can and must be performed just to establish a plateau from which scholarship on Soviet politics can grow free from the encumbrances of those stereotypes of which I spoke. The vigorous and devoted labor of a handful of scholars following the model of the man to whose memory these essays are dedicated has not yet dispelled the atmosphere of sensationalism and exoticism surrounding the subject of Soviet affairs.

Has the intelligent layman in the West come to understand the Russian Revolution the way he has absorbed the essential meaning of the French Revolution or of the American Civil War? Of course not. We have had some very good and perceptive studies of the momentous event. But since they appeared, we have been presented, again ultimately courtesy of Mr. Khrushchev, with a plethora of new facts. And of course our perspective has changed, for in the last few years we have come to *feel* what a revolution is about, and in our own bailiwick, not just read about it. Even within our once sheltered academic life we have encountered quite a few Kerenskys and an occasional Makhno, but perhaps fortunately, no Lenin.

At the near end of the time scale we can now see much more vividly how the Soviet Union is being governed than in the days when the vast country was ruled through mystification as much as by anything else, when the tyrant in the Kremlin kept his closest collaborators, not to mention the Soviet public or the outside world, ignorant of his basic motives and designs. We can perceive the basic dilemmas of the Soviet administrator more clearly than in the days when many official statistics were systematically falsified and when the most fundamental problems of political and economic organization were veiled in mystery and double-talk. And some of the things which the government still refuses to tell us are being supplied through the writings of Soviet dissenters. Soviet Russia is still very much a closed society, but we can now appreciate much better its complexity. We can now eschew those ritualistic and oversimplistic questions which used to color and distort Soviet studies, for example, "Are the Soviet rulers motivated by the ideology or by power considerations."

Concerning foreign policies, hitherto the most secretive aspect of Soviet government insofar as policy-making is concerned, we are in a position to profit greatly by the assiduous if somewhat malicious kibitzing that the Chinese Communists pursue over the shoulders of their dear Kremlin colleagues. It is amazing how little use has been made in the West, whether by scholars or governments, of this often invaluable source of information. True, one must not believe everything the Chinese have said about the Russians (or vice versa); still, we are being provided with a lot of "leads" and helpful hints for our own endeavors.

This brings us to another and potentially fruitful line of study. Is it possible to understand Mao's China without a thorough knowledge of Stalinist and post-Stalin Russia? To be sure, there are vast differences but also striking similarities. No one who has read Chou

En-lai's speech at the Tenth Chinese Party congress, asserting that further internal crises and struggles are inevitable, could fail to be reminded of Stalin's famous dictum that the closer one gets to socialism the sharper becomes the character of the class struggle. The extent to which problems of other Communist societies and parties are affected by the historical experience and the present position of the Soviet Union is again a subject of vast dimensions and one which we have hardly begun to explore in depth.

And so, much of what has already been done ought to be done again and better, taking account of our more ample information and experience. There also are fresh and enticing subjects beckoning to the contemporary political scientist, urging him to moderate his passion for abstract models and methodology and not to neglect the living reality of a hugely important and interesting political system. It is not superfluous to stress the importance from the national point of view of a continued and vigorous growth of Soviet studies in this country. Whatever the future of Soviet-American relations, what happens in Russia will continue to be one of the determinants of U.S. foreign policy, and not only toward the USSR. Soviet developments will continue, as in fact they have since 1945, to affect our daily lives. And so we do need to learn much more about Russia, and the foundations of that knowledge must come not from news dispatches, travelers' observations, the columnists' homilies on dissent in the USSR or on the coup the Soviets pulled in the grain deal, but from the patient and unremitting labors of the scholar.

# PART TWO

## Political Leadership and Power

# Political Leadership
# in Soviet Historiography:
# Cult or Collective?

## NANCY WHITTIER HEER

2

The cult cannot be regarded as a collection of phenomena concerning Stalin alone. The cult was a negation of Leninism. The cult must be ridiculed and suppressed. It is essential to reestablish in every particular the atmosphere of the first years of Soviet power—simplicity and approachability . . . There is no need for a cult of Khrushchev or Bulganin or anybody else. There is no need for a Lenin personality cult either.

*Political Diary,* no. 30 (March 1967), as quoted in *Survey,* Summer 1972, p. 213

The structure and style of leadership remains one of the most elusive elements of any political system. For the USSR this proposition is a truism. Our knowledge of the Soviet political elite consists fundamentally in what that group wishes to display—a bare stage set which must be furnished out of clues and props in the memory and imagination of the observer.

But this is not new in Russia. The legacy of Tsardom is a tradition of mystical, secretive autocracy, wielding an arbitrary power which could occasionally serve progressive ends but which all too frequently degenerated into intrigue and fanatic brutality of legendary proportions. Against this backdrop was played out a culminating revolution both populist and Marxist, spontaneous more than "scientific," of gigantic scope—for which the Communist Party has subsequently taken full historical credit.

Since the Bolshevik triumph the Russian autocratic heritage has become interwoven with Marxist concepts as well as Leninist and Stalinist practice, to form the intricate pattern of Soviet leadership. The interrelationships of these strands are now so complex and so obscured by official semantics and doctrinal rationale—to say nothing of the intentional and unintended distortions and confusions produced by the furtive style of Kremlin politics—that the precise nature of leadership continues to elude scholarly definition. Direct information, interviews, the quantitative data of voting patterns, the speculations of a more open press, must be compensated in part by indirect or refracted sources. The most obvious danger is that of distortion and misperception of this partial information; the only sure correctives would seem to be continual checking against whatever open factual materials exist, and a large dose of humility. One important refracted source of insight into contemporary and perhaps future political questions concerning the leadership is Soviet political historiography, which can be valuable as a mirror of actual events as well as a clear view of official explanations and doctrinal interpretive theories about politics. With a state-controlled press and academic establishment, published historiography becomes not merely a record of happenings but an official mythology and the foundation of public aspiration.

## THE FUNCTIONS OF SOVIET HISTORIOGRAPHY

Elsewhere the author has developed the thesis that, given the particular systemic restrictions and demands for ideological orthodoxy placed upon historians—as well as the very special role assigned to history itself by Marxism-Leninism—historical writings in the Soviet Union have come to perform vital sociopolitical functions of a degree and scope perhaps unique and certainly beyond those found under other political systems.[1] These functions may be categorized as formal (officially stated) ones and those informal (publicly unacknowledged) ones that operate by virtue of the very nature of the Soviet political system. In the first instance, Soviet political history is formally charged by Party and state to be the repository of Soviet tradition and legend—specifically and especially for the education of the youth—and to act as exhorter and agitator promoting approved behavior by the masses. Among the informal functions of Soviet historiography we may count legitimation of the Party and the entire state bureaucratic system, and rationalization of their policies. Official Soviet histories are attitudinal prisms through which the current leadership projects its own political intentions upon past heroes and their deeds. The story of Stalin's career could thus be used as a political weapon by Khrushchev against his own rivals. In this category of unacknowledged functions there are also some usages of history unintended by the regime. History is perceived by the reading public as well as the elites to be a barometer of the actual (as distinct from the advertised) political climate and a clue to future shifts. It can also become a vehicle for covert ideological and political discussion among elite groups and historians.

Soviet historiography, in carrying out its official didactic and legitimating mandate in a closed ideological environment, has come also to invade forbidden precincts. By holding up a mirror of an idealized past in which the citizenry is to read the record of Lenin and the early years as a morality play of heroic progress, Party historians are also displaying ideal standards against which subsequent leaders are to be judged and perhaps condemned. Whether the judgmental function is performed intentionally or inadvertently by various historians, Soviet history in this manner becomes a mode of conscience and a projection of the future. The performances and the ideas of victorious leaders are weighed not only against the "should have been" of historical materialism, but sometimes also against the "might have been" of forbidden political and economic alternatives advocated by their vanquished rivals.

Each historical personality—Trotsky and Bukharin as well as Lenin and Stalin—becomes a veritable magnetic field of Soviet politics, forever surrounded by the policies and attitudes that he promoted in life. Each one serves as a permanent representational device for a specific cluster of alternatives. For this reason discussions in both published and underground historiography concern not only the leader personally; they also implicitly revive political issues long since exorcised as "anti-Party," "revisionist," or "petty bourgeois." Thus for Khrushchev to unmask Stalin at the Twentieth and Twenty-Second Party Congresses was to repudiate very specific policies of terror. Similarly, before the Twenty-Third Congress early in 1966 when rumblings of top-level rehabilitation of Stalin were abroad, fiery protests sent to Brezhnev and the Central Committee urged renewed denigration of Stalin to symbolize continued toleration of liberal intellectuals.

THE CONTINUING CULT OF LENIN

There are several sound reasons why the role of any individual leader, and indeed the whole question of political leadership and its relationship to the Party rank and file and the population, pose enormous and perhaps insoluble difficulties for Soviet historians and social theorists. The Marxist theoretical denial of the personal hero, and reliance on class struggle as the locomotive of evolutionary change and revolution; the regime's avowed determination to reject the Tsarist history of personal autocracy; the nightmare experience of Stalinism; Khrushchev's attack on the personality cult as anti-Leninist; and the continuing worship of the person of Lenin are facets of this conundrum. Ironically perhaps, Marxist historical scholarship has facilitated the most compelling and persistent heroic legends of this century: Lenin, Stalin, Mao. In the Soviet Union, the cults of Lenin and Stalin stand in inverse and interdependent relationship to one another, one cult rising at the expense of the other, manipulated by the contemporary leadership for its own glorification. The cult of Mao increasingly replaces that of Stalin as the prime example of distorted leadership, at a more comfortable distance.

It must be observed that the adulation accorded Lenin in the mass media and large-edition history texts and ideological pamphlets, as well as in more serious and select professional journals and historical studies, has since 1964 remained at essentially the pitch of frantic intensity to which Khrushchev brought it.   The praise of Lenin has increased steadily since Stalin's death, accentuated by the 100th anniversary of his birth in 1970. Undeniably habit and inertia combine with other elements to perpetuate the worship of Lenin. But his successors find the cult positively useful: the verbal references peak during the succession crises of 1953–1955 and 1964–1965 to promote a public image of solidarity among a quarreling elite group and then to legitimate the victories first of Khrushchev and then of Brezhnev. At any time, reference to the words and actions of the dead founder can serve not only to sanctify the innovative policies of later leaders and help discredit attacks from ambitious rivals, but also to blur responsibility and mask the real origin of specific controversial policies and programs.

Lenin—like Stalin in earlier years—appears in many guises in historical literature. He is omnipresent in Soviet historiography: the revered leader of a quasi-religious cult, revolutionist, unique party organizer and administrator, socialist theorist and creative adapter of Marxism to Russian conditions, historian of the early years and the

Revolution, and the final role model for all socialist revolutionists, theorists, and political leaders to come.

But if the historical Lenin can be used as a primary authenticating source for the political leadership, this gigantic figure created by the regime can also be useful to revisionist historians and political dissidents. Several political programs and critical tracts appearing in samizdat contend that their proposals for socialism and communism, not those of the Party, deserve Lenin's mantle.

Unique in samizdat literature is the powerful attack on Lenin mounted by Solzhenitsyn. The Lenin portrayed in *Gulag Archipelago* is the logical historical predecessor of Stalin, rather than his antithesis. It was Lenin who created the institutional machinery of the Cheka to eradicate his opponents; Stalin only took this course to its logical end. Acceptance of Solzhenitsyn's historical account would, of course, destroy the Lenin cult and indeed the legitimacy of the Party. There is not only official antipathy to Solzhenitsyn's view of Lenin, but also a good deal of resistance among samizdat writers, many of whom reject the historical interpretation of Lenin presented in *Gulag*.

STALIN'S PLACE IN HISTORY SINCE 1964

The fate of the historical Stalin and his cult is quite another matter, since 1956 a torment to all concerned. Much has been made by some observers of an alleged re-Stalinization of history to pace a tightening of domestic policies by Khrushchev's successors, but the facts do not bear this out. There has been an effort to drain the whole issue of Stalin's leadership of the heavy emotional charge and vitriolic abuse generated by Khrushchev; and this has been accomplished in part by some "positive" evaluations, notably of Stalin's actions during the war. But there has been no restoration of the cult of his person nor a reelevation of his rank to historical superhuman.

Any decision as sensitive as the reappraisal of top leaders must, of course, be signaled and carried to the mass media by the political elite itself; Soviet historians do not take unlicensed initiatives in this area, although demonstrably some are capable of probing interpretive actions during periods of elite uncertainty or conflict over the historical image of Stalin.[2] The low-key treatment of Stalin by Khrushchev's successors can be observed in all official, that is published, histories of the Party; the best indicator is probably the six-volume *Istoriia kommunisticheskoi partii sovetskogo soiuza* now being issued under the auspices of the Central Committee through the Institute of Marxism-Leninism. Volume 5, book 1, deals with the period of high Stalinism, the years after the Purges, and World War II (1938–1945), and was published in October 1970. This particular version of Stalin's leadership could hardly be more authoritative or responsive to the wishes of the current political elite; moreover, it treats that period of Stalin's rule most susceptible to patriotic feelings: the war years. Yet Stalin, while not the devilish monster of the Secret Speech, remains essentially a negative figure.

Stalin appears in this account visually only twice, and in both instances as part of a group: seated at a round table with Roosevelt, Churchill, and numerous aides at the Crimea Conference in 1945 [3] and at the center-front of a large group photograph of the victorious Soviet military leaders taken in March 1946.[4] The book's index shows twenty-six entries under his name, many more than accorded any other individual then alive, but less than half the number given to Lenin. Most references are in connection with foreign rather than domestic policy; many show Stalin's name in alphabetical order, as one of several members of some Party body. Other citations refer in a brief and factual manner to some new wartime appointment, a piece of international correspondence, or a report given by him.

A tremendous furor was stirred up among historians and Party ideologues in 1966 and 1967 by the Nekrich study of the beginning days of the war,[5] which charged Stalin's guilt in the unpreparedness of Russia. As far as the new Party history is concerned, this debate might as well not have happened. Two or three bland sentences tell the reader that Stalin, buying time to prepare for war, did not order the military onto an active footing for fear that the Nazis would use this as a pretext for attack. This lack of action, the account reads, was perceived by the armies near the Western frontier as a reflection of the lack of danger—hence their complete surprise at the Nazi advance.[6] This circuitous bit of reasoning presumably absolves both Stalin and his commanders from any charges more serious than miscalculation of Hitler's timetable; but no explicit interpretation or judgment of any kind is made. This version, apparently adumbrated in late 1965,[7] is the product of a slow and at times harrowing process of discussion among historians in journals and conferences, published military and diplomatic memoirs, samizdat sources, and a stream of official accounts. It seems now to be generally adopted as the official formula.

Neither stupid nor actively guilty, Stalin nonetheless is no hero. Never does he emerge as the towering, guiding, symbolic, military figure in command of the fate of the country. His name appears just often enough to make the account barely accurate in factual terms;

but the contrast to Western historical treatments of Roosevelt and Churchill is marked. The glory for victory is clearly ascribed to the Party as a disciplined and dedicated whole, rather than to Stalin personally or as a popular leader. For Nekrich, incidentally, the heroic force of victory was the ordinary Soviet people.

This volume of the *Istoriia* contains no index entry to the cult of personality, but the reader is certainly alerted to its evils: for example, in a section dealing with the strengthening of Party organizations on the eve of the war, we read that "the course of further development of internal party democracy would have seen much greater successes had not the Leninist norms of party life been broken by the so-called cult of personality of Stalin." [8]

The historical appraisal of Stalin is quite literally a time-charge explosive on three levels—first, the immediate *political* danger that the Secret Speech presented to his little circle of rivalrous successors; second, the continuing debate among historians and ideologues over the precise nature and extent of Stalin's crimes as they relate to contemporary *policy* alternatives; and third, the surfacing of some unintended and ultimate *systemic* questions as to the legitimacy and basic nature of the Soviet polity. I have touched on the first two, which are in any case evident from the flow of events. For some insights into the third and most obscure aspect of the discussion of Stalin, we need to turn to unauthorized sources.

A far darker portrait of Stalin than the faceless bureaucrat of the post-Khrushchev histories continues to emerge from underground literature. Attacks on Stalin as the anti-Lenin, the ravager of Soviet society, were removed from the political and historical press even before Khrushchev's ouster; and the strongly negative historical portrayals which peaked in 1961 and 1962 were finally forced out of the literary journals as well with the curbing of *Novy mir* in 1965.[9] But samizdat historiography has maintained the denunciation of Stalin at a high pitch. It is as impossible to deny the social and political impact this stream of history has on legally published accounts as it is to specify and quantify the precise points of contagion. Roy Medvedev's major analysis of Stalin,[10] completed in 1968 and published only in the West, can be seen as an attempt to use historical evidence in documentation and judgment of Stalin's rule; it is also a political argument about the nature of socialism. The book can be read as a monumental scholarly footnote on Solzhenitsyn's remarkable poetical explication of the tyrant seen briefly late at night in his Kremlin office.[11]

Medvedev is especially interesting because he attempts to deal seriously with the dangerous question at the center of the quarrel over Stalin's ghost, the question only hinted by most Soviet historians. Was Stalin historically inevitable? He rejects as too simplistic a series of variants on the classical Marxist historical thesis which argue that certain specifiable economic and social preconditions for a socialist revolution were absent in Russia of the twenties, creating a fatal lag that foreordained the Stalinist bureaucratic repressions. History, for Medvedev, seems to run on probabilities, possibilities, even accidents; this is, of course, a profoundly non-Marxist, even anti-Marxist, position. "I proceed from the assumption that different possibilities of development exist in almost every political system and situation," [12] he tells us. Thus, Lenin's early death reversed the order of immediate probabilities from "the victory of genuinely democratic and socialist tendencies" to the triumph of Stalin.[13] In the larger sense, however, he reverts to the standard Manichean dichotomy: "It was an historical accident that Stalin, the embodiment of all the worst elements in the Russian revolutionary movement, came to power after Lenin, the embodiment of all that was best." [14] Moreover, any one of several leaders of the twenties and thirties could have led the Party forward "much faster and better than Stalin." [15]

Why, then, is Medvedev's analysis unacceptable to the regime and its censors? The answer would seem to lie in his rambling and unsystematic attempt to explain the very process of Stalin's usurpation of power. "The cult did not spring up overnight"; rather, Medvedev insists that the cultist atmosphere and religious psychology spread upwards from the Party membership as a whole—inculcated with the notion of Party infallibility—to members of the Politburo, until by the end of the twenties almost every local chieftain was supported by a regional personality cult.[16] Finally, Stalin topped them all on his fiftieth birthday in December 1929.

There is a complex causality at work in Medvedev's account: a reciprocal and mutually reinforcing relationship between the cult and Stalin's well-organized terror. The dreadful fact is that "not only the punitive organs but the entire Party and government *apparat* participated actively in the campaigns of the 1930s." [17] The continued silence of those Bolsheviks who one after another saw where Stalin was leading; and the absence of any significant resistance from Party officials, or the remnants of the Mensheviks and Essars, surrounded Stalin with a conspiracy of silence until 1956.

At a meeting in early 1966, historians discussing A. M. Nekrich's controversial study of World War II, *22 June 1941*, reportedly raised similar questions about the ultimate origins and responsibility for the Stalin cult, pushing beyond the individuality of the leader to probe the system that spawned him: "Because of us, the little people, Stalinism began . . ."[18] To ask whether Stalin's guilt was total or limited is still a typical attitude of the personality cult. One is still concentrating on Stalin. We should look into the problem more deeply . . . We must analyze the process which allowed Stalin, who was not equal to his task, to become head of the Party and the state, with unlimited powers." [19] This is essentially the task that Medvedev took upon himself as part of his historical analysis.

In blaming the Party—and the political opposition—Medvedev stops just short of explicitly calling in question the one-party system, *any* one-party system.

Stalin's destruction of all opposition groups was not, as some dogmatic historians claim, a "great victory" . . . It was precisely in this period of "unprecedented unity" that Stalin adopted a policy of mass crimes, which damaged the Party so badly that it has not yet fully recovered . . . And the opposition itself shares a good deal of the responsibility. The tragedy of the Party was not only that a man like Stalin led the Central Committee in the twenties but also that the opposition was led by men such as Trotsky, Zinoviev, and Bukharin, who could not offer an acceptable alternative to Stalin's leadership.[20]

Here is a rather sophisticated treatment of the problems of the twenties, in which the issues of the quality of leadership, Party structure, and the role of opposition groups are conjoined. Medvedev seems to be advocating a kind of loyal Leninist opposition at least within the Party, because very real social benefits accrue from viable political alternatives. In so doing, of course, he is implying an ideal model of leadership for mature socialism, and suggesting that Lenin tolerated or could have developed such a pluralist type of leadership had he lived into a more stable political period.

HISTORICAL DISGUISES AND DISCUSSIONS OF POLITICAL QUESTIONS

It is in the attempt to specify the correct Leninist stance toward other individual leaders and the political groups and parties on the left, that the Soviet historian—whether his work is published or circulated as samizdat—encounters more general political issues, such as the proper Party structure to ensure internal democracy and nonauthoritarian leadership, the nature and origins of the single-party system in the USSR, whether there is any acceptable scope and positive role for political competitors or opposition groups in a socialist system. And, as is usually the case in Soviet historiography, open exploration of these difficult questions takes place in historical journals and the small-edition monographs as a prelude to (or perhaps instead of) the modification of popular histories. These articles are in effect the public professional conversations among historians and Party theoreticians about Party leadership, and they have presented some interesting facets during the past few years.

### The Non-Bolshevik Opposition

Ever since the 1956 Burdzhalov heresy, which raised the issue of Bolshevik-Menshevik cooperation in 1917 and demanded a more accurate portrayal of the Mensheviks during the revolutionary period,[21] historical judgment of the Bolsheviks' rivals on the left has been undergoing spasmodic scholarly revision. It seems that as we move from right to left—from the Right Essars, to the Mensheviks, to the Left Essars, and the Trotskyites—we pass into ever darker precincts. The appraisal of these parties has not altered appreciably from that set out during the Khrushchev era, and has followed the general trend toward depersonalization of all historical actors. We are now grappling with bumbling and antagonistic socialist parties, movements, tendencies; not the giant figures of Trotsky, Zinoviev, and Bukharin who in themselves personified evil for Stalin's historians. Evidently the political groups on the left are more denigrated because they represent political alternatives which are considered to be still dangerous in the contemporary world of the 1970s.

There continues in the historical journals a pattern of steady and serious research on the opposition parties of the left, an effort marked by notably improved sourcing and methodology. There is evidently being built up a body of research as well as the beginnings of more sophisticated political categories regarding political parties. Reporting on a conference held in late 1971 on historiography of the October Revolution, one noted authority expresses pride in the accomplishments of Soviet historians despite the fact that "the ideology and politics of bourgeois and petty-bourgeois parties . . . have been widely studied only in recent years." A number of studies using "a rich documentary basis" have concerned themselves with the following aspects of these parties: ". . . their activities in Russia, their ideologies, policies, aims, social base, composition, class interests . . . their interconnections . . . the struggle of V. I. Lenin and the Bolsheviks against their anti-popular policies." [22]

Another, more conservative historian puts forward a definition of political parties that includes the class factor, but as only the last of three categories: (1) definite programs and aims, (2) an organized and centralized leadership, (3) a class basis. He cautions that despite the Leninist principle that "parties reflect class," the basis of any party is not class interests, but the objective and material factors of class *identity*. Individual party leaders and members do not always correctly perceive the appropriate class interests, and thus some party platforms carry goals inimical to their class—as for example the Russian socialist parties frequently championed national and religious causes while trying to appeal to the working class.[23] If political parties (except, of course, the Bolsheviks) do not always follow their class interests, analysis of the political scene even in Russia of the early twentieth century is much more complicated than Soviet historians have hitherto believed.

As would be expected, there is considerable difference of opinion among specialists over the extent to which the bourgeois parties can be, or should be, studied as focal points in themselves. At least one of the most prolific and prestigious historians of these parties is willing to argue that they deserve independent analysis in the interest of developing "many aspects of the contemporary world revolutionary process, the correct definition of tactics of the working class and Marxist-Leninist parties." He denigrates the former practice of discussing the bourgeois parties only "in the course of showing the struggle of the Bolsheviks against these parties." [24] Very interesting, in terms of the subject at hand, is the less schematic treatment of the structure and leaderships of these parties which is emerging in some studies. As historians delve into local archival materials, at official urging, they expose a picture of political forces that does not fit any neat stereotype or periodization.

## Opposition within the Party

Not only the elites of other parties, but the Bolsheviks themselves, are revealed as internally split over key issues—particularly in relation to the soviets; and often the central elite is at odds with regional leaders and the rank-and-file.[25] One striking example should perhaps be noted here: a careful detailing of the split within the Rostov Bolshevik leadership that occurred on the eve of the October Revolution and persisted afterwards.[26] The issue was the extent to which cooperation with other local party organizations was permissible. The Central Committee line allowed for cooperation only with the Left Essars; but several Bolshevik leaders in Rostov and elsewhere in the

Don area are shown as eager to work with the Mensheviks and Right Essars as well. These disobedient leaders are not passed off as either traitorous or stupid; rather they emerge as strong men who seriously differed with the center in their appraisal of local conditions. Indeed, their reasoning is spelled out quite fully.

By contrast, Trotsky remains outside the pale of credible political alternatives. His policies were too outrageous, his person dictatorial and egocentric. But he is no longer portrayed as having sold out to capitalism to betray the Russian people. From a simple opportunist, he is said to have developed into a committed proponent of his own coherent program in opposition to Lenin. A new feature in some published discussions is the focus on his leadership style, now presented as one of his most glaring sins. The key concept in party organization for Trotsky is seen as "centrism," or personal authoritarianism—the antithesis of democratic centralism—which inevitably results in intrigue, splitting, and political adventures. This aspect of Trotskyism, as well as his ideas of permanent revolution and notions of the effects of economic backwardness on the building of socialism, are accorded a more sophisticated and detailed (if not objective) treatment than they received even a few years ago. There is evident concern to argue substantively against Trotsky's policies and to analyze what one writer calls the "class and ideological sources of Trotskyism as a political force," rather than merely to denigrate it as demonic cunning.[27] It is Trotsky as the intellectual force behind Mao, even more than the historical Trotsky, who remains a threat.

### Bolshevik Hegemony and the One-Party State

The matter of the historical place of the non-Bolshevik left is, of course, very intimately linked with the whole process of Bolshevik monopolization of power, or to use the Soviet phraseology, the formation of the single-party system in the USSR. Gone is the very abbreviated Stalinist historical account, which asserted that the unmasking of rival leaders and parties as anti-revolutionary in 1917 and 1918 was almost immediately followed by public rejection and their destruction as political factors. The Soviet public is now told that while this is quite true with respect to right-wing parties, several socialist parties continued on the political scene for some months after the October Revolution, until they too repudiated the policies of the Bolsheviks and lost popular support.

Behind this rather bland formula in the mass-edition histories and reference works is a lively debate in professional circles. With respect to the precise instant when the Bolsheviks acquired absolute hegemony in the Soviet state and the related issue of their methods, there are virtually as many opinions expressed as there are investigators. In general, earlier dates are put forward by historians who come down hard on the other parties, while longer post-Revolutionary periods of multiparty coexistence and even cooperation are described by more liberal scholars. Three examples in historical journals may point this up. The most orthodox of these relies chiefly on Lenin's recounting of events and places blame on the anti-Revolutionary policies of the opposition itself for its failure. The author states flatly that objective conditions (the repudiation by the Left Essars of their alliance with the Bolsheviks) created a single-party state as early as the second half of 1918.[28]

Documented tabulations on eighty-eight local soviets are presented in quite a different type of article, also in a historical journal, which discusses the disagreement among Party historians over the growth of Bolshevik power in the soviets.[29] Guseinov quotes Academician I. I. Mints as claiming an absolute majority of 250 Bolshevik and sympathetic deputies in the Moscow Soviet as of March 1917, which is contradicted by data showing that not until June 1 (1917) did this bloc reach 230 members. He is cautious in taking on a man of the power of Mints, but his work is meticulous and shows clearly that in many instances the Bolsheviks required the support of the Left Essars and non-Party delegates at least until October.

Even more revisionist of the standard popular treatment is the third example to be cited, which provides quite a bit of verbal analysis and commentary along with statistics.[30] Gimpelson explains that studies of the Bolshevik sharing of power are needed to refute bourgeois fabrications of Bolshevik "seizure of power," and he mentions that Lenin never took the position that a one-party state was necessary during the dictatorship of the proletariat; rather, Lenin expected the participation of other parties during the transition period. He shows that in many soviets the Left Essars held the key fraction—up to 30 percent of the deputies—until the summer of 1918, and that they and other parties continued to oppose the Bolsheviks legally even after they were excluded from the soviets in 1918. His is a much more complicated picture of the various parties and their internal splits than is usually found in the literature. On the basis of tables of percentages of local and all-Russian soviet memberships from 1918 to 1922, Gimpelson concludes that not until 1922–1923 were the Bolsheviks in sole command of the soviets. The elections of 1920–1921 were the turning point to a single-party Soviet state.

The matter holds some historical interest, for it begins to clarify a murky picture of the early years of the Soviet regime and its gradual extension of power to the hinterland. In addition, it carries real political significance because Lenin's personal presence at the helm during these early months or years encourages the presumption that he at least tacitly tolerated a multiparty system, and possibly approved it in principle. The implicit question becomes: if Lenin anticipated an indefinite period of peaceful competition for popular support among socialist parties during the dictatorship of the proletariat, could not the prerequisite conditions equally well occur or recur under mature socialism? If Stalin imposed a mistaken rigidity upon the interim period following the Revolution, perhaps the fierce Bolshevik hegemony during full socialism may also have been his personal anti-Leninist error. As Stalin's crimes have shaken the idea of Party infallibility—despite the best precautions of the regime—so his theoretical mistakes may in time come to be used by reformers to erode the Party's claim to monopoly of power.

### The Possibility of Legitimate Political Opposition

Lenin emerges from recent official Soviet historiography as a leader unwilling to stoop to Stalin's methods of dealing either with opposition parties, or with such rivals as Martov outside the Party and Trotsky the enemy within. There is never any doubt in these historical narratives that the Bolsheviks will win power in the twenties, but the setting has become more political than military, and the struggle is now peopled with not mere saboteurs, but opponents capable of challenging Lenin's political skills.

An outstanding utilization of the early Soviet experience and the figure of Lenin to further a political argument, as well as to make a specific historical interpretation, occurs in a volume of essays put out by the Philosophy Institute of the USSR Academy of Sciences.[31] The essay contributed by Plimak caused considerable ferment precisely because of his unorthodox treatment of the question of political opposition, both as a philosophical and a historical phenomenon. Although other essays are criticized, Plimak's Chapter 6, "The Leninist Approach to Intra-Party Disagreements (On the Basis of Materials of the Seventh and Tenth Congresses)," has come in for a great deal of critical attention. According to his critics, Plimak commits several distinct but related sins. These can be very briefly summarized as follows:

(1) Plimak "does not always correctly characterize Lenin's posi-

tion"; that is, he shows similar or identical policies of the Bolsheviks and their rivals within the Party. Thus Lenin's stand on a revolutionary war in April 1917, before the Brest Treaty, is made indistinguishable from that later espoused by the Left Communists.[32]

(2) Plimak leaves the distinction unclear between criticism of the Party by the intra-Party opposition and "reasoned" criticism (sources of such approved criticism are not specified).[33]

(3) He offers his interpretation of gnoseological roots of the views of oppositionists to explain—even to justify—actions which were objectively wrong. "In the interpretation of E. G. Plimak one finds that the opposition stood on party positions, but obsolete ones, and for that reason Lenin blamed them not for their views, but only because they applied 'non-Party, alien means of solving differences.' "[34]

(4) Plimak goes further and offers sociopolitical reasons for the rise of opposition groups within the Party, none of which reasons are in the framework of Marxism-Leninism. The reviewers charge: "In the opinion of the author, the 'workers' opposition' arose to a great extent as a reaction to the growth of the bureaucratic tendency in the management of the economy." [35]

(5) Most serious of all, Plimak makes an implicit argument for toleration of political dissent by citing Lenin's mild treatment of the worker Kutuzov, who had joined the workers' opposition, commenting, "Lenin specifically explained the necessity of such a constructive approach to the opposition . . ." [36] One wonders whether in fact Kutuzov would have been so gently dealt with if he had been a rival leader of stature rather than a simple worker. It is thus impossible from this passage to say that Plimak sees Lenin's approach to internal and external opposition leaders as the same. He does not introduce the example of Lenin's rather gentle treatment of Martov.

(6) The critical article notes disapprovingly that the author "explains differences within the party as natural and unavoidable, saying they were 'completely natural to the life of the party and the direction of the revolutionary process.' " [37] This argument would imply that intra-Party disputes are an integral part of the historical dialectic, enabling the Party to make correct policy choices among alternatives. It occasions a long passage from the reviewers, which cites several sources to prove that Lenin saw oppositionist views as detrimental and dangerous to the Party's revolutionary mission.[38]

As part of the campaign against the *Leninist Methodology* volume, the Bureau of the Division of Philosophy and Law of the USSR Academy of Sciences organized a huge "discussion" in May of 1970, attended by three hundred persons. From the published account, the twenty-eight speakers had some disagreements but the general tenor of the meeting was sharply critical of several chapters, including that by Plimak. His response was to consider reformulating the issue of his essay in light of the discussion—in terms of the opposition's "narrowness of theory, especially as perceived by several figures at a moment of gigantic broadening of revolutionary practice. This may show itself in their continuing to adhere to old slogans or persist in mistaken concepts . . ." [39] Surely any recasting by Plimak of point 3 above is of form rather than substance. And in the process of discussion meetings and journal articles touched off by this volume the question of the proper limits for political opposition within the Party has been ventilated to an unusual extent.

COLLECTIVE LEADERSHIP AS A HISTORICAL MODE

In line with the slogan of Stalin's successors, "Back to Leninism!" there has been great emphasis placed on collective leadership and inner-Party democracy, which is presented as the historical pattern of Party organization in fact, as well as its ideal norm. Stalin's unique contribution to leadership theory, if mentioned at all, is quickly disposed of as a temporary and rather unimportant aberration. When one searches for clues as to the relative standing of the lesser angels and devils of the past, a significant trend becomes apparent. Now, rather than the careful group pictures of leaders around Lenin and Stalin—in the tradition of Russian Orthodox iconography which ranked the Church fathers visually by the precise location of their images in relation to the central figure of Christ—we find in official histories of the Soviet Union and the Communist Party the faces of ordinary workers, soldiers or peasants, rank-and-file Party members, or middle-rank bureaucrats and regional Party functionaries. Individual portraits set in rows across the page, rather than the politically revealing groups, predominate. This is pictorial evidence of what can only be termed the depersonalization of Soviet history, begun during Khrushchev's ascendancy and intensified under his successors: the strange obscurity into which all former leaders save Lenin have been swallowed. Nor have the figures of Brezhnev and Kosygin grown to gigantic size to replace earlier heroes.

The stress on collective leadership may be seen as the positive aspect of the post-Stalin historical mop-up operation, and one that has remained a constant feature since 1953: Khrushchev's efforts at self-aggrandizement in the histories produced during his tenure never attained the proportions of a cult, nor is Brezhnev playing this game.

But Mao's personal leadership is frequently cited in historical sources as a horrifying counterpoint to the Leninist model of Party democracy.

One writer makes an interesting linkage of collectivity with infallibility by asserting that Lenin thought "only collective leadership . . . would protect [the Party] from serious mistakes." [40] This means not just that the substance of Stalin's policies was wrong, but that his method of policy-making in itself created errors. Pushed to its ultimate conclusion, such an observation calls for some kind of institutionalization of collective leadership for the Party.

SOME CONCLUSIONS

As with other dimensions of Soviet policy, the Brezhnev leadership has attempted to cast aside the passions and excesses of the Stalin and Khrushchev periods and strike a more rational and coherent posture. It is not the less difficult stance for being undramatic. While continuing to repudiate the evils of the personality cult, the top Party spokesmen have made amply clear their rejection of ideological coexistence and their intent to silence dissenters—including historical revisionists, defined as those who "by definition, reject the leading role of the Communist party . . . [who] deny any necessity in that leadership . . . [and whose position] is supported by bourgeois ideology and all antisocialist elements." [41] As long as the détente and stepped-up trade with the West continue abroad, the regime may be expected to push ideological conformity at home, as its first line of defense against contamination from increased foreign contacts and influences. Despite this hardening, the post-Khrushchev regime has increased the number of trained historians, their publications, and their organizational and research base.[42] The historians are functionally useful to the Soviet leadership—whether despotic or collective—as legitimizers and educators. But they can be dangerous in the long run even while ostensibly fulfilling short-term tasks for the leadership. And their suggestive portrayals of past leaders, particularly the various oppositionists, remain on the record as a reminder of past political alternatives.

# Permitted Dissent in the Decade after Stalin: Criticism and Protest in *Novy mir*, 1953–1964

DINA SPECHLER

In the excitement about the voluminous underground or samizdat writing that has surfaced in the Soviet Union since the mid-1960s, the literature of dissent that preceded it, published in the journals of official institutions, has been largely ignored or forgotten. Yet the appearance of this "permitted" dissent constituted an equally, if not more important, phenomenon in the development of the Soviet regime and society. It indicated a major change taking place in the political system. It significantly altered our conception of totalitarianism and raised serious doubts as to the appropriateness of that term for the Soviet Union. The emergence of this dissent formed a necessary preliminary to the current samizdat activity: the regime's tolerance of public criticism both emboldened those with grievances and raised their hopes for possible reforms. Moreover, for the student of Soviet society the public dissent permitted in the first decade after Stalin provided an acquaintance with the outlook of a sizeable portion of the intelligentsia. The views expressed were not, for the most part, the original ideas of those who voiced them, but opinions that had already acquired a substantial following.[1] To Western observers this dissent offered a different and important perspective from which to evaluate the Soviet system—the perspective of those who lived under it and best knew its strengths and shortcomings. Finally, the dissent of 1953–1964 appeared at the time to have won sympathy and exerted influence in high places.[2] It may yet be a force for change—at least in such spheres as cultural policy and economic administration, if not in other areas of the political system.

This essay examines the major and most consistent voice of dissent in 1953–1964, the literary magazine *Novy mir*. It describes the content, targets, and apparent motives of that dissent and the way in which they evolved over that decade. At the same time it tries to demonstrate the limits within which the dissenters had to work—the rules which the writers, critics, and editors had to obey and against which they periodically rebelled. It also shows how, and speculates why, these limits differed at different times.[3]

APRIL 1953–AUGUST 1954: RIGID RESTRICTIONS, DISSENT UNDETERRED

Stalin's death in March, 1953, had no immediate effect on *Novy mir*. An analysis of the issues that appeared in the months after that event reveals little one would call dissent. Such an analysis does, however, provide considerable insight into the requirements that continued to be imposed on writers and editors by Stalin's successors. One can see that the vast majority of the stories and articles enunciated certain criteria and conformed closely to them. These resembled, not surprisingly, the literary and artistic standards proclaimed by Party Secretary Andrei Zhdanov and later pronouncements applying his policies in 1946–1948 and 1951–1952, and might therefore be called "Zhdanovite criteria." They related primarily to the content of fiction, poetry, plays, and essays, yet they also included prescriptions for literary technique. They comprised the limits within which the first dissent of the post-Stalin era had to be expressed.

*Zhdanovite Criteria for Content and Technique*

For a year and a half after Stalin's death, and particularly from April through October 1953, a clear demonstration of ideological-political orientation was apparently required of *Novy mir* contributors. The writer, it seemed, had to state his position on any question of ideology or current policy his work touched on. When he failed to do so, an editor stepped in to supply the missing declaration. The contributors seemed to be obliged to make at least some characters obvious spokesmen for themselves and to endow these characters with correct ideological and political viewpoints, no matter how this marred the characterization.

The *Novy mir* editors of this period were careful to include a display of *partiinost* ("Party spirit") in every issue and most individual works. The Party was depicted as omniscient, omnipresent, and infallible, responsible for all the great accomplishments of the Soviet Union from the Revolution to the present and supremely sensitive to the needs and interests of the masses. Party members and especially leaders were paragons of virtue who placed service to the Party and the people above all personal goals.

A requirement often articulated and consistently observed by *Novy mir* was that all essays, stories, and even poems contain an educational message. Writers were reminded that their purpose must be "to educate and transform man in the spirit of Communism," that they were "the engineers of human souls." The stories they turned out provided clear lessons concerning, for example, the moral superiority of the laboring classes and their historic vanguard, the inevitable outcome of the worldwide conflict of progressive versus reactionary forces, and the advantages of socialism.

The rejection of bourgeois culture and values and the espousal of Soviet patriotism also seemed to be mandatory. The *Novy mir* articles dealing with the work of Western writers treated their ideas as bankrupt at best, savage at worst, an insidious source of infection threatening the healthy socialist society. Works on the Soviet Union, its culture and people had, on the other hand, to be effusively complimentary. The achievements of the Soviet system were enumerated at great length, and intense pride in them was evinced by authors and characters alike.

The *Novy mir* contributors were apparently obliged to convey a sense of optimism and of progress, to instill in their readers the conviction that life was moving forward and tomorrow would be brighter than today. Essays and reviews preached the importance of optimism, and stories embodied it. Writers were warned that "the philosophy of *Weltschmerz* is not our philosophy," that their disposition must be bright and joyful. Only citizens of dying and moribund societies had the right to grieve, it was asserted.

Stories or articles centered around any time other than the present were extremely rare. Writers were told to focus on "burning" contemporary issues and problems. Nothing, one infers, could be allowed to distract the reader from the tasks at hand.

Most *Novy mir* works in the year and a half following Stalin's death prescribed or conformed to certain criteria of literary technique, as well as of content. The most important of these was the employment of pure character types rather than complex or contradictory figures. Individuals were usually endowed with an impressive set of essential attributes and attitudes, uniformly good or bad from the regime's point of view. Everything about the character was shown to result from these essential features, and he was readily identifiable as a model of good behavior or a suitable target for attack. The author's attitude toward these character types was unambiguous: sympathetic to the good, hostile to the bad. Moreover, these types had to be presented in the proper proportions. There had to be both positive and negative types, but there could not be too many of the latter, and they could not be the center of the story. They were transient figures who would not long remain part of Soviet life and could exert little influence on it.[4]

## Dissent within the Limits

As restrictive as these rules were, writers in the first year and a half after Stalin's death found ways to criticize the regime without flagrantly violating them. Their "dissent within the limits" was of two general types. The first might be called *social pragmatism.* The authors described serious defects in various parts of the Soviet system, then attempted to analyze their consequences and causes. Their apparent concern was with the efficiency of the system: they were alarmed by its failures or shortcomings and wanted to make it work better. The second general type so closely resembled a major style of nineteenth-century Russian fiction that it might legitimately be called *critical realism.* In this instance the focus was not so much the system itself as its impact on the lives of the people. The authors seemed primarily concerned that the system be just and that it bring happiness—prosperity, security, personal fulfillment—to those who lived under or participated in it. The function of these essays and stories was to expose the injustice inflicted and unhappiness created by the system.

Between June 1953 and August 1954, a group of stories that belonged to one or both of these general types was published in *Novy mir.*[5] These works collectively mounted a thoroughgoing attack on the Soviet system of rule and administration in the economic sphere. They examined conditions on Soviet farms, enterprises, construction sites, and technical research institutes, found them deplorable, and looked to the bureaucracies and the men who held power in them as the source of the problems they saw.

The defects in the system of bureaucratic rule and administration cited by the *Novy mir* authors were legion. Centralization of power and decision-making had been carried to ludicrous extremes, they charged. The result was that most important policies were made by people who had no knowledge of the conditions in which they would be applied; uniform policies were foolishly imposed in the most diverse circumstances; and all initiative and creativity was stifled at levels below the central authority. Innovation was systematically discouraged, the *Novy mir* writers maintained, because only with the approval and resources of the center could new discoveries and inventions be put to use. Those who could authorize their application were either indifferent—unwilling to be bothered, timid, and afraid to take risks or committed to the status quo. But it was not merely new proposals that were thwarted. By the sheer complexity of their structure and procedures the bureaucracies tended to obstruct action of any kind. A multiplicity of authorities, each of whom had to be consulted, was responsible for every aspect of production, procurement, and distribution. No administrator could act on his own; each had to obtain the approval of, and submit endless reports to, associates and superiors. Countless man-hours that should have been spent in productive activity were wasted on checking and inspecting.

The bureaucracies in agriculture and industry were shown to be as inept in recruiting and assigning personnel as in their daily operations. *Novy mir* contributors V. Ovechkin, G. Fish, and G. Troepolsky decried what they saw as a pervasive tendency to appoint and keep on incompetent cadres. This was partly due to faulty selection criteria: officials placed too much emphasis on academic knowledge and certification, rather than practical experience or familiarity with the locality. More typically they disregarded formal criteria altogether and selected or retained unqualified personnel on the basis of friendship or other personal ties. The presence of ignorant, inexperienced, and inept managers was made all the more serious by forces in the system of economic administration which consistently led to wrong and harmful decisions. There was, for example, constant, extreme pressure for favorable reports. Yields were reduced, crops destroyed, and fields ravaged because officials, harassed to show quick results, compelled their subordinates to take irrational shortcuts.

Certain features of the system of rule and administration were criticized as much because they were dishonest, unfair, or humanly destructive as because they were economically unsound. One of these was the pretense of democratic decision-making. While much was said about the vital role of the "collective" in deciding production questions, workers and peasants were never allowed to participate in the resolution of important issues. Writers like Ovechkin and Troepolsky were ashamed of and embarrassed by this hypocrisy. *Novy mir* contributors also despised the ritual of criticism–self-criticism repeated regularly at kolkhoz, enterprise, and institute meetings. At its most innocuous, Troepolsky showed, the practice was an absurd formality —an occasion for making lavish displays of feigned contrition. But it also could be devastating to a person's self-confidence and integrity: Bek and Loiko's characters were forced to repudiate their most deeply held views to keep their jobs and salaries. Similarly repulsive to *Novy mir* writers was the atmosphere of suspicion pervading the system of economic administration. Officials in the works of Ovechkin, Zalygin, and Tendriakov automatically regarded one another and the people they supervised as swindlers or saboteurs. The characters in these stories thus lived in constant fear, knowing their most innocuous error could bring on accusations of "wrecking" or "criminal negligence."

The new works of social pragmatism and critical realism were left uncondemned by the literary and political authorities and were, in fact, generously praised in the press.[6] This success was a tribute to the authors' political skill. While attacking important Soviet institutions, they managed to convey a strong sense of their loyalty to the system and their faith in its ultimate success. They adroitly chose their targets of criticism, focusing on problems that the new leadership recognized and was eager to solve.[7] Thus they did not appear to violate the Zhdanovite criteria and did not antagonize the regime.

*Protest against the Limits*

Not all the *Novy mir* contributors were content to work within the established limits, however. A small number of them,[8] possibly encouraged by the journal's chief editor, Aleksandr Tvardovsky,[9] apparently saw Stalin's death as an opportunity for them safely to challenge those limits. Their protest against the Zhdanovite criteria belonged to the third major type of dissent to appear in *Novy mir* in 1953–1962. This type might appropriately be termed *cultural liberalism*. The authors of this dissent sought the loosening or removal of restraints on both the producers and the consumers of culture. They tried to show that the existing restraints harmed these groups and why this was so. They fought to make the entire Soviet cultural heritage and that of the West accessible to Soviet citizens.

In the most important example of this type of dissent in the year and a half after Stalin's death Vladimir Pomerantsev[10] argued that the chief criterion of the quality of a literary work was not the Zhdanovite principles, but the sincerity of the author. He was willing to accept the idea that literature should educate the reader, but most of the other Zhdanovite criteria he either explicitly or implicitly rejected. He showed, in effect, that when they were imposed on writers by literary critics and officials, they led to distortions of the truth (thus to departures from sincerity) and hindered the writer's efforts to educate his readers.

Critics have so often chastised writers for creating characters which are "not typical," Pomerantsev complained, that Soviet literature has been inundated with pure types—superheroes who do not speak but deliver orations, who have not human motives, but Stakhanovite impulses. These are not believable characters who can hold the reader's interest; they are so dull they drive the reader away, convincd he can learn nothing from books. Moreover, Pomerantsev intimated, a writer could neither express his sincerity nor provide any insight into real life if he tried to observe a preordained proportion between positive and negative phenomena. "The shortcomings of life and human vices cannot be 'elements' of plays and novels," he wrote. "And one cannot balance them with other 'elements' . . . love of labor, kindness, optimism, and so forth. An artistic production must be organic, not constructed out of the positive and negative." [11]

Pomerantsev implicitly suggested that critics must not impose on writers the criterion of correct ideological orientation, when this is taken to mean blind acquiescence to the policies of the regime. The authorities could be quite wrong, for example, in their views of what would promote progress toward Communism, and writers must point this out if they are to contribute to that progress. Similarly, if rejecting the Party's definition of truth in favor of the writer's own implied deficient partiinost, Pomerantsev apparently wanted critics to tolerate such a violation of the Zhdanovite criteria. Moreover, the critic must not, in the name of partiinost, compel writers to pretend that the Party was without faults or that its cadres were uniformly the most valuable members of society. Pomerantsev condemned critics who demanded patriotism in a literary work. He deplored the "embellishing" of Soviet reality, a practice typical of writers wishing to avoid the reproach of being "antipatriotic." He took critics to task for insisting on contemporary focus in novels and stories. This, he claimed, led to a kind of encyclopedic fiction in which political, technical, economic, and other facts abounded, but people and their experiences were neglected and the thoughts and emotions of the author omitted.

The reaction to *Novy mir*'s expression of cultural liberalism was swift and strong. In articles in the press, speeches, and discussions with writers, Party and literary authorities made it known that the Zhdanovite criteria were still very much in force and that writers and editors who opposed them were committing a grave political error. The *Novy mir* editors were told that in printing Pomerantsev and the other cultural liberals they had "used the pages of [the] magazine to attack the ideological foundations of Soviet literature." For this sin chief editor Tvardovsky was dismissed in August 1954.[12]

If Party and literary officials were so clearly determined to prevent any challenge to the prevailing restrictions, how is it *Novy mir* could publish these works in the first place? One can only speculate that Stalin's death created a very special situation. It would appear that the new leadership, preoccupied with nonliterary affairs, failed to indicate what its cultural policy would be, and the conservatives who dominated the Writers Union and censorship apparatus were unsure whether they could continue to impose the old limits. Thus a courageous editor like Tvardovsky, too prominent a member of the literary establishment to be outvoted by his more conservative subordinates, was able for a brief period to test the intentions of Stalin's successors.[13]

SEPTEMBER 1954–DECEMBER 1956: EFFORTS AT COMPLIANCE, UPSURGE OF DISSENT

*Novy mir* responded to this reimposition of the Zhdanovite criteria with a tactical retreat.[14] It resumed publication of the first two types of dissent, social pragmatism and critical realism, to which the regime had not objected, and which could readily be expressed without challenging or seriously violating the Zhdanovite rules. Now, moreover, the authors employed several devices to reduce the sting of their criticisms. They tended to avoid suggesting the causes of the problems they exposed, thus protecting themselves against possible charges that they disparaged the government's policies. Often they set the date of the story or essay in the past and failed to indicate whether the phenomena criticized still persisted. By condemning the situation in agriculture compared to industry, they paid an indirect compliment to the achievements of the latter and indicated that improvement was possible in the former. In addition, the primary targets of attack were now subjects about which the regime had invited discussion and indicated dissent was permissible: the shortcomings of the men who administered agriculture (as opposed to the system of administration) and of the work of the Party in training and appointing supervisory cadres in that field.

As the months passed *Novy mir* submitted less and less to the Zhdanovite restrictions. In the wake of Khrushchev's Secret Speech to the Twentieth Party Congress in February 1956 it ceased altogether to do so. The assault on the Stalin cult by the First Secretary was taken as a sign that the Zhdanovite limits would no longer be enforced. They were, after all, a legacy of the Stalin era. Would they be retained when so much else in that period was being repudiated?

Once again there was a resurgence of cultural liberalism in the pages of *Novy mir*. The new chief editor, Konstantin Simonov, and a well-known literary historian, A. Metchenko, employed a new and clever strategy to discredit the Zhdanovite criteria. They argued that socialist realism, the style prescribed for all Soviet writers, did not require the writer to conform to any particular standards. It was only under "the period of the personality cult" that what was originally a descriptive concept was erroneously transformed into a normative one. In fact, "socialist realism [was] not a collection of aesthetic dogmas, not a normative aesthetics." Did it require anything at all? Only "belief in socialism and faith in its victory." The Zhdanovite rules could be ignored, Simonov implied, so long as this minimum criterion was met.[15]

In the months following the Twentieth Congress the *Novy mir* editors felt free to publish protests against the persistence of Stalinism in numerous areas of Soviet life and society. A new type of dissent appeared, which might be called *moral humanism*. This was moral protest against the character of Soviet society—the goals it proclaimed and sought, the sort of men it produced, and the kinds of relationships that existed among them. For the authors of this type of dissent the individual human personality was the highest value. But unlike the critical realists they were not primarily concerned with the happiness, prosperity, or security of the individual or the ability of the government to promote these things. They wanted man's spiritual worth to be recognized, his moral sense to be developed and refined, and his capacity and will to do good to be strengthened. They attacked what they saw as the failure of Soviet institutions and ideology, shaped in the Stalin era, to put these matters right.

An example of this fourth type of dissent was the protest against the dishonesty that the humanist writers believed had come to pervade Soviet life. They described instances of dishonesty in the Party, ministries, and press, in literature, scholarly journals, research institutes, and schools.[16] While most of the contributors seemed unable to explain why it arose and persisted, D. Granin made an effort in this direction. In a story entitled "One's Own Opinion" he analyzed the bureaucratic pressures that gave rise to dishonesty and the psychological processes that sustained it. His young engineer Olkhovsky discovered that a new engine designed by a renowned academician was extremely uneconomical. He wrote an article demonstrating this defect and sought the support of his superior Minaev to get it published. Neither Minaev nor the bureaucrats in the numerous state and Party agencies to which he subsequently appealed would help him. Privately they acknowledged Olkhovsky was right, but publicly they acted as if his arguments were groundless. "Why should we print a scientific article that is caustic or controversial?" he was asked. "We might have to answer for it, we might be rebuked for it. But if we turn the article down, no one will ever hold us responsible." Knowing suppression of the truth thus could be explained, Granin indicated, by its never being penalized in Soviet bureaucracies.

Moreover, Soviet citizens had developed reliable mechanisms to assuage their consciences. Minaev told himself that once his promotion was confirmed, he would support Olkhovsky: "[Then] he'd be able to maintain his own opinion against anyone at all. It wasn't enough just to have opinions. You had to be in a position to do something about them. Such thoughts usually soothed Minaev. They always arose obligingly whenever events took an unpleasant turn." [17] Minaev's promotion didn't change things. "A certain instinct which he had developed over the years held him back from a premature attack on [the powerful academician]. He needed to consolidate his position." In fact the same thing had happened to Minaev (and not only to Minaev) many times before. It had always been too early to be honest.

Granin believed that three psychological states or processes combined to bring about dishonesty on the part of Soviet bureaucrats. One was lack of faith in the power of truth, unaided by position or status, to convince people and win allies. The second was self-deception. A person could imagine he was devoted, at least inwardly, to truth, when in fact he was devoted to nothing more than his own career. The third was belief in the innocence of silence, of keeping quiet while others told what one knew were lies. Thus someone could avoid overt falsehoods and assure himself that he had maintained his own views in spite of all pressure. "Silence," Granin declared, "is the most convenient form of lying. It keeps you at peace with your conscience; it craftily preserves your right to withhold your personal opinion on the grounds that someday you will have a chance to express it." [18]

Another aspect of Soviet society condemned in *Novy mir* was its materialism. Vladimir Dudintsev delivered the strongest criticism of this phenomenon in "Not by Bread Alone," his story of a tenacious physics teacher who overcame an endless series of bureaucratic obstacles to get his design for a pipe-casting machine accepted.[19] Dudintsev created and contrasted two main types of characters, representing two sorts of personalities found in Soviet life and institutions. One was the materialist—either a consumer, preoccupied with acquiring and enjoying material goods, or a producer, dedicated to providing more and more goods for his own and others' consumption. Dudintsev was contemptuous of the consumer who, he said, was "mankind at its worst, always striving to seize as much as possible and always corrupt. Once [he] gets hold of something, [he] immediately grows fat and bloated with a snout instead of a face." He also detested the producer, who believed the most valuable human quality was "the ability to work well, to create the greatest possible quantity of necessary things." Why was the materialist so despicable? Because of his exclusive pursuit of goals unworthy of the human spirit, of what Dudintsev called "first-floor values," because he lived for and by bread alone. It was the second type of character that received Dudintsev's approval. This was the inventor, the sort of man who could not be made happy by a car, a nice apartment, or a bedroom suite, but only by the freedom to use his imagination, to innovate and to perform challenging and fulfilling labor.

The inventor was for Dudintsev a prophet, a man who had a true vision of what Communist society could be like. The materialist, "whose heart [was] in the good things of life," "expect[ed] from Communism merely the filling of his belly." But the inventor knew that the essence of Communism was not increased consumption, that in fact "under true Communism many objects of crazy luxury, born out of the idleness of the rich, will be abolished." He saw that the essence of Communism lay in the substitution of free creative labor for alienated work (routine tasks performed not for their own sake, but for the sake of consumption). As Dudintsev's inventor-hero Lopatkin put it, Communism would not be a time when he could get things for himself, but when there would be nothing to prevent him from freely giving of himself.

In what sense was all this an attack on the regime—its policies, institutions, or ideology? Dudintsev condemned the regime for lauding and rewarding men of the first type. Materialists were allowed to dominate the bureaucratic hierarchies in science and industry. They were given power, prestige, and secure jobs, while men of the second type —inventors, who represented the best potentialities of Soviet society— were shunted aside, ignored, or repressed. The regime also encouraged a materialist outlook, advertising the joys of consumption on "huge household insurance poster[s]" and luring citizens with "objects of crazy luxury." At the same time it failed to provide what was really important to the human spirit, opportunities for creative labor. Only outside of official institutions—factories, research institutes—could Lopatkin and his like-minded friends find it. Worst of all, the regime failed to see that this was what it should provide in the society of the future. It inferred from Marxist doctrine only a mandate "to expand the material basis" and create a Communism of abundance. (One character cited the *Short Course on the History of the Party* to bolster this interpretation of Marxism.) It thus neglected the true and morally highest meaning of Communism.[20]

The expressions of moral humanism appearing after the Twentieth Party Congress constituted a stronger type of dissent than the earlier social pragmatism and critical realism. Unlike the earlier dissenters, those of 1956 tended to make a special point of showing that what they were attacking were general and widespread phenomena, not single instances. The consequences of the regime's policies appeared to them more serious: in the stories of 1956 the lives of good men were broken, their talent destroyed, and their thought stifled, whereas in earlier works such people were usually only thwarted in their efforts to improve the system. The dissenters of 1956 tended to put themselves more squarely in opposition to the values and aims of the regime than their predecessors. Nothing comparable in its challenge to official goals had appeared previous to Dudintsev's rejection of "goulash" Communism. Similarly, some of the regime's proudest claims, such as its ability to produce a new, more moral Soviet man, were questioned in 1956. The system of economic administration, whose inefficiency and lack of humaneness were attacked in 1953–1955, was not, by contrast, so great a source of pride for the post-Stalin leadership. Finally, the works of 1956 were much more pessimistic than those of 1953–1955. They described lone individuals who opposed the evils they saw, but found no coherent groups or social forces that might ultimately eliminate them, whereas the earlier stories and essays usually expressed the faith that the shortcomings they reported could be eliminated.

The upsurge of dissent in 1956 was short-lived. At the end of the year literary authorities, later joined by top Party leaders, initiated what became a violent campaign of abuse directed against the cultural liberals, the moral humanists, and ultimately the *Novy mir* editors as well. Once again the attack was made in terms of the Zhdanovite criteria. Simonov, it was said, displayed a grave deficiency of partiinost. His redefinition of socialist realism was a "politically immature" attempt to cast doubt on the correctness of the Party line in literature.

Granin had been inexcusably pessimistic and derogatory in his treatment of Soviet reality. Dudintsev's "dramatic poetization of asceticism" was an unacceptable ideological deviation: he had scorned "the lofty social ideal" of Soviet society. Furthermore, he had failed to balance his numerous "warped" and negative characters with positive heroes of the proper sort.[21]

It is hard to say whether the content alone of these works provoked the attack on them. One cannot ignore the fact that they stimulated an unprecedented outpouring of verbal dissent and expressions of sympathy within the Soviet literary community and received considerable attention from the Western press. There is evidence that important literary officials were greatly perturbed by this. Moreover, the dissenting pieces were printed just before the uprisings in Hungary and Poland. We know that these events alarmed the Soviet leadership, as did the role that disaffected intellectuals played in them. Quite possibly dissent that would otherwise have seemed harmless appeared quite ominous in the light of the upheavals in the Bloc. Perhaps it was not so much the authors' violation of the Zhdanovite criteria that led to a new enunciation of them as the reception the works received and the timing of their publication.

## 1957–1959: RETREAT AND RECOVERY

The campaign against *Novy mir* lasted until the middle of 1958. During this period (January 1957–June 1958) dissent virtually dropped out of the magazine altogether, and *Novy mir* reached its nadir as a liberal organ in the decade after Stalin. Dissent had been possible, apparently, only so long as the top leadership as a whole, or at least a powerful individual, had been willing to tolerate it. Now this was no longer the case. Although his speech to the Twentieth Party Congress had played a major role in encouraging the new upsurge of dissent, by early 1957 Khrushchev was in a far less tolerant mood. Personally frightened by the unrest in Eastern Europe, he also found himself in need of support from conservative Party and military officials against his Presidium opponents. Thus in a series of speeches to cultural figures he personally reiterated the Zhdanovite criteria and warned writers against misconstruing his Congress speech as a license to criticize. In this new political climate, a change in *Novy mir*'s policy was unavoidable.

In June 1958 Simonov was removed as chief editor, and the post was restored to Tvardovsky. His appointment was probably a sign that at least some portion of the top leadership was unwilling to stamp out dissent completely. At any rate, Tvardovsky chose to interpret it that way. Very slowly and cautiously over the next year and a half he began to reintroduce dissenting works into the journal. Examples of social pragmatism and critical realism and even hints of cultural liberalism began to reappear in small quantities. Ilya Ehrenburg employed Aesopian techniques to protest Soviet literary controls. His essay, "On Rereading Chekhov," was purportedly a study of the latter's work and views, but Chekhov's ideas were selected, arranged, and endorsed in such a way that they formed a systematic critique of the current regime's policy toward literature. Taking the dismissal of a number of conservative literary officials in the spring of 1959 as a sign of some liberalization in the attitude of the leadership, Tvardovsky ventured to publish some dissent of the fourth type—moral humanism. However, the most prominent of these works, N. Ivanter's "August Again," was sharply denounced in the press, indicating that the conservatives still had the regime's backing.[22]

## 1960–1964: DISSENT REVIVED AND SUSTAINED

The years 1960–1962 witnessed a striking resurgence of dissent in the pages of *Novy mir*. But unlike that of 1953–1954 and 1956 this new outburst of protest cannot be correlated with a change in the top leadership or a major policy declaration. Possibly it can be explained by the balance of power between liberal and conservative writers that emerged in this period, a balance in which the liberals held control of more key organizational and editorial positions than at any time since the 1920s.[23] To Tvardovsky this situation must have indicated an increased willingness on the part of Khrushchev, if not other top leaders, to let writers speak their minds. He was, apparently, courageous enough to embark on a new course without any clearer signal that it would be acceptable.

Critical realism and moral humanism reappeared, sometimes combined in a single work. The situation in the countryside was again a target of protest. This time, however, the emphasis lay less on the system of administration than on the piteous condition in which the regime's policies had left the peasant. There was a variety of new topics. Careerism, allegedly rampant in Soviet society, was exposed and attacked by S. Zalygin, V. Kaverin, and other contributors. N. Dubov and E. Rzhevskaia were two of many writers who sympathetically described the malaise of Soviet youth, portrayed as uninspired and even repulsed by the regime's goals and representatives. Zalygin and Kaverin, among others, dwelt on the conflict of generations in Soviet life. Despite official claims to the contrary, they showed this to be a very real and possibly insoluble problem for the regime.[24]

In questioning the wisdom of Soviet economic development and technological advance and in describing their harmful impact on the population, *Novy mir* writers criticized a fundamental ideological tenet and policy of their government. The worst thing about economic progress, several claimed, was the single-minded attention the regime had given it, to the exclusion of other vital social goals. The government had been indifferent to the aesthetic and emotional development of Soviet citizens, it had ignored and even thwarted their moral and spiritual growth. The Soviet people had been raised on a production ethic, Fomenko and Ehrenburg protested. They had been taught to scorn traditional virtues like honesty, concern for others, kindness. They had learned to think that the only things that mattered were results—projects built, plans fulfilled, and never the means by which they were obtained. The consequence of this upbringing was the alarming discrepancy that currently existed between the level of Soviet technology and the moral development of the Soviet people. "I have too often come across extraordinarily complicated machines and incredibly primitive men with the prejudices and crude reactions of cavemen," Ehrenburg exclaimed.[25]

Ehrenburg was responsible for much of the revived cultural liberalism and moral humanism expressed in *Novy mir* in the early sixties. He took it on himself to fill in what an earlier *Novy mir* contributor had called the "blank spots on the map of Soviet [culture]." As late as 1960 many of the great writers, playwrights, directors, and painters of the years immediately preceding and following the Revolution were still unpublished, unexhibited, and unmentioned or only alluded to abusively in some textbooks and encyclopedias. Ehrenburg insisted that their failure to meet the criteria currently imposed by the regime was no reason to censor the works of these artists or consign them to oblivion. In a series of vignettes, character sketches and literary and artistic analyses he and a half dozen other contributors brought to life people like Tsvetaeva and Mandelstam, Pasternak and Pilniak, Kirshon and Afinogenov—in all more than thirty cultural figures ignored or anathematized under Stalin. They also provided many readers with their first reasonably accurate view of the variety of literary, artistic, and dramatic schools that flourished after the Revolution and were later suppressed in the name of socialist realism.[26]

Along with a few other writers Ehrenburg resumed the attack initiated by Pomerantsev in 1953 against the Zhdanovite criteria. The group asserted the irrelevance of these rules as criteria of good art and their ultimate incompatibility with artistic creation. Going a good deal farther than Pomerantsev, they argued that not merely these particular rules, but any rules at all were inherently bad, and they urged an end to official control of what writers could write and readers read. All judgments in the sphere of art are relative, individual, and unstable; hence there can be no objectively or permanently optimum form, style, or subject matter, Ehrenburg insisted. Party control of the arts, he thus implied, was no more than the arbitrary imposition of the tastes of the current leadership. It was, moreover, an effort doomed to fail. As Ehrenburg saw it, to shape all art on a single model, to enforce "the monopoly of a single trend" was impossible. The urge to experiment was inherent in the creative process. One could, through terror, suppress it, but one could never extinguish it.

Ehrenburg found support in the writings of Lunarcharsky for the idea that "true freedom" should be granted the artist. V. Maksimovoi introduced an even more prestigious authority in support of this position. Citing a hitherto unpublished memorandum written by Krupskaia at the end of 1919, he demonstrated that she was strongly opposed to official censorship of literature. The Soviet regime, she maintained, did not know what the people needed or wanted to read, and it should let them decide that for themselves. Every writer should be guaranteed the right to present his work to the people—to have a certain number of copies of it printed. "We must not close the door," she wrote, "to any form of artistic creativity, no matter how naive or alien to current trends it may seem." [27]

In the years 1960–1962 *Novy mir* printed not merely bolder versions of the types of dissent it had published previously, but a new and fifth type, which might be called *historical revisionism*. While it had considered the general influence of Stalinism on Soviet life and society, the magazine had hitherto largely remained silent about Stalin himself and specific policies associated with him. Now for the first time it undertook the job of destroying the Stalin myth, of reevaluating the man and his works. *Novy mir* writers sought to show that the man who had been worshipped for over a quarter of a century deserved rather to be despised, that policies long considered great accomplishments or at least wise and necessary measures were in fact only sources of gratuitous suffering and grave harm to Soviet society, culture, and economic progress. Contributors attempted, too, to rewrite Soviet history, to put back into the record what was eliminated by Stalinist historians, to enter what they omitted and to excise their invented fictions.

Just as he had signaled to potential contributors in 1953 that he was willing to print expressions of cultural liberalism, so in May 1960 Tvardovsky published a poem in which he subjected the Stalin era to critical scrutiny and invited others who knew both "those years and these" to do likewise.[28] Those who did this in the next year and a quarter employed marked restraint and caution. They seemed hesitant to investigate any particular aspect of Stalin's rule too deeply. Some tried to say a good word about Stalin along with the bad. Generally they wrote in a veiled, indirect, or evasive manner, avoiding the use of Stalin's name and explicit references to the deaths he caused or other punishments he inflicted. In the fall of 1961, with the Twenty-Second Party Congress approaching, Tvardovsky apparently sensed that this caution was no longer necessary. Analyses became more extensive and bluntly critical; the "balancing" of Stalin's good and bad features was virtually abandoned; the language became unambiguous (writers spoke of Stalin, not "the cult," camps, not "there," deaths, not "repressions"), the range of sensitive subjects dealt with widened considerably and the volume of anti-Stalin works doubled.

With incredulity, anger, and horror writers such as Ehrenburg and Tvardovsky, M. Simashko and V. Lakshin attacked the style and methods of Stalin's rule and the character and attitudes of the man himself. They tried to give the reader some sense of the virtual limitlessness of Stalin's power, of the enormous range of affairs he personally directed or in which he intervened. They voiced their resentment at his inaccessibility and arbitrariness, at the irrationality of his decision-making and his disregard for facts. They described his terrible indifference to human beings—"mere puppies, nonentities too trivial to constitute the goal of his life." They attacked his megalomania and his chauvinism. They depicted his personal paranoia and the paranoid mentality he imposed on the whole of Soviet society.[29]

*Novy mir* authors condemned nearly all the policies for which Stalin had been reviled in the West, often in terms no softer and examples no less vivid than those employed abroad. E. Dorosh, E. Gerasimov, and V. Rosliakov exposed the brutality of the collectivization campaign and the massive loss of human and animal lives it entailed. Stalin's destruction of the creative intelligentsia was the subject of numerous works. Nekrasov, Ehrenburg, and Gladkov were among those who bitterly recalled the artistic bankruptcy experienced by those who tried to placate Stalin and the persecution and death that were the lot of those who could not do this. A. Solzhenitsyn, I. Bondarev, and M. Popovsky were a few of the many contributors who joined Ehrenburg in describing and analyzing various aspects of the terror: the groups who were its major targets, the role of the hated secret police in implementing it, the ordeals of its victims in prisons and camps, the devastating impact it had on all social relations and on the lives of everyone who lived through it. Stalin's foreign policies were severely attacked. Ehrenburg recounted his outrage at the dictator's delay in aiding the Spanish Republicans, at his prewar pact with Germany, and at his subsequent efforts to appease Hitler. Novelists Kaverin and Bondarev joined Ehrenburg and others in condemning Stalin's war policies: his failure to prepare the army and country for the Nazi attack, his crippling purge of the military and his responsibility for the massive slaughter both of civilians abandoned in occupied territory and of soldiers ordered to confront the invaders virtually unarmed. Indignation was expressed by Tvardovsky and Ehrenburg at Stalin's nationality policy—his wartime and postwar deportation of whole minority groups and his frenzied effort to wipe out Jewish culture.[30]

*Novy mir*'s denunciation of Stalin and his crimes, for all its thoroughness and passion, was not entirely original. Some of the phenomena the journal described and condemned had been attacked by Khrushchev himself at the Twentieth and Twenty-Second Party Congresses. Should one, then, still consider the *Novy mir* works dissent? I believe one should. In the first place, these works presented a devastating indictment of Soviet leadership, policies, and institutions. They reflected profound dissatisfaction with the society, values, and political system which had prevailed in the USSR for more than two decades—for nearly half the period in which the Soviet state had existed. Such writing by its very nature deserves to be called dissent, even if similar dissatisfaction was occasionally voiced from high places. Too, *Novy mir*'s exposé of Stalin and his era appears to have been unacceptable to highly influential men in the top leadership.[31] The anti-Stalin works constituted dissent against the views of these conservatives, subsequently dominant as to permissible ways to treat the Stalin years. Thirdly, Khrushchev had stressed that it was the exclusive responsibility of the Party to expose the excesses of the "cult of personality"; writers and artists were supposed to concentrate on positive aspects of the Soviet past. For *Novy mir* to take the function of critic on itself was thus an act of dissent against Khrushchev's proposed division of labor.[32] Moreover, the *Novy mir* works went a good deal farther than Khrushchev had gone. They cast aspersions on policies which, even after the Twenty-Second Congress, official sources still condoned (Stalin's policy in Spain, the pact with Hitler); they revealed facts the Party had been unwilling to admit (the widespread use of force against poor peasants in the collectivization drive, the scope of

Stalin's purge of the creative intelligentsia, the scale of the terror); and they made far more sweeping denunciations than could be heard from Party spokesmen (of police surveillance, for example, no matter how restrained, as a method of controlling the population). It should be remembered, too, that many of Stalin's policies, such as persecution of unorthodox writers, maintenance of labor camps for political criminals and discrimination against minority nationalities, were still being implemented when *Novy mir* attacked them. Thus the works in that journal may be read as dissent against the slow pace of de-Stalinization and the retention of Stalinists, responsible for obstructing change, in the Party and state bureaucracies.

The dissent of 1960–1962 did not, for the most part, elicit strong reaction from the press and Party officials when it first appeared.[33] Khrushchev seemed to be protecting the authors and editors of these works. The attacks on Stalin meshed nicely with his own efforts to dissociate himself from the policies of the dictator and to brand his opponents as Stalinists. By the end of 1962, however, Khrushchev's position had been significantly weakened. His erratic agricultural policies, his drastic reorganization of the Party and the economic-administrative structure, and his insistence on reducing the size of the Soviet ground forces aroused the opposition of his Presidium colleagues, as did his policies in China, Berlin, and Cuba. As his position declined, that of his chief rival, Frol Kozlov, became stronger. Kozlov was a conservative on cultural matters, and with his increased eminence, it became harder for Khrushchev to maintain his tolerant attitude toward dissent. Moreover, there were signs that the First Secretary himself was disturbed by the results of this tolerance. Along with the other Soviet leaders, he was beginning to fear that the prestige and authority of the Party would be undermined by criticisms of its policies and revelations of crimes it had failed to prevent.

A turning point in official treatment of dissent came in December 1962 when Khrushchev's criticisms of unorthodox painting during a visit to the Manezh sparked a crackdown on cultural activity of all kinds. Whether Khrushchev was unable to prevent this development, prepared to go along with it to mollify his opponents, or genuinely in favor of it, we cannot be sure. (Probably all three interpretations are partly correct.) What we do know is that in 1963 *Novy mir* became a major target of a broad campaign to strengthen Party control in the arts and to defend the record of Party leaders in the Stalin era. Works of critical realism and moral humanism by Iashin, Tendriakov, and A. Nekrasov[34] were attacked. The strongest denunciations were directed at the contributions of Ehrenburg, V. Nekrasov,

Solzhenitsyn, and Bondarev—memoirs, essays, and stories which challenged Party authority in the arts or other spheres of Soviet life or which exposed the ugliest aspects of the Stalin years. Three Zhdanovite criteria were invoked against these writers. Some critics accused them of pessimism, of focusing exclusively on negative phenomena, failing to show the forces (like the Party) that opposed and would ultimately triumph over everything bad in Soviet life. Others berated them for their lack of positive heroes, people worthy of emulation, who typified the best in Soviet citizens. (Unlike the *Novy mir* heroes, it was alleged, the "genuinely typical" Soviet man never lost faith in the eventual triumph of justice or the ability of the Party to restore it.) Party leaders and reviewers upbraided these writers for taking "ideologically defective" positions—or no positions at all—on Party leadership of youth. Their views on the Party's guidance of culture and its complicity in Stalin's evil deeds were similarly said to constitute erroneous ideological and political positions.[35] As in the past, authors who had created the greatest stir at home or abroad tended to receive the most criticism. In comparison with the campaigns of 1954 and 1957, however, this one was less well orchestrated. There were many dissonant voices in the press and public meetings. Liberal writers were determined to prevent a strict reimposition of the Zhdanovite criteria, and the regime, still headed by a man committed to de-Stalinization, was reluctant to use more than verbal pressure to win their acquiescence. By the summer of 1963, the attacks had ended without having made a sustained impact on the character of *Novy mir* or the dissent it published.

CONCLUSION

An examination of *Novy mir* in the first year and a half after Stalin's death suggests that its editors and contributors were laboring under a set of rules relating to the content and technique of literary works. Had these rules, which might be called "Zhdanovite criteria," been imposed with the same rigor throughout the period 1953–1964, very little dissent would have appeared in *Novy mir*. As it was, their enforcement fluctuated. The regime allowed the rules to be broken for a time, then vehemently restated them, chastising and otherwise punishing some of the writers and editors who violated them.

Why were these rules not uniformly imposed at all times? The answer lies partly in the exigencies of political struggle and partly in the intrinsic usefulness of dissent to the leadership as a whole. To Khrushchev, as we have seen, it was a weapon in his fight for ascendancy. When his position was sufficiently secure, he could employ this weapon, only to find it necessary or prudent later to abandon it. Yet there are reasons why Khrushchev's colleagues, too, might have been willing to relax control at times and apply the Zhdanovite criteria less rigorously. Khrushchev was not alone in his determination to prevent a return to the worst abuses of the Stalin era. Not only to him, but to others on the Presidium as well, dissent may have seemed worth tolerating because it created a climate of opinion that made such a return more difficult. At the same time, toleration of dissent made a favorable impression on Western intellectuals and the leaders of Western Communist parties at a time when their support for Soviet foreign policy was greatly desired. Furthermore, dissent in an official journal may have been accepted in order to forestall illegal, underground protest. This would be harder to monitor, channel, and control, and might eventually become the basis of a full-fledged political movement. These reasons might explain why dissent was periodically allowed to appear—until it seemed too bold an assault on ideology (as in 1954), too grave a threat to the security of the regime (as in 1957) or too strong a challenge to the authority of the Party (as in 1963). The Zhdanovite criteria were not imposed uniformly because they were the reflection not merely of the aesthetic preferences, but also of the momentary political will (or wills) of the leaders. As that will varied, influenced both by political developments at home and abroad, and by the content of the dissent which was published, so the use of these criteria varied.

Five major types of dissent appeared in *Novy mir* in the decade after Stalin. First to emerge, both in 1953 and after each period of repression, were social pragmatism and critical realism. The former was the safest sort of dissent—the closest to constructive criticism in its identification with the goals of the regime and its focus on problems that concerned the leadership itself. This type was thus the least offensive to the authorities. They may even have desired this kind of aid from writers in exposing problems and mobilizing the population to solve them. Works of critical realism, which evaluated aspects of the Soviet system in terms of their impact on the lives of the people, raised questions such as, are the people happy, are they treated justly? This dissent was somewhat more sensitive, suggesting as it did that some segments of the population were unhappy, that some groups were neglected, exploited, or otherwise victimized. However, the works of this sort conveyed a strong basic loyalty to the ideals of Soviet ideology (in whose name they criticized the reality of Soviet policy) and probably for that reason were not too harshly condemned. The third type of dissent, cultural liberalism, was more directly a challenge to Soviet ideology and institutions. It questioned the relevance of ideologically derived artistic standards and the wisdom of Party supervision of the arts. Both Party and literary authorities felt highly threatened by this dissent and were always quick to denounce it. They were similarly aroused by works of moral humanism, a type of dissent that was not grounded in official ideology and that upheld values external to it: the worth of the individual as an end in himself; the unacceptability of immoral means to obtain social ends; the importance of personal morality under all circumstances. Perhaps the most sensitive dissent of all was the fifth type, historical revisionism. While oriented to the past, it raised disturbing questions about the responsibility of present leaders for that past and about their willingness and ability to renounce former policies and methods of rule. It was also the strongest, most unqualified and explicit rejection of Soviet values, institutions and policies—those associated with the Stalin era.

The character of permitted dissent evolved between 1953 and 1964: types that were weaker, less challenging to the regime appeared at the beginning of the decade and were later supplemented by stronger, more challenging types. The moral humanism that was expressed in 1956 and 1960–1964 and the historical revisionism that emerged in the latter period evinced, in comparison with the social pragmatism and critical realism of 1953–1954, deeper disaffection with a broader range of official values, institutions, and policies; more uneasiness as to whether these could be changed; and greater frankness and boldness in revealing the evils of Soviet rule.

This evolution did not continue in the decade that followed. In 1965 the Brezhnev-Kosygin regime initiated a new, far more determined and enduring effort to curb dissent than had ever been undertaken by Stalin's first successors. *Novy mir* was one of the first and prime targets of this new policy. For several years the journal fought valiantly to keep dissent, particularly the most controversial fifth type, alive in the official press. But it was a losing battle, whose ultimate result was the second dismissal of *Novy mir*'s crusading chief editor, Tvardovsky. In the decade after 1965 *Novy mir*'s struggle was increasingly taken up in samizdat. It was in illegally reproduced magazines, manuscripts, and manifestos that one could now find examples of the cultural liberalism, moral humanism, and historical revisionism which *Novy mir* had introduced into Soviet intellectual life after Stalin. Among certain groups of the intelligentsia *Novy mir* had helped to create a lasting habit or culture of protest, a firm determination to speak out against social and political ills, even when threatened with imprisonment and exile. The repression of intellectuals by the police, which has continued unabated since the arrest of the writers Siniavsky and Daniel in September 1965 has not extinguished dissent, but only driven it underground.

# Toward a Theory of Soviet Leadership Maintenance

## TERESA RAKOWSKA–HARMSTONE

For students of Soviet politics the enforced retirement on October 14, 1964, of Nikita Sergeevich Khrushchev raised a number of questions. How was it possible to remove a man who, as First Secretary of the Communist Party of the Soviet Union and Chairman of the Council of Ministers of the USSR, had reached the apex of power, and who so obviously enjoyed its uses? It seemed incredible that he was removable at all while in control of two key bureaucracies that had served Stalin well and seemed to many to be the key to power in the Soviet Union. Was Khrushchev a lesser man than Stalin or were there other requirements that he failed to meet? Or had the system changed to the point that tried-and-true methods no longer worked? How would any new demands affect Khrushchev's successors?

An examination of these and related questions may provide some insights into the requirements for leadership maintenance in the Soviet Union. It may also help to further our understanding of the dynamics of the relationships among personalities, factions, group pressures, social tensions, and policy problems, the interplay of which has been crucial to the system's adaptability and change. Soviet political leaders, like leaders elsewhere, have to be able to meet the basic demands of their system successfully. Some of these demands figure in all political systems; others apply more specifically to a Marxist-Leninist one-party state.

Three factors are crucial in outlining the systemic context of this analysis. The first factor, which cannot change without altering the nature of the system itself, is the one-party monopoly of power. This is expressed through the exercise by the Party of the *leading role* within the society. The second crucial factor is Marxism-Leninism, from which springs the ideological source of systemic legitimacy. Third is the lack of any provision for political succession. These three major characteristics mark the Soviet system as—in Melvin Croan's terminology—"pre-institutional." Not only has it no mechanism for effective long-term sharing and transfer of leadership at the top, but, in addition, the leading Party role is exercised "without benefit of regularized procedures for the presentation of social forces or even very effective consultation with those special interests upon which it must depend for the attainment of the high level of economic performance *and* social control it seeks." [1] The system is also "postrevolutionary" insofar as the ideologically motivated transformation of society has already taken place, transforming Marxism-Leninism from a revolutionary creed into a "preserver and legitimizer of the status quo."

The three characteristics mentioned above, as well as the demands for success in problem solving and conflict resolution common to any body politic, impose a set of basic requirements that a Soviet political leader—or group of leaders—has to meet in order to maintain mastery of power. These requirements fall into three broad, overlapping categories: (1) personal as well as systemic legitimacy; (2) control of the institutional mechanics of power; and (3) success in policy making.

The first requirement concerns the legitimacy indispensable for the maintenance of leadership in any society but generated, in this case, within the constraints of an ideological political system; [2] ideology substitutes for the sanction of periodic popular approval, and a leadership struggle substitutes for the constitutional transfer of power.

In the context of one-party power, monopoly control over the institutional levers is the second crucial requirement. The leading role of the Party precludes alternative sources of power, but its exercise under the operational principle of democratic centralism [3] depends on powerful bureaucracies. Divided along functional, branch, or territorial lines, each bureaucracy has strong interests of its own. If manipulated skillfully, the bureaucracies can serve as instruments of control in the hands of a ruler; under collective leadership, however, they tend to balance one another. A balance that depends on shifting coalitions and factional agreements is inherently unstable, but if the contending forces have roughly equal strength, the balance can be maintained indefinitely. Nonetheless, a shift in the balance for or against a contender or a holder of power can make or break him. Such shifts are invariably connected with shifts in policy.

Success in policy making is thus the third vital requirement for leadership maintenance. In a modernizing and increasingly professionalized Soviet society, the policy-making process has increased in complexity, but the political framework within which it is carried out has remained unchanged since the early days of the system. The test of policies still lies primarily in their implementation. No adequate mechanisms exist to evaluate proposed solutions in terms either of technical adequacy or social acceptability. As major domestic and foreign policy issues are tackled and resources are allocated, the decisions bear on each leader's relative power standing. The demands of key bureaucracies and functional groups can be ignored only at peril because their support is vital and their cooperation necessary for policy implementation and feedback. The satisfaction of basic social needs builds support for the system, induces the people to carry out required social and economic tasks, and prevents frustrations from accumulating to the point of explosion. While forced to respond to demands in an increasingly practical manner, the leaders are also aware that giving in to pressures tends to erode the Party's leading role and hence their own power. The search for a golden mean in trading off solutions, group satisfactions, and authority was evident in Khrushchev's "subjectivism" and rapid policy changes. It is still present now in the compromises adopted by his successors, in their simultaneous emphasis on practical approaches to policy problems, and in their preoccupation with ideological orthodoxy and social engineering.

LEGITIMACY [4]

Legitimacy concerns the title to rule, that is, a belief by those subject to rule that the ruler has a right to it. Legitimacy is necessary to support the possession and exercise of authority or command if such authority is to be obeyed willingly and exercised without coercion. The dependence of authority on the attitudes of the governed suggests that, in the words of Carl Friedrich, "the degree of effective obedience to a given rule is directly proportionate to the degree of legitimacy which such a rule possesses." [5]

Max Weber identifies three "pure types of legitimate authority" that are analytically distinguishable but empirically overlapping. These are: rational-legal, based on a belief in the legality of patterns of established normative rules; traditional, based on a belief in the sanctity of tradition; and charismatic, "resting on devotion to the specific and exceptional sanctity, heroism, or exemplary character of an individual person, and of the normative patterns or order revealed or ordained by him." [6] Ideologies, which have proved to be effective legitimizers of rule in this century, particularly in the case of totalitarian systems, do not easily fit into Weberian categories. Marxism-Leninism, however, spans the three categories: it originated with a charismatic leader of a movement; its normative content supplies rational-legal authority; and, in the passage of time, it has also acquired the sanctity of tradition.

Lenin's leadership of the Communist movement represents a case of legitimacy derived from charismatic authority, combining revolutionary action directed against the established order with the conviction of carrying out *the* mission of history.[7] The prescription of just how this mission was to be accomplished was provided by the leader in a body of doctrine that adapted the philosophical premises of Marxism to the Russian heritage,[8] and provided new norms. The system established to fulfill the mission embodied a set of institutions that fit the traditional patterns of Russian authority remarkably well,[9] and thus the new order was rooted in tradition. To its claim to rule, already established by the leader's charisma, the Party added claim to rational-legal and traditional authority as the infallible interpreter of the doctrine and the implementer of the new order. After Lenin's death the ideology was reinforced by the "founder's myth," [10] but from the late thirties until 1956 the Lenin myth was overshadowed by the myth of Stalin.[11]

The fifty years of existence of the Soviet political system testify to its ability to develop and to maintain legitimacy, although its history also indicates that the system has yet to meet the ultimate test of non-coercive obedience by the majority of its subjects. Much of this stability results, in my judgment, from Lenin's infusion of Tsarist patterns of authority into the theory and practice of the system. In the ideological context, on the other hand, signs of erosion appeared as the system matured. This ideological erosion affected particularly the legitimacy of succession and the Party's right to rule based on its claim to be the sole possessor and interpreter of ultimate historical truth. In the Weberian sense, the personal charisma of the founder became "routinized" insofar as his charismatic mission was transformed into an "office of a bureaucratic character" [12]—the Party—within the Soviet state. But because the personal charisma of Stalin, as Lenin's successor, overshadowed the Party's routinized legitimacy, the leadership of the movement (and thus the succession) did not "routinize" in the sense of becoming "impersonally separable from particular individuals," (a quality that, according to Weber, bestowed legitimacy on the Roman

Catholic Church and the popes).[13] This failure to "routinize" the office of the leader has resulted in a periodic recurrence of the struggle for succession. In the absence of objective attributes of the office, there is a need for each leader to attempt to generate personal charisma. Because the Party was for so long identified with Stalin, the 1956 explosion of the Stalin myth undercut the Party's claim to infallibility, and this in turn broke the continuity on which its post-Revolutionary legitimacy was based.

The key functional problem, "that of maintaining the authority of the original point of reference—as in a divine mission—and yet meeting the changed conditions," [14] also remains. Ironically, the Party's social relevance has failed to keep up with the process of change it initiated and carried out. In ideological terms, the justification for the leading role of the Party became more tenuous with the social and economic transformation of Soviet society. In practical terms, moreover, the Party's role as a total mobilizer has become increasingly dysfunctional to the needs of newly differentiated social groups, because its structural and operational rigidity acts as an impediment to change.

The need to stop the erosion of ideological legitimacy and to restore the image of Party infallibility and technical competence confronted Khrushchev after 1956, and it continues to preoccupy his successors, for the leading role is crucial to their raison d'être and to the Party's claim to the leadership of the world Communist movement. The revival of the Leninist founder's myth receives top priority in an effort to restore legitimacy and continuity.[15] The myth has become the touchstone of orthodoxy in policy as well as in behavior. At the same time, in proper dialectical usage, it gives a degree of flexibility needed for the justification of new policies. The founder's myth has been particularly important in combating revisionism and reformism at home and abroad. The leading role of the Party, a key Leninist concept, is also emphasized with special reference to the Party's revolutionary roots and its historical mission.[16] A continuing intensive political socialization of the elites is complemented by regular indoctrination campaigns directed at the masses.[17]

Because neither the cult of Lenin nor the socialization campaigns seem to have done much to overcome growing uncertainties, Khrushchev's successors have embarked on partial re-Stalinization in order to restore, in the words of Richard Lowenthal, "the authority of the regime, and to justify their personal part of service under Stalin by stressing the unbroken continuity of legitimate Party rule." [18]

Efforts to restore the Party's ideological legitimacy are reinforced by a new emphasis on rational-legal and traditional aspects of state authority. The stress on "socialist legality" has, in fact, furnished the dissidents with a weapon in their unequal fight for the exercise of civil rights.[19] Symbols of democratic legitimacy are increasingly manipulated, even though frequent periodic exercises in electoral mechanics serve the purpose of socialization rather than that of providing an outlet for expression of popular preferences.[20] The emphasis on the participatory role of deputies in the network of the soviets has grown steadily since the Twenty-Second Party Congress; leaders have been increasingly paying lip service to popular preferences in enunciating or justifying policy decisions, and have been actively seeking to satisfy the more pressing demands of major social groups. An appeal to Russian nationalism helped Stalin to legitimize his rule in traditional terms at points of stress, such as in World War II, and there was a revival of Great Russian symbolism at the Twenty-Fourth Party Congress. Russian nationalism, however, is counterproductive in the socialization of the half of the Soviet population that is not Great Russian. In fact it has provoked the growth of ethnic nationalisms, as non-Russian political elites seek legitimacy within their own traditions.[21]

In this context of renewed emphasis on the maintenance of systemic legitimacy, the individual leaders must now compete to create, maintain, and maximize personal charisma in their quest for the top position. In this attempt, ideological factors are emphasized: to be successful à la Lenin and Stalin, one must become *the* interpreter of the doctrine and *the* center of a "cult of personality." Given the over-all gray homogeneity of the current leadership,[22] however, tangible success in tactical infighting and policy making also has grown in importance. Zbigniew Brzezinski argues that Lenin's charisma derived from his being the chief ideologist, chief organizer (and founder) of the Party, and chief administrator of the state, and that although Stalin succeeded in eventually holding all three of these positions, the feat may not be repeated because the division of functions is now jealously guarded.[23] Khrushchev succeeded for a brief period only; his efforts to acquire charisma as an ideologist included the famous de-Stalinization policy (which proved counterproductive), a major attempt at a reformulation of the doctrine (as reflected in the 1961 Party Program),[24] and an effort to build his own cult of personality. On balance, it was an impressive attempt but it proved inadequate to offset failures in policy making and in control of power mechanics.

In the collective leadership that succeeded Khrushchev, the three charisma-generating posts were filled by three different people: L. I.

Brezhnev became chief Party organizer, A. N. Kosygin chief state administrator, and M. A. Suslov assumed the role of chief ideologist. In the seventies, however, Brezhnev appears to have made considerable progress in making himself doctrinal spokesman and in starting his own cult of personality. In doctrinal matters he offers no startling innovations but has become the foremost authority on the leading role of the Party and on the concepts of détente and "proletarian internationalism," reflecting, respectively, the twin aspects of his foreign policy vis-à-vis the capitalist world and world progressive forces.[25] He is the one Politburo member with a number of volumes of collected works (Suslov and Kosygin have published only one volume apiece).[26] The admiration of Brezhnev's "Leninist" policies and the invocation of his words to legitimate policy have multiplied. The same cannot be said of any of his colleagues, all of whom have participated in the adulation of Brezhnev but in varying degrees.[27] The praise heaped on Brezhnev at the Twenty-Fifth Party Congress (February 25–March 5, 1976) may have exceeded that bestowed on Khrushchev before the latter's downfall, as speaker after speaker referred to the General Secretary as "the most outstanding political figure of our epoch," "a bright and inspiring example," and a man of "excessive modesty and brilliant talent." [28] In the years since Khrushchev's ouster, it is Brezhnev who has been identified with most policy successes and who has benefited from tactical infighting.[29]

In the context of authority, charisma can accrue only to an individual, and it has to be "proved" by being recognized as genuine by his followers.[30] For an aspiring Soviet leader, such recognition has become an almost impossible goal in the absence of "routinized" succession (which would bestow attributes of the office on the incumbent) and the need to meet the requirements of success in conditions of factional balance of power. The legitimacy of the collective leadership depends on the Party's legitimacy, which has been eroded both ideologically as well as instrumentally. Nevertheless, traditional authority appears to have been a strong compensating factor for the system's survival and stability. But the "tsar" is missing, and it is perhaps the traditional demand for a supreme ruler as much as the internal logic of a successionless ideological system that affects the dynamics of power within the collective leadership of the Party.

## THE MECHANICS OF POWER

There are few actors in the Soviet top leadership arena, the Party's Politburo. Functionally, they are all at the apex of the few powerful bureaucracies that run the country. It is essential for an aspiring leader on his way up to manipulate support of these bureaucracies and, for the one who has already gained supreme power, to keep them in balance and to ensure that they cannot satisfy their objectives except through him. The careers of Stalin and Khrushchev stand as cases in point, the first as a success, the second as a failure. Each bureaucracy represents entrenched institutional interests; it also serves to aggregate special interests within its structure and in coalition with similar interests outside. Special interests within the Soviet Union are neither formally recognized nor provided with procedures to facilitate contacts with decision makers, and bureaucracies provide the necessary framework in the search for influence. Nonetheless, group dynamics may operate around an issue or a leader, or in response to current functional or career needs within, as well as across, bureaucratic boundaries.[31] Factional coalitions, "packing" of key bodies, administrative reorganizations, and trade-offs in favors and penalties have all been featured in leadership contests within the institutional setting of the key bureaucracies.

An ultimate aggregator, the Party has customarily been regarded as the key instrument of power, the control of its apparat an essential condition for a leader. But other powerful bureaucracies—the all-Union agencies, the secret police, and the armed services, all with vertical structures controlled from the top—have proved to be a useful counterweight. The Party was explicitly conceived as a unitary structure[32] and its apparat[33] retains a high degree of cohesion. A small group in relative terms, estimated at approximately 250,000 functionaries[34] (out of a Party of 15 million members and a total population of over 240 million people), these are the people who in effect carry out the Party's leading role, using a triple mechanism: incorporation of members of local elites into Party decision-making structures[35] through control of appointments (*nomenklatura*); maintenance of executive organs parallel to the executive organs of state and other bureaucracies; and the use of Primary Party Organizations as instruments of control within all other organizations and institutions. Whether the leading role should take the form of guidance or "substitute management" in relation to other bureaucracies has been the subject of a raging controversy and changing policies,[36] as has been the role of Primary Party Organizations within state agencies. Less explicit, if nonetheless vital, is a controversy over whether the Party should be an integrator or merely a coordinator of group interests. A homogeneous group, the Party functionaries have as their main interest the perpetuation of their political role and privileged position; they are jealous of their prerogatives, and close ranks against outside interference. In pursuit of special interests dictated by their responsibilities, however, they divide, joining similarly motivated bureaucrats in coalitions directed against fellow functionaries and their allies.

The governmental bureaucracy is far larger and less cohesive than the Party apparat, and differentiates along federal-republican, and functional and production-branch lines. The all-Union agencies, particularly the functional conglomerate around the USSR Council of Ministers and the production-branch bureaucracies of the economic ministries, carry substantial political weight. In the latter, cohesion runs along vertical lines, including not only the officials, but also managers and technocrats, as well as scientists and professionals in subordinate institutions and enterprises. Officials of industrial ministries tend to polarize along heavy industry–light industry lines; the former have greater community of interests with the military establishment and with Party officials in charge of both (the "steel-eaters" group) than they do with light industry bureaucrats whose views tend to favor consumer interests. Nonetheless, "modernizers" in the armed forces have more in common with the reform-minded consumer lobby than with military traditionalists, and planners and technocrats in all agencies have interests in common. Agricultural administrators deal with a specific set of problems and tend to see eye to eye with Party counterparts and any group that favors related objectives (chemical industry officials, for example).

The interests of the union republics aggregate laterally and unite republic, Party, and state agencies against the central authorities in matters of resource allocation and distribution or jurisdictional disputes, with overtones of ethnic nationalism. The power base in the major republics, as well as in the two major cities—Moscow and Leningrad—is of importance in the leadership contest. The secret police and the armed services, also representing specific interests, are unique instruments in the power dimension, as both employ troops with military hardware. The functions and role of the secret police are too well known to need discussion in this essay. This organization was Stalin's key instrument of control; downgraded after L. P. Beria's abortive bid for power in 1953, it has gradually regained some of its importance. The armed services' aspirations as a whole are seen to complement closely the interests of the Party and are felt to be served best through it.[37] The political influence they acquired after World War II has tipped the scale at least twice in the leadership struggle.[38] Nevertheless the military differentiate by function as well as by attitudes—as between traditionalists and modernizers.

A lifelong career as Party functionary (even if one has been temporarily assigned to other hierarchies) has so far been an essential condition for the rise to the top. A classic pattern of ascent to power—
pioneered by Stalin, followed by Khrushchev, and thus far by Brezhnev—leads up the Party apparat: through control of key appointments
which, in turn, control nomenklatura of other agencies; "packing" of
the Central Committee; co-opting supporters into the Politburo; and,
finally, elimination of rivals. The secret of success in the maintenance
of power, if the two cases so far are indicative, is the ability to control
the Party once the summit is reached. Using terror as a means to
eliminate real and potential rivals, Stalin downgraded the Party
apparatus (through elevation of other bureaucracies) to the point
where its officials held only one out of ten of the voting membership
in the Presidium (Politburo) reconstituted following his death. The
one member was Khrushchev, who became First Secretary when G. M.
Malenkov, unable to keep both posts, opted to retain the chairmanship of the Council of Ministers.

Khrushchev's rise to power remains so well known that only high-
lights need to be recalled. Beria's downfall in July 1953 removed the
secret police as one of the Party's rivals. Khrushchev's appointees in
posts of provincial and republican Party secretary enabled him to win
the 1957 showdown in the Central Committee over the sovnarkhoz
reform, against his state-based rivals, the "anti-Party group," members
of which were desperate because the reform removed their power base
in the all-Union economic ministries. By March 1958 Khrushchev completed the consolidation of personal power by additionally assuming
the chairmanship of the Council of Ministers. He was supreme and so
was the Party, but no bureaucracies remained powerful enough to
challenge its power. The terror option was foreclosed to Khrushchev.
His way of controlling the apparat was bureaucratic manipulation. He
broke the unity of the central apparat through the creation of separate bureaus, two of which were functional, and three regional; vertically, the structure was "bifurcated," in November 1962, into separate
industrial and agricultural branches. Khrushchev also tried democratization by opening Party meetings and ranks to experts, and institu-
tionalizing turnover and tenure in Party positions.[39] All of the new
measures antagonized his erstwhile followers in the Central Committee and Presidium; coupled with failures in other policy areas, this
lack of support cost him the leadership in October 1964.

His successors lost little time restoring *status quo ante*. Bifurcation
was repealed a month after Khrushchev's downfall, and functional
and regional bureaus soon faded into oblivion. Only the RSFSR

Bureau survived another two years, apparently because Brezhnev attempted to use it, unsuccessfully, to build up a personal power machine.[40] Turnover and tenure provisions were also scrapped,[41] and a new restrictive membership policy slowed down the Party's growth pattern.[42] The restoration of centralized economic ministries in September 1965 [43] returned many of the old faces to Moscow. The Party-state representation, stabilized in the Politburo, was headed, respectively, by Brezhnev and Kosygin, even though signs began to multiply of Brezhnev's attempts to consolidate his institutional position. He started by removing rivals from the Secretariat, where they stood in the way of his building a base in the Central Committee.[44] As of 1976 one could discern four stages in Brezhnev's effort to consolidate power (see table 4.1). Brezhnev won the struggle with N. V. Podgorny, an old rival from the Ukraine, at the December 6, 1965, plenum, when Podgorny lost his position as Central Committee secretary (assumed at the ouster of Khrushchev) and was "kicked upstairs" to become the head of state.[45] The year 1965 also saw the decline in position of another rival Central Committee secretary, A. N. Shelepin (the only Politburo member still left at that time with a position also in the state hierarchy), who lost the chairmanship of the Party-state Control Commission (which was abolished) [46] and the deputy chairmanship of the USSR Council of Ministers. Shelepin was removed as Central Committee secretary in the second stage of consolidation in 1967, when he was downgraded to the chairmanship of the Trade Unions' Council.[47] Brezhnev strengthened his position in the Secretariat further by replacing Podgorny in 1965 with A. P. Kirilenko (presumably as Central Committee secretary for cadres), a member of his own "Dnepropetrovsk" faction. The only other secretary who stands in the way of Brezhnev's complete control of the apparat is M. A. Suslov.[48] In 1970 rumors reached the Western press of an abortive challenge to Brezhnev which involved Suslov and Shelepin with D. S. Polyansky and K. T. Mazurov in support,[49] but there was no change in status of either of the leaders mentioned. Nonetheless new faces in the Politburo following the 1971 congress reflected a strengthening of Brezhnev's position.

Politburo members involved in the third stage of consolidation (1971–1972) were G. I. Voronov and P. E. Shelest.[50] Both of these men were "retired." D. S. Polyansky was moved to head the Ministry of Agriculture from the position of Kosygin's first deputy in February 1973,[51] a demotion.

The decline in the power of Podgorny and Polyansky, and the removal of Voronov, all of whom were considered close to Kosygin on

TABLE 4.1   Changes in the Politburo/Presidium and Secretariat, 1961–1976.

| Presidium 22nd Congress, October 31, 1961 | Presidium November 17, 1964, Plenum | Politburo 23rd Congress, April 8, 1966 (Ranking according to Congress protocol) |
|---|---|---|
| Politburo members (voting) | Politburo members (voting) | Politburo members (voting) |
| N. S. Khrushchev [a,c] First Secretary Central Committee Chairman, Council of Ministers, USSR Chairman, Bureau, RSFSR | L. I. Brezhnev First Secretary, Central Committee Chairman, Bureau, RSFSR | L. I. Brezhnev General Secretary |
| L. I. Brezhnev Chairman, Presidium, Supreme Soviet, USSR | A. N. Kosygin Chairman, Council of Ministers, USSR | A. N. Kosygin Chairman, Council of Ministers, USSR |
| A. N. Kosygin First Deputy Chairman, Council of Ministers, USSR | M. A. Suslov Secretary, Central Committee | N. V. Podgorny Chairman, Presidium, Supreme Soviet, USSR |
| N. V. Podgorny First Secretary, Ukraine | G. I. Voronov Chairman, Council of Ministers, RSFSR | M. A. Suslov Secretary, Central Committee |
| M. A. Suslov Secretary, Central Committee | A. I. Mikoyan [a,d] Chairman, Presidium, Supreme Soviet, USSR | G. I. Voronov Chairman, Council of Ministers, RSFSR |
| G. I. Voronov Deputy Chairman, Bureau, RSFSR | D. S. Polyansky Deputy Chairman, Council of Ministers, RSFSR | A. P. Kirilenko Secretary, Central Committee |
| F. R. Kozlov [e] Secretary, Central Committee | N. M. Shvernik [a,d] Chairman, Control Commission | A. N. Shelepin Secretary, Central Committee |
| O. V. Kuusinen [e] Secretary, Central Committee | A. P. Kirilenko First Deputy Chairman, Bureau, RSFSR | K. T. Mazurov [b] First Deputy Chairman, Council of Ministers, USSR |
| A. I. Mikoyan First Deputy Chairman, Council of Ministers, USSR | A. N. Shelepin Secretary, Central Committee Deputy Chairman, Council of Ministers, USSR Chairman, Party-State Control Commission | D. S. Polyansky First Deputy Chairman, Council of Ministers, USSR |
| D. S. Polyansky Chairman, Council of Ministers, RSFSR | P. E. Shelest First Secretary, Ukraine | P. E. Shelest First Secretary, Ukraine |
| N. M. Shvernik Chairman, Control Commission | | A. J. Pelshe [b] Chairman, Control Commission |

**TABLE 4.1** (Continued)

| Presidium 22nd Congress, October 31, 1961 | Presidium November 17, 1964, Plenum | Politburo 23rd Congress April 8, 1966 (Ranking according to Congress protocol) |
|---|---|---|
| **Politburo candidate members (nonvoting)** | **Politburo candidate members (nonvoting)** | **Politburo candidate members (nonvoting)** |
| V. V. Grishin Chairman, Central Committee, Trade Unions | V. V. Grishin Chairman, Central Committee, Trade Unions | P. N. Demichev Secretary, Central Committee |
| V. P. Mzhavanadze First Secretary, Georgia | V. P. Mzhavanadze First Secretary, Georgia | V. V. Grishin Chairman, Central Committee, Trade Unions |
| Sh. R. Rashidov First Secretary, Uzbekistan | Sh. R. Rashidov First Secretary, Uzbekistan | V. P. Mzhavanadze First Secretary, Georgia |
| K. T. Mazurov First Secretary, Belorussia | K. T. Mazurov First Secretary, Belorussia | Sh. R. Rashidov First Secretary, Uzbekistan |
| V. V. Shcherbitsky [a,f] Chairman, Council of Ministers, Ukraine | L. N. Yefremov [a,b] Deputy Chairman, Bureau, RSFSR | D. F. Ustinov [b] Secretary, Central Committee |
| | P. N. Demichev Secretary, Central Committee | V. V. Shcherbitsky [b] Chairman, Council of Ministers, Ukraine |
| | | D. A. Kunaev [b] First Secretary, Kazakhstan |
| | | P. M. Masherov [b] First Secretary, Belorussia |
| **Secretaries (nonmembers)** | **Secretaries (nonmembers)** | **Secretaries (nonmembers)** |
| B. N. Ponomarev | B. N. Ponomarev | Yu. V. Andropov |
| P. N. Demichev [i] | L. F. Ilyichev | B. N. Ponomarev |
| L. F. Ilyichev | Yu. V. Andropov [b] | I. V. Kapitonov [b] |
| I. V. Spiridonov [a] | A. P. Rudakov [b] | F. D. Kulakov [b] |
| | | A. P. Rudakov [a,e] |

TABLE 4.1 (Continued)

| Politburo 24th Congress, April 10, 1971 (Ranking according to Congress protocol) | Politburo April 26–27, 1973 Plenum | Politburo 25th Congress, March 5, 1976 |
|---|---|---|
| Politburo members (voting) | Politburo members (voting) | Politburo members (voting) |
| L. I. Brezhnev General Secretary | L. I. Brezhnev General Secretary | L. I. Brezhnev General Secretary |
| N. V. Podgorny Chairman, Presidium, Supreme Soviet, USSR | N. V. Podgorny Chairman, Presidium, Supreme Soviet, USSR | N. V. Podgorny Chairman, Presidium, Supreme Soviet, USSR |
| A. N. Kosygin Chairman, Council of Ministers, USSR | A. N. Kosygin Chairman, Council of Ministers, USSR | A. N. Kosygin Chairman, Council of Ministers, USSR |
| M. A. Suslov Secretary, Central Committee | M. A. Suslov Secretary, Central Committee | M. A. Suslov Secretary, Central Committee |
| A. P. Kirilenko Secretary, Central Committee | A. P. Kirilenko Secretary, Central Committee | A. P. Kirilenko Secretary, Central Committee |
| A. J. Pelshe Chairman, Control Commission | A. J. Pelshe Chairman, Control Commission | A. J. Pelshe Chairman, Control Commission |
| K. T. Mazurov First Deputy Chairman, Council of Ministers, USSR | K. T. Mazurov First Deputy Chairman, Council of Ministers, USSR | K. T. Mazurov First Deputy Chairman, Council of Ministers, USSR |
| D. S. Polyansky First Deputy Chairman, Council of Ministers, USSR | D. S. Polyansky [a,j] Minister of Agriculture | V. V. Grishin First Secretary, Moscow |
| P. E. Shelest [g] First Secretary, Ukraine | A. N. Shelepin [a,k] Chairman, Central Committee, Trade Unions | D. A. Kunaev First Secretary, Kazakhstan |
| G. I. Voronov [g] Chairman, Council of Ministers, RSFSR | V. V. Grishin First Secretary, Moscow | V. V. Shcherbitsky First Secretary, Ukraine |
| A. N. Shelepin Chairman, Central Committee, Trade Unions | D. A. Kunaev First Secretary, Kazakhstan | F. D. Kulakov Secretary, Central Committee |
| V. V. Grishin [b] First Secretary, Moscow | V. V. Shcherbitsky First Secretary, Ukraine | A. A. Grechko [i,k] Minister of Defense |
| | F. D. Kulakov Secretary, Central Committee | A. A. Gromyko Minister of Foreign Affairs |

64

TABLE 4.1 (Continued)

| Politburo 24th Congress, April 10, 1971 (Ranking according to Congress protocol) | Politburo April 26–27, 1973 Plenum | Politburo 25th Congress, March 5, 1976 |
|---|---|---|
| Politburo members (voting) | Politburo members (voting) | Politburo members (voting) |
| D. A. Kunaev [b] First Secretary, Kazakhstan V. V. Shcherbitsky [b] Chairman, Council of Ministers, Ukraine F. D. Kulakov [b] Secretary, Central Committee | A. A. Grechko [b] Minister of Defense A. A. Gromyko [b] Minister of Foreign Affairs Yu. V. Andropov [b] Chairman, KGB | Yu. V. Andropov Chairman, KGB D. F. Ustinov [b] Secretary, Central Committee G. V. Romanov [b] First Secretary, Leningrad |
| Politburo candidate members (nonvoting) | Politburo candidate members (nonvoting) | Politburo candidate members (nonvoting) |
| Yu. V. Andropov [b] Chairman, KGB D. F. Ustinov Secretary, Central Committee P. N. Demichev Secretary, Central Committee Sh. R. Rashidov First Secretary, Uzbekistan P. M. Masherov First Secretary, Belorussia V. P. Mzhavanadze [a,g] First Secretary, Georgia | D. F. Ustinov Secretary, Central Committee P. N. Demichev Secretary, Central Committee Sh. R. Rashidov First Secretary, Uzbekistan P. M. Masherov First Secretary, Belorussia M. S. Solomentsev [b] Chairman, Council of Ministers, RSFSR B. N. Ponomarev [b] Secretary, Central Committee G. V. Romanov [b] First Secretary, Leningrad | P. N. Demichev Minister of Culture Sh. R. Rashidov First Secretary, Uzbekistan P. M. Masherov First Secretary, Belorussia M. S. Solomentsev Chairman, Council of Ministers, RSFSR B. N. Ponomarev Secretary, Central Committee G. A. Aliev [b] First Secretary, Azerbaizhan |
| Secretaries (nonmembers) | Secretaries (nonmembers) | Secretaries (nonmembers) |
| I. V. Kapitonov B. N. Ponomarev M. S. Solomentsev [b] K. F. Katushev [b] | I. V. Kapitonov K. F. Katushev V. I. Dolgikh [h] | I. V. Kapitonov K. F. Katushev V. I. Dolgikh M. V. Zimianin [b] K. U. Chernenko [b] |

(Continued)

TABLE 4.1   (Continued)

---

a Removed.

b Newly appointed.

c Retired at the October 14, 1964 Plenum.

d Retired.

e Retired and died.

f Not included in the October 15, 1964, list.

g Retired at the April 1973 Plenum.

h Appointed after the April 1973 Plenum.

i Appointed Minister of Culture, November 14, 1974; relieved of duties as Secretary, Central Committee, at the December 16, 1974, Plenum.

j Not reelected at the Twenty-fifth Congress; removed as Minister of Agriculture, March 6, 1976.

k Died, 1976.

Personnel changes occurred in the various plenums. On *October 15, 1964,* Kirilenko became a member of the Presidium and Shelest and Yefremov became candidate members. A secretary (Polyakov) was appointd but was not listed in November 1964. Andropov, Rudakov, and Titov were appointed Central Committee secretaries. On *March 26, 1965,* Mazurov became a member of the Presidium and first deputy chairman of the Council of Ministers, USSR. Shelepin was dropped as chairman of the Party-State Control Commission and as deputy chairman of the Council of Ministers, USSR. Yefremov, Ilyichev, and Titov were also dropped. On *December 6, 1965,* Shcherbitsky was appointed candidate member of the Presidium; Polyansky became first deputy chairman of the Council of Ministers, USSR (October 2, 1965); Podgorny was removed as secretary of the Central Committee and became chairman of the Presidium of the Supreme Soviet, USSR; and Kapitonov was appointed secretary of the Central Committee.

On *December 12–13, 1966,* Solomentsev was appointed secretary of the Central Committee. On *June 20–21, 1967,* Grishin became first secretary, Moscow City, and was released as chairman of the Central Committee, Trade Unions, in June. Andropov was appointed candidate member of the Politburo and Chairman of the KGB and was released as secretary of the Central Committee. On *September 26, 1967,* Shelepin was released as secretary of the Central Committee and became chairman of the Central Committee, Trade Unions. On *April 9–10, 1968,* Katushev was appointed secretary of the Central Committee.

On *November 22–23, 1971,* Solomentsev was appointed candidate member of the Politburo and was relieved as secretary of the Central Committee. He was also appointed as chairman, Council of Ministers, RSFSR. Voronov was relieved as chairman, Council of Ministers, RSFSR, and was appointed chairman of the State Control Commission in July 1971. On *May 19, 1972,* Ponomarev was appointed candidate member of the Politburo. In *April 1973* Shelest was removed as first secretary, Ukraine, and was appointed deputy chairman, Council of Ministers, USSR. Mzhavanadze was relieved as first secretary, Georgia. Polyansky was relieved as first deputy chairman, Council of Ministers, USSR, and was appointed Minister of Agriculture in February 1973.

policy issues, appears to have weakened the latter's faction. The fourth stage, 1973–1976, reflected further gradual consolidation of Brezhnev's power. The changes of the April 1973 plenum increased the representation of functional interests in the Politburo: the armed forces are represented by Marshal Grechko, the KGB by Yu. V. Andropov, and the foreign ministry by A. A. Gromyko. All of the men involved either closely cooperated with Brezhnev or were his appointees. The inclusion directly in the Politburo of the heads of the two key power bureaucracies balanced the ascendancy of Party functionaries there and reduced Brezhnev's vulnerability to removal by the apparat. The payoff may have come already in the apparent crisis of December 1974–January 1975. Brezhnev's seven weeks' disappearance (explained as "a cold") was accompanied by a hardening of the line in foreign and domestic policies,[52] including rejection of the 1972 trade agreement with the United States.[53] Moscow rumors and Western specialists speculated about various factional combinations within the Politburo as probable challengers or successors to Mr. Brezhnev.[54] However, Brezhnev reemerged in mid-February to greet the visiting Harold Wilson of Great Britain, and his reappearance was accompanied by a reaffirmation of the policy of détente.[55] In April 1975 Shelepin was finally removed from the Politburo, and the July 1975 Helsinki Conference on Security and Cooperation in Europe, a major triumph for the Soviet Union, vindicated the policy of détente. The changes in the Politburo and Secretariat in the Twenty-Fifth Party Congress further consolidated the General Secretary's leadership. Polyansky was dropped from the Politburo; [56] two new members were elevated from candidate status: G. V. Romanov, first secretary of the Leningrad city Party organization, and D. F. Ustinov, the Central Committee secretary in charge of defense matters. One new candidate member was added, G. A. Aliev, first secretary of the Azerbaijan Party organization, thus restoring representation to the Caucasus, lost with the removal of Mzhavanadze in 1973; two new Central Committee secretaries were appointed. On balance, in early 1976, ten out of sixteen full members of the Politburo were Brezhnev's appointments, including key functional and regional representatives and three Central Committee secretaries; so were three out of six candidate members, and all of the five Central Committee secretaries who were not included in the Politburo. The General Secretary's main rivals, Podgorny, Kosygin, and Suslov, appeared weakened and, in the case of at least one of the first two, isolated. In line with the system of checks and balances first developed by Stalin, Brezhnev appears to have "packed" most of the key posts in the central and regional Party apparat and power bureaucracies with "his" people, and to have balanced, in the top decision-making body, the Party with functional interests and central with regional representatives.[57] Chances of his removal, barring a major policy disaster, appear remote. But as age and rumored poor health may intervene, the stage is set for a new round of "collective leadership."

Leaders of key institutions, particularly those of the apparat and state bureaucracies, have been selectively represented in top Party bodies in the past; since 1964, there has been a trend toward stabilization of a representation pattern reflected in stronger regional as well as functional contingents. The Politburo has always included the three key posts: the Party's first (general) secretary, and the heads of state and of the government. Other positions have fluctuated. Since 1964 regional interests are recognized by the inclusion of more first secretaries of republics and of Moscow and Leningrad; and functional interests, by the inclusion of representatives of key bureaucracies. The Party-state representation ratio, which underwent a radical shift under Khrushchev (from 1:4 in July 1953 to 7:3 in June 1957), stabilized in the 1964–1976 period at 2:1, with the balance tipped in favor of the Party.[58] Representation in the Central Committee is more institutionalized: membership always includes top officials of the Council of Ministers and Party central apparat, as well as virtually all first secretaries of RSFSR province Party committees and central committees of the republics and a few selected top regional state administrators, heads of social and cultural organizations, and token "toilers." Its complexion changes with the change of incumbents. In the post-Khrushchev decade the Party-state representation in the Central Committee stood at approximately 4:3, with the largest Party contingent coming from the regions, and the largest state group from the all-Union bureaucracies.[59]

The over-all pattern shows the Party carrying greater weight than the state, but less so than under Khrushchev, and the representation of professional bureaucracies at the highest Party level indicates a challenge to its supremacy. While this is a factor in the perpetuation of the collective leadership, the relative power balance makes for stability (as well as for "immobilism" in policy making).[60] It is, however, no safeguard against one man's manipulation of institutional mechanics, a task which Brezhnev appears to be successfully pursuing.

## POLICY MAKING

Effective policy making requires success in dealing with major policy issues, in responding to social pressures, and in meeting key group demands. The test of implementation requires decisions to be technically sound and acceptable to the implementers as well as to the groups affected by them. In the Soviet Union major occupational and "opinion" groups have direct access to decision makers, but broad social groups, such as workers, peasants, consumers, students, the creative intelligentsia, and most nationalities have indirect access, at best through bureaucratic feedback. The attitudes of these latter groups nevertheless bear directly on the fulfillment of tasks planned by the leaders and on the success or failure of their policies. Lessons of Eastern Europe have not passed unnoticed, and satisfaction of key social demands as well as an improved feedback [61] have come to assume some importance for Soviet leaders. At the same time, their individual power requirements remain at least as important as their perception of issues and social needs. In policy alignments both power needs and issues count, and policy shifts in the struggle for power are common. Intense disputes are generated over policy issues as each person's attitude is shaped by a complex matrix of functional responsibilities, career conditioning, ideological perceptions, and personal power requirements. Democratic centralism supplies the "rules of the game." Unless there is a showdown, policy differences within the Politburo emerge only in subtle hints. Polemics within and between bureaucracies and in the media are possible and may be vigorous (if kept within the confines of basic systemic consensus), but no challenge to central bodies and no appeal to broader constituency [62] is tolerated once the decision is made.

Chronic problems always in need of resolution occur in three major areas: the economy, social relations, and foreign policy. In recent decades the key economic problem has been the decline in the growth rate because of the failure of the economy to change from an extensive to an intensive growth pattern. Any decision to resolve the problem, however, inevitably runs into the conflict between the systemic requirement of political primacy and objective economic needs, a conflict present in decisions on resource allocation and economic priorities, economic reforms, and basic problems of incentives and labor productivity.

Social problems are rooted in the tension between group and individual demands for greater autonomy and the constraints imposed by the Party's leading role. This tension constricts the range of disagreement among the leaders. Ideological and political imperatives preclude real differences, as shown in the retreat of the advocates of reform and partial liberalization in the face of the "snowball" effect of concessions and the impact of the East European experience. Responses to pressure lack imagination and repeat old remedies: repressive measures (albeit half-hearted compared with Stalin's times) are punctuated with agitprop exhortations. At the same time there is a recognition that better standards of living may go a long way in defusing frustration about lack of freedom. Still, the demands of functional groups always take precedence over those of the consumer.

Foreign policy problems are related directly to the leaders' perceptions of USSR power requirements as well as to the Party's leading world role. In the transition from the Cold War through peaceful coexistence to détente, relations with the West, with the "Socialist Commonwealth," and with the Third World have formed interrelated areas of concern. The first problem has been shaped by the USSR-U.S. rivalry over spheres of influence, power, and nuclear capability, with the settlement of the World War II legacy in Europe as the crucial question. Maintenance of Soviet control in Eastern Europe and political stability there, and the crisis in relations with China are key problems in relations with the Communist countries. The rivalry with China in Asia has come to loom as large as the European question in Soviet foreign policy.

Khrushchev's policy mistakes were the major factor in the erosion of his power.[63] New and largely untested methods, sweeping shifts in allocations and in policy direction, and faith in the curative effects of reorganization caused shortfalls and dislocations, and substituted new problems for the old ones. Unrealistic goals were imposed on Soviet planners of industrial policy, and unwarranted redirection of investments was implemented. In agriculture, administrative reorganization was used as a sovereign remedy; the famous Virgin Lands scheme threw significant resources into marginal lands; and the U.S.-inspired corn-growing campaign caused huge shortages of grains. Small gains by the consumer failed to compensate for a retreat from the 1957 Thaw into repressive policies and intensive "vigilance" campaigns. The 1956–1957 concessions to national republics awakened expectations which were then denied in the post-1959 purges of national hierarchies. The emphasis on missiles in preference to conventional weapons perturbed military traditionalists. Arbitrary changes also marked Khrushchev's foreign policy. Friendly overtures to the West alternated with threats, and the ill-conceived Cuban confrontation brought deep humiliation. The 1955 concession to the Yugoslavs of "their own road to socialism" encouraged revisionism, polycentrism in Eastern Europe, and the events of 1956. De-Stalinization and the head-on conflict with China split the world Communist movement altogether.

Khrushchev's "harebrained scheming, hasty conclusions, rash decisions and action based on wishful thinking, boasting and empty words, bureaucratism" [64] served to antagonize, one by one, every bureaucratic elite in the country. They found their vested interests violated, their routine destroyed, their security of tenure eroded, and at the same time they had to cope with the results. In the final analysis it was Khrushchev's penchant for generating problems through attempted solutions that bred the coalition that removed him from office.

The Brezhnev-Kosygin team made a serious effort to restore balance in policy making by approaching problems in a less spectacular but more practical manner, steering a middle course between group demands. A new Five Year Plan scaled down Khrushchev's goals to manageable proportions; a new approach to planning and management recognized some market forces; and more emphasis was placed on neglected consumer and agricultural sectors. "Kosygin's" September 1965 reform was a compromise. At the micro-level, local managers were given new initiatives but the command planning system remained intact.[65] Performance improved, but the effects of the reform were offset by its partial character, by resurrection of old methods, and by the unwillingness of most managers, trained in the Stalinist school, to learn new ways.[66] The April 1973 Industrial Association Law reflected partial failure of the reform and a new effort to streamline economic management. Indicative of the same trend is the emphasis on computers, which are to inject rationality into planning processes without prejudice to controls from the top. Recognition of consumerism represents slightly higher allocations for the neglected sectors but certainly no shifts in priorities. Allocations for the group B (light) industries (traditionally 10 percent of the total) increased from Khrushchev's 13 percent (1961–1965) to 15 percent in 1966–1970, and shortfalls were forecasted for the Ninth Five Year Plan.[67]

Prompt and major policy changes, however, came in the crisis-ridden field of agriculture. With Brezhnev as the spokesman for the new line, the March 1965 plenum of the Central Committee doubled agricultural investment, established higher prices for state deliveries, and substantially raised peasant income by wage increases, a guaranteed minimum wage, and extended social security coverage. The expected increase in productivity did not materialize sufficiently, however, to offset rapid growth in agricultural subsidies: agriculture is still undercapitalized and undermechanized, and given the competition for allocations from other sectors, notably defense,[68] it is unlikely that even the current rate of subsidies will be maintained. Peasant attitudes are crucial on the productivity-incentives front. The link (zveno) conception advocated by Voronov (which would have restored group profit motive) lost out in favor of a revival of the old concept of agricultural cities (agrogorod) involving resettlement and the formation of "factories in the fields." This is implied in the new scheme of

farm councils (agriculture's answer to industrial associations) introduced in 1973.[69] An improvement in living standards is to compensate
for further tightening of controls on freedom of expression and for
intensifying the persecution of dissidents, even though methods and
timetables vary. Discussion of the problems inherent in the nationalities question continues, but it seems there is no agreement on how
best to deal with it, and thus no decision has been made.[70]

The lower profile and more cautious approach of the Brezhnev regime in foreign policy brought a substantial extension of influence in
the Third World, particularly at the periphery of China and in the
Middle East, and established Soviet military presence in the Mediterranean and the Indian Ocean, made possible by extensive build-up
of naval forces, particularly the submarine fleet. Brezhnev's policy of
détente achieved the long-sought *de jure* recognition of the Soviet
presence in Eastern Europe and the division of Germany; it also
brought trade gains and some progress in disarmament negotiations.
There have, however, been ups and downs (connected with President
Nixon's problems and the two Middle East wars) and the policy of
détente has strong critics in the Politburo. These critics warn against
the détente-bred danger of "infection" with Western ideas and point
out that the policy failed to bring about the expected technology
transfer.[71] The December 1974–January 1975 crisis was clearly triggered by detractors of détente as seen in policy statements made at
the time of Brezhnev's "illness," [72] but the Soviet commitment to
détente, to the continued development of trade exchanges and to
Vladivostok SALT II agreements, was restated with Brezhnev's reemergence in February [73] and the July Helsinki Conference. At the
same time a new emphasis has emerged on the Soviet Union's role as
the supporter of "national liberation movements" throughout the
world. In bloc relations, the Czech crisis of 1968 and Warsaw Pact
troop intervention (after six months of indecision in the Politburo)
undermined Party credibility as world leader of Communist forces,
but helped to preserve the leading role at home. The "Brezhnev
Doctrine" enhanced Brezhnev's image as a strict advocate of Soviet
hegemony and its enforcement in bloc affairs and introduced a new
emphasis on East European integration.[74] No progress was made toward settlement of the dispute with China or resolution of Soviet-
Chinese rivalry for the allegiance of world Communist parties.

In foreign policy, as in the choice of allocations at home, the dividing lines in the Politburo are neither clear-cut nor permanent, and
major policy shifts by individuals are not uncommon when power
positions are at stake. In functional terms only Secretary Brezhnev

TABLE 4.2 Politburo and Central Committee secretaries (March 1976).

| Party | | All Union | State |
|---|---|---|---|
| Central | Regional | | Regional |
| L. I. Brezhnev PB | V. V. Grishin  Moscow PB | *Central* | M. S. Solomentsev RSFSR PB |
| A. P. Kirilenko PB | G. V. Romanov  Leningrad PB | A. N. Kosygin PB | |
| A. J. Pelshe PB | D. A. Kunaev  Kazakhstan PB | K. T. Mazurov PB | |
| M. A. Suslov PB | V. V. Shcherbitsky  Ukraine PB | N. V. Podgorny PB | |
| F. D. Kulakov PB | P. M. Masherov  Belorussia PB$^c$ | | |
| D. F. Ustinov PB | Sh. R. Rashidov  Uzbekistan PB$^c$ | *Branches* | |
| B. N. Ponomarev PB$^c$ | G. K. Aliev  Azerbaijan PB$^c$ | Iu. V. Andropov PB | |
| I. V. Kapitonov$^s$ | | A. A. Grechko PB | |
| K. F. Katushev$^s$ | | A. A. Gromyko PB | |
| V. I. Dolgikh$^s$ | | P. N. Demichev PB$^c$ | |
| M. V. Zimianin$^s$ | | | |
| K. U. Chernenko$^s$ | | | |

PB, Politburo member; PB$^c$, candidate member; $^s$, Secretary, Central Committee, not a member of the Politburo.

73

carries an over-all responsibility, as well as being the head of the apparat and the main architect of foreign policy. In addition to a major policy area, almost every one of the top leaders carries responsibility for some minor ones, frequently combining domestic and foreign concerns. Moreover, they each have less obvious functional, regional, and ideological ties developed through their past careers, as well as ties of national origin. The latter may be misleading, however, as some minority nationals are counted among the Russifiers, as in the case of Marshal Grechko. Western analysts generally see a basic dichotomy in the Politburo between the "hard-liners" (the military, heavy industry, security, and orthodox ideological wing) and the "reformers-modernizers" (technocrats, consumer industry, and agricultural interests) defined by Vernon Aspaturian as a "security-productionist-ideological" coalition and a "consumptionist-agricultural-public sector" coalition.[75] In view of overlapping functional differentiation, the dichotomy tends to oversimplify the picture. Samizdat sources offer an attitudinal rather than functional classification into three basic groups: a dominant group of conservative moderates, a smaller group of "neo-Stalinists" on the right, and on the left a fringe of Marxist-Leninist "democrats." Another division offered is along the following lines: "dogmatists," "careerists," and "liberals." [76]

As befits an ambitious leader, Secretary Brezhnev steers a middle course. His enthusiasm for economic reforms was doubtful, but he spearheaded the 1965 and 1973 agricultural measures, and is identified with the policy of détente. At the same time, as the author of the "Brezhnev Doctrine" and promoter of controls at home, he projects a stern orthodox image. On the whole his policy performance offers something to all groups and resembles the manipulation pattern of Stalin and Khrushchev on their road to power. His career history, however, puts him squarely in the hard-line camp: his decade's consolidation of power runs parallel to the decline in influence of the "reformers" and of Kosygin personally. His identification with the policy of détente is so close, however, that its collapse might cost him power, although the events of 1975 appear to have reaffirmed both his power and the policy. In the case of foreign policy failures it would be difficult for Brezhnev to assign the blame to a "supporting leader" as happened to Voronov and then to Polyansky in agricultural policy.[77] Kosygin's personal identification with economic reforms has weakened him even though part of the blame for lack of success was assigned to Voronov; Kosygin's foreign policy achievements (such as the 1966 Tashkent agreement) are now forgotten. Except for Suslov, identified as the ideologist, no other leader has built a clear policy-connected image, except for obvious functional ties. It is too early to say which one, if any, of the supporting actors now in the Politburo may move forward.

Since 1964 the collective leadership has on the whole done well in domestic problem solving, but none of the policies provide long-range solutions, and thus crises will recur. It has been very successful in foreign policy. Caution and compromise have been characteristic of the group decision making, marked by some stalemates and immobilism. None of the leaders seems either bold or creative or powerful enough to try radically new solutions at home, which might move the country forward and might assure the leadership for the innovator.

There are differences in the requirements of the ascent to power and its maintenance. For an individual on the way up, the mechanics of control are of primary importance, as an institutional base is essential for access to decision making, and charisma follows in the wake of success. Once at the top, however, success in policy making becomes the crucial variable; without it a leader can neither retain his base nor reinforce his charisma. In the long run, however, given the experience so far, it is only the accretion of genuine charisma that grants security of tenure. Because it performs the Party-leading role the apparat is still the essential instrument for the rise to power; in power maintenance other bureaucracies may and do supplement and balance its effectiveness. But within the context of the system no other bureaucracy may serve as the arena of the leadership context.

Systemic constraints and growing complexity of meeting the requirements appear to favor the collective over one-man leadership, but a collective arrangement, which depends on a dynamic balance of contending factions, is unstable and inherently generates the contest for supreme power. Aspirants for the top leadership may continue to trade, balance, and compromise for prolonged periods, as demonstrated in the years since 1964. Compromises are the rule in decision making (only a total stalemate may necessitate an appeal to outside agents—the Central Committee, conceivably the armed forces), and a mechanism exists for absorbing policy failures by blaming an individual who is then removed, and co-opting another without prejudice to the stability of collective arrangements. But a tendency toward coalescence of power does eventually emerge as one of the contenders is consistently better able than the others to meet the challenges of power and policy. The struggle for ascendancy within the collective leadership remains the systemic feature as long as members' selection and tenure is not institutionalized, even though the room for maneuver is severely constrained.[78] The system's dynamics generate periodic pendulum swings on a continuum between a collective leadership and one-man ascendancy. Historical experience so far is inadequate to draw valid conclusions, but it seems that periods of collective leadership are bound now to predominate. The Soviet leadership selection process does not seem to favor men with the spark that is needed to acquire genuine charisma for lifelong ascendancy, and the growing complexity of the national and international environment maximizes the potential for policy failures.

In the aftermath of the Twenty-Fifth Party Congress it appears that Secretary Brezhnev made significant progress on the road to personal power. At some point between 1971 and 1976 the pendulum seems to have swung from the stage of an "oligarchic" [79] to a "pluralistic" [80] model to that of a model of "limited personal rule." [81] Whether it will continue to move toward full ascendancy and, if so, for how long, remains to be seen.

It is sometimes assumed that a growing recognition of occupational-functional-group interests in decision making may eventually lead to the gradual institutionalization of pluralism and the evolution of the system away from the Marxist-Leninist model. But developments do not seem to point in this direction. So far interest articulation is channeled within the Party and there are no signs of the formation of independent foci of political influence. In terms of future dynamics it is well to remember that by virtue of its ideological and traditional legitimacy, the system—and the Party—has proved remarkably durable, and that a reaffirmation of orthodoxy is considered the condition of survival not only by the current leaders but also by the future ones who are now being groomed as they rise through the Party committees. Whatever their disagreements in policy making, the top leaders stay well within a basic consensus on the system's key features. Reforms undertaken in response to group pressures are always weighed in terms of their cost to the system's survival and particularly to the survival of the leading role of the Party. The central predicament of the Party—in a changing society—is that its legitimacy will increasingly be measured by its pragmatic performance. But if the Party becomes merely the coordinator of specific interest group demands, it loses its leading and ideological role, hence its claim to the monopoly of power. None of the ruling Communist parties has yet shown any inclination to withdraw gracefully, either in terms of ideology or of power, in the face of growing pluralism.

# Office Holding
# and Elite Status:
# The Central Committee
# of the CPSU

## ROBERT V. DANIELS

5

The subject of Soviet politics lends itself to the subdiscipline known as "elite studies" remarkably well. This is so because the Soviet political structure is capped by an elite stratum institutionalized as the Central Committee of the Communist Party. It is the aim of this essay to explore the makeup of the Central Committee as an elite defined by the rules of the Soviet system, and to derive whatever propositions may be reached thereby concerning the operational principles of the Soviet regime.

Since the mid-1960s a multitude of American works on Soviet politics, reflecting the encroachments of the behavioral revolution on the precincts of Kremlinology, have addressed themselves to the analysis of the Central Committee of the CPSU as an institutionally defined elite.[1] In good behavioral style and with much statistical sophistication these works have explored the educational and career backgrounds of Central Committee members and probed the channels for "recruitment" or "co-optation" into that body.[2] They have weighed the "representation" of functional entities such as the Party apparatus, government bureaucracy, military, intelligentsia, and such, as well as various geographic regions and social groups, in the makeup of the Central Committee membership.[3] Almost never, however, and only by indirection if at all, has this school of investigation actually inquired into the exact composition of the Central Committee and the specific posts that are associated with Central Committee status.[4]

## JOB SLOTS AND THE MAKEUP OF THE CENTRAL COMMITTEE

The membership of the Central Committee is arrived at, of course, neither by free election nor by random appointment. The single list of proposed members, presented at each Party congress and voted in unanimously as a matter of routine, proves on close analysis to be very carefully made up in accordance with a system of unwritten (or at least unannounced) rules. Except for a few special cases, these rules (extending back to the early years of the Stalin era) guarantee Central Committee status to holders of elite-status bureaucratic offices—Party, governmental, and military—with a sprinkling of the top figures in the other sectors of society (trade union, academic, cultural, and so forth). There is in practice an organic and automatic connection between this specific set of offices and the Central Committee status of their incumbents. It is therefore possible to view the Central Committee as a well-defined and quite stable set of leading job slots whose occupants enjoy the elite status conferred by Central Committee membership as long as and only as long as they occupy their respective offices. Invariably an individual appointed to a position carrying Central Committee status will be nominated and elected to the Central Committee at the next Party congress. Conversely, a member of the Central Committee who is removed from the job that conferred Central Committee rank and is not appointed to another position of like status will almost always be dropped from the Central Committee at the next Party congress. By the same token, a man is never dropped from the Central Committee unless he has previously been removed from the job that gave him that rank.[5]

So close is the association between membership on the Central Committee and holding an office of Central Committee rank that it may be questioned which is really the most important and which is derivative. For individuals in the Party apparatus and government, at least, it is probably fair to say that the true basis of elite status is appointment to one of the set of leading jobs in the central and provincial administration. The automatic membership in the Central Committee that follows would then be more the visible badge of status than its source.

Since membership on the Central Committee is governed by previous appointment to a job slot carrying Central Committee status, it follows that the composition of the Central Committee is determined not at the time of the congress, but over the entire period elapsing since the previous congress during which particular decisions were made to remove, install, or retain particular individuals in particular Central Committee-level slots. With a few possible exceptions the make-up of the Central Committee is the reflection of a series of previous decisions about the composition of the elite, that are merely revealed in the formal election at the congress.[6] How such decisions are actually arrived at, of course, is one of the best-kept secrets of the Soviet political process; one must assume that they are made at the level of the Politburo with staff assistance or recommendations from the responsible heads of the Party Secretariat.

Another type of decision may be made more closely in conjunction with the congress itself—namely the decision as to which additional jobs will be awarded Central Committee status or promoted thereto, and how the representational balance of functional and geographical areas may be altered. Such decisions are evidently taken in a fairly restricted context, in a stable and long-term tradition, with change occurring in one direction only: upgrading of jobs, not downgrading (with rare exceptions), and steady expansion of the over-all size of the Central Committee (see table 5.1). What is obviously going on is a progressive lowering of the criteria for membership in the Central Committee (or for candidate status or membership on the Central Auditing Commission), as jobs of marginally lower importance are accorded elite status at each successive congress. Thus a sort of long-term inflation in the status value of Central Committee membership is going on. This extension of status symbols is based, as far as any data indicate, on the significance imputed to the various job slots that are next in the line of intrinsic importance, and not on the identity of the individuals who happen to hold those jobs. The following analysis of the increment to the Central Committee between 1966 and 1971 makes this job-status criterion quite clear. The only significant areas of discretion that the decision-makers appear to allow themselves are (1) how much to expand the various ranks at any one congress, and (2) the apportionment of the resulting gains among the various functional areas represented in the Central Committee.

The widely entertained notion that the Central Committee is apportioned to "represent" various functional and geographic interests has a firm basis in actual Soviet practice. However, this apportionment of representation operates not in terms of individuals, fundamentally, but of job slots. The unwritten code allocates to each functional hierarchy and to each union republic (and often province) a proportion of the seats in the Central Committee corresponding to the imputed status and importance of the particular institution or region. These seats, in turn, are permanently attached to the highest-status job slots in the institution or region. The holders of these job slots, whoever they may be, are then recognized by election to the Central Committee at the Party congress.[7]

TABLE 5.1   Expansion of the Central Committee.

|  | 19th Congress (1952) | 20th Congress (1956) | 22nd Congress (1961) | 23rd Congress (1966) | 24th Congress (1971) |
|---|---|---|---|---|---|
| Full members | 125 | 133 | 175 | 195 | 241 |
| (Increase) | — | (6.4%) | (31.6%) | (11.4%) | (24.6%) |
| Candidate members | 110 | 122 | 156 | 165 | 155 |
| (Increase) | — | (10.9%) | (27.9%) | (5.8%) | (−6.1%) |
| Central Auditing Commission | 37 | 63 | 65 | 79 | 81 |
| (Increase) | — | (70.3%) | (3.2%) | (21.5%) | (2.5%) |

FUNCTIONAL REPRESENTATION AND STATUS

A fine sense of status differentials emerges in the apportionment of Central Committee seats to the various constituencies. In the functional breakdown the Party apparatus (the hierarchy of professional Party secretaries) naturally has the lion's share—99 out of 241 (41 percent) at the Twenty-Fourth Party Congress in 1971, with the civil government (not counting the military, police, and diplomats) somewhat behind—76 (32 percent) in the same year. These two hierarchies, Party and governmental, have between them consistently occupied close to three-fourths of the Central Committee. Small delegations hold the seats for the other institutional categories—the military (twenty or 8 percent in 1971), the diplomats (sixteen or 7 percent, mainly ex-Party secretaries in Communist capitals), the cultural and scientific sector (eight or 3 percent), the police agencies (two—KGB Chairman Andropov and the head of the newly established Union Ministry of Internal Affairs, N. A. Shchelokov), and the trade unions (two—Chairman Shelepin and the then Chief Secretary V. I. Prokhorov), in descending order of magnitude and implicit status for each group. Geographical balance is observed within the Party and governmental groups (the others being too small for this breakdown), with a careful assignment of seats to central and regional job slots corresponding to the importance of both the job and the region. Table 5.2 summarizes the allocation of seats to the various functional areas in 1966 and in 1971.

In the Party apparatus, apart from a bloc of seats (twenty in 1971) for the central secretariat and its staff, Central Committee membership is accorded to local Party secretaryships on the basis of the importance of their jurisdictions. Full Central Committee rank is enjoyed by the first secretaries of thirty-two out of the fifty-five oblasts and krais in the RSFSR—including all of the more populous and important ones —and the first secretaries of the seven largest of the fifteen ASSR in the RSFSR. The list further includes the first and second secretaries of the independent city of Moscow, the first secretary of Leningrad city, and the second secretary of Leningrad province, reflecting the special importance of these two centers.[8]

Also accorded Central Committee status are the first secretaries of all of the fourteen other union republics, plus subordinate secretaries and selected oblast secretaries in numbers commensurate with the importance of the republic. There were in 1971, in addition to the first secretaries of the respective republics, twelve seats for the Ukraine, five for Kazakhstan, two for Belorussia, one extra for Uzbekistan, and (an apparent exception to the status rule) one for the second secretary of Turkmenia.

In the civil government, the bulk of the Central Committee seats (58) are assigned to ministries and ministry-level agencies in the Union government. Seven seats are allocated to the government of the RSFSR, including the Politburo-level seat of its prime minister. A few other seats are reserved for the prime ministers of the more important union republics (the Ukraine, Kazakhstan, Belorussia, Uzbekistan, and Georgia) and chairmen of the presidium of the Supreme Soviet of the first four of the above groups, plus Estonia for reasons that are unclear and discussed further on. One anomalous case completes the list—a provincial government chief from the Ukraine, who had earlier attained Central Committee rank as a mass representative.

The system of apportionment evidenced by the distribution of Central Committee seats in the Party apparatus and in the government strongly suggests the existence of a complex matrix of unacknowledged but strongly felt status relationships in the Soviet political system. These relationships hold not among individuals, but among job slots, which continue to be ranked and represented in highly stable and predictable ways however much their individual tenants may come and go. By the device of Central Committee rank, status differences are systematically and sensitively recognized among types of function and among geographical units as well as between obviously superior and subordinate offices. The fine and enduring observance of these distinctions of rank is made even more apparent when the analysis takes account of the apportionment of candidate membership in the Central Committee, and of seats on the Central Auditing Commission, of which more to follow.

There are two small groups in the Central Committee membership where the job-slot rule does not apply. One is the category of retired dignitaries, former leaders usually of Politburo rank who managed to avoid being bracketed with one "anti-Party group" or another. (Only one man, Mikoyan, remained in this category at the Central Committee level in 1971.) The other, larger group consists of the "honored workers," industrial executives, milkmaids, and the like, who are presumably nominated to the Central Committee to give it the flavor of popular participation. Sixteen such individuals were elected in 1971 (a marked increase, incidentally, over the eight of 1966). Inclusion in this group depends neither on personal officeholding nor (so far as is discernible) on individual renown, but on the good fortune of selection to represent a social category. Within these terms the rules of representation continue to apply, with apportionment of these "mass representatives" among economic sectors and regions of the country roughly in relation to the importance imputed to each. All sixteen mass representatives in 1971 came from the Russian Republic except for two Ukrainians. Four were directors of factories (including the Magnitogorsk Combine, regularly holding a seat); ten (including two women) were workers in industry or construction; while only two, a kolkhoz chairman and a kolkhoz brigade leader, represented the agricultural sector. It is difficult to regard the mass representatives as persons of influence, and in fact they tend to be replaced at each congress by comrades from the same constituency, at a much higher rate of turnover than the Central Committee as a whole.

STATUS RULES IN THE EXPANSION OF THE CENTRAL COMMITTEE

The status-ranking nature of the Central Committee's membership is made particularly clear by analysis of the periodic expansion in the body. The secular trend, observable at each Party congress, is to increase the size of the Central Committee and thereby confer the status of Central Committee membership on an additional group of job slots (see table 5.1). The 1966 Central Committee of 195 was increased by forty-six in 1971, reflecting the net gain after fifty-seven slots were upgraded from candidate status or newly created, and eleven were downgraded to candidate status or left unfilled.

Gains in the Central Committee were apportioned as follows: The central Party apparatus, +2 (10 percent); the Party in the Russian Republic, +5 (13 percent); the Party in the other republics, +6 (20 percent); the central government, +17 (41 percent); the government of the Russian Republic, no changes; government in the other republics, +1 (10 percent); the military, +6 (43 percent); the diplomats, +2 (14 percent); the police, +1 (100 percent). The cultural-scientific sector was held constant at eight members, while the trade unions were cut from three to two. Two retired dignitaries (Shvernik and Voroshilov) died without replacement; one seat was awarded to a newly created post fitting none of the above categories, the chairmanship of the Committee of Soviet Women (held by the cosmonaut Valentina Nikolaeva-Tereshkova); and the mass representatives, as noted above, were doubled in number.

A close look at these increments of Central Committee representation is particularly revealing as to the status distinctions governing these awards. In the central Party apparatus, the net change, apart from some reshuffling among the department heads of the Central Committee staff, was the extension of Central Committee rank to the First Deputy Chairman of the Party Control Commission (by transferring an incumbent member, K. N. Grishin, to the job) and the upgrading of the post of Assistant to the General Secretary (by promoting the incumbent, G. Ye. Tsukanov, directly from Central Auditing Commission status). In the Russian Republic four growing or strategic oblasts (Amur, Penza, Sakhalin, and Vologda) were raised to Central Committee status by the promotion of their incumbent first secretaries from candidate rank, and the same was done to increase the list of autonomous republics of Central Committee rank from three to seven. These moves were partially offset by downgrading three relatively stagnant central Russian oblasts—Belgorod, Kursk, and Orel (accomplished by transferring or dropping the incumbent first secretaries and awarding their successors only candidate rank). In the Ukraine three oblasts* and the fourth secretaryship of the republic were upgraded, offset by the downgrading of the Crimean oblast (evidently an anomaly in its status of 1966–1971). In Kazakhstan the Karaganda oblast was upgraded to join the capital region of Alma-Ata and two

* Including Kiev, normally at Central Committee rank until 1966.

other oblasts in the Virgin-lands area. The first secretary of the Tuva Autonomous oblast (S. K. Toka) was rewarded with full membership after long service at candidate rank, and the second secretary of Turkmenia (V. N. Rykov) was elevated in a nonconforming move that perhaps presaged his transfer to a higher post.

The Central Government was the beneficiary of the largest single bloc of promotions in 1971, adding to the forty-one ministers and equivalent officials holding Central Committee membership in 1966 a list of nine ministers and chairmen of state committees (ranging from the Minister of the Chemical Industry to the Chairman of the All-Union Farm Machinery Association) promoted in office, three ministries upgraded with new incumbents, and eight ministerial positions newly organized since 1966 (against three dissolved or unfilled). In the Russian Republic the governmental chief of the Moscow Province (N. T. Kozlov) was promoted to the Central Committee, which rank had already been enjoyed by the "major" of Moscow (V. F. Promyslov) but by no other local government official. The rising importance of Kazakhstan was reflected in the elevation of the chairman of the Presidium of its Supreme Soviet (S. B. Niyazbekov) to the Central Committee, to correspond with his counterparts in the Ukraine, Belorussia, and Uzbekistan. Chairman of the Presidium of Estonia's Supreme Soviet, A. P. Vader, was jumped from the Central Auditing Commission to the Central Committee in an exceptional move that bears no logical relation to the importance of the republic, but balanced the retirement of Central Committee member P. V. Ruben from the Supreme Soviet of Latvia. Conceivably Vader and his predecessor were selected as class representatives of the governmental chieftains in the minor republics.

Four military slots were upgraded in 1971—the Chief of Air Defense (who was also made a Deputy Minister of Defense, a status regularly carrying Central Committee rank); the commanders of the Leningrad and Central Asian military districts (joining the Moscow district at Central Committee rank); and the commander of the Soviet forces in East Germany. These adjustments obviously reflect military priorities. In addition, a new (third!) First Deputy Minister of Defense was created at the Central Committee level. Marshal Bagramian retained his Central Committee rank as he joined Marshal Konev in the honored retirement status of Inspector General. In the police sector, the one previous membership for the KGB chairmanship was supplemented by the re-created Union Ministry of Internal Affairs.

In the diplomatic sector three interesting adjustments were made by the Twenty-Fourth Party Congress, adding to the roster of ambassadors to the bloc countries the ambassador to the most powerful non-Communist country (in the person of A. F. Dobrynin, promoted from candidate), and the ambassadorships to two promising Latin American allies, Chile and Cuba—the one post filled with a sitting Central Committee member (A. V. Basov), the other with the one ex-member (N. P. Tolubeyev) to have been restored in 1971. In the trade-union sector the Ukraine lost the special distinction of Central Committee membership for its chairman. The literary world gained an additional member in the person of G. M. Markov, the new secretary of the Writers' Union, while the representation of the director of the Institute of Philosophy lapsed. Finally, among the mass representatives, four workers and one kolkhoznik were promoted to full membership and three additional worker slots were filled.

CENTRAL COMMITTEE CANDIDATES AND THE
CENTRAL AUDITING COMMISSION

A study of the apportionment and expansion of the full members of the Central Committee by no means exhausts the possibilities for analysis of the principles of elite selection in the Party. The same rules of job-slot apportionment, at lesser levels of status, govern the selection both of candidate members of the Central Committee (155 in 1971) and of the members of the Central Auditing Commission (CAC) (81 in 1971). The latter institutional curiosity, whatever fiduciary functions it may exercise, is not primarily what its name suggests. Its make-up shows it to be a sort of honorable-mention category for jobholders whose slots fall just short of candidate status.* With the inclusion of the CAC, there are thus three distinct ranks (plus the two super-ranks of Politburo and Politburo Candidate membership) in the institutionally defined Soviet elite that in 1971 totaled 477 individuals.

Job slots are classified among the various ranks of the elite with remarkable finesse to give their tenants the appropriate status. The status principle holds throughout, among the various functional hierarchies and among the territorial divisions of the Union as well as between people of different formal rank in particular institutions.[9] To illustrate, these allocations of status among the three ranks are

---

* The chairman of the Central Auditing Commission, currently G. F. Sizov, enjoys a status, according to the evidence of career patterns and press references, equal to a Central Committee member or perhaps almost to the Secretariat (*Pravda*, April 9, 1966). He alone has no regular function apart from his CAC work, and is probably a party control official in fact.

traced in the 1971 Central Committee, with note made both of the degree of consistency and of occasional exceptions.

In the central Party apparatus, along with the twenty full Central Committee members there were in 1971 eleven candidate members and fourteen members of the CAC—for the most part heads of lesser departments, editors of Party journals, and the first deputy heads of certain key departments whose heads were full members.[10] From the Party in the Russian Republic, in addition to the forty-three full members, there were thirty-three candidates, mostly first secretaries of lesser oblasts from Archangel to Yaroslavl together with the first secretaries of seven ASSR. Also included at candidate rank were the first secretary of Novosibirsk City (reflecting its size and scientific importance), the three Moscow men mentioned earlier, and one individual, a woman raikom secretary from Volgograd oblast, who fits no obvious criterion for elite status except possibly as a class representative of the lower party apparatus. The six RSFSR members of the CAC were a miscellaneous group: the first secretaries of the two remaining oblasts, Kamchatka and Murmansk, and the last ASSR, the Mordvin, together with the first secretary of the largest National Area, the Evenki; plus the second secretary of Leningrad City and a second woman representative of the lesser apparatus. (The Evenki appointment, first made in 1966, again reflects the occasional practice of extending token elite status to selected representatives of certain categories of offices not normally accorded such rank.)

Among the Union Republics the distribution of apparatus seats at the candidate and CAC levels, like the full memberships, reflected the importance imputed to each republic. The Ukrainian Party apparatus along with its thirteen Central Committee memberships of 1971 received eight candidate slots—the last two of its central secretaries, four oblast first secretaries in addition to the eight of full member rank, the first secretary of the capital city of Kiev, and one lesser figure, the first secretary of the city of Dneprodzerzhinsk (presumably as a token representative of the local apparatus). To these were added one further oblast secretary (Kirovograd) at the CAC level, leaving twelve of the smaller and more rural oblasts without representation in the Central Committee elite.

The Party in Kazakhstan had, in addition to its six full memberships, six candidate positions, five assigned to major oblast secretaries and one to a representative of the local apparatus (a raikom secretary in the Virgin Lands area). The one CAC membership went to the third secretary for the Kazakh Republic. Five lesser oblasts in Kazakhstan failed to be represented.

TABLE 5.2  Allocation of Central Committee seats, 1966 (in parentheses) and 1971.

| | Full members | Candidate members | Central Auditing Commission | Total |
|---|---|---|---|---|
| Party Apparatus | (86) 99 | (69) 68 | (30) 26 | (185) 193 |
|   Central | (18) 20 | (13) 12 | (15) 14 | (46) 45 |
|   Russian Republic | (38) 43 | (36) 33 | (8) 6 | (82) 82 |
|   Other republics | (30) 36 | (20) 24 | (7) 6 | (57) 66 |
| Government | (87) 114 | (75) 63 | (35) 35 | (197) 212 |
|   Central | (41) 58 | (30) 22 | (11) 19 | (82) 99 |
|   Russian Republic | (7) 7 | (9) 8 | (4) 1 | (20) 16 |
|   Other republics | (10) 11 | (16) 16 | (10) 7 | (36) 34 |
|   Military | (14) 20 | (17) 12 | (4) 3 | (35) 35 |
|   Police | (1) 2 | (1) 2 | 1 | (2) 5 |
|   Diplomatic | (14) 16 | (2) 3 | (6) 4 | (22) 23 |
| Other sectors | (11) 11 | (7) 11 | (8) 7 | (26) 29 |
|   Trade unions | (3) 2 | (4) 4 | (3) 3 | (10) 9 |
|   Scientifc/intellectual | (8) 8 | (2) 6 | (5) 4 | (15) 18 |
|   Miscellaneous | 1 | (1) 1 | | (1) 2 |
| Mass represenatives | (8) 16 | (13) 12 | (6) 9 | (27) 37 |
| Retired leaders | (3) 1 | (1) 1 | | (4) 2 |
| Position undetermined | | | 4 | 4 |
| Total | (195) 241 | (165) 155 | (79) 81 | (439) 477 |

In Belorussia one apparatchik at the candidate and CAC levels (the Mogilev and Brest obkom secretaries, respectively) joined the three full members. For Uzbekistan it was three candidates (the secretaries for Tashkent and Samarkand oblasts and the Karakalpak ASSR) along with the two full members. Georgia, Azerbaidzhan, Kirgizia, Moldavia, Tadzhikistan, and Latvia placed their second secretaries as candidates; the second secretaries of the remaining small republics (Estonia, Lithuania, and Armenia) were put on the CAC. Throughout, the ranking of apparatus assignments in the Central Committee corresponded closely both to the importance of the republic or region, and the relative status of the particular job.

Turning now to the civil government we can observe essentially the same principles of status distribution, although with much more emphasis on the central functions. The Union government, with fifty-eight full memberships, was assigned twenty-two candidate slots in 1971, going to a variety of specialized ministries together with five particular functionaries (the secretary of the Presidium of the Supreme Soviet, the editor of *Izvestia,* the chairman of the Novosti Press Agency, the director of the space program, and the third of four "first" deputy chairmen of Gosplan (the first two along with the chairman enjoying full member status, and the last sitting on the CAC). At the CAC level the central government had altogether nineteen memberships, for a wide miscellany of positions ranging from the Minister of the Meat and Dairy Industry and the chairman of the Central Statistical Administration to the editor of "Village Life" and the business manager of the Council of Ministers. Every central minister save one (the minister of the "medical industry"—*not* health) and every chairman of a State Committee or other functionary of cabinet rank was included as a member of the Central Committee or at least of the CAC.

A comparable number (twenty-four and eight respectively) of candidate and CAC slots was apportioned among the Union Republics. The government of the Russian Republic in addition to its seven full memberships had eight candidate slots (five deputy prime ministers, the deputy chairman of the presidium of the republic Supreme Soviet, and the government chiefs of the province and city of Leningrad) plus one CAC membership (the Minister of Social Security, D. P. Komarova, perhaps singled out to add some representation for women in the bureaucracy). The Ukrainian government had two candidate members (both deputy prime ministers). Kazakhstan had a candidate slot for its first deputy prime minister in addition to its two full governmental members; Uzbekistan had CAC rank for its corresponding first deputy. All republics—nine of them—whose premier was not a full member had candidate status for him. Similarly, the same group of republics (except Estonia) whose chairman of the Presidium of the Supreme Soviet was not a full member had either candidate rank (Moldavia, Tadzhikistan, Latvia, Lithuania) or CAC rank for him.

Beyond the Party apparatus and the government bureaucracy, representation at the candidate and CAC levels drops off sharply just as it does among the full members. The military had twelve candidate positions and three memberships on the CAC in addition to their twenty full members, with most of the lower slots going to commanders of military districts as well as three political officers. Incidentally, and not surprisingly in view of the over-all system of status correspondences in the Soviet elite, Central Committee rank and military rank are interleaved: all Marshals of the Soviet Union, almost all the Generals of the Army, and a few Colonel-Generals are full members of the Central Committee; candidate members and members of the CAC are with a few exceptions Colonel-Generals or the equivalent.

Other groups apart from the military had only a token sprinkling of candidate and CAC posts: for the police, in addition to their two full memberships, two candidate slots and one CAC membership for deputy chairmen of the KGB; for the diplomats, in addition to the sixteen full memberships, three candidate slots and four CAC memberships, all ambassadorships except for (third) Deputy Foreign Minister V. S. Semenov. (The particular ambassadorships included reflect particular diplomatic interests of the Soviet Union—ally Egypt and neighbor Finland are at the candidate level; two major Western powers, Britain and Italy, and the two smaller Asian Communist governments, North Korea and North Viet Nam, were at the CAC level. All the ambassadors to Communist governments—except Albania— were thereby included at some level in the elite.) The trade unions, limited to two full members, received four candidate slots (three central secretaries and the Ukrainian union chief) and three CAC memberships (the heads of three leading unions—railroad workers, metal workers, and agricultural workers). Along with the union people might be listed the chairman of the Cooperative Organization, a candidate member. In the scientific and cultural sector the eight full members were joined by six candidates (editors, institute directors, and the president of the Kazakh Academy of Sciences) and four members of the CAC (secretaries of cultural workers' unions and the director of the Institute of the USA). One candidate—Marshal Budenny —remained in the retired-leaders category. Finally, the mass representatives, increased from eight to sixteen at the full member level, were adjusted from thirteen to twelve candidates and from six to nine members of the CAC, duly distributed among men and women (in a 5:1 ratio), various sectors of the economy (mainly industry among the members and candidates, half agricultural among the CAC members), and the national minorities (three Ukrainians, two Belorussians, a Kazakh shepherd, an Uzbek sovkhoz employee, and a kolkhoz chairman from the Jewish Autonomous Oblast). (To these numbers probably there should be added the four CAC members, three of them women, of unidentified occupation.)

POLITICAL RANK AND THE REPRESENTATION OF STATUS

The foregoing tabulation of positions in the Central Committee has been presented in detail to demonstrate the consistency with which status and representative considerations are followed in determining the over-all makeup of the institutionally defined elite group in Soviet society. Numbers of Central Committee seats at all three ranks are allocated to the functional bureaucracies in proportion to their imputed importance. Union republics and regions are represented, if at all, in numbers and at ranks proportionate to their importance, and in lesser numbers or at lower levels in bureaucracies that are less important. Where a given territorial entity qualifies for a number of seats for its Party or government officialdom, Central Committee ranks are always distributed in a manner consistent with the relative job status of the officials to be included—first secretary equal to or ahead of second secretary, prime minister ahead of or equal to chairman of the Presidium of the Supreme Soviet, and so on. At the same time Party precedence over the government is always maintained: first secretary of republic or oblast always equal to or ahead of the respective government chief. Tables 5.3 and 5.4 illustrate the operation of the status matrix in two particular cases, one simple (the cities with Central Committee representation) and the other fairly complex (the Union Republics). Note the consistent downward steps in rank proceeding both horizontally (left to right) through the job hierarchy and downward through the pecking order of cities or republics as the case may be.

Where a few anomalies crop up in this close-knit matrix of status relationships they suggest a supplementary principle at work, of token representation of certain social categories. Evidently the "mass representatives" are not the only ones who accomplish this function. Most notable besides them are the five people (two of them women) who

TABLE 5.3  Status matrix: cities with Central Committee representation, 1971.

| City | 1st Sec. | Chairman, Executive Committee | 2nd Sec. | 3rd Sec. | 4th Sec. |
|------|----------|-------------------------------|----------|----------|----------|
| Moscow | PB | CC | CC | Cand. | Cand. |
| Leningrad | CC | Cand. | CAC | — | — |
| Kiev | Cand. | — | — | — | — |
| Novosibirsk | Cand. | — | — | — | — |
| Dneprodzerzhinsk (token) | Cand. | — | — | — | — |

PB, Politburo; CC, Central Committee; Cand., candidate; CAC, Central Auditing Commission.

seem to represent the lower Party apparatus—and who are again distributed by importance of nationality (three to the Russian Republic, including one non-Russian; one to the Ukraine; and one to Kazakhstan).

CONCLUSIONS

The basic proposition advanced by the foregoing analysis is that the Soviet elite identified by membership in the Central Committee of the CPSU (including the Central Auditing Commission) is chosen according to a set of unannounced rules that display a fine and complex sensitivity to a variety of interlocking status relationships. The Central Committee thus constituted consists of a carefully defined set of job slots, in which the rank of any individual member of the elite depends on the status assigned to his job, or (in a few instances) on the imputed status of the social category of which he is a token representative.

For most members of the Central Committee it would appear that any real personal influence they may exercise is based on the jobs to which they have been bureaucratically appointed, rather than on the derivative status of their Central Committee rank. It follows that the influence of a particular individual is more or less directly proportionate to the importance of his specific job. Numerous members of the Central Committee—the mass representatives, many nationality representatives, other token figures, and probably most of the incum-

TABLE 5.4   Status matrix: Union Republics with Central Committee representation, 1971.

| | 1st Sec. | Prime Minister | 2nd Sec. | Chairman, Presidium | 1st Deputy Prime Minister | 3rd Sec. |
|---|---|---|---|---|---|---|
| RSFSR | — | PB | — | CC | CC (2) | — |
| Ukraine | PB | Cand. PB | CC | CC | Cand. | CC |
| Kazakhstan | PB | CC | CC | CC | Cand. | CAC |
| Uzbekistan | Cand. PB | CC | CC | CC | CAC | — |
| Belorussia | Cand. PB | CC | CC | CC | — | — |
| Georgia | Cand. PB | CC | Cand. | CAC | — | — |
| Latvia | CC | Cand. | Cand. | Cand. | — | — |
| Moldavia | CC | Cand. | Cand. | Cand. | — | — |
| Tadzhikistan | CC | Cand. | Cand. | Cand. | — | — |
| Turkmenia | CC | Cand. | CC | CAC | — | — |
| Azerbaidzhan | CC | Cand. | Cand. | CAC | — | — |
| Kirgizia | CC | Cand. | Cand. | CAC | — | — |
| Estonia | CC | Cand. | CAC | CC | — | — |
| Lithuania | CC | Cand. | CAC | Cand. | — | — |
| Armenia | CC | Cand. | CAC | CAC | — | — |
| Tuva autonomous oblast | CC | — | — | — | — | — |

bents of technical government ministries—cannot be regarded as people of significant political weight. Consequently the Central Committee taken as a whole cannot be considered a collective leadership of fundamentally equal individuals. If there is any significant collective leadership at work it must be a smaller group within the Central Committee holding inherently influential posts (and most likely people who have held such posts for some time). Recent expansions of the Central Committee, leaning to token jobholders and mass representatives of little influence, have probably diluted the influence of the Central Committee as a whole and enhanced the importance of the putative leading group within that body. Research to try to identify such a group—perhaps twenty to thirty individuals in addition to the twenty-five making up the Politburo (including candidates) and the Secretariat—might yield interesting results.

Whatever the political weight of the Central Committee as a whole, the job-slot basis of membership lends a measure of tenure to the individual member and of stability to the body as a whole. The weight of bureaucratic tradition, if nothing else, makes it difficult to remove or demote a large number of individuals suddenly or capriciously, since the rules of the game would require that they be replaced in their specific jobs at the same time. Such removals would involve questions of relations with the local or functional constituency and the over-all effectiveness of the system. Probably for reasons of convenience, if not salutary neglect, some Central Committee members in ministerial positions and minority republics have held their office and rank for extraordinarily long periods of time—the Minister of Railroads Beshchev since 1948, the First Secretary of Lithuania Snieckus ever since the Soviet takeover in 1940 (both put on the Central Committee in 1952). To be sure, the top leadership has the power of discipline over the Central Committee by removing any jobholder from the position that confers membership—but if this power were used too broadly and abruptly, threatening the entire membership at once, it is conceivable that the Central Committee could mobilize its statutory authority to depose the leadership as it was called on to depose Khrushchev in 1964. The top leadership and the Central Committee elite thus stand in a position of mutual vulnerability.

The discretionary power of the top leadership over the membership of the Central Committee is further restricted, in addition to these practical limits on its powers of removal, in the choice of replacement members and in those it may add by expanding the membership at the time of the Party congress. The unwritten rules of the system call for replacing a fallen member of the Central Committee with the person who assumed his Central-Committee-ranked job, and with minor exceptions at the lower ranks, these rules have been followed closely. In effect, the decision about a Central Committee membership becomes a commitment at the time the aspiring functionary is appointed to a job carrying a Central Committee rank, possibly years before the next Congress formalizes the individual's status. While it might appear that expanding the Central Committee (substantial in 1961 and in 1971) would offer the leadership an opportunity to pack it with individuals of their choice, the network of unwritten rules and expectations about Central Committee rank and job status very narrowly restricts the options of the leadership in opening up new membership slots. There is an overwhelming weight of practice and tradition governing the assignments of new memberships at all three levels to the jobs next in line according to rank or territorial importance within each functional hierarchy, while respecting the basic existing proportions of representation among the functional hierarchies and the territorial units. If the leadership made its decision to expand the Central Committee at the time of the Party congress, it would largely be restricted in its choice of new members at each rank to the incumbents of the jobs that were most logically ready for promotion in status. The analysis earlier of the expansion of the Central Committee between 1966 and 1971 amply illustrates this point, although the same conclusion would be sustained by detailed analysis of the expansion ordered at the three preceding congresses. Consequently, if the leadership wishes to introduce or promote a particular group of new people, it is necessary to see that they are appointed well before the congress to jobs bearing the appropriate rank or to jobs that can plausibly be promoted. But here again the leadership runs into the political and practical problems of trying to make too many changes too fast in its vital bureaucratic hierarchies. Here perhaps is an institutional explanation of the trend to elite stability discernible under Brezhnev's leadership.

The job-slot conception of Central Committee membership, and the evident rules of apportionment, representation, and ticket-balancing that govern the make-up of the body, lend considerable substance to the "interest group" approach to Soviet politics. It must be borne in mind, of course, that Soviet "interest groups" are not the kind of independent private pressure groups of a pluralist society originally subjected to this particular analysis, but correspond more to the competing functional interests discernible within the governmental bureaucracy of a non-Communist country. The difference is that the whole social system in the USSR is organized under such bureaucratic structures, all of which are subsumed and integrated through the central and local committees of the Communist Party.

All this being understood, it is nevertheless clear that special political interests are advanced by the various functional bureaucracies in the Soviet system, and that through the principle of representation in the Central Committee all these bureaucracies and the local branches of the major ones have a voice or at least an ear in the central councils of the decision-making process. Further, the representation of these functional and territorial groups, in proportion to their importance, is firmly established according to the unwritten code of Central Committee membership, and must be a matter of basic expectation within the various bureaucratic units. The level and amount of Central Committee representation actually defines the institutional weight to be accorded each functional and territorial interest group in Soviet society. Any attempt to tamper fundamentally with this representative principle could conceivably have serious consequences for the effective functioning of many segments of the Soviet system.

# The Problem of Succession

## JOHN H. HODGSON

The replacement of Khrushchev by a duumvirate in October 1964 was seen by most political scientists in the West as merely the first step on the old road to one-man rule,[1] a view consistent with the assertion by a prominent scholar that a "dog-eat-dog" bitterness accompanies the Soviet struggle for advancement.[2] Even now in the 1970s there is strong sentiment that one-man rule will again emerge in the Soviet Union, and a noted Kremlinologist goes so far as to argue that the alternative to one-man rule is a disintegration of the Soviet political system.[3] After more than a decade of experience with a duumvirate, however, others might be willing to concede that the Soviet system has matured sufficiently to permit, although not guarantee, a lasting division of labor between the general secretary and the prime minister.

A decision to keep the two posts in separate pairs of hands may have taken the form of a closed circular letter issued by the CPSU Central Committee.[4] However, the division did not necessarily imply equality. In view of the fact that the Party has been described by Soviet leaders as the core of all public and state organizations, or as the conductor of an orchestra that includes the state apparatus and public organizations,[5] it is not surprising that the general secretary ranks higher than the prime minister on the political totem pole. In fact, the imprecision of the line dividing what one author calls policy and nonpolicy questions frequently causes Party leaders in the Soviet Union to go beyond leadership (*rukovodstvo*) and direction (*napravlenie*) and to supplant (*podmeniat*) state authorities through parallelism and the merging of functions.[6] At the highest level there have been inward pressures working upon the general secretary of the Party to assume concurrently the position of prime minister, which is the most powerful and the most coveted state office,[7] although in recent years it would appear that the impetus for assuming both positions has diminished in intensity. If there is any truth to the statement of Todor Zhivkov, general secretary of the Bulgarian party and former chairman of the Council of Ministers, that over-all responsibility for both the state and the party apparatus is too demanding a task for a single individual in even his smaller country,[8] it is little wonder that leaders of the world's second most powerful nation may have accepted in principle and practice the existence of a duumvirate. This accommodation with the reality of governing a large industrialized nation, coupled with the absence of a formal and open process of leadership selection, certainly complicates the task of predicting what leader(s) will emerge center stage following the death, ouster, or voluntary resignation of an incumbent ruler. Now, unlike previous leadership crises when first Stalin and then Khrushchev became a "supreme ruler," [9] one must identify a duumvirate or two political successors. The problem of prediction can nonetheless be reduced in magnitude through identification of power and policy ingredients in what one might call a Soviet recipe for succession.

CONSIDERATIONS OF POWER

It is of course true that some leaders, Soviet as well as non-Soviet, strive harder than others to reach the apex of political power. It may be that leaders who advance to important positions at an early age are among the most ambitious contenders for top billing. However, the crises of 1953, 1957, and 1964 in Soviet Russia suggest that neither extreme on the age spectrum—very young or very old—steps into the limelight. Khrushchev was five years older than the median age of fifty-three for the twenty-five full members of the Presidium (Politburo) selected at the Nineteenth Party Congress, one year older than the median age of fifty-seven for the probable members of an inner "Bureau of the Presidium" formed soon after the Nineteenth Party Congress, and two years older than the median age of sixty-one for the eleven Presidium (Politburo) members in the summer of 1957 when he consolidated his power against the anti-Party group. Seven years later, when Khrushchev was replaced, Brezhnev was four years and Kosygin one year younger than the median age of sixty-one for the ten full members of the Presidium (Politburo) who faced the October crisis. As a rule of thumb one might say, with some confirmation from past history, that the two major posts in Soviet politics may well go to men whose dates of birth place them within a five-year span from the median age for full members of the Politburo.

Age nonetheless takes a back seat to nationality when determining the outcome of a succession crisis. It was no accident that Stalin in his famous toast of 1945 singled out the Great Russians as the "leading force" among all the peoples of the Soviet Union, and no coincidence that his successor liked to refer to the Great Russians as the "older brothers" in a friendly family of peoples.[10] Khrushchev's efforts to bring Ukrainians, too, into the Soviet political elite are well known,[11] not to mention the more recent shift of influence from Ukrainians to White Russians.[12] In the eyes of one noted authority the three Slavic peoples together perform the vital function of leadership in the Union of Soviet Socialist Republics.[13] Indeed, the fact that other nationalities are not the political equals of the Slavs, and that the Kremlin follows a calculated policy of political inequality, is readily apparent at the Union-Republic level.

Over a span of twenty-three years, 1952–1975, there have been forty first secretaries at the Union-Republic level,[14] and with the exception of four first secretaries in Kazakhstan (the Great Russian Brezhnev, for example) and two first secretaries in Moldavia (the Ukrainian Z. T. Serdiuk, for example) all Union-Republic first secretaries have been natives.[15] On the surface this contradicts the notion of political inequality among Soviet nationalities. As reported by a responsible staff worker in the Party Central Committee apparatus, however, a native first secretary (a natsmen) cannot effect the dismissal of his second secretary,[16] who in fact is the real master.[17] It is generally the second secretary who wields practical control over the entire Union-Republic Party apparatus,[18] and this position has been carefully and consciously reserved for political figures of Slavic origin. Of the fourteen Union-Republic second secretaries now in office, one is a White Russian, three are Ukrainians, and ten are Great Russians. Only in the Ukraine and White Russia, moreover, can one find a natsmen sitting as both first and second secretary,[19] which is strongly suggestive of what one authority calls the favored status of the three Slavic nationalities.[20]

With respect to the Politburo of the Party Central Committee, a natural springboard to power during a succession crisis, one can hardly challenge the proposition that this organ has for more than half a century been a preserve for the Slavic peoples, who in the 1970s constitute 74.0 percent of the population (53.4 percent Great Russian, 16.9 percent Ukrainian, 3.7 percent White Russian). Of the twenty-eight full members of the Politburo from 1919 until its reorganization in 1952, sixteen were Great Russians (Khrushchev and Malenkov, for example) and eight were either Russified Jews (Trotsky and Kaganovich, for example) or Russified Georgians (Stalin and Beria, for example).[21] Moreover, thirty-four of the fifty people who have served on the Politburo (Presidium) as full members since 1952 have been Great Russians. If the notion of a political elite is expanded to include members of the Party Secretariat as well as the Politburo (Presidium) over the life span of the two organs, 1919–1976, little doubt remains about the locus of power. Of one hundred and two members, eighty-six have been of Slavic origin (seventy-six Great Russians, eight Ukrainians, and two White Russians).[22] Nationality is clearly a factor taken into account, implicitly or explicitly, when the Kremlin selects a new leader.

Experience in the Party and state apparatus is also a prerequisite for advancement to the highest positions of power in the Soviet Union, and it is likely that the chosen few will at the time of their promotion be either full voting members of the Politburo,[23] or candidate members whose Politburo position is strengthened by concurrent membership in the Secretariat. In addition, previous training gained through occupancy of one or more of thirteen critical administrative posts seems mandatory. Leading candidates for the position of general secretary will in all probability have directed the Party Cadres Department of the Central Committee and/or have worked as first secretary of the Ukrainian Party apparatus, as first secretary of the Communist Youth League (Komsomol, which is said to be a more important position than that held by any obkom first secretary [24]), or as first secretary of one or more committees with the largest and most influential delegations at recent Party congresses (the Moscow gorkom, the Leningrad obkom, the Moscow obkom, the Rostov obkom, the Gorky obkom, the Sverdlovsk obkom, and the Krasnodar kraikom).[25] Viable candidates for the prime ministership may well have worked as a first secretary, although the most critical consideration for selection to the government post will be previous experience as prime minister of the RSFSR, as deputy prime minister of the USSR, or as first deputy prime minister of the USSR. Tables 6.1–6.3 indicate what can be learned from using the criteria of age, nationality, and work experience in an identification of potential successors on the eve of two real and one hypothetical instances of succession.

It is apparent from table 6.1 that of the twenty-seven leading contenders for Stalin's mantle (full members of the Politburo or candidate members also sitting in the Secretariat), approximately two-thirds could have been eliminated from consideration if in the sorting-out process one applied the formula of age (a span of five years from the

TABLE 6.1  USSR: potential successors to Stalin, March 1953.

| Name and year of birth | Nationality | Party background [a] | State background [b] | Politburo/ Secretariat membership |
|---|---|---|---|---|
| V. M. Andrianov 1902 | Great Russian | First Secretary, Sverdlovsk obkom, 1938–1949; First Secretary, Leningrad gorkom and obkom, 1949–1950; First Secretary, Leningrad obkom, 1949–1953 | | Politburo |
| N. A. Bulganin 1895 | Great Russian | | Prime Minister, RSFSR, 1937; Deputy Prime Minister, USSR, 1938–1941, 1947–1953 | Politburo |
| N. G. Ignatov 1901 | Great Russian | First Secretary, Krasnodar kraikom, 1949–1952 | | Politburo,[c] Secretariat |
| N. S. Khrushchev 1894 | Great Russian | First Secretary, Moscow gorkom, 1934; First Secretary, Moscow gorkom and obkom, 1935–1938; First Secretary, Ukrainian Central Committee, 1938–1947, 1947–1949; First Secretary, Moscow obkom, 1949–1953 | | Politburo |

| | | | | |
|---|---|---|---|---|
| G. M. Malenkov 1902 | Great Russian | Head of Party Cadres, CPSU Central Committee, 1934–1946 | Deputy Prime Minister, USSR, 1946–1953 | Politburo |
| V. A. Malyshev 1902 | Great Russian | | Deputy Prime Minister, USSR, 1940–1956 | Politburo |
| M. G. Pervukhin 1904 | Great Russian | | Deputy Prime Minister, USSR, 1940, 1950–1955 | Politburo |
| M. Z. Saburov 1900 | Great Russian | | Deputy Prime Minister, USSR, 1941, 1947–1955 | Politburo |

Six potential candidates (full members of the Presidium or candidate members of the Presidium also serving on the Secretariat) were eliminated because of age (L. M. Kaganovich, N. A. Mikhailov, L. G. Melnikov, V. M. Molotov, N. M. Pegov, K. E. Voroshilov), six because of lack of requisite experience (A. B. Aristov, S. D. Ignatiev, D. S. Korotchenko, V. V. Kuznetsov, P. K. Ponomarenko, M. A. Suslov), four because of age and a lack of requisite experience (L. I. Brezhnev, D. I. Chesnokov, M. F. Shkiriatov, N. M. Shvernik), two because of nationality (L. P. Beria, A. I. Mikoyan), and one because of age, nationality, and a lack of requisite experience (O. W. Kuusinen).

ª Includes only ten possible positions: Head of Party Cadres, CPSU Central Committee; First Secretary, Ukrainian Central Committee; First Secretary, Komsomol; First Secretary, Moscow gorkom, Leningrad obkom, Moscow obkom, Rostov obkom, Gorky obkom, Sverdlovsk obkom, Krasnodar kraikom.

ᵇ Includes only three possible positions: First Deputy Prime Minister, USSR; Deputy Prime Minister, USSR; Prime Minister, RSFSR.

ᶜ Candidate membership.

TABLE 6.2  USSR: Potential successors to Khrushchev, October 1964.

| Name and year of birth | Nationality | Party background [a] | State background [b] | Politburo/ Secretariat membership |
|---|---|---|---|---|
| L. I. Brezhnev 1906 | Great Russian | Head of Party Cadres, CPSU Central Committee, 1959–1960, 1963–1964 | | Politburo, Secretariat |
| A. P. Kirilenko 1906 | Great Russian | First Secretary, Sverdlovsk obkom, 1955–1962 | | Politburo |
| A. N. Kosygin 1904 | Great Russian | | Prime Minister, RSFSR, 1943–1946; Deputy Prime Minister, USSR, 1940–1953, 1953–1956, 1957–1960; First Deputy Prime Minister, USSR, 1960–1964 | Politburo |

| N. V. Podgorny 1903 | Ukrainian | First Secretary, Ukrainian Central Committee, 1951–1963 | Politburo, Secretariat |

Two potential candidates (full members of the Presidium or candidate members of the Presidium also serving on the Secretariat) were eliminated because of age and a lack of requisite experience (N. M. Shvernik, G. I. Voronov), one because of age and nationality (A. I. Mikoyan), one because of age (D. S. Polyansky), and one because of a lack of requisite experience (M. A. Suslov).

[a] Includes only ten possible positions: Head of Party Cadres, CPSU Central Committee; First Secretary, Ukrainian Central Committee; First Secretary, Komsomol; First Secretary, Moscow gorkom, Leningrad obkom, Moscow obkom, Rostov obkom, Gorky obkom, Sverdlovsk obkom, Krasnodar kraikom.

[b] Includes only three possible positions: First Deputy Prime Minister, USSR; Deputy Prime Minister, USSR; Prime Minister, RSFSR.

TABLE 6.3 USSR: potential successors, 1976.

| Name and year of birth | Nationality | Party background [a] | State background [b] | Politburo/ Secretariat membership |
|---|---|---|---|---|
| V. V. Grishin 1914 | Great Russian | First Secretary, Moscow gorkom, 1967– | | Politburo |
| A. P. Kirilenko 1906 | Great Russian | First Secretary, Sverdlovsk obkom, 1955–1962 | | Politburo, Secretariat |
| K. T. Mazurov 1914 | White Russian | | First Deputy Prime Minister, USSR, 1965– | Politburo |
| D. F. Ustinov 1908 | Great Russian | | Deputy Prime Minister, USSR, 1957–1963; First Deputy Prime Minister, USSR, 1963–1965 | Politburo, Secretariat |

Three potential candidates (full members of the Politburo or candidate members of the Politburo also serving on the Secretariat) were eliminated because of age (N. V. Podgorny, G. V. Romanov, V. V. Shcherbitsky), three because of a lack of requisite experience (Iu. V. Andropov, A. A. Gromyko, B. N. Ponomarev), two because of age and a lack of requisite experience (F. D. Kulakov, M. A. Suslov), one because of nationality and a lack of requisite experience (D. A. Kunayev), and one because of age, nationality, and a lack of requisite experiencee (A. J. Pelshe).

[a] Includes only ten possible positions: Head of Party Cadres, CPSU Central Committee; First Secretary, Ukrainian Central Committee; First Secretary, Komsomol; First Secretary, Moscow gorkom, Leningrad obkom, Moscow obkom, Rostov obkom, Gorky obkom, Sverdlovsk obkom, Krasnodar kraikom.

[b] Includes only three possible positions: First Deputy Prime Minister, USSR; Deputy Prime Minister, USSR; Prime Minister, RSFSR.

median age for full members of the Politburo), nationality (Slavic), and work experience (an apprenticeship in one or more of the thirteen most important Party and state positions). Of the eight remaining contenders listed in table 6.1, two became head of the Party (Malenkov briefly in 1953, Khrushchev 1953–1964) and together with a third also served as prime minister (Malenkov 1953–1955, Bulganin 1955–1958, Khrushchev 1958–1964). As chairman of the State Economic Commission, Pervukhin became for a short period of time (1956–1957) an "overlord of overlords" with two first deputy chairmen and four deputy chairmen in what amounted to "a sort of second government." [26] The remaining candidates were less prominent in the years 1953–1964, although Malyshev became one of Pervukhin's first deputy chairmen in 1956 and Saburov (like Pervukhin) joined the anti-Party group of 1957 in an unsuccessful attempt by Politburo members to remove Khrushchev from office. Party secretary Ignatov also managed to advance: from Gorky obkom first secretary in 1955–1957, he was elevated to full membership in the Politburo (1957–1961). Only Andrianov suffered immediate political eclipse in the wake of Stalin's death.

Applying the same criteria of analysis in table 6.2, the number of candidates for the positions left vacant by the involuntary retirement of Khrushchev in October 1964 can be reduced to four men, only one of whom had experience in that branch of government constitutionally responsible for highest executive and administrative power in the USSR and extra-constitutionally responsible for the initiation of most Soviet legislation.[27] One might say that Kosygin was the logical choice for the position of prime minister. Of the three other candidates, Brezhnev and Podgorny held an edge over Kirilenko for the top Party position by virtue of their seniority, as revealed for example through membership in both the Politburo and the Secretariat. More recently, however, Kirilenko (a five-time winner of the Order of Lenin) has gained membership in the Secretariat as well as the Politburo, and his present stature in the apparatus is indicated by the fact that only Brezhnev (General Secretary of the Party), Kosygin (Chairman of the Council of Ministers), and Podgorny (Chairman of the Presidium of the Supreme Soviet) received more nominations than Kirilenko in the 1974 election to the Supreme Soviet of the USSR and in the 1975 elections to the Union-Republic Supreme Soviets.[28] If a succession crisis were to occur at the present moment, Kirilenko would join Grishin, Mazurov, and Ustinov as possible choices for a new leadership based on the three criteria of age, nationality, and work experience (see table 6.3).

POLICY CONSIDERATIONS

The assumption is fairly widespread among specialists on Soviet politics that during a succession crisis policies are sponsored less on their merits than on their utility in a struggle for power. One noted Kremlinologist goes so far as to argue that power is "an all-consuming passion" for Soviet leaders.[29] However, a word of caution was voiced by Merle Fainsod when he referred in his classic study of Soviet politics to the danger inherent in viewing the struggle for succession as merely a series of maneuvers for power and place. Coalitions are, he argued, cemented by principle as well as by calculation of advantage.[30] If the situation were otherwise, identification of a new leadership in the Kremlin would be a well nigh impossible task.

Stalin is perhaps the epitome of a power-seeking leader, although it may be an exaggeration to suggest that it was primarily or solely for this reason that he emerged as Lenin's successor. It has been argued that Stalin's chief rival, Trotsky, was "a poor strategist as well as a poor tactician" and that it was due to Trotsky's "ineptness" and "incapacity" for political in-fighting that he lost out to Stalin,[31] a harsh commentary indeed about the father of the Red Army and the man once described by Stalin as the person mainly responsible for the success of the November Revolution.[32] With perhaps equal justification one could posit the hypothesis that it was Trotsky's commitment to a policy position, the principle of primitive socialist accumulation (*pervonachal'noe sotsialisticheskoe nakoplenie*), that made him a less acceptable candidate than Stalin for Lenin's mantle, in spite of Lenin's clear preference for Trotsky over Stalin.[33] Trotsky's belief in the urgency of rapid industrialization at the expense of the peasantry was well-known and may even have led to a compromise at the 1923 party congress whereby Trotsky, setting aside Lenin's personal instructions,[34] refrained from attacking Stalin on the nationality question in return for a last-minute decision permitting Trotsky to draft and deliver a statement about industrialization.[35] However, the Party was not yet ready for acceptance of primitive socialist accumulation, which in many respects resembled Marx's harsh description of primitive capitalist accumulation.[36] One might well have predicted that Trotsky's dedication to a policy calling for national sacrifices in the early and mid-1920s would make him a less successful candidate than Stalin for control over a country that had only just begun to experience domestic tranquillity after years of war and domestic upheaval. Thus, to put it another way, Trotsky's interest in building socialism subverted his desire for personal power.[37]

Stalin's subsequent turn to primitive socialist accumulation is often equated with Khrushchev's switch three decades later to policies resembling Malenkov's program of 1953–1955. There is a tendency to see both reversals in policy as confirmation of the theory that policy consistency is the victim of a struggle for power and that Soviet politicians use policies only as a means of struggle in their quarrel over power.[38] One proponent of this view argues that Khrushchev was virtually forced into a "left" position after the death of Stalin by the mere fact that Malenkov took what could most easily be attacked as a right view, so that any alternative contender for power would have to rely on the opposite argument.[39] This approach rules out the possibility that many Soviet leaders believe in the intrinsic value of a given policy and that they can shift positions over time for reasons other than personal ambition. In the case of Malenkov and Khrushchev, there was a clear commitment to certain policies that in the short run led to Malenkov's demise and in the long run to the ouster of Khrushchev.

## Malenkov's Demise

Stalin's death opened up to Politburo members a wide range of policy choices as an attempt was made to solve the difficult problem of economic stagnation. Of the Soviet leaders listed in table 6.1 it was Malenkov and Khrushchev who spearheaded the major programs for change.

Malenkov's primary focus in the policy arena was on the industrial sector of the economy, although he shifted somewhat from Stalin's obsession with the development of heavy industry to a concern for increased rates of growth in industries producing consumer goods. Even though Malenkov may have felt, like other Kremlin leaders, that de-Stalinization would speed up the development of Soviet society, it is unlikely that he was enthusiastic about revealing publicly the extent to which the Party and the nation had been subjected to Stalin's terror machine.[40] Malenkov's reservations about de-Stalinization would of course be natural in view of his position as deputy head of Party cadres during the Great Purge, a position that made him Ezhov's right-hand man in the eyes of at least one noted authority,[41] and his more recent role in the Leningrad Affair involving the execution of Politburo member A. Voznesensky in 1950.

If power takes precedence over policy,[42] it is difficult to comprehend Malenkov's selection of issue positions. His interest in the production of consumer goods alienated the long-favored bureaucrats in heavy industry, who sensed a potential reduction of funds and influence. There is no reason to suppose that the military, already unhappy with Malenkov's declaration that an atomic war would mean the end of world civilization,[43] were any less concerned about the projected shift in the direction of the Soviet economy. Malenkov's apparent reluctance to accept sweeping de-Stalinization and the rehabilitation of thousands of Party members by the Military Collegium of the Supreme Court was surely a further irritant in the eyes of the Soviet officer corps, an elite group whose ranks had been reduced during the Great Purge by as much as 30 percent.[44] Malenkov had little to gain and much to lose by enunciating an economic program that was at variance with Stalinist priorites. Even a coalition with Beria, who fits rather well the Kremlinologist profile of Soviet leaders "wildly scrabbling for power," [45] could not rescue Malenkov from the abyss into which he had thrown himself by electing to be a champion of consumer goods while at best a reluctant supporter of de-Stalinization as a means to accelerate the development of Soviet society.

By way of contrast, Khrushchev's remedy for economic stagnation in the Soviet Union did not upset Stalin's industrial priorities. Khrushchev sought to resuscitate the economy through an agricultural program of extensive farming and through an attack on the administrative violence, mass repressions, and terror engaged in by Stalin during the last two decades of his rule. It can be argued, to be sure, that Khrushchev chose agriculture as his main concern in order to strike a blow at Malenkov, who had borne heavy responsibility for agricultural policy under Stalin and who is alleged by Khrushchev to have falsified grain statistics by somewhat more than 40 percent in a report to the 1952 Party congress,[46] but Malenkov's direct link to Stalin's failures in agriculture may have been no more than of secondary or tertiary importance to Khrushchev. One need only recall that Khrushchev came from Kursk, an agricultural oblast where starvation had been a common occurrence in 1947,[47] and that he had a certain amount of expertise in agricultural matters. More than any other Soviet leader, Khrushchev had personal knowledge of the sufferings that had accompanied Stalin's policy of taking what he needed from the farms (with little or no compensation) in order to feed the growing urban population and to gain foreign exchange from the export of agricultural products. Stalin's horizon did not go beyond marketings, which in the case of grain had not climbed much beyond the levels reached in 1937–1938, and at the time of his death it was clear to at least Khrushchev that agriculture had become the Soviet Union's chief economic problem. The Virgin Lands Program represented his immediate solution to the need for a quick expansion of both production and marketings in a much neglected sector of the Soviet economy.

Khrushchev's decision to deliver the Secret Speech of 1956, which Mikoyan asserts was "carefully planned" and "no accident," [48] can be seen as something other than a commitment to a policy designed to promote, as Khrushchev asserted at the Twentieth Party Congress,[49] a freer exchange of views concerning issues of "a practical character." There are unmistakable signs in the speech of an effort to discredit Malenkov while making a play for support from the military by absolving it of responsibility for "the threatening danger which hung over the Fatherland in the first period of the war." Khrushchev portrayed Malenkov as Stalin's alter ego who answered the master's telephone and who refused at a critical time in the war to send arms to Khrushchev on the Kiev front. Nonetheless it is unlikely that the de-Stalinization campaign in general, or the Secret Speech in particular, resulted wholly or primarily from a dedication to "plot, counterplot, and intrigue." [50] As Palmiro Togliatti, the former leader of the Italian Communist Party, stated in his controversial analysis of the Secret Speech, a denunciation of Stalin's errors had become a mandatory first step for leading Soviet society from the torpidity caused by the cult of Stalin.[51]

## Khrushchev's Ouster

Khrushchev's concern with policy matters became even more evident and much bolder following the support that he received in the summer of 1957 from the Central Committee. The anti-Party group of Malenkov forces was condemned, and the decision of an "arithmetic majority" in the Presidium to remove Khrushchev from office was overturned. The Stalin succession had been resolved. Khrushchev could move more freely, and he proceeded to act on many fronts, seemingly oblivious to the realities of power. A series of policy initiatives, many of which were later branded "hare-brained schemes," succeeded in alienating the major power clusters in Soviet society, including the all-important Party apparatus, the state apparatus, and the military.[52]

Khrushchev established parallel Party organs in almost all oblasts and krais, one organ for industry and one for agriculture, offering as his rationale for this "bifurcation" of the Party apparatus a concern over the campaign method of guidance by Party cadres (*kampaneiskii kharakter v partiinom rukovodstve*), a synonym in 1962 for a preoccupation by central committees in the republics, by obkoms, and by kraikoms—even those in the most industrialized parts of the country—with directives about agriculture.[53] Like many bureaucrats, Khrushchev was "organization happy" and was following the guiding principle of "When in trouble, reorganize,"[54] coming up with a reform of the Party apparatus that he hoped would bring industry, transport, and construction back into focus without disrupting the campaign to improve agriculture. The results of bifurcation were unwanted and unanticipated, however. A lack of coordination between the agricultural and industrial units of the Party, which reached the point of absurdity in the field of public health,[55] convinced top Party leaders that the reform was ill-conceived, and secretaries at the oblast/krai level who had rescued Khrushchev from the anti-Party group in 1957 were no longer willing in 1964 to stand up and be counted with the man who had reduced the scope of their authority through the bifurcation reform.[56]

Khrushchev's faith in the utility of reorganization as a means to solve economic problems can also be seen in his tampering with the state apparatus, which was subjected to a severe shake-up in the years 1957–1964, commencing with the abolition of most All-Union, Union-Republic, and Republic ministries. In their place Khrushchev substituted a system of economic councils (sovnarkhozy) set up on a territorial basis and charged with responsibility for industrial production within a given geographic area. Of the 105 economic councils created in 1957, seventy were located in the RSFSR and all but three of the seventy corresponded exactly with the boundaries of existing oblasts, krais, and Autonomous Republics. This arrangement gave a certain amount of credibility to the argument that the reform was motivated by a desire on Khrushchev's part to wrest control of the state apparatus from Malenkov's forces by sending staff personnel from the ministries into the field where they could be more closely observed and controlled by obkom/kraikom first secretaries or sovnarkhoz Party committees. One would do well, however, to ponder the proposition that a preoccupation with "assumed power struggles" obscures the strong possibility that Khrushchev's dismantling of the centralized ministerial system was motivated by a concern for economic efficiency.[57]

By early 1958 the economic councils accounted for almost three-quarters of industrial production in the Soviet Union,[58] a figure that must have risen considerably in late 1962 when the city soviets lost control over local industry, which in the case of Leningrad had accounted for 80 percent of the city soviet's budget in 1960.[59] Real or imagined economic advantages accompanying the reform were nonetheless overshadowed by the growth of localism (*mestnichestvo*) and by a breakdown in coordination. The danger of localism was met by a restructuring of the economic councils, first reducing their number from 105 to 47, and then by adding an RSFSR Sovnarkhoz, a Ukrainian Sovnarkhoz, a Sovnarkhoz for Kazakhstan, three Inter-Republic Sovnarkhozy, a Sovnarkhoz for the USSR, and, finally, a Supreme Sovnarkhoz for the USSR.

The problem of coordination was less amenable to solution, however. In one geographic area, which encompassed two oblasts and an Autonomous Republic, it was necessary to set up a coordinating (*koordinatsionnyi*) council that brought together the chairman of the sovnarkhoz, the chairmen of the two *oblispolkoms*, and the chairman of the Autonomous Republic Council of Ministers in a fruitless attempt to resolve matters of jurisdiction between state organs.[60] Coordination between Party organs was apparently no more successful. The Northern Caucasus Sovnarkhoz, for example, had a Party committee that refused to deal with either the Rostov gorkom or the Rostov obkom for industry. It went directly to the top, to the RSFSR's Bureau for Industry in the Central Committee of the Party.[61] If one further considers the absence of coordination in technical matters between, say, tractor plants under the jurisdiction of different sovnarkhozy,[62] it is little wonder that the state and Party apparatus lost patience with Khrushchev.[63]

It is significant that a number of defense-related ministries were exempted from Khrushchev's reorganization of the state apparatus, although it would be misleading to conclude that the military was satisfied with Khrushchev's policies. A struggle of unknown dimensions had preceded the ministerial victory for the professional soldiers,[64] and they stood on the threshold of an open conflict with the first secretary. Khrushchev's abrupt removal of Marshal Zhukov from positions of influence in the state apparatus (Minister of Defense) and the Party apparatus (Presidium member) was followed in the post-1957 period by a resurgence of political controls in the military. The voluntary study of Marxism-Leninism by the officer corps, a policy that had been adopted soon after Zhukov had taken Beria's vacant seat on the Central Committee in 1953, became obligatory study. As Minister of Defense in 1955, Zhukov had authorized the removal of some 30,000 political officers (*zampolity*) at the company level, but in the first half of 1958 Khrushchev proceeded to increase by 30 percent the number of Party organizations in the army and navy.[65] The view that a military man should be a soldier first and an ideologist second, a view that Zhukov had openly expressed after becoming a member of the Presidium in 1956–1957, was attacked when it reappeared in 1962 in Marshal Sokolovsky's book about military strategy.[66] To assist what two Soviet reviewers of the Sokolovsky book called the Leninist subordination of the military point of view to the political, a former high-ranking secret police officer, A. A. Epishev, had been named by Khrushchev in May 1962 to head the Main Political Administration of the Ministry of Defense. Another peak had been reached in the long-standing conflict between Soviet military commanders and political functionaries.

In the wake of Zhukov's removal from power, the military also discovered that Khrushchev no longer shared its thinking on matters related to strategy and tactics. Khrushchev's statement to the Twentieth Party Congress that war had ceased to be "fatalistically" inevitable, coupled with his view that the living would envy the dead in a nuclear exchange, may have triggered memories of the policies that Malenkov had unsuccessfully sought to sell to the military in the early years of the Stalin succession crisis. Khrushchev's awareness of the awesome power of nuclear weapons had caused him to accept a revision of Leninist doctrine, and it also led him to favor rockets and missiles over traditional military forces. Khrushchev stressed the need for "firepower" as opposed to "army greatcoats," called for a drastic cut in conventional troop levels, and even raised the specter of a return to a territorial militia,[67] a philosophy of defense that had resulted in much friction between professional soldiers and Party leaders in the early years of the Soviet regime. These policy statements were received with deep resentment and much bitterness by leaders of the Soviet military establishment,[68] and it was perhaps with a feeling of satisfaction that Marshal Malinovsky, who once described the formation of a separate Strategic Rocket Force as a personal decision made by Khrushchev,[69] was able to report at the Twenty-Third Party Congress that balance had been restored to the development of Soviet military strength.

The policies that flowed from Khrushchev's emphasis on peaceful coexistence and détente also called for a resurrection of Malenkov's program for the consumer, which evoked stiff resistance from "some comrades" whom Khrushchev described as having "an appetite for metals." [70] One could easily have anticipated the military's reaction to cuts in the defense budget intended to release scarce capital for investment in light industry and agriculture. Defense Minister Malinovsky presented a vigorous case for the maintenance of high levels of defense spending in the May 1962 issue of *Kommunist*. However, his arguments did not deter Khrushchev from signing the partial test ban treaty of 1963, an agreement that was anathema to both the Soviet and American military establishments but which fostered an ˌatmosphere of détente so necessary for further cutbacks in defense spending.[71] Malinovsky's arguments failed also to prevent Khrushchev from announcing the consideration of new troop reductions for 1964.[72] In 1957 the military had come to the defense of Khrushchev when he faced the anti-Party group, but within seven years approbation had turned into open hostility, and it was not by accident that the military became Khrushchev's most virulent critic after his ouster from power at the October 1964 plenum of the Central Committee.[73] This is not to say, however, that there was a grand conspiracy by the military against Khrushchev. The military were merely one of several power clusters that had opted for a change in Party leadership for the Soviet Union. What is surprising is not that Khrushchev was removed from office with the concurrence of the military but that he lasted so long despite one policy blunder after another.[74]

PROSPECTS

The ouster of Khrushchev resulted in promotions for the four men listed in table 6.2, three to the very top (general secretary, prime minister, and president) and one to membership in the Secretariat (as a supplement to his seat in the Politburo). A satisfactory division of labor between Brezhnev and Kosygin made possible the establishment of a duumvirate that has successfully directed Soviet politics over a decade. Nevertheless, it is only natural to anticipate a change at the top before the end of the 1970s in view of the duumvirate's lengthy tenure in office, in view of the reported health problems of both Brezhnev (heart and liver) and Kosygin, and in view of the rumor that Brezhnev would like to establish the precedent of retiring from office on a strictly voluntary basis. If the existence of a duumvirate has been accepted by the Kremlin as a principle of Soviet government, which is not improbable, two leaders will emerge as replacements for Brezhnev and Kosygin. Indicators of power (the age, nationality, and previous work experience of Politburo members) reduce the number of likely candidates to the four men listed in table 6.3. The choice of one man over another for the position of either general secretary or prime minister can be further refined by examining what is known about the policy views of these four candidates and by relating this information to the circumstances that will eventually result in a succession crisis.

If Brezhnev or Kosygin were to die in office or to retire voluntarily, there is a good chance that the policies of the last decade would in all major respects be continued by the Kremlin. Under this set of circumstances there is a strong possibility that a succession crisis at the present time would result in Brezhnev's replacement by Kirilenko,[75] whose present ranking in the Party hierarchy is senior to his competitor Grishin, and Kosygin's replacement by First Deputy Prime Minister Mazurov. In their election speeches of 1974 Kirilenko and Mazurov stressed Brezhnev's "personal contribution" (*lichnii vklad*) to Soviet successes on the domestic and foreign fronts,[76] which in itself is suggestive of a certain compatibility with the Brezhnev-Kosygin line not to be found in the election statements of all members of the Politburo and Secretariat. Kirilenko and Mazurov agree with Brezhnev that détente must become "irreversible" (*neobratimyi*).[77] There is no indication that their economic priorities differ from those of the present leadership, Mazurov having worked closely with Kosygin as his only first deputy prime minister since Dimitri Polyansky was relieved of a similar post in 1973 in conjunction with his appointment to the post of USSR Minister of Agriculture.[78]

Brezhnev and Kosygin could be removed from office, however, by Politburo members wishing a change in Soviet policy at home and abroad. There is obvious disagreement among Politburo members over the desirability of détente with the United States, a fact that can be seen from the promotion of Defense Minister Grechko and Foreign Minister Gromyko to membership in the Politburo after the dismissal in 1972 of hard-liner P. Shelest, as well as from the more recent removal of A. Shelepin, who on the eve of his ouster from Politburo membership stated that he could see only the beginnings of détente (*razriadka napriazhennosti*) and that Soviet defense capabilities needed to be strengthened.[79] One is perhaps justified in assuming that the opponents of détente are also dissatisfied with the present allocation of scarce financial resources. The current Soviet leadership has lifted the ceiling set by Khrushchev on investment in agriculture and light industry, a limit that Khrushchev had justified on the basis of minimal needs in heavy industry,[80] and the duumvirate has also "resolutely" (*reshitel'no*) rejected the idea that a rise in military expenditures is consonant with a policy of détente.[81] In line with this thinking, there has been a steady decline over the last decade in the percentage of state funds allocated through the central budget to the category called defense (see table 6.4).

TABLE 6.4  USSR state budget expenditures, 1964–1974.

| Year | (1)<br>Total budget<br>expenditures<br>(billions of rubles) | (2)<br>Defense expenditures<br>(billions of rubles) | Column 2 as<br>percentage of<br>column 1 |
|---|---|---|---|
| 1964 | 92.2 | 13.3 | 14.4 |
| 1965 | 101.6 | 12.8 | 12.6 |
| 1966 | 105.6 | 13.4 | 12.7 |
| 1967 | 115.2 | 14.5 | 12.6 |
| 1968 | 128.6 | 16.7 | 13.0 |
| 1969 | 138.5 | 17.7 | 12.8 |
| 1970 | 154.6 | 17.9 | 11.6 |
| 1971 | 164.2 | 17.9 | 10.9 |
| 1972 | 173.8 | 17.9 | 10.3 |
| 1973 | 184.3 | 17.9 | 9.7 |
| 1974 | 193.9 | 17.6 | 9.1 |

Sources: Budget figures come from the Soviet statistical yearbook *Narodnoe khoziaistvo SSR* (1964–1973) and from a report by Minister of Finance V. F. Garbuzov to the seventh session of the Eighth USSR Supreme Soviet (December 1973).

The figures in column 2 do not, of course, reflect total defense spending by the Soviet government. Total expenditures, including money spent for scientific research related to military research and development (social and cultural category) and money allocated to defense industries (financing the national economy), are probably in the neighborhood of 21–24 billion rubles annually. See George Modelski, *World Power Concentrations: Typology, Data, Explanatory Framework* (Morristown, 1974), pp. 6–7, 10; *The Military Balance, 1972–1973* (London, 1972), p. 9; Stanley H. Cohn, "Economic Burden of Defense Expenditures," in *Soviet Economic Prospects for the Seventies: A Compendium of Papers Submitted to the Joint Economic Committee Congress of the United States* (Washington, D.C., 1973), pp. 148–149, 158. It is interesting to note that allocations to science from the All-Union budget have fluctuated very little over the decade as a percentage of total budget expenditures (reaching a high of 4.4 percent in the 1960s and a low of 4.1 percent in the 1970s). The figures suggest that the military may be holding on to a constant share of the growing economic pie when it comes to allocations for research and development, although one should not overlook the existence of stiff competition for research and development resources between military and civilian purposes, which could over time effect a reduction in the percentage of scientific outlays going to the military establishment.

A conscious shift to policies more reminiscent of the Stalin era might elevate Grishin, who has been described as unsympathetic to Brezhnev personally and as opposed to détente,[82] to the position of general secretary, and Ustinov, who has been characterized as un-sympathetic to urban consumer welfare as well as détente,[83] to the position of prime minister. Grishin would bring with him four years of experience as second secretary of the Moscow obkom (1952–1956), eleven years as Chairman of the Central Council of Trade Unions (1956–1967), and seven years as first secretary of the Moscow gorkom (since 1967). Ustinov, by way of credentials, holds the title of Hero of Socialist Labor (the highest civilian award), is a five-time winner of the Order of Lenin, and has been the recipient of high military awards (Orders of Suvorov and Kutuzov First Class). His experiences as Minister of Armaments under Stalin and Chairman of the USSR Supreme Economic Council under Khrushchev, combined with his special concern for the "A" or heavy industry sector of the economy,[84] make Ustinov a logical choice for prime minister in the event that the Politburo decides to replace Kosygin with a man less amenable to the foreign and domestic policies of the present duumvirate. Given the absence of any visible sign that the "hawks" are about to gain the upper hand in the Kremlin, a Grishin-Ustinov combination is a less likely alternative to the Brezhnev-Kosygin duumvirate than is the combination of Kirilenko and Mazurov. Considerations of power and policy are too complex, however, to justify a finite statement about the outcome of the next succession crisis in the Soviet Union. Unan-ticipated developments may well strengthen Hegel's judgment that the Owl of Minerva begins its flight only when dusk is falling.[85]

# Party "Saturation"
# in the Soviet Union

## JERRY F. HOUGH

7

From a comparative standpoint, perhaps the most distinctive feature of the Communist Party has been the nature of its membership policy. Lenin insisted upon a party in which a prospective member had not only to accept the Party's basic philosophy but also to work full-time to achieve its goals. The demand that the Party members be professional revolutionaries became anachronistic after 1917, but it evolved into the requirement that they devote their entire life to the construction of socialism and then communism. The result of this membership policy has, of course, been the admission of only a relatively small minority of the total population into the Party. Soviet authorities term the Party a "vanguard" of the Soviet people, a collection of the "best representatives" of the Soviet people; Westerners often call it "an elite, not a mass organization." [1]

Yet to label the Communist Party of the Soviet Union an "elite" organization represents a dangerous undertaking, for the word conjures up quite different images for different people.[2] In one well-known study T. B. Bottomore defines "elite" broadly—"functional, mainly occupational groups which have status (for whatever reason) in a society"—and he suggests that this definition is widely employed.[3] Explicitly or implicitly, however, other scholars use the concept much, much more narrowly. Thus, "elite studies" in the Soviet-East European field frequently focus upon Central Committee membership, while the chapter on the Soviet Union in a book entitled *World Revolutionary Elites* is limited to an examination of the Politburo.[4]

What then is the type of elite that we should have in mind when we think of the Communist Party of the Soviet Union? Is it the rather narrow elite implied in such phrases as "a secular priesthood" or even "the leading personnel of any organization or group, the commanders and their essential staffs . . . with a general sprinkling of industrial workers and a very small peasant component"?[5] Or is it a broad elite—perhaps even "the attentive public," to use a familiar phrase from American political science?

### SATURATION BY SOCIAL GROUP

The most obvious way to determine the relative exclusiveness of the Party elite in the Soviet Union is to calculate the degree of Party "saturation" in Soviet society—the percentage of Party members among Soviet citizens or special groups of Soviet citizens.[6] One could simply divide the number of Party members (14,821,031 on January 1, 1973, including 450,506 candidates) by the number of Soviet citizens. And, in fact, if this is done, the Party saturation in the population as a whole turns out to be 5.8 percent on that date, 6.0 percent if the candidates are included.[7] The percentages produced by this method seem rather low, and it is not surprising that they have been most often cited in works emphasizing the closed nature of Party membership.[8]

In at least one respect, however, it seems misleading to use the total Soviet population as the denominator in a calculation of Party saturation. One-third of the population is under eighteen years (the earliest permissible age for admission to the Party), and many scholars exclude these persons from their analysis of Party statistics. In this view, the real saturation level is the percentage of Party membership (including candidates) among the *adult* population, and it should be put at 8.9 percent in 1973, not 6.0 percent.[9] This figure suggests a somewhat broader Party membership and it was the one Brezhnev used at the Twenty-Fourth Party Congress in 1971.[10]

Despite official Soviet endorsement of this second method, I would, nevertheless, like to argue that it too fails to create the appropriate impression of the degree of Party saturation in Soviet society.

In the first place, while the age of eighteen is the theoretical minimum for Party admission, in practice few Soviet citizens enter the Party at such an early age. We have no complete Soviet data on this question, but we can find illumination on this subject by examining the biographies of the deputies to the Supreme Soviet. If anything, these deputies should be atypically "political" in their attitudes and behavior, but those deputies of the last fifteen years who joined the Party after 1946 did so at the average age of 29.4 years. Only 8 percent of the deputies joined before the age of 23, 18 percent before the age of 25. The data further suggest—although the deputies may well be unrepresentative on this point—that the age of Party admission has risen somewhat in recent years. The 293 deputies who joined the Party in 1960 or later did so at the average age of 31.7 years.[11]

The limited information available on Party age distribution clearly supports the conclusions drawn from the data on Supreme Soviet deputies, at least to the extent of indicating that the mid- and late-twenties is the earliest age at which substantial numbers of Soviet citizens enter the Party. While 20 percent of the adult population were between the ages of 18 and 25 in 1973, only 5.7 percent of the Party members were in this under-26 age group.[12] The 1973 Party saturation in this group can easily be determined by dividing the number of adults of this age into the number of Party members in the group, and, as indicated in Table 7.1, it proves to have been only 2.5 percent.

If we subtract the total population and the Party members in the 18–25 age group from the statistics for the adult population as a whole, we can place the Party saturation in the age group of 26 and over at 10.5 percent, in contrast to 8.9 percent for the adult population as a whole. The level of Party saturation was also low among those persons between the ages of 26 and 30 and among those over 60. If these groups are also subtracted from the total, 1973 Party saturation

TABLE 7.1 Party saturation, by age group, 1973.

| Age group | Total population | Party members | Party saturation (%) |
|---|---|---|---|
| 18–25 | 32,939,000 | 834,166 | 2.5 |
| 26–30 | 13,869,000 | 1,101,794 | 7.9 |
| 31–40 | 36,736,000 | 4,588,939 | 12.5 |
| 41–50 | 33,406,000 | 4,329,005 | 13.0 |
| 51–60 | 19,725,000 | 2,425,048 | 12.3 |
| 61+ | 29,613,000 | 1,542,079 | 5.2 |
| Total | 166,288,000 | 14,821,031 | 8.9 |

Sources: The number of Party members by age is found in *Partiinaia zhizn*, no. 14 (July 1973), p. 19. The population data are extrapolated from *Narodnoe khoziaistvo v 1972 g.* (Moscow: Statistika, 1973), p. 34.

rises to 12.6 percent among adults aged 31 to 60, as can be calculated from table 7.1.

A second reason for not limiting our analysis to Party saturation within the adult population as a whole is the great imbalance in the number of men and women in the Party. As has often been noted, women are grossly underrepresented in the Party, comprising 3,412, 029 (or 23.0 percent) of the 14,821,031 members and candidates in 1973.[13] However, the converse of this statistic has usually been ignored —the gross overrepresentation of men in the Party, and, therefore, the higher saturation rates among men than among the population as a whole. If the number of males in the adult population (that is, those 18 and over) is divided into the number of males in the Party, the result is a saturation figure of 15.6 percent in 1973, quite a difference from the 8.9 percent in the over-all adult population.

Obviously, the patterns of Party membership by age and sex, when taken together, produce even higher figures for the percentage of men between the ages of 31 and 60 who are Party members. Unfortunately, information is not published on the age distribution of Party membership for each sex, and we are compelled to rely upon some assumptions in making estimates on this subject. The most obvious and easiest assumption is that the age distribution among men and women Party members is the same, but there are some difficulties with this supposition. In the first place, 35 percent of all women are over the age of 50 compared with 23 percent of the men,[14] and this might lead one to suspect a disproportionate number of older women Party members. In the second place, young women with children may find the responsibilities of Party membership particularly burdensome, and they may put off joining the Party until they have reached an age when they have more time. In the third place, on the other hand, the percentage of women admitted into the Party has been increasing in recent years: 18.0 percent of the new candidates in 1956–1961, 21.7 percent in 1962–1965, 25.7 percent in 1966–1970, and 29.0 percent in 1971–1972.[15] If Party admission occurs at the same average age for men and women, there should be larger percentages of women in younger age brackets. In the fourth place, the sex ratios among educated citizens are quite different at different ages. In the 20–29 age group in 1970, there were 22 percent more women than men who had a complete secondary education or better, but in the over-50 group there were 6 percent more men, despite the far greater number of women in general of this age.[16] Given the association of Party membership and education, this too might lead one to hypothesize a disproportionate number of younger women Party members.

TABLE 7.2   Party saturation among men, by age group, 1973.

| Age group | Total population | Party members and Party saturation | | |
|---|---|---|---|---|
| | | Methodology A | Methodology B | Methodology C |
| 18–25 | 16,727,000 | 640,000    3.8% | 682,000    4.1% | 592,000    3.5% |
| 26–30 | 6,884,000 | 849,000    12.3 | 893,000    13.0 | 792,000    11.5 |
| 31–40 | 17,985,000 | 3,531,000    19.6 | 3,692,000    20.5 | 3,438,000    19.1 |
| 41–50 | 14,909,000 | 3,333,000    22.4 | 3,358,000    22.5 | 3,380,000    22.7 |
| 51–60 | 7,821,000 | 1,869,000    23.9 | 1,792,000    22.9 | 1,940,000    24.8 |
| 61+ | 8,754,000 | 1,187,000    13.6 | 992,000    11.3 | 1,267,000    14.5 |
| Total | 73,080,000 | 11,409,000    100 | 11,409,000    100 | 11,409,000    100 |

Methodology A assumes an identical age distribution for men and women Party members. Methodology B attempts to correct this distribution for the difference in the age distribution of men and women as a whole. Methodology C assumes that the age distribution varies with the percentage of women admitted into the Party when each age group was around 30. It assumes 29 percent women in the 18–25 group, 28 percent in the 26–30 group, 25 percent in the 31–40 group, 22 percent in the 41–50 group, 20 percent in the 51–60 group, and 18 percent in the over-61 group.

TABLE 7.3  Party saturation among women, by age group, 1973.

| Age group | Total population | Party members and Party saturation | | | | | |
|---|---|---|---|---|---|---|---|
| | | Methodology A | | Methodology B | | Methodology C | |
| 18–25 | 16,212,000 | 194,000 | 1.2% | 152,000 | .9% | 242,000 | 1.5% |
| 26–30 | 6,985,000 | 253,000 | 3.6 | 209,000 | 3.0 | 310,000 | 4.4 |
| 31–40 | 18,751,000 | 1,058,000 | 5.6 | 889,000 | 4.7 | 1,150,000 | 6.1 |
| 41–50 | 18,497,000 | 996,000 | 5.4 | 974,000 | 5.3 | 950,000 | 5.1 |
| 51–60 | 11,904,000 | 556,000 | 4.7 | 636,000 | 5.3 | 485,000 | 4.1 |
| 61+ | 20,859,000 | 355,000 | 1.7 | 552,000 | 2.6 | 275,000 | 1.3 |
| Total | 93,208,000 | 3,412,000 | 100 | 3,412,000 | 100 | 3,412,000 | 100 |

There is no way to determine which of these distortions are most important, but, fortunately, they work at cross purposes and may tend to cancel each other out. Even more important, as tables 7.2 and 7.3 indicate, the use of different assumptions in calculating the rates of Party saturation among men and women does not change the results in a major way, in particular among those in the 31–60 age group. Whichever method is used, it turns out that 21–22 percent of the men between the ages of 31 and 60 were Party members in 1973. If we make a few more assumptions, then we can estimate that this figure rises to the vicinity of 25 percent for men in this age group in urban areas.[17] (Of course, as table 7.3 indicates, the proportion of women who are Party members is correspondingly low.)

As has been repeatedly reported, Party membership in the Soviet Union varies not only with age and sex, but also with socioeconomic variables such as education and occupation. Thus, in 1973, 32 percent of those with a complete higher education were Party members, compared with 11.7 percent of those with incomplete higher education, 12.1 percent of those with complete secondary education, 6.7 percent of those with incomplete secondary education, and 2.6 percent of those over the age of 9 without any high school education.[18]

While these statistics correctly indicate the correlation of Party membership and education, they are misleading, for they are not adjusted for age and include persons in school, even elementary-school pupils over the age of 9. They exaggerate some of the differences in the saturation rates among persons of different educational backgrounds, for all of the college graduates are old enough to be admitted into the Party, while all the other educational groups include younger persons. (For example, the explanation for the relatively low Party saturation among those with incomplete higher education is that this group includes large numbers of people still in college— people who generally are below the age at which most admission into the Party takes place.)

Data on the age distribution of those with different levels of education are not available for 1973, but they were published in the 1970 census. The over-all saturation levels were a bit lower in 1970 (10.6 percent among those over 30, compared with 10.8 percent in 1973), but the differences are small enough that the 1970 statistics should be quite adequate for our purposes. What they clearly demonstrate, as table 7.4 shows, is that Party membership really begins to take on a mass character among those persons over 30 years of age who have at least a high school education. Of this group 27 percent are Party members, and this figure includes women as well as men.

TABLE 7.4   Party saturation among persons over thirty, by level of education, 1970.

| Level of education | Total population | Party members | Party saturation (%) |
|---|---|---|---|
| Complete higher | 6,377,000 | 2,265,000 | 35.5 |
| Incomplete higher | 945,000 | 285,000 | 30.2 |
| Complete secondary | 17,097,000 | 4,033,000 | 23.6 |
| Incomplete secondary | 22,915,000 | 3,037,000 | 13.3 |
| Complete and incomplete elementary | 67,495,000 | 2,556,000 | 3.8 |
| Total | 114,829,000 | 12,176,000 | 10.6 |

Sources: Data for Party members were extrapolated from *Partiinaia zhizn,* no. 4 (July 1973), p. 16; total population, *Itogi vsesoiuznoi perepisi naseleniia 1970 goda* (Moscow, Statistika, 1972), III, 6–7.

When we attempt to distinguish between levels of Party saturation among men and women of different educational levels, we are on less certain grounds in our extrapolations. We must make assumptions not only about the similarity or dissimilarity of the general age distribution among men and women Party members, but also about that of the educational distribution among Party members of different sexes. Again, as tables 7.5 and 7.6 demonstrate, we face the problem that the various educational groups within the population as a whole are not divided proportionately among men and women. There are nearly 20 percent more men with higher education, but nearly one and three-quarters times as many women as men with elementary education. In particular, in 1970 there were 24,350,000 women over the age of 55 who never attended high school, compared with 10,495,000 men,[19] and this interaction of the uncertainties in age and education distributions of Party members is a worrisome fact.

Nevertheless, any attempt to explore the consequences of our assumptions reveals that, as in the case of age distribution, it would take very extraordinary irregularities to affect the saturation rates by more than a few percentage points. Thus, Methodology B of tables 7.5 and 7.6 produces an estimated Party saturation of 10.8 percent among women over 30 with at least a secondary degree, compared with 44 percent of the men with these characteristics. If we made the extreme assumption that the number of women Communists over 30

TABLE 7.5  Party saturation among men over thirty, by level of education, 1970.

| Level of education | Total population | Party members and Party saturation | | | |
|---|---|---|---|---|---|
| | | Methodology A | | Methodology B | |
| Complete higher | 3,464,000 | 1,744,000 | 50.3% | 1,870,000 | 54.5% |
| Incomplete higher | 525,000 | 219,000 | 41.7 | 237,000 | 45.1 |
| Complete secondary | 7,869,000 | 3,105,000 | 39.5 | 3,116,000 | 39.6 |
| Incomplete secondary | 10,746,000 | 2,338,000 | 21.8 | 2,364,000 | 22.0 |
| Complete and incomplete elementary | 24,506,000 | 1,968,000 | 8.0 | 1,787,000 | 7.3 |
| Total | 47,110,000 | 9,374,000 | 19.9 | 9,374,000 | 19.9 |

In methodology A, it is simply assumed that 77 percent of the Communists in each education group are men. In methodology B, an attempt is made to adjust for the differences in the distribution of men and women in each group.

with a secondary degree were to be 50 percent greater (that is, 2,040,000 such women instead of 1,360,000, 73 percent of all women Communists instead of 49 percent), the saturation rate among this group would rise only to 16.2 percent and that among comparable men would decline only to 38.3 percent. Even if there were not a single woman Party member without a secondary degree (which obviously is untrue), then 32 percent of all men over 30 with a secondary degree or better would still be Party members.

In short, when we talk about Party membership among men in the Soviet Union, we are talking about a political activity that is extremely widespread in comparison with the typical levels of political activity in the West—particularly among men who have at least ten years of schooling (the amount required for a secondary school degree) and who have reached the age of "settling down." [20]

It could be argued, of course, that this essay places far too much emphasis upon Party membership among men and that very high rates of membership among educated males over 30 says little about the dispersion of potential influence—except that it is not dispersed to women. However, at a minimum, the relatively late age of Party admission and the male-female imbalance within the membership do have the consequence of ensuring a far wider representation of mature family units within the Party than is indicated by over-all Party statistics. If there is frequent communication within the family, if

TABLE 7.6   Party saturation among women over thirty, by level of education, 1970.

| Level of education | Total population | Party members and Party saturation | | | |
|---|---|---|---|---|---|
| | | Methodology A | | Methodology B | |
| Complete higher | 2,913,000 | 521,000 | 17.8% | 395,000 | 13.6% |
| Incomplete higher | 420,000 | 66,000 | 15.7 | 48,000 | 11.4 |
| Complete secondary | 9,228,000 | 928,000 | 10.1 | 917,000 | 9.9 |
| Incomplete secondary | 12,169,000 | 699,000 | 5.7 | 673,000 | 5.5 |
| Complete and incomplete elementary | 42,989,000 | 588,000 | 1.4 | 769,000 | 1.8 |
| Total | 67,719,000 | 2,802,000 | 4.1 | 2,802,000 | 4.1 |

husbands pass on "inside dope" received through the Party channel of communication, if they use their access to communicate the grievances of their respective wives and children as well as their own, then the large proportion of men enrolled in the Party implies that the benefits of Party membership are much more broadly diffused among family units than we have realized.

Moreover, even the participation rates among women over 30 with at least secondary education—as low as they are in comparison with those of Soviet men—are fairly comparable with rates found in the West, at least if membership were to entail considerable activity. To think of such a Communist Party as a "priesthood" makes no sense at all, and even to call it "an elite" requires us to recognize that it is, indeed, "an elite of a rather peculiar kind." [21]

*Party Saturation over Time*

The analysis of Party saturation in this paper has thus far been essentially limited to one point in time. Yet, major longitudinal questions obviously are close to the surface, for the percentage of Soviet citizens with higher and secondary education is rising rapidly. If the levels of Party saturation among the respective educational groups remain the same, then the size of the Party must also increase rapidly. Conversely, if Party membership does not grow sufficiently, then the saturation levels among the better-educated citizens inevitably will decline.

The possibility of a change in the levels of Party saturation reported in this paper is raised even more strongly by a reduction in the rate of growth of Party membership over the last decade.[22] In July 1965 the Central Committee passed a decision "About Serious Deficiencies in the Work of the Kharkov Oblast Party Organization in Party Admission and the Training of Young Communists," which called upon lower Party organs to take greater care in admitting new members— implicitly to raise their standards.[23] Following this decision, the number of persons admitted into the Party did decrease. In the period 1962–1965, 760,000 persons a year became candidate members of the Party, but this figure dropped to 600,000 a year in the period 1966–1970 and to 493,000 in 1971 and 469,000 in 1972.[24]

Yet, these figures can be—and often have been—misleading to the outside observer. In the first place, even with the reduced rates of admission, the number of Party members increased 26 percent from 1965 to 1973, compared with only 11.2 percent for the adult population (as measured by the number of persons registered to vote in the elections).[25] In the second place—and even more important, of course —Party members are not admitted from the population as a whole, but for the most part from a relatively narrow band of the population: those between their mid-twenties and their mid-thirties. Because of the very low birth rates during World War II, there has been an abnormally small age cohort affecting the various institutions through which it passes, and over the last decade it has been reaching the age of Party admission. Quite aside from questions of Party policy, the number of admissions into the Party would have dropped sharply unless the saturation rates among young adults had increased rapidly.

The nature of the "World War II baby" problem can easily be gleaned from an examination of the statistics on age distribution in the 1970 census. In that year there were nearly 25 million persons in the 5–9 and 10–14 age groupings and 22 million between the ages of 15 and 19. However, there were only 17.1 million persons between the ages of 20 and 24 and 13.8 million in the 25–29 group. The 30–34 age group, on the other hand, contained 21 million people.[26] The meaning of this "trough" in the population for the level of Party saturation is clearly indicated in table 7.7: the number of persons admitted into the Party could decline sharply, but the saturation rates among the age groups during which admission usually occurs could remain fundamentally unchanged.

It should be noted that the significance of the demographic factor for the pattern of Party admission is not limited to the last decade. For example, at least a small part of the explanation for the major increase in Party membership in the late 1950s and early 1960s must lie in the size of the generation following the one that suffered the brunt of World War II. There were 57 million persons between the ages of 20 and 34 in 1959, an average of 3.8 million for each year, while there were but 2.2 million persons for each year in the 35–44 age group (the one that had been knocking on the doors of the Party in the previous decade).[27]

Similarly, the 1970 census figures already cited make it perfectly clear that the Soviet leadership will soon face a very basic decision with respect to the nature of Party membership. By 1950 the effects of World War II had ended, and for 15 years thereafter nearly 5 million babies a year were born and survived. In the mid-1970s this group is just beginning to reach the age of large-scale Party admission. If the intake of new members were to continue to drop (or even to rise very slowly), the saturation rates would be affected significantly.

The question of the stability of Party saturation among men and among education groups is much more difficult to discuss. As has been seen, the percentage of women admitted to the Party has been increasing in recent years, but the exact meaning of this change is unclear. The saturation levels among those over 40 has been rising during the last decade, and conceivably some of the increase in the percentage of women members is reflected in this fact, for, of course, these are the age levels at which women begin to outnumber men. The percentage of women among political and administrative officials

TABLE 7.7   Party saturation, by age group, 1965, 1967, 1973.

| Age group | 1965 [a] | 1967 | 1973 |
|---|---|---|---|
| 18–25 | 3.1% | 2.2% | 2.5% |
| 26–40 | 11.0 | 11.5 | 11.2 |
| 41–50 | 10.7 | 11.8 | 13.0 |
| 51 + | 5.5 | 6.5 | 8.0 |
| Total | 7.9 | 8.3 | 8.9 |

Sources: *Partiinaia zhizn*, no. 10 (May 1965), p. 13; no. 19 (October 1967), pp. 9, 16; no. 14 (July 1973), p. 19. The 1965 and 1967 age distributions were extrapolated from the 1959 and 1970 census data. The age distribution for 1973 came from *Narodnoe khoziaistvo v 1972 g.*, p. 34.

[a] The age categories in the data were actually 18–25, 26–39, 40–49, and 50 +.

has risen from 27 to 34 between 1959 and 1970, that among enterprise officials from 14 to 17,[28] and conceivably many such women are being admitted into the Party in middle age when their children have become older and they have more time for outside activities. However, this is merely speculation—and not very confident speculation at, that— and the plotting of the actual trend in saturation rates among men (which at the most still involves a change of not over a percentage point or two in the younger age brackets) is too sensitive to the methodological differences embodied in tables 7.2 and 7.3 to be done with any assurance at all. In any case, if the trend toward the admission of more women were to continue, obviously the maintenance of the existing saturation rates among men would require a larger intake of new members than would otherwise be necessary.

Trends in Party saturation among educational groups are even more difficult to discuss, for information about the age distribution of persons with various levels of education, vital because of the continuing sharp rise in the educational level of those in their twenties, is available only at the time of the census. If we forget about age distribution and simply divide the number of Communists with a given education level by the total number of persons with that education, we find (as table 7.8 demonstrates) that Party saturation among college graduates has remained essentially stable in the post-Khrushchev period, despite the increase in the proportion of young people in this group. (The variations in table 7.8 are statistically insignificant, for they could simply be the result of rounding in the data.)

TABLE 7.8 Party saturation among college graduates of all ages, 1959–1973.

| Year | Communists with higher education | Persons with higher education | Party saturation (%) |
|------|------|------|------|
| 1959 | 1,047,864 | 3,800,000 | 27.6 |
| 1965 | 1,763,262 | 5,600,000 | 31.5 |
| 1967 | 2,097,055 | 6,400,000 | 32.8 |
| 1971 | 2,819,642 | 8,800,000 | 32.0 |
| 1973 | 3,209,605 | 10,000,000 | 32.1 |

Sources: *Partiinaia zhizn*, no. 5 (May 1965), p. 11; no. 19 (October 1967), p. 4; no. 14 (August 1973), p. 16; *Narodnoe khoziaistvo v 1964* g., p. 33; *1967* g., p. 34; *1970* g., p. 23; *1972* g., p. 38.

By contrast, the saturation rate among those who have only graduated from secondary school or who have incomplete higher education has been declining fairly steadily. (See table 7.9.) However, it is not altogether clear what this decline means, for the category includes many young persons who would not normally become Party members. Thus, of the 39,500,000 persons with complete secondary education in 1970, 14 percent were under the age of 20, and another 37 percent were between the ages of 20 and 29. Partly because of Party emphasis on universal secondary education, partly because of the differences in the birth rates during and after World War II, the number of such young people with secondary education has increased enormously in the post-Khrushchev period. (The number of those in the "complete secondary education" category rose 2,687,000 a year in the period 1965 to 1973, compared with 800,000 a year from 1959 to 1965.) [29]

The real question about the levels of Party saturation among those over 30 with secondary education is, as it often has been in previous analyses, the policy of Party admission to be followed in the near and intermediate future. The bulge of post–World War II babies, whose leading edge is 27–28 years of age in 1975 is also (perhaps with a few years' delay) also the bulge of secondary school graduates approaching the age of Party admission. However, if we make the rather modest assumption that 65 percent of those between the ages of 10 and 19 in 1970 will eventually complete at least the ten years of schooling required for a secondary degree (and 53 percent of those in the 20–29 age cohort in 1970 had already done so),

TABLE 7.9  Party saturation among persons of all ages with incomplete higher and complete secondary education, 1959–1973.

| Year | Communists with incomplete higher and complete secondary education | Persons with incomplete higher and complete secondary education | Party saturation (%) |
|------|------|------|------|
| 1959 | 2,334,958 | 19,500,000 | 12.0 |
| 1965 | 3,843,260 | 25,000,000 | 15.4 |
| 1967 | 4,319,104 | 29,200,000 | 14.8 |
| 1971 | 5,270,953 | 41,800,000 | 12.6 |
| 1973 | 5,672,926 | 46,900,000 | 12.1 |

then the maintenance of the existing saturation rates for educational levels would eventually require two and a half times as many Party members from the cohort as from the 20–29 age cohort in 1959 even though the younger group is only some 21 percent larger in size. (See table 7.10.) If one attempted the dubious projections necessary to distinguish between those with higher education and those with secondary education, the number of Party admissions required for stable saturation would be even higher.

It would be interesting to try to predict the policy of Party admission to be followed in the future. Surely the number of admissions

TABLE 7.10  Hypothetical number of Communists among three ten-year age cohorts, 1959–1970.

| Level of education | Persons with indicated education | Hypothesized Party saturation (%) | Hypothesized Communists |
|---|---|---|---|
| *20–29 age cohort, 1959* | | | |
| Secondary or higher | 8,711,000 | 27.0 | 2,350,000 |
| Incomplete secondary | 12,380,000 | 13.3 | 1,650,000 |
| Elementary or less | 17,433,000 | 3.8 | 660,000 |
| Total | 38,524,000 | | 4,660,000 |
| *20–29 age cohort, 1970* | | | |
| Secondary or higher | 16,251,000 | 27.0 | 4,390,000 |
| Incomplete secondary | 11,058,000 | 13.3 | 1,470,000 |
| Elementary or less | 3,567,000 | 3.8 | 140,000 |
| Total | 30,876,000 | 27.0 | 6,000,000 |
| *10–19 age cohort, 1970* | | | |
| Secondary or higher | 30,225,000 [a] | 27.0 | 8,240,000 |
| Incomplete secondary | 14,000,000 [a] | 13.3 | 1,860,000 |
| Elementary or less | 2,000,000 [a] | 3.8 | 750,000 |
| Total | 46,225,000 | | 10,850,000 |

Sources: The hypothesized Party saturation rates are taken from table 7.4, the population data from *Itogi vsesoiuznoi perepisi naseleniia, 1970 goda*, III, 6–7, and *Itogi vsesoiuznoi perepisi naseleniia 1959 goda, SSSR* (Moscow: Statistika, 1962), pp. 74–75.

[a] Estimates are based on the assumption that 65 percent of the cohort will eventually receive a secondary degree or better and that the number without any high school education will continue to decline. Some small mortality is also assumed.

will soon begin to rise, but the degree of the increase is the crucial variable. When this question was raised with several highly-placed Soviet social scientists who should be in a position to know, they gave every indication of never having thought of the implications of the changes in birth rates for levels of Party saturation—or, indeed, of not having thought much at all about saturation levels by age and educational group, particularly among men. One such scholar insisted that he would certainly have heard about a debate on this question within the upper echelons if it were occurring and that he has heard nothing.

Whatever is decided or not decided in the future (and the absence of a decision permitting a rise in admissions would be the most drastic change in policy), we in the West must be very careful in our analysis of what is occurring. In particular, we must be keenly aware of the implications of the fluctuations in the size of age cohorts produced by World War II. It would be very easy to interpret an increase in Party admissions as a movement toward a more open Party when, in fact, a small increase in admissions might denote lower saturation rates among groups that, in fact, have had fairly free access to the Party in the past.

CONCLUSION

To the extent that membership in the Communist Party has meaning, the mass character of the "elite" Party is a key fact about the USSR that has not been sufficiently absorbed into our understanding of that country. Some might contend, of course, that the degree of Party saturation, whether among men or women, has little importance and that the entire statistical exercise in which we have been engaged is basically trivial. And, certainly, it is true that every Soviet citizen could be enrolled in the Party tomorrow and that such a development might have little more meaning than the universal participation of Soviet adults in elections to the Supreme Soviet.

Yet, so far as can be judged, membership in the Party usually is quite a different matter than voting in elections to the soviets. It involves the obligation to take on "Party assignments" (frequently participation and leadership in activities of non-Party institutions and committees), and it provides the member with the opportunity to receive certain information that is not published in the press. When a number of people do begin to participate in this type of political and social activity and do become knowledgeable about it, everything that we have learned about the political process suggests that responsible officials will sometimes be responsive to some of the input, if nothing else than for reasons of morale.

While many Party members remain relatively inactive,[30] the proportion of adult men in the Party is very high in comparison with the proportion of politically active adults in the West, and the number of Soviet citizens who participate in non-Party institutions is even higher.[31] Large numbers of Party members could be relatively inactive or without influence, and there still would be ample room for the type of limited direct citizen impact on decisions found in the West by such scholars as Robert Dahl. In the past, we have simply assumed that "the Soviet regime . . . uses political participation to control its people [and] the controls produced by political participation flow in one direction only." [32] At least part of the burden of proof lies on those who make such assertions.

# PART THREE

# The Policy Process:
# Administration and Control

# The Scientific–Technical Revolution and the Soviet Administrative Debate

## ROBERT F. MILLER

In the preface to the revised edition of *Government and the American Economy* Merle Fainsod and Lincoln Gordon noted that "the energies released by modern industrialism and democracy have given shape and content to the multiplying obligations of government in the economic realm." They expressed "the conviction that effective economic or other criteria of desirable public policy can be most fruitfully developed when there is a vivid realization of the potentialities and limitations of the political context in which they must be applied." [1]

Unlike the American economic system, where the full acknowledgment of government involvement has come rather late, and grudgingly, the Soviet system, from its very inception, assigned the state a dominant role in the organization and operation of the economy and society. Yet in the last few years it would not be difficult to find sentiments similar to those expressed by Fainsod and Gordon implicit in the writings of the more candid among Soviet politicians and social scientists. For in their current preoccupations with "economic methods" and the "scientific and technical revolution" there is tacit acknowledgment of the limitations, as well as the potentialities, that the political and socioeconomic subsystems pose to each other.

The role of the administrative bureaucracy in the relationship between political leadership and society has always been crucial. In classical Weberian theory the bureaucracy occupies the strategic "space" between the policy makers and the producers and consumers of the goods and services that are the ultimate objects of policy.[2] However, as the processor and purveyor of most of the information on which policy is based, and as the main instrument by which policy is manifested, the bureaucracy is itself heavily involved in the policy formation process. The conception of administration as simply the implementation of decisions made by others (political leaders, factory owners, and so forth) has long been rejected by Western students of administration. Even in the Soviet Union, where the top Party leaders have so assiduously endeavored to preserve their monopoly of decision making, a categorical separation between policy-making and administrative roles has customarily been avoided.[3] The ready transferability of leadership personnel between Party and state apparatuses, as well as the uniformity of their training at the highest levels (for example, at the Higher Party School of the Central Committee), is an implicit denial of the feasibility or desirability of strict compartmentalization.

This conscious blurring of political and administrative roles may, of course, be interpreted primarily as a technique for maintaining Party dominance over administration, rather than as a recognition of the complexity of the administrative function. Whatever the explanation, however, there are grounds for suggesting that the denial of role specificity may be becoming increasingly untenable.

PRE-REVOLUTIONARY THEORETICAL HERITAGE

Before proceeding with an analysis of the changes in the Soviet conception of the role of administration I should say a few words about the scope of the institution to be discussed. For reasons of space I make general observations on the Soviet administrative apparatus as a whole rather than to focus in detail on a specific segment of that apparatus. Accordingly this essay is concerned with the entire group of so-called Employees of the Soviet State Apparatus, the approximately (in 1970) 13.5 million administrative officials engaged in mental, but not "purely creative, work" in Party, governmental, economic, social, military, and judicial institutions, but especially the 2 million in responsible leadership positions.[4] Their general function is customarily defined as the management of the *persons* who produce the *things* (goods and services of various kinds) consumed by Soviet society. Excluded are the personnel of the so-called "public organizations," such as the trade unions, the Komsomol, and voluntary organizations, whose acts usually carry no formal state authority. For obvious reasons, the Communist Party, the most important public organization of all, cannot be thus ignored. Its 200,000-strong apparat contains the main segment of the political leadership group whose interaction with the administrative apparatus is a basic theme of this essay.

The Marxist-Leninist heritage of Soviet administrative theory is a curious amalgam of analytical sophistication and rather naive utopianism. The normative impact of most of the utopian projections —for example, the transcending of the division of labor and the withering away of the state—has all but vanished in the light of subsequent political and technological developments. However, many of the more concrete analytical and prescriptive elements have had considerable practical influence.

Like Marx and Engels, Lenin had foreseen the need for strong, efficient administration under socialism, at least for the first postrevolutionary phase. Yet their often brilliant analyses of the sociology and politics of bureaucracy under capitalism produced surprisingly unsophisticated projections of the role and character of administration under socialism. On the eve of the Revolution Lenin professed to see but little difficulty in taming and recasting the majority of the existing bureaucrats into faithful servants of the proletarian dictatorship.[5] Under socialism the administrative apparatus, staffed mainly by holdovers from the Tsarist administrative and economic bureaucracy —the so-called "bourgeois specialists"—would be transformed as if by magic into a Weberian organizational automaton. A few selected excisions, threats of material or physical sanctions, the placement of reliable Bolshevik cadres in key leadership positions, and continuous supervision by intelligent proletarian controllers provided everything needed to ensure faithful, efficient compliance.

To the extent that it was sincere, and not merely a polemical rejoinder to those who were skeptical of the Bolshevik capacity to rule, Lenin's depiction of the new socialist bureaucracy obviously rested on an oversimplified, static conception of administration and of the tasks of socialist construction that lay ahead. His prescriptions would have been more appropriate for a German revolution, perhaps, than for the Russian Revolution.

PRACTICAL IMPERATIVES

Lenin's casual approach to problems of administration was bound to change after the Revolution. The Civil War, naturally, left little time for theorizing, although it did provide practical experience in crisis management. With the return to peace, the evaporation of the cherished hopes of fraternal assistance from successful revolutions in the advanced Western countries, and daily immersion in the enormous tasks of economic and social rehabilitation, Lenin found it necessary to devote increasing attention to the principles and practice of administration.

Although, according to Azrael, there was reason for general satisfaction with the performance of the industrial bureaucracy, and its large complement of bourgeois specialists,[6] the same could not be said of the state administration as a whole. Lenin characterized its work as "pitiful, not to say disgusting." [7] With the sole exception of the Commissariat of Foreign Affairs (also, incidentally, staffed largely with experts from the old regime), the central administrative machine had become so inefficient and unresponsive, in Lenin's view, that the implementation of Party policy was seriously threatened.[8]

The diseases of bureaucracy had especially heavily infected RAB-KRIN, ostensibly the chief watchdog agency of proletarian control. Lenin seized upon reform of this agency as the key to regeneration of the entire bureaucratic system. He proposed to reshape it into a super-agency of Party and state control with the dual function of organizational research and systematic inspection. At its core he proposed the recruitment of a staff of 300–400 experts in public administration and scientific management, fully conversant with modern Western management techniques.[9] To increase its leverage and enhance its political authority it was to be fused with a revitalized Central Control Commission. In Lenin's view, this linkage would provide opportunities for the injection of scientific administration not only into the state bureaucracy, but into top Party deliberative bodies as well. It would help, he said, "to reduce the influence of purely personal and casual circumstances and thus to lower the danger of schism" in the Central Committee.[10]

Lenin's fascination with scientific administration and structural reorganization as a cure for the ills of the evolving political system is striking, especially in view of his criticisms of Trotsky in his famous "Testament." It is difficult not to agree with Schapiro that Lenin's approach reflected a profound lack of understanding of the political transformation that Stalin was bringing about at precisely this time.[11] On the other hand, Lenin was far from naive in his awareness that, whatever the Party's power configuration, the quality of administration could not be a matter of indifference, particularly for a country in Russia's position, where foreign and domestic enemies were allegedly watching for the slightest signs of weakness. He had come to realize that management of an entire system the size of Russia's required special skills that Bolshevik willpower alone could not hope to provide. Western managerial techniques seemed to offer magnificent opportunities for a planned, centralized system such as Lenin envisioned.[12]

## THE STALINIST APPROACH TO ADMINISTRATION

Lenin's prestige was such that his suggestions for reform were dutifully enacted before he died. However, the evolving political environment made the kind of systematic theory development and technical experimentation Lenin specified increasingly irrelevant. As Paul Cocks has shown, RABKRIN was soon relegated primarily to the role of a research organization.[13] Some of its theoretical and experimental studies of public administration and production processes were interesting and potentially useful.[14] But to the Stalinist political cadres ascending to positions of leadership during the late twenties and early thirties, such efforts were not worthy of serious attention.

Azrael has aptly described the change in the climate of decision-making and management that accompanied the forced-draft industrialization campaign.[15] Once again Bolshevik élan replaced technical rationality and scientific consistency as leadership values. Mobilization, rather than efficient management, became the primary function of the administrative system. The distinction between political and administrative roles was, accordingly, substantially eroded, and reliable organizers were shuffled continually between Party and governmental bureaucracies. To a certain extent this interchange promoted the mutual assimilation of skills, Party officials acquiring a modicum of technical knowledge and administrators acquiring habits of the "Party style" of political leadership. But there can be little doubt that technical expertise (legal, agronomic, economic, for example, as well as industrial) suffered serious depreciation in the exchange. Given the increasing politicization of Stalin's style of leadership during the thirties, political "perspective" was deemed more valuable than mere technical competence. An example of contemporary priorities is the following passage from Stalin's report to the Eighteenth Party Congress in March 1939:

It may be confidently stated that if we succeeded in training the cadres in all branches of our work ideologically and in schooling them politically to such an extent as to enable them easily to orientate themselves in the internal and international situation; if we succeeded in making them quite mature Marxist-Leninists capable of solving the problems involved in the guidance of the country without serious error, we would have every reason to consider nine-tenths of our problems already settled.[16]

One of the most important results of the Great Purge was the formation of a new corps of "red specialists" trained under Soviet conditions and imbued with loyalty to Stalin.[17] Having substantially completed the construction of an industrial base and a society organized and conditioned to serve it, Stalin encouraged the development of an appropriate managerial apparatus. The administrative profession accordingly regained much of its status as the repository of a specialized body of knowledge, mainly of an engineering character. Except at the apex of the system, where Stalin retained absolute decision-making authority, a fairly precise division of labor between Party and administrative roles was established. The authority of the Party apparatus to interfere in administrative matters was greatly circumscribed. The new Soviet managers could be trusted to fulfill their responsibilities to Party and state without undue interference, although, it goes without saying, their loyalty was not entirely taken for granted.

Under Stalin's style of leadership, in which the dictator himself performed the role of supreme ideological and theoretical legislator, administrative science along with the social sciences in general (and many of the natural sciences as well) suffered an almost total eclipse. As I have suggested elsewhere, administrative theory became the preserve of administrative law specialists, whose main function was to elaborate on Stalin's pronouncements and to provide ideological justifications for the occasional reorganizations of the administrative structure.[18] A sample of their theoretical contributions can be found in the following passage on personnel selection from a popular textbook on administrative institutions published in 1951: "Comrade Stalin teaches [us] to select and assign cadres in accordance with political criteria, that is, does the given official deserve political trust, and also in accordance with businesslike criteria, that is, is he suitable for the proposed job." [19]

Khrushchev found the practical performance of this system far from satisfactory. Considerations of Kremlin political infighting aside, Khrushchev's radical reorganizations of bureaucratic structure and functions were to have a tremendous impact, both directly and indirectly, on the Soviet administrative system.

On balance, the *post factum* characterization of Khrushchev's reign by his erstwhile colleagues as an era of "hare-brained schemes" and "hasty decisions" is not entirely unjustified. Although his analyses of

the bureaupathology[20] of the Stalinist administrative system were often very cogent, the bumptiousness and impatience of his personal
leadership style—doubtless aggravated by the vigorous political opposition he encountered at every turn—engendered a pattern of solutions more often than not ill-suited to the specific problems he had
diagnosed. The disruptive effects of Khrushchev's incessant structural
reorganizations, particularly upon the professional and careerist sensibilities of the bureaucrats affected, were at least as important as his
substantive policies in coalescing the disparate forces that ultimately
overthrew him.

Khrushchev's contempt for administrators and administrative processes went beyond mere tactical, political considerations. His attitude
was clearly manifested in the recklessness with which he dismantled
the established division of functions and subordinated administrative
institutions to direct Party leadership and control. A common element
in the reorganizations of agriculture in 1953, industry in 1957, and
the entire provincial Party and governmental systems in 1962 was the
insertion of Party officials directly into the administrative chain of
command.[21] The Party apparatus itself was not immune to his attacks
on the principle of functional specificity. Beginning in 1959 he introduced a series of experiments with "non-staff" instructors and com-
missions of rank-and-file Party members to aid the regular apparatus
in carrying out its functions. In 1962 he reintroduced Lenin's idea of
combining Party and state control functions in the form of a hierarchy
of Party-State Control Committees to involve ordinary workers in the
supervision of the bureaucracy.[22]

To a certain extent these changes represented a return to the principle of Bolshevik élan as the prime attribute of leadership, but not
entirely. For under Khrushchev's new "production principle" of Party
organization, concrete economic performance became the ultimate
criteria of successful leadership.[23] Political considerations aside, the
placement of Party officials in positions of direct responsibility was
designed to stimulate energetic compliance with central plans and
directives: in short, to pinpoint responsibility for performance, rather
than to conceal it, as the previous administrative system was alleged
to have done.

That the new system placed tremendous demands on the local Party
secretaries is obvious. But just as obvious was the fact that the Soviet
economy and society were no longer what they had been in the
thirties. In addition to the vested interests of the entrenched managerial and technical cadres, Party officials had to contend with a
rapidly growing technological complexity which rendered the simple

"Party style of leadership" increasingly ineffectual. Party leaders had literally to be engineers and managers themselves if they were to be able to intervene effectively in administration. In the words of a secretary of the Perm' Gorkom, "If you don't know production, it's hard to get close to it." [24]

Khrushchev's eclectic and oversimplified view of administration was reflected in his general attitudes toward science. His interest and encouragement were limited primarily to those scientific developments that promised immediate practical or military benefits. The more abstract theoretical contributions were likely to meet with his indifference or downright scorn. Sometimes this attitude was relatively beneficial, as in the case of his attacks on the academic economists in 1956.[25] But its effects could just as well be harmful, as in the cases of his treatment of the research workers of the Ministry of Agriculture in 1961 and his continued sponsorship of the quackery of T. D. Lysenko.

The most favorable thing that can be said of Khrushchev's policies toward science and technology was that he permitted and sometimes actively encouraged the discussion of divergent opinions on topics that had long been taboo. The so-called "Liberman proposals" immediately come to mind. For our purposes the most significant development was the first timid steps in the revival of work on administrative theory. The discussion of such "bourgeois" sciences as cybernetics and information theory now became legitimate. Some of the early works on administration even managed to smuggle in eclectically a few Western social science concepts, such as structural-functionalism for analyzing Soviet practice.[26] Also, for the first time in over twenty-five years, Soviet scholars began serious and systematical discussion of the social structure of a communist society, in line with the new Party Program published in 1961.[27]

THE REBIRTH OF ADMINISTRATIVE SCIENCE

As if in reaction to Khrushchev's persistent denigration of administrative professionalism, a veritable flood of discussions on scientific management followed his ouster in the fall of 1964. At first this development was overshadowed by more spectacular changes, such as the reimposition of traditional patterns of Party and state organization.[28] But gradually it became evident that there would be no simple return to Stalinist practices; a qualitatively new approach to administration was evolving. The most visible manifestations of change were the major reforms in agriculture and industry in the spring and fall of 1965. These reforms involved more than mere structural reorganization (in fact, the old production-branch ministerial format was restored virtually intact). Substantial changes were attempted in the methods of planning and management. In the economic realm, at least, the thrust of the reforms was soon relatively clear: to attack the increasing problems of stagnation and inefficiency by long-term qualitative improvements in the technological level of administration and performance evaluation.

A measure of the change in atmosphere was the level of the discussions on administrative questions which began to appear with increasing frequency in Party and professional journals. An early harbinger was the publication, on the eve of the industrial reform, of a discussion of social theory in *Kommunist*, the Party's main theoretical journal. The initial article in the series was an essay on "The Scientific Direction of Social Processes" by V. G. Afanas'ev, a professor of philosophy in the Central Committee's Academy of Social Sciences, who would eventually become one of the most prominent middle-of-the-road proponents of a scientific approach to administration.[29] The major themes he discussed as germane to the science of administration are worth listing here, for they constitute the basic issues around which conflicting political and professional viewpoints have tended to cluster in recent years. These themes, not necessarily in order of presentation or importance, were as follows:

— the content of the administrative function (*upravlenie*) and its relationship to the primary leadership function (*rukovodstvo*);
— formal and informal relationships between the structures mainly associated with these functions, namely, the state organs of administration (including economic management) and the Party leadership organs, respectively;
— the nature of the decision-making process in a mature socialist society, and the relationship between the "subjective factor" and "objective conditions" in decision-making and administration;
— the different areas of administration and the specific disciplines involved; also, the value of "bourgeois" developments in these disciplines and their applicability to socialist conditions;
— problems in the collection, processing, and application of social information;
— appropriate systems of recruitment, training, and placement of administrative personnel.

Underlying these themes was the fundamental issue of the leading role of the Party in the "age of the scientific and technological revolution." Discounting this "exogenous variable" from the debates, a foreign observer might be forgiven for thinking that he was witnessing a continuation of the argument between traditionalists and behaviorists that had so preoccupied Western social sciences in past decades.

Even considering cases of more or less transparent political special pleading, the quality of the debates has been quite high. Party stalwarts have been forced to defend their interests on a relatively high theoretical plane, for the rules of the game have evidently prohibited the rejection out of hand of the new conceptual framework. In many cases, moreover, political and professional traditionalists have raised valid methodological and theoretical issues.[30]

In his article initiating the discussion Afanas'ev presented a definition of administration involving a curious blend of modern systems concepts and historical materialism. "Administration in its most general sense is the ordering and regulation of a system under the conditions of a continuously changing internal and external environment, and the bringing of the system into conformity with the requirements of its characteristic objective laws." [31] Only the retention of the concept of objective laws really separates this formulation from Western theories of open systems.[32] True, the formulation does not go as far as A. A. Bogdanov's turn-of-the-century model of Tektology, the super-science.[33] But it should be remembered that Bogdanov's theories had been explicitly condemned by Lenin in 1908 and have remained on the official Index ever since.[34] In this sense, the Afanas'ev formulation represented a highly significant ideological, as well as conceptual advance.

A particularly striking aspect of the definition was its comprehensiveness. In the discussion that followed in the November issue of *Kommunist*, A. K. Belykh, the conservative chairman of the Department of Scientific Communism at Leningrad State University, criticized theorists who failed to distinguish between the administrative function and the political-organizational function.[35] This criticism was, perhaps, not fully applicable to Afanas'ev, who had a special place for the function of Party-political leadership as the epitome of the "subjective factor" at the apex of his administrative model.[36] A more appropriate target perhaps was formulations such as those of V. Komarov, an instructor at the Leningrad Electro-Technical Institute of Communications, who went far beyond the traditional division of functions:

Leadership and administration in principle coincide only in socialist society. Now the task obviously consists in maximally approximating the content of leadership to the objective tendencies of social administration and self-regulation . . . The object of leadership is controlled (*upravliaetsia*) in its development by certain laws, independently of the subject of leadership. And this subject will be really leading (*deistvitel'no rukovodiashchim*) when its conscious, volitional activity is determined by these laws of 'self-regulation' in the object.[37]

Komarov's conception of objective laws implied serious constraint on the "subject of leadership."

Of direct importance to this question about the division of administrative labor was the discussion of the subdivision of the administrative function. A basic threefold division has been posited: economic administration, sociopolitical administration (concerned with the management of class, group, nationality, and territorial distinctions in society), and "spiritual" administration (concerned with the management of scientific, educational, cultural, and attitude-formation processes). The three subdivisions are subsumed under the concept of social administration, as the master, integrating science.[38] The political and professional traditionalists have tended to be the most concerned with the maintenance of boundary lines and the supremacy of social administration. Not only is the latter considered the most comprehensive and, hence, the most appropriate sphere for the continued dominance of Party decision-making, but it is also conceded to be the least susceptible to quantitative methods of analysis and determination. Thus, computer technology, especially for information processing, automatic control theory (cybernetics), information theory, and mathematical modeling are conceded to be appropriate tools for economic administration but they are not, the conservatives argue, applicable to the broader questions of total societal regulation.[39] General systems theory, at least on the terminological level, appears to be considered less threatening in this respect, since it bears many surface similarities to historical materialism.

Those who have taken refuge in such abstractions, were bound to be somewhat disturbed, however, by assertions such as the following by V. A. Iadov, the director of the sociological research laboratory at Leningrad State University and one of the most unabashed behaviorists in Soviet social sciences: "There exists the point of view that there are social processes which are not amenable to quantitative analysis . . . The question is not that there are processes which are not amenable to precise analysis, but that we have not learned how to do it yet." [40] Afanas'ev, although stressing the importance of "concreteness," was not prepared to go nearly this far. Indeed he criticized not only the administrative lawyers, but cyberneticists, sociologists, and economists as well, for their preoccupation with narrow areas of administration and for imputing to their own disciplines a paradigm-like quality for administrative science as a whole.[41] And he himself had expressed skepticism about the possibilities of quantification in many areas of social science.[42]

The commitment to a scientific approach to administration implied a massive assimilation of the most up-to-date conceptual and technical tools. Given the relative underdevelopment of many of the Soviet branches of the relevant sciences, it was perhaps natural that Soviet specialists would turn to the West. Wholesale borrowing carries the danger of vulnerability to accusations of "selling out," "convergence," "embourgeoisement," and the like, whether from Western, Eastern, or conservative domestic critics. But a solution was found in shrouding the process of borrowing with a web of qualifications and justifications: namely, that the assumptions and conclusions of bourgeois social sciences and managerial research were erroneous and useless; only (some of) the techniques were suitable. Ultimately refuge was found in the formula that bourgeois techniques, while sometimes useful and promising, could never be maximally applied in a social system ridden with class conflict and based on anarchistic market forces. Only under a fully planned, totally integrated, mature socialist system could the possibilities immanent in these techniques be fully realized.[43]

Afanas'ev himself had nothing to say directly on the issue of technical borrowing in his initial essay. However, in the brief bibliography supplied at the end of the essay he included a work by Dzherman Gvishiani on this topic.[44] Gvishiani, Kosygin's son-in-law, has become one of the main Soviet exponents and managers of the process of "safe" borrowing from the West.

A seeming anachronism in the discussions was the repeated appearance of the traditional Marxist concepts of "the subjective factor" and "objective conditions." In the traditional formulation the subjective factor (read: the top-level Party and governmental decision-makers) is essential to the realization of the potentialities inherent in the objective conditions at each historical stage. Indeed, the conscious, properly organized activity of the subjective factor can overcome the impact of superficially unfavorable objective conditions.[45] Only in a mature socialist society, it is asserted, can full advantage be taken of these potentialities.[46] Under the conditions of the scientific and technical revolution these potentialities are greatly enhanced. But potentiality is not automatically translated into actuality. Current conditions place exceptionally great responsibilities on the subjective factor. On the one hand, this can be used to justify an enhanced role for Party leadership; but, on the other hand, it can also be interpreted, as Komarov's comments suggest, as imposing serious constraints on the freedom of action of the Party leaders. For the increasingly precise mechanisms of "the object"—part of the objective conditions—do not permit of arbitrary tampering and manipulation.

A vital aspect of the subjective factor and ultimately, perhaps, the crucial variable in the entire political-administrative equation is the cadres question. The scientific and technological revolution imposes tremendous demands for highly trained personnel at all levels of the administrative hierarchy. There appears to be increasing recognition that no amount of short-term retraining can equip top-level Party and government leaders for the complete mastery of the complex processes involved in the management of society. Former patterns of co-optation and interchangeability of political and technical cadres are increasingly obsolete. The specialist co-opted into the political elite soon loses touch with advanced developments in his area of special competence. Accordingly, the loyalty and "political maturity" of the specialists who are assigned to responsible positions in their areas of competence have become a matter of great concern to political leaders. Indeed, a rough measure of the conservatism of individual writers and of the temper of a particular period is the order of priorities assigned to political and professional criteria in the selection of responsible officials. Afanas'ev, in his 1965 article, presented the traditional Leninist formulation: "dedication to the cause of communism, a high sense of responsibility to the people, principled behavior, knowledge of business matters." [47] A lead editorial in *Kommunist* in July 1972 substantially changed this order of priorities; placing "businesslike" (*delovye*) qualities ahead of "political" and "moral" qualities.[48] This editorial, it is true, was primarily about economic leaders, but the traditional formulation had always applied to them as well. The emendation was obviously "not by accident."

The theses discussed in the preceding pages have continued to occupy the focus of attention in subsequent debates on the role and characteristics of administration. Limitations of space preclude a full analysis of the various viewpoints. In the remaining pages I shall merely summarize important developments in the argument and shifts in the official line.

The new freedom for the behavioral and managerial sciences led to an immediate flourishing of research and publishing activity. Institutes and bureaus of concrete sociological research sprang up throughout the country. By 1968 there were at least a hundred of them, mainly connected with academic institutions. Local Party committees hastened to set up their own "bureaus of concrete sociological research," and soon there existed what might be called a separate Party sociology to provide hard data on attitudes and social conditions in particular localities.[49] A rich monographic and periodical literature began to appear on specific aspects of administrative and social processes. Of particular interest are the annual compendia *Man and Society*, published by Leningrad University, and *Scientific Administration of Society*, edited by Afanas'ev under the imprimatur of the Higher Party School and Academy of Social Sciences of the Central Committee. The sponsorship of the latter publication has not been as restrictive as one might expect, especially in the most recent period, reflecting the changes in official perspectives. However, most of the contributions maintain a fairly high level of abstraction, even where such topics as cybernetic applications are discussed. This is not true of the Leningrad publication, which regularly presents the findings of research and experiments in the fields of sociology, social psychology, information theory, and mathematical modeling.[50]

The new approaches have by no means gone unchallenged. A conservative reaction soon made its appearance. What the conservatives especially criticized, particularly in the Leningrad studies, was the tendency to ignore the basic tenets of historical materialism in thinking through research problems and in methodology. A similar complaint was directed against the more radical of the systems theorists. Academician A. Rumiantsev, for example, attacked latter-day Bogdanovites for absolutizing structural and processual features of administration in general, without regard to the characteristics of specific sectors.[51] Afanas'ev himself evidently found it necessary to execute a partial retreat in 1967, warning that concrete sociological research must be firmly grounded in Marxist-Leninist methodology.[52]

The Central Committee decree "On Measures for the Further Development of the Social Sciences and Enhancement of Their Role in Communist Construction," published in mid-1967, gave the conservatives substantial encouragement. It placed the social sciences in a clearly instrumental role in combating bourgeois ideological penetration, and demanded an increase in the ideological content of education and personnel management. It specifically criticized sociological research for being too empirical in its methodological and conceptual orientation.[53]

One of the high points in this campaign was the attack in 1970 by the conservative philosopher G. Glezerman on Iu. A. Levada, one of the leading empirical sociologists in the USSR, whom he accused of blind adoption of Western methods and concepts and of brazen disparagement of historical materialism.[54] In other areas as well, conservatives continued to reject mathematical models in economics and to stress the importance of the class approach to all social phenomena.[55]

The liberals held their ground, however, and continued to publicize their work. In 1970 Iadov launched a rather sophisticated counterattack in the form of a proposed division of theoretical labor between historical materialism and empirical social theory. In his formula the former was relegated to a level of generality that effectively rendered it irrelevant to empirical research.[56]

The very vigor and duration of the debates suggest that the Party elite had not yet come to a final decision. In this sense the Twenty-Fourth Party Congress in March–April 1971 represented a watershed in official policy. In his Report at the Congress Brezhnev came out foursquare for the scientific and technical revolution, characterizing it as the key to economic development, "not only from the standpoint of present tasks, but also the long-term perspective." [57] The conscious fostering of scientific and technological progress was elevated to the status of a primary continuing responsibility of Party cadres. Brezhnev gave his full endorsement to the application of modern science and technology to the processes of administration.[58]

This firm commitment to modern methods brought the issue of the character of the Party's leadership role into sharp focus. Further elaboration of the problems and dangers involved came in the ensuing months. In July the editors of *Kommunist* found it necessary to warn against the "fetishization" of automatic control methods in the management of the economy. The new commitments, they argued, did not diminish the role of conscious direction.[59] Suslov made similar remarks with respect to social administration the following January. Scientists, he asserted, must be given their head in applying modern methods to Communist construction, but their work should be informed by the spirit of Marxist-Leninist partisanship.[60] Nevertheless, there could be no return to the status quo. At about the time of the Congress Glezerman conceded defeat by tacitly accepting the division of theoretical labor presented by Iadov.[61]

Under the new dispensation the traditional Party prerogative in personnel matters assumed particular importance. Given the likelihood of slippage in Party influence on many areas of policy, control over the appointment of responsible specialists and continuous monitoring of their behavior in office became probably the most important single aspect of Party dominance. In the past local Party organs had allegedly been rather timid in interfering in the professional affairs of scientific and technical personnel.[62] The extension of the right of control (*pravo kontrolia*) to Party organizations in scientific research and educational institutions and design bureaus by the Twenty-Fourth Party Congress was obviously motivated by these considerations. But the question was, what kind of interference would be appropriate under the new conditions.

Even apart from these political issues, the technical requirements of the new commitment necessarily placed the cadres problem in the center of attention. In addition to recruiting new appointees, an immediate problem was the upgrading of skills of the existing corps of managers in order to enable them to assimilate the anticipated revolution in techniques. It was estimated that 5 percent of the 2 million incumbents of managerial posts would have to be replaced each year because of retirements alone. This meant training about 150,000 managerial recruits, essentially from among specialists already employed, each year in the projected one–two year courses.[63] In the immediate postreform period, management retraining, particularly in short-term courses, had been largely a Party responsibility. For officials in noneconomic branches of administration it has tended to remain so. Both the full-time and correspondence branches of the Higher Party School of the Central Committee and the republic and inter-oblast higher Party schools increased their attention to systematic upgrading of the technical knowledge of Party, government, trade union, police, and other administrators. In November 1972 the Central Committee decreed the introduction of a special course on "Principles of Scientific Administration of the Socialist Economy" in the curriculum of the central Higher Party School.[64] The extensive retraining programs in managerial techniques throughout the Party educational system are an indication of the seriousness with which the new challenge is viewed.

However, there has been considerable criticism of the entire system of administrative training.[65] The Party-centered system is obviously designed to provide merely introductory knowledge of the new techniques. The traditional retraining system, based on the individual ministries, was poorly coordinated, insufficiently financed, and lacking in standards. To remedy this situation a number of special management training institutes have been established at higher educational institutions in recent years. And in February 1971 a special Institute of Administration of the National Economy began operation under the State Committee for Science and Technology. Its functions include the training of management specialists and the coordination of training practices and methodologies.[66] The modernizing influence of Gvishiani, who is deputy chairman of the state committee, is undoubtedly strongly reflected in the program of the Institute.

The new stress on rational, scientific criteria has even penetrated the sacrosanct area of personnel recruitment in recent years. Several writers have been suggesting the use of standardized selection methods, such as psychological and personality testing, and a greater reliance on competitive procedures (konkursy) for recruitment of managerial cadres. Relatively conservative writers, such as Iu. A. Tikhomirov, would restrict these procedures to technical personnel and middle-level specialists, leaving top management to be selected "by careful study by the appropriate services," as in the past.[67] This is obviously a sensitive issue, for it could reduce the Party's ability to manipulate personnel matters through the nomenklatura. No one has ventured to question the nomenklatura system itself; indeed, there seem to be fewer inhibitions in discussing it, albeit always positively, than in past periods. But some writers have shown themselves to be bolder than Tikhomirov in suggesting the application of standardized professional selection criteria for managerial personnel.

The dangers to the traditional system of Party control have obviously been recognized by Soviet leaders in their decision to link their society to the scientific and technological revolution. They are evidently willing to accept the risk.

CONCLUSIONS

In many ways the Soviet administrative system has come full circle. The highly trained scientific and technical intelligentsia of today are the functional equivalent in professional respects of the bourgeois specialists of Lenin's day. And the present leaders' appreciation of the importance of their contribution to the effective functioning of the socioeconomic system is similar to Lenin's in the last years of his life, in contrast to the attitudes of Stalin and Khrushchev. Historical parallels are never exact, to be sure. There are obviously tremendous differences, in addition to the political, between the status of the present-day bureaucrats and that of their counterparts fifty years ago. Not the least important cause of this difference is the quantum jump in the content of expertise. The paradigm of the socioeconomic system is no longer the machine but the cybernetic system, with its complex of interrelationships and its various feedback mechanisms. The scope of involvement of specialists from various disciplines expands ever more widely in the complex of administrative systems, overspreading the established boundaries between administration and policy-making.

What do these changes in the role and characteristics of the administrative bureaucracy portend for the ways in which—to paraphrase the title of Merle Fainsod's magnum opus—Russia will be ruled? Skeptics will probably answer that very little has changed or will change in the future. Party leaders, they may point out, are well aware of the challenge to their control and are bound to take whatever measures are necessary to preserve it, either by mastering the necessary skill themselves or by co-opting trustworthy specialists with such skills into the Party apparatus. Perhaps. But the "knowledge explosion" and the consequent narrowing of specialization today makes it questionable whether this traditional method of keeping up with the times can be successful in the long run. The evidence offered in this essay suggests that Party leaders themselves are no longer sanguine about this possibility. In his latest book, published in 1972, Afanas'ev, while continuing to proclaim the leading role of the Party and casting it as the main integrating force in society, places his main emphasis on specialization and the division of labor as the watchwords of the present era.[68] Indeed, the precise content of the Party's leadership functions is perhaps the weakest part of his analysis. The chief distinguishing characteristics of the leader in his formulation appear to lie in the shadowy realm of personal qualities: the Party leader must have different qualities from the economic administrator, he says without substantial elaboration.[69] This is obviously a tenuous basis for the maintenance of authority in the age of the scientific and technological revolution.

A somewhat less obvious objection to my argument concerns the durability of the current infatuation with scientific progress. While the reversal of this commitment does not seem likely, particularly in the area of industrial management—although it is not impossible there either—there exists the danger that the scientists and their champions may have oversold themselves. They may have exaggerated the extent to which their concepts and techniques can in fact solve the problems of social administration. Gvishiani's recent shrill criticisms of Western management scientists for giving up the battle and taking refuge in existentialism smack suspiciously of special pleading. His assurances that socialist conditions eliminate the indeterminacies which have stymied bourgeois managers are not altogether convincing.[70] The partial rejection of McNamara's systems-analytic methods in defense procurements and the reaction against urban planning in the United States suggest that the revolution in techniques has not been entirely victorious. It is not inconceivable that a similar reaction could occur in the Soviet Union and that the Russians will look once again to a *krepkii khoziain* to solve their social and economic problems for them. Russian history offers few grounds for rejecting such an outcome out of hand.

But even if the commitment to science and technology is profound and long-lasting, it does not follow that the liberalization of Soviet society will necessarily result. Andrei Amalrik's pessimistic character-ization of the new Soviet intelligentsia on this score surely deserves thoughtful consideration.[71] There is no reason to believe that the overwhelming majority of the new technocrats will be dissatisfied with the professional, material, and status rewards that the regime seems quite willing to offer them. Moreover, the assertion that rational, scientific decision-making and administration will enhance the attain-ment of humanistic goals and individual self-fulfillment remains to be proven. In the words of Afanas'ev in his latest book:

The achievement of the most effcient functioning of the system is the main task of administration, and the more educated, the more qualified the indi-vidual, the basic component of the social system, the more successfully this task is accomplished. This type of person, if we may say so, is easier to ad-minister, since he performs his functions more accurately, more skillfully, and has more initiative.[72]

Were it not for the likelihood that this type of system will never be fully attained, the prospect would be chilling indeed.

# The Policy Process
# and Bureaucratic Politics

## PAUL COCKS

The interplay of power and policy in the Kremlin has long been a subject of speculation and debate among Western observers. Views about the nature of decision making in the USSR, moreover, have altered considerably over the years in accord with changing Western perceptions of Soviet society and the political system. With the movement in recent years to link comparative politics and Communist studies more closely, more and more students of Soviet affairs have begun to apply various approaches and assumptions that have been derived from the experience of Western and developing societies. This trend has become particularly pronounced in studies of the policy process and bureaucratic politics.

Generally speaking, there have been two principal approaches to decision making in Western administrative thought and practice. For purposes of this essay, these may be called the "group approach" and the "systems approach." While the former emphasizes bargaining, the latter stresses hierarchy in the workings of government.[1] Each approach revolves fundamentally around quite divergent and conflicting sets of values, issues, and influences. These, in turn, have given rise to oscillating tides of centralizing and decentralizing administrative change in the history and theory of public administration.[2]

In studies of the Soviet policy process, applications of group theory and pluralist models have been very much in the ascendancy among Sovietologists since the late 1960s. Some scholars argue, in fact, that pluralist features have become so dominant in the polity and society that a new, essentially "pluralist" model—even a paradigm—of the Soviet system as a whole is called for.[3] But the use of systems theory, especially the movement toward PPBS (Planning-Programming-Budgeting System) which became so fashionable in the West during the sixties, has not figured prominently in the current literature on Soviet decision making. Though generally not used by Western analysts of Soviet affairs, the systems approach is equally if not more useful than group theory as a guide and aid in understanding recent developments in the politics of oligarchy in the USSR.[4]

Indeed, modern systems theory with its sophisticated analytical methodology, managerial technology, and centralizing bias has increasingly attracted Moscow's attention.[5] Eager to improve their own system of planning and management, Soviet authorities have again shown growing interest in and enthusiasm for the "superiority of capitalist technique," to borrow a phrase from Lenin. Moreover, it is not so much pluralism and spontaneity per se in the American system that capture their eye. Rather it is the ways in which decision makers in Washington and the White House have tried to curb and control these phenomena in the pursuit and conduct of national policies. Like Washington in the sixties, the Kremlin in the seventies exhibits a peculiarly keen fascination with "forecasting," "technological assessment," "scientific management," and the "systems approach." In a sense, the Party under Brezhnev's leadership seems to be struggling to engineer and negotiate its own brand of PPBS revolution in decision making and bureaucratic politics as it seeks to harness the so-called "scientific and technological revolution" to the aims and interests of the regime.

BUREAUCRATIC BARGAINING, PLURALISM, AND INCREMENTALISM:
THE GROUP APPROACH TO SOVIET DECISION MAKING

The dominant imprint of bureaucratic features on the shape and functioning of the Soviet system is today unmistakable. The passage of more than two decades since Stalin's death has cast into clear relief a basically bureaucratic character that previously was overshadowed by the preponderant image of an omnipresent and omnipotent supreme leader. A dense atmosphere of arbitrary terror likewise concealed and constrained the workings of administrative rationality and byways of bureaucracy. With the demise of Stalin, however, the "cult of personality" has steadily given way to a "cult of oligarchy" and "collective leadership," the Soviet euphemism for what Zev Katz aptly calls rule by the executive committee of the ruling class. The process of industrialization has also led to an increasingly complex economy and differentiated society whose management requires enhanced dependence on the advice and knowledge of technical experts and administrative specialists. A new stratum of managerial technocrats, sometimes referred to as "the second New Class," has gradually risen alongside the new ruling class of political bureaucrats. Together they struggle to maintain and manage what is now called in official parlance "a developed socialist society."

More and more, then, the Soviet Union displays, as Fainsod noted after Khrushchev's fall, "many of the signs of a mature and immobile society not easily moved from the grooves" into which it is settling.[6] A decade later, the character of these signs of maturity continue to agitate and divide Western observers. For some analysts the present regime seems to be hopelessly sunk in a state of bureaucratic immobilism and oligarchical petrification. Others, on the contrary, see a more dynamic and adaptive bureaucracy, moving forward cautiously and pragmatically by disjointed and incremental steps.[7] In any case, all agree that the pace of building socialism has slowed perceptibly while the process has become increasingly bureaucratic in nature and outcome.

In line with this evolution of Soviet society, there has been a marked shift in the focus of inquiry and framework of assumptions by Western specialists regarding the policy process. Previously, primary emphasis was placed on the concentration and exercise of power at the top of the political pyramid. While the concept of totalitarianism captured well the hypercentralized nature of Stalin's rule, it tended to obscure, if not deny, the play of pluralist pressures and the role of intermediate actors in the policy process. There was the strong impression, as Jerry Hough notes, that all persons below the pinnacle of power were simply "acted upon" rather than having any impact on the making of policy and settling of disputes.[8] Or, as Gordon Skilling says, there was almost exclusive concern with "outputs," namely, the imposition of binding decisions, and little attention to "inputs." [9] Mass organizations were regarded as mere "transmission belts"—means of transmitting policy *to* groups rather than as sources originating and shaping policy.[10] Administrative organs and groups within the various bureaucracies were likewise seen to play predominantly an administrative role.[11]

With the "deconcentration of power" [12] since Stalin's death and especially since Khrushchev's ouster, increasing attention has been paid to the devolution of authority to the major institutional centers and bureaucratic subsystems in Soviet society. To be sure, the various strategic elites have been given a greater voice in policy making. Particularly marked is the change in the amount of operational autonomy enjoyed by state officials and elite groups within the areas of their professional competence.[13] These developments have led some Western specialists to use terms such as "institutional pluralism," [14] "bureaucratic pluralism," [15] "participatory bureaucracy," [16] and "pluralism of elites" [17] in describing the Soviet Union. Gradually, a new image of the political system has evolved, one in which ideas and power are seen to flow up the administrative hierarchies as well as down.[18] Rather than as mere objects of manipulation by the top Party bosses and leadership factions, institutions and groups are seen to be influential and semiautonomous participants in making and executing policies and are considered to be at least somewhat responsive to broader societal forces.[19] Bureaucratic officials are depicted as "men who are driven to represent many of the interests of their clientele and low-level subordinates." They tend to identify with professional standards and with the programs they administer.[20] Or, as Fainsod observed, they "build their loyalties and hopes around the complex of concerns that have been entrusted to their care." [21] The image of politicians, too, has become less rigid and inflexible as they are seen to be men who strive "to juggle and reconcile a multiplicity of conflicting pressures from both above and below." [22]

Along with rising emphasis on group activity and policy inputs, there has been more and more attention to political conflict and less and less to political controls. Far from being "monolithic" and "conflictless," society and the political system are characterized by a multiplicity of diverse interests and competing forces. Conflict, in fact, is regarded as a crucial and central feature of post-Stalin politics.[23] Hough, for example, describes the political process as revolving "around conflict among a complex set of crosscutting and shifting alliances of persons with divergent interests." [24] Darrell Hammer also states succinctly, "Policy is the outcome of an ongoing political conflict." [25] No longer is conflict narrowly interpreted as "mere personal struggle for power, largely divorced from questions of policy or ideology, or from the interests of social groups" or as taking place mainly at the top levels of the Party.[26] Azrael, in fact, speaks of the "reemergence of politics" after Stalin's death with the rise of political assertiveness by major social groups and the increase in official responsiveness to both popular claims and institutional demands. The division of power along fundamentally bureaucratic lines that was created by Stalin's heirs, not to mention Khrushchev's successors, also contributed to inevitable conflict within the ruling elite and to the bureaucratic character of the struggle over power and policy.[27] In a similar vein Hammer talks about the change from "autocratic politics" to the "politics of oligarchy." [28]

The accent on group interest and conflict has, in turn, been accompanied by mounting stress on bargaining rather than hierarchy in Soviet decision making. Despite personal initiatives of individual leaders, including Khrushchev, Kremlin policies are seen as growing generally out of "compromises and adjustments among diverse bureaucratic groups and their interests in society." [29] The highly centralized and authoritarian nature of the system notwithstanding, Soviet policies and lack of policies, Bill Taubman points out, "mirror the clashes and compromises of bureaucratic agencies and their representatives, and . . . Soviet governmental behavior reflects not only the Politburo's deliberate political purpose but also the mode of operation of complex large-scale organizations that even a powerful central leadership cannot always and everywhere control." [30] According to Hough, politics has become "a set of give-and-take interactions in which each side bargains for a set of more or less limited objectives." [31] Rather than as policy initiators, politicians are also depicted from this perspective as serving essentially as political brokers that mediate the competing claims of powerful interests.[32] In order to fulfill their brokerage function, Party secretaries have had to acquire "a balancing, incremental perspective on many issues and to develop bargaining techniques." [33] In fact, Hough suggests that incrementalism has become the "hallmark of the system." [34]

From the perspective of those using a group approach, decision making in the Soviet Union resembles substantially, therefore, the "muddling through" approach characteristic of the so-called "incremental-bargaining" model that dominated American administrative theory and political practice before the advent of PPBS.[35] The major attributes of this model include emphasis on political pluralism, organizational process, interest group competition, and bureaucratic bargaining. The accent is on achieving consensus, maintaining stability, and limiting the scope and intensity of conflict. There is typically a neglect of outcomes and an avoidance of goal specification and priority setting that tend to exacerbate conflict. The activity by which bargains are struck and allocations negotiated among competing powers and claimants is the salient feature of this mode of decision making. Instead of trying to maximize some consistent set of policy objectives and priorities, a "satisficing" or suboptimal approach is pursued whereby everyone is partially satisfied and no one is wholly alienated. Policies and programs emerge primarily as the derivatives and aggregates of special, limited group interests through a process of incremental adjustments and mutual compromises. Consequently, there are no radical departures from the established status quo, and change is gradual and piecemeal. Underlying the system is an almost deus ex machina faith in the efficacy of the group process and bureaucratic interplay to produce favorable outcomes.[36]

To be sure, Soviet decision making does manifest many features of the Western incremental-bargaining model. While elements of group competition and bureaucratic politics have always occupied an important place in the interplay of power and policy in the Kremlin, they seem to have become more pronounced and visible in the period since Khrushchev. The restoration of the ministerial system and retreat from Khrushchev's policy of excessive Party involvement and interference in economic management have permitted the growth of autonomy and departmentalism in the economic bureaucracy. After Khrushchev's arbitrary ways, "adventurist" policies, and dynamic inspirational leadership style, a bureaucratic "muddling through" approach probably provided welcome relief to a constantly harassed officialdom eager for greater stability, security, and order.

Certainly there is no disputing the potential use of group theory to explain a great deal of the policy process and bureaucratic politics in the Soviet Union. Such a theory, moreover, can add to our understanding in ways that are not readily achieved by other models of Soviet politics.[37] As Gordon Skilling rightly points out, the group approach "sensitizes the observer to a realm of political activity that has gone almost unnoticed." [38] It is indeed an important contribution to our understanding of the Soviet system to emphasize the role of groups and pluralist pressures and to begin to analyze them systematically.

At the same time, an appreciation of the value of the group approach should not obscure the limitations and deficiencies of group theories and pluralist models for both their applicability to the Soviet experience and their own merits as well. As regards the former, Janos has emphasized the dangers inherent in making cross-national and cross-cultural comparisons.[39] Franklyn Griffiths has pointed to the "variety of conceptual and methodological difficulties encountered in defining Soviet interest group subsystems and determining their influence." [40] While group activity is a vital part of the policy process, it cannot be regarded as the "central phenomenon in Soviet policymaking." [41]

It must also be said that in trying to rectify some of the biases and blindspots of those using other models, champions of the group approach have themselves often adopted a too one-sided and partial view. By concentrating almost exclusively on group activity at the intermediate levels and neglecting factional politics and leadership conflict at the top, they create an image of the policy process that is as unrealistic and incomplete as that projected by pure totalitarianism. The Soviet political system is neither "topless" nor "bottomless." By focusing predominantly on groups who allegedly are "primarily interested not in attaining power but in seeking to influence the policy pursued by the powerholders," [42] some analysts try to separate the inseparable. They commit the cardinal sin of administrative theorists who try to divorce power from policy. They forget that individuals and groups struggle for power in order to shape policies and that they also frame policies in order to secure power.[43]

Similarly, some Sovietologists who have used the group approach have also tended to divorce policy from administration, two inter-related parts of the same political process. Preoccupied with "inputs," they have concentrated on policy-making aspects. Problems of implementation and execution, of organization and administration, have been generally excluded from their analyses.[44] Yet administrative theory teaches that "a choice of organization structure is a choice of which interest or which value will have preferred access or greater emphasis." [45] Like users of the incremental-bargaining approach generally, scholars working with this model in Soviet studies have been concerned "mainly with the fact that individuals and groups with differing values exist, with the power they possess, and with the processes of adjustment among these groups in the workings of government." [46] The performance of government has figured little in their complex of concerns. For the most part, they have been interested in the question of "who governs?" rather than in the notion of "how is a system governed?"

Evidence suggests, however, that the performance of the Soviet system and administrative personnel, especially their capacity to cope effectively with the growing complexity of a modern industrial society, is a major and mounting concern of Kremlin leaders.[47] The need to switch to what Moscow calls an "intensive" stage of development and methods of management places rising importance on efficiency of governmental operations. "Outputs" are, then, of crucial significance for the current leadership. Moreover, it may be argued that it is precisely here where the diminution of terror since Stalin has had its greatest effect. The thrust of group analysis has been to emphasize the impact of declining terror on policy inputs, that is, the rising assertiveness of groups to express their interests more freely and to press their demands more forcefully. The dominant stress has been on the resulting fragmentation and diffusion of power, not on the erosion of authority and declining ability of decision-makers and administrators, particularly at the center, to enforce their decisions and carry through on policies and programs.

Deficiencies of the group approach to Soviet decision making are manifest on another level as well. It is an innate supposition of this approach that the policy process is fundamentally "subsystem dominant." That is, it views and explains the functioning of the system as a whole in terms of the interactions of its subparts. However, Griffiths argues eloquently, "Subsystem-dominant theories of group politics are of limited use in helping us to understand the overall process of policy-making in the contemporary Soviet Union." [48] More appropriate, he claims, is a system-dominant perspective which sees the policy process as the integrated activity of the whole and the subordination of its integral and interacting parts.[49]

Certainly for purposes of studying national policy making, a systems view seems essential. Yet the recent trend in Soviet studies and of applications of group theory has become increasingly microanalytical. Research has focused more and more on very specific areas of activity and on separate parts of the political system. The "articulation" rather than the "aggregation" of interests has received primary attention. General overviews of the spectrum of Soviet politics and macrostudies of the policy process have appeared much less frequently in the current literature.[50] That is, scholars applying group theories have focused basically on representation and participation by various group actors in decision making. Problems and processes of integration and regulation, the cornerstones of executive leadership and the traditional functions of the Party apparat, have been generally neglected or deliberately downplayed. Concentrating almost exclusively on the growth and consequences of pluralist tendencies within the Soviet system, they are sometimes unaware of or underestimate centripetal forces and centralizing trends also at work, seeking to impose limits on pluralism and groupism. In fact, forces aiming at strengthening the capability of central authorities to plan, coordinate, and implement *national* policies and program priorities have grown steadily since 1970. They provide the main impetus behind the burgeoning systems movement in the Soviet Union today.

Finally, mention should be made of certain weaknesses of the incremental-bargaining model that are particularly relevant for understanding current decision-making trends and pressures in the Kremlin. Yehezkel Dror, for example, observes that for a basic strategy of incremental change to persist three general conditions must pertain: (1) the results of present policies must be in the main satisfactory; (2) there must be a high degree of continuity in the nature of the problems; (3) there must be a high degree of continuity in the available means for dealing with the problems.[51] Suffice it to say that belated discovery of the scientific revolution sweeping the West and of Russia's technological backwardness has generated rising dissatisfaction among the Soviet ruling elite with the outcomes resulting from established processes and procedures, at least in some issue areas. Brezhnev in particular has spoken out more and more forcefully since 1970 about the need to adjust managerial attitudes, organizational structures, and administrative techniques to the changing conditions and new demands of the modern age.[52] Efforts have mounted, therefore, to adjust the system of planning and incentives to the new claims of efficiency and technical progress, to develop more sophisticated analytical tools as well as a broader information base and better data processing capability to support more systematic and comprehensive planning and policy analysis.[53] The partisan mutual adjustment process is also unlikely to throw up the least cost or most optimal solution to a given policy problem.[54] Again it should be noted that with the growing squeeze on resources, Moscow's interest in optimal planning and management has risen appreciably in recent years.

One special sphere of decision making exists where incrementalism is seen to be notably deficient and inferior to a broader systems approach. This area concerns issues of innovation and obsolescence in program development—questions of major importance for the Kremlin today which is bent upon modernizing the economy and promoting technological reconstruction along a broad front. Modernization entails the creation of new sectors of industry, the development of new skills, and the application of new techniques. These often do not receive sufficient attention, let alone active support, within the framework of existing institutions and programs. In fact, innovative approaches and new programs become direct competitors for resources with ongoing programs and established methods, which already have their own entrenched devotees and sources of group pressure. There is also need to reappraise the purpose and effectiveness of existing programs, to expand, redirect, or curtail given areas of activity in light of their newly perceived relevance or obsolescence. This often requires shifting highly prized and jealously guarded resources—not only manpower, materials, and money but also political power and privilege—from some sectors and organizations to new areas and groups. For purposes of facilitating these decisions about determining existing or approaching obsolescence, incrementalism acts more as a barrier than as a bridge to progress.[55] Evidence suggests, moreover, that it is precisely in this sphere of decision making that existing Soviet procedures and structures are found to be increasingly deficient.[56]

THE SYSTEMS APPROACH TO SOVIET DECISION MAKING:
PPBS COMES TO THE KREMLIN

The "systems approach" and PPBS are identified with the so-called "rational-comprehensive" model of decision making and a new kind of politics. Here the main focus is not on bureaucratic bargaining and the group process per se but on what results from it. In fact, a principal aim of this approach is to transcend and circumvent group politics, to refocus and broaden managerial perspectives, to reassert the primacy of general interests, values, and needs of the "system" as a whole over the special and limited interests of bureaus, organizations, and regions. It seeks to shift the axis of problem solving, policy making, and resource allocating away from input-oriented, partisan-motivated interest groups on to national objectives, actual outputs, and program alternatives. Designed as an antidote to counteract and contain increasing fragmentation of decision making and compartmentalization of government, PPBS stresses a more centralized and integrated administrative structure to ensure more comprehensive and coherent policy making and policy implementation.[57] As such, modern systems analysis is an integral and continuing part of a body of Western administrative thought which has emphasized "hierarchies of objectives, lines of authority, division of labor among organizational units, coordination of policies and programs, and systems efficiency." [58]

Significantly, since the onset of the seventies, there has been increasing emphasis in the Soviet Union on the "systems" concept and growing official clamor, led by the General Secretary, for more comprehensive planning, integrated structures, and unified management along the lines of PPBS in the West.[59] Here the basic aim of policy makers in Moscow is similar, it seems, to that of their Western counterparts. That is, they are primarily interested in enhancing their analytical and administrative capabilities in order to be able to cope better with problems of uncertainty and choice that are compounded in an age of growing complexity and rapid change.

Intensified efforts to modernize the industrial base and administrative infrastructure have placed rising importance on organization and management. "It is no exaggeration to say," admits one high official, "that the pace of our advance hinges on organization and capabilities in the system of management. Fusion of the latest developments in science and technology with the most up-to-date achievements in organization and management is an imperative of the contemporary scientific and technological revolution." [60] A statement by Brezhnev that the "science of victory in building Communism is in essence the science of management" has become a slogan capturing the new demands of the times.[61] As issues of organization and management have moved to the forefront of domestic policy moreover, deficiencies in the integrative capability of central authorities have surfaced as major areas of official concern. "The greater the differentiation in the system of ministries and departments becomes," explains one Soviet analyst, "the more difficult it is to unify their activities and the more complicated it is to carry on such general organizational functions as planning, coordination, and supervision on the scale of the state administrative apparatus as a whole. In addition, there is an increasing tendency toward departmental dissociation and growing difficulty in achieving integrated solutions to interbranch and interdepartmental problems." [62] Capabilities for program definition and systems management appear to be particularly deficient in the more backward and depressed civilian and consumer-related sectors of the economy, and research and development outside of the defense, space, and atomic energy areas.

Consequently, there has been since 1970–1971 a mounting effort not unlike that in the United States in the mid-sixties to harness the organizational and managerial experience of the defense sectors, where systems methods have been most developed, to improve planning and management elsewhere in the economy.[63] Growing realization of Russia's backwardness and of the need to overcome it has led some official circles to advocate more and more strongly the application of methods used in the development and management of modern weapons systems as appropriate and necessary for the promotion and management of technological progress more broadly.[64] The planned reorganization of industrial management, decreed in March 1973, which will create within the ministerial system large research and development complexes and science-production associations, seeks basically to extend to the economy more broadly organizational forms and managerial practices that have been used extensively or on a trial basis in the more efficient military-oriented rocket, aviation, heavy machine-building, electronics, and instrument-making industries. In fact, these pace-setting branches have been made models for all industry.[65]

A shift to a modern systems approach to planning and management is perceived by many in the Kremlin to hold the key to Russia's mounting administrative ills. "What interests us," the deputy chairman of the USSR State Committee for Science and Technology explains with regard to systems analysis, "is its basic conclusion as to the need for a complex, all-round approach to management and the disclosure of its integrative function." "This approach makes it possible," he says, "to see the whole managed system as a complex set of interrelated elements, united by a common aim, to reveal the integral properties of the system, its internal and external links." [66] Academician N. P. Fedorenko also claims that PPBS-type techniques "will make it possible to solve key national economic problems in a more purposeful and internally coordinated way and to ensure the unity of all aspects of planning and management of the socialist economy." [67] According to a prominent Soviet authority on science policy, "Program-type planning with a clear objective and schedule, a single source of financing, and unified management—such as the programs for development of the hydrogen bomb or for Gagarin's space flight —are able to coordinate the efforts of many industries and departments." [68] Indeed, as the regime confronts more and more directly the issue of administrative rationalization and the bureaucratic obstacles to technological innovation, the remedy is seen to lie necessarily in "a systems approach which encompasses all levels and echelons from the shop floor to the ministry." Only such an approach, some contend, "prevents complex scientific, technical, and organizational problems from being dismembered into separate parts or being solved in isolation from problems as a whole." [69]

Generally speaking, the conditions underlying current Soviet interest in the systems approach and PPBS-type techniques resemble in many respects the circumstances that contributed to the rise of PPBS in the United States in the 1960s.[70] Just as PPBS was pushed principally by the Bureau of the Budget and the Executive Office of the President, so in the USSR its chief backers appear to be the General Secretary, key officials in the Central Party Secretariat like Ustinov, who are closely connected with heavy industry, machine-building, and defense, and the new technocrats and systems analysts in the military establishment, all of whom have extensive experience in modern management and vested interest in mastering technology. To be sure, considerations of economic rationality play an important role in the growth of the systems approach. Rising awareness of the need to switch to more intensive methods of planning and management and to allocate more effectively scarce manpower, facilities, and fiscal resources has pushed to the forefront the issue of outcomes and need for priority-setting, more substantive planning, and tighter control. But the main motivations underlying and dominating the systems movement appear to be *political*. That is, it is being promoted in large part by central authorities, especially those around Brezhnev, as a political device against a sprawling and brawling bureaucratic establishment that is fragmented, inefficient, and unresponsive to changing conditions and new demands.[71] For the Kremlin, as for the White House, more integrated planning and management appears to be a means by which to bring under closer scrutiny and effective control the administrative machinery that implements national policies and programs.

To phrase the issue somewhat differently, official espousal of the systems approach and PPBS-type techniques in Moscow in the seventies, like Washington in the sixties, is basically a reaction against the prevailing system of "muddling through" a search for more viable and effective methods of decision making and administration. There is a strong desire to break away from and to go beyond the narrow bureaucratic politics and incremental-bargaining mode which seem to have steadily dominated Kremlin decision making since Khrushchev. Like proponents of PPBS in the United States, advocates of the systems approach in the USSR also appear to be interested in extending the parameters of political choice, to expand the range of opportunities and options available to central decision makers. In the United States, for example, officials in the Bureau of the Budget and the White House found that by the time the budget reached them most of the decisions had already been made for them in the form of existing programs and incremental bureau claims. Similarly in the Soviet Union, despite its system of central planning, incrementalist and pluralist tendencies in decision making narrow the range of choice and constrain the powers of initiative enjoyed by Kremlin authorities. Branch ministries and departments have a large degree of autonomy so that plans and policies do develop to a great extent spontaneously, separately, and incrementally. Such planning "from the achieved level," the December 1973 Central Committee plenum emphasized, holds back progressive changes in the economy and perpetuates an obsolete technical base.[72] In addition, existing procedures and arrangements restrict the possibility for political decision makers not only to choose but also to evaluate the progress and effectiveness of programs.

On another level, the impetus behind the systems movement can be traced to mounting dissatisfaction among the top leadership with the outcomes resulting from the economic reforms introduced in 1965. On the one hand, elements of pluralism and spontaneity developed in the process of implementing the reforms at both the enterprise and ministry levels.[73] These have made more difficult unity of leadership and uniform policies both within and across ministerial lines. They have made more difficult horizontal integration and coordination of interbranch programs at a time when the need for such integration has risen. The new success indicators also did not sufficiently motivate production managers to introduce new technology, reduce production costs, and raise product quality—factors of growing importance as the regime moves into the seventies.[74] On the other hand, the feeling also arose that the individual enterprise itself, the main focus of the 1965 reforms, is fundamentally an inadequate unit on which to base the current modernization effort. It is simply too small and lacks the financial assets, research and technical base, liaison with other organizations, and administrative ability to carry out the kinds of specialized and integrated activities that are required at the present time. More concentrated and centralized research and development complexes and industrial associations, which have greater planning, programming, and budgeting capabilities and over-all managerial control, are perceived by Kremlin authorities to be more appropriate instruments to accomplish the manifold and formidable tasks involved in the technical modernization and automation of industry.[75]

Finally, quite apart from personal and political motivations among the ruling elite, which admittedly are almost impossible to verify, and the peculiar conditions and demands facing science policy today, the growing prominence of the systems approach with its centralizing bias should also be viewed as part of a more general pattern and cyclical phenomenon in Soviet history. Much as in the United States, there have been alternating periods of centralization and decentralization.[76] These have been directed at overcoming particular deficiencies and myopic tendencies (under the general rubrics of "departmentalism" and "localism") that are inherent in certain modes of organization and management of the economy. In the case of the USSR the pendulum has swung constantly between a highly centralized ministerial system of functional and branch administration, on the one hand, and a more decentralized system organized along regional lines, on the other. The whole system tends to oscillate "back and forth in slow motion; adjustments and readjustments are introduced when one particular reform has caused too many and too serious troubles at one administrative level or another." [77] On another plane, however, this process gives rise to a continuous struggle over how to offset the fragmentation of government which results under *both* branch and territorial forms of planning and management and how to unify the policies and administration of separate centers of power. Here the issue revolves basically around the problems of balancing the need for and values of strong executive leadership with the interests and values of organizational autonomy and initiative, of bureaucratic representation and participation in the making and execution of policy.

From this perspective, the systems movement, which has steadily gained ground since 1970, should be seen as part of a general drive to counter pluralist tendencies and particularistic forces of vertical hierarchy which have grown in the interval since Khrushchev's ouster. Indeed, since the restoration of the industrial ministries in 1965 many of the familiar "departmental evils" of branch planning and management have reappeared to plague political decision makers at the center. In many respects the task that confronts Brezhnev today resembles that which Khrushchev faced two decades ago—namely, to overcome bureaucratic inertia and ministerial resistance to program innovations, fresh approaches, and new methods in order to enhance his own capacity (and of central authorities more generally) for executive leadership. Just as Khrushchev sought a remedy in the abolition of the ministries in 1957 and the creation of regional economic councils, Brezhnev, too, has pushed increasingly for the formation of industrial associations and changes in the administrative system. Though within the ministerial structure, the new production associations and research and development complexes are best characterized as forms of organization and management by area and integrated activity as opposed to the prevailing system of functional departments and compartmentalized branch administrations. While the justification for this change is couched in terms of raising "efficiency," it is aimed principally it seems, at strengthening executive leadership. In his conflict with the branch ministries, Brezhnev, like Khrushchev, seems also in part to be making common cause with strong local leaders in order to garner support for his policies.[78] Closely related to this coalition-building with local executives is the General Secretary's promotion of a more activist and interventionist role for Party agencies in supervising the implementation process. Again reflecting a more general pattern in Soviet history and similarity with Khrushchev, the Party apparatus itself is being used more and more extensively by its leader as a counterweight to complacency and bureau-cratism in the government.[79]

## THE SYSTEMS APPROACH AND SCIENCE POLICY:
## THE QUEST FOR NEW TECHNOLOGY AND MODERN TECHNIQUES

Given the Kremlin's enhanced interest in modernizing the economy, it is not surprising that the systems approach is being promoted and applied especially in the area of science policy. The modernization of industrial structures and the development of new natural-resource bases involve tasks for which systems planning and management are particularly appropriate. As John Hardt notes, "What we are dealing with now are highly complex projects involving advanced technology and skilled manpower, with relatively long lead-times and high in-divisibility of resources." [80] Because of the high costs involved, the limited supply of investment resources, and the highly interrelated nature of numerous projects, there is a strong imperative for Soviet planners and politicians to try to optimize both the planning and management of the development process.[81] In short, Hardt explains, "What is required to speed up development and the introduction of new technology is the integrated management of a number of related and sequential activities and facilities." [82] The systems approach pro-vides a means of integrating into a consistent whole various spheres of decision making and administration that have traditionally been conducted separately and in isolation from each other.[83]

Grappling with problems of speeding technological progress has caused Kremlin policy makers to take a new look at the linkages be-tween science, technology, and production. In the process they have come to see the research and development cycle as a complex process of interdependent parts and interlocking relationships. "This is not a mechanistic chain," writes Academician Rumyantsev, "but a unified, complex system with direct communication and feedback among its elements." [84] More and more "the problem of ensuring *continuity* of the process at every stage of research and development work, includ-ing introduction into mass production, is now being brought to the fore as the most complex organizational task." [85] The new science and production associations integrating research activities and manu-facturing operations are designed to give institutional expression and coherence to this process. Some science policy analysts in Moscow argue, in fact, that only through such research and development com-plexes can the "research *to* production" process be effectively carried on from beginning to end.[86]

A number of shortcomings in the existing system have prompted this movement toward greater integration, conceptually and administratively, in the area of research and development. Of particular importance is the extreme fragmentation, horizontally and vertically, of the innovation and diffusion process which gives rise to a host of bureaucratic bottlenecks and conflicts that impede and drag out the process, even in the case of excellent innovations. Above all, fragmentation has resulted in both divided responsibility and diluted authority. Each individual and institutional participant in the process takes a very narrow view of his role, responsibilities, and interests. No one has any incentive or responsibility to see an innovation through from its inception to its implementation in production. Indeed, the Soviet research and development cycle has been very much a mechanistic chain, broken into separate links, with little communication and cooperation between them. A major aim of the drive to form science and production associations is to concentrate managerial responsibility and authority for the research and development process as a whole, to centralize decision making in order to achieve greater unity and order and to eliminate endless wrangling and delays that can occur at every stage of the cycle. Through the associations the leadership hopes to reshape the attitudes of research and development personnel and to create a coincidence of interest among all participants in the smooth and accelerated transfer of technology. Instead of being guided by its own special interests and parochial perspectives, each unit is to be motivated by common objectives, by "only one concept: ours." The new associational forms are seen as means by which to transform "awkward external cooperation into harmonious intrafirm cooperation." [87]

Applications of a systems approach and PPBS-type techniques are also discernible in the area of science planning. Until quite recently, Kremlin leaders simply lacked the necessary organization, techniques, experience, and authority to cope with problems of comprehensive planning of research and development on a national scale.[88] Recent efforts have centered particularly on finding more effective ways of integrating research and development planning with general economic planning.

On one level, this has entailed rising emphasis on long-range science policy planning, an area in which the existing system has been especially deficient.[89] Belated discovery of the scientific revolution has wrought a radical change, Gvishiani acknowledges, in Soviet views on the space-time parameters of progress.[90] This has led to rising stress on the need to expand the time horizons of planners from the narrow confines of a single year to a more flexible multi-year frame-work. Like their Western counterparts, Moscow decision makers have become more and more aware that with planning on a predominantly annual basis almost all options are foreclosed by previous commit-ments. A longer time span enhances opportunities for planning and analysis to have greater impact on future expenditures and opens more options. Long-term planning provides, above all, a means by which to overcome myopic tendencies of planners and administrators with respect to "time," which manifest themselves in the form of creeping "incrementalism."

Along with stress on long-range planning, there has been burgeon-ing interest in forecasting and futurological studies in the Soviet Union. Until the mid-sixties there was little differentiation in ap-proaches to problems of the future. Nor was this seen to be an ur-gent task.[91] Like U.S. decision makers, however, Kremlin authorities have become increasingly aware of the need to anticipate and eval-uate the future impact of science and technology on society, the eco-nomy, and the polity. "Such forecasting is essential," says Gvishiani, "if only to prevent some of the negative consequences entailed by scientific and technological progress, or at least to mitigate them."[92] Much as in the West, "technological assessment" is being promoted as a device to provide planners and politicians with a kind of "early warning system" which will make them ready and capable of respond-ing more effectively to changing conditions and contingent events.[93]

A number of factors have fed the growing stress on the need for long-range planning and forecasting. Because of the usually long lead-times involved before the application of their results, research and engineering are particularly difficult to plan and evaluate on a yearly basis. More effective long-term planning is needed to accom-modate the kinds of investment allocation decisions and program planning tasks involved in overcoming technological backwardness. At the present time the Soviet leadership is deeply engaged in for-mulating a fifteen-year economic development plan for the USSR covering the period 1976 to 1990. The methodological and analytical problems associated with this undertaking reinforce emphasis on the quality and pertinence of strategic planning.

Steps have also been taken to shift from an essentially department-oriented structure of planning to more goal-oriented, program-type planning in the area of science policy. Program planning is seen as a means by which to counterbalance the growing predominance of the so-called "branch-departmental principle of planning" and pluralistic patterns of decision making in research and development, dominated by the ministries. The peculiar biases and priorities of this system have produced the regional imbalances and sectoral disproportions in technological development which today the leadership is keen on overcoming, in part at least. Even Gosplan, which should be guided by statewide interests and a systems perspective, has come under increasing criticism for its narrow "departmental approach." [94] Through more program planning political authorities hope to change the style of managerial thinking, to refocus it on national objectives and to reduce departmental prejudice in planning and management. Cooperation and coordination are simply not the norm between agencies of government in any country, least of all the USSR. Integration cannot spring forth spontaneously. For decision makers in the Kremlin, therefore, program planning and management by objectives represent devices by which they can promote more effectively a macroanalytical approach to planning with an accent on national goals and coherent programs that cut across the interests of competing agencies.[95]

Significantly, it is in the area of introducing new technology that a systems programming approach is being increasingly applied. The incorporation of scientific advances into practice has long been the weakest link in the research and development cycle. Among the obstacles to technological innovation and diffusion is the "production orientation" of the planning system which has traditionally favored the expansion of existing patterns of production rather than the introduction of innovations based on research and development.[96] For the most part, only the stages of the research and development process up to experimental design and testing work have been objects of comprehensive and central planning, and in exceptional cases the production of prototypes. That is, the planning process for all practical purposes has stopped short of series production.[97] Significantly, only in *1973* were the *first* comprehensive and integrated programs for the introduction and diffusion of new products, machines, and technological processes of national priority drawn up and confirmed together with the annual economic plan. These programs, for the first time, provided for the construction-installation work, materials, equipment, manpower, and financial resources that are required to complete the assimilation process.[98] This kind of "packaging" of the various components needed to implement programs in the area of new technology is a prime example of the systems approach and of official efforts to overcome some of the deficiencies and fragmentation of the existing system of planning and management.

REMAKING THE SOVIET MODEL:
THE USES AND ABUSES OF WESTERN MODELS

In general, both the group and systems approaches to decision making, which are found in Western theory and practice, provide useful perspectives from which to view the Soviet political process. Despite underlying differences in philosophy, organizational approach, and points of emphasis, Soviet leaders have grappled with much the same set of problems and have grasped for similar kinds of remedies in framing policy as have their Western counterparts. Many of the same issues and concerns that have motivated policy makers and animated political debate in Washington have also been keenly felt in Moscow. As for the two approaches, we are dealing essentially with differences in relative emphasis, not with pure dichotomies. Each focuses on a different set of values, attitudes, and interests, *both* of which are very real and generate competing pressures in any administrative system. If not used together, each gives a very one-sided and incomplete view of the decision process. The two approaches are, then, not alternative and mutually exclusive but complementary though conflicting guides to understanding the nature and dynamics of decision making. Indeed, it is the conflict of values and tendencies that provides the dynamics around which power and policy constantly turn. Even in highly authoritarian regimes, like under Stalin and Hitler, elements of bargaining exist at certain stages down the bureaucratic hierarchy. They are an intrinsic part of the decision process and impose limits on the function and power of top political leadership. At the same time, it may be said that extensive and excessive bargaining connotes the impotence or absence of a single center of command and control.

In recent years a discrepancy has emerged in the views emanating from inside and outside the USSR regarding the Soviet political process and the direction of its development.[99] Western spectators, on the one hand, have begun more and more to apply group theories and pluralist models in their analyses. They have concentrated on the play of pluralist pressures and on tendencies toward bargaining and autonomy in the Soviet system. The growth of these tendencies has led some observers to conclude that the model of "a directed society," which has long dominated Western studies of the Soviet Union, is no longer appropriate. A pluralist paradigm incorporating much of the Western incremental-bargaining model is more fitting, they claim, as an aid to understanding Soviet reality. Writing in a society whose political culture places a high value on political bargaining, compromise, and subsystem autonomy, they tend to overestimate these values and the forces of pluralism in the USSR. They also fail to see or appreciate conflicting forces at work not only in the Kremlin but also in Western society which emphasize hierarchy, concentrated authority, and system dominance. They forget that in the West hierarchy has long been used as an instrument to achieve coherent policy making, to reduce the necessity of relying upon interminable processes of bargaining to arrive at policy decisions.[100]

Political decision makers in the Kremlin, on the other hand, have shown growing interest in applying modern systems theory and scientific management techniques to improve the policy process and to construct a more tightly organized planning and management system to deal more effectively with national problems and priorities. Like proponents of PPBS in the West, they seek basically to use hierarchy as a means of imposing new limits on bureaucratic bargaining and group pluralism. With its centralizing bias, systems theory is consistent with the Leninist model of organization and a political culture that stresses the teleological nature of the system and the legitimization of the concentration of authority in a single command center.[101] The growth of the systems movement reflects the persistence of a centralist-command mode of integrating an increasingly differentiated and complex society. It is an example of the traditional penchant for grand macrosolutions and grandiose schemes. In short, adaptations of the systems approach signify not the "passing of a directed society" but, on the contrary, efforts by a determined leadership to maintain —or perhaps more accurately speaking to regain—the momentum and march of an administered society.[102]

At the same time, the systems movement in the Soviet Union should not be seen as simply a campaign to replicate Western methods, to transplant them wholesale into Russian soil. The Soviet model of PPBS should not be taken as a mirror image of PPBS-type techniques in the U.S. Though such terms as "systems analysis," "management science," and "network planning" are becoming more and more a part of the Soviet managerial idiom, they necessarily acquire different meanings in Russian translation and practice.

Indeed, Soviet scholars themselves are being constantly warned about the uses and abuses of Western models, about the dangers of "mechanical borrowing." The emulation of advanced foreign methods, official spokesmen stress, must not result in the imposition of "alien" models. Fedor Burlatsky, for example, observed in July 1972 that a number of Russian scholars combing Western manage-

ment literature "scoop up a cupful of conceptions, terms, and categories, without any attempt to connect them with our realities." "A
fashion has set in," he said, "to make a show with a whole mass of
words, which when translated into the Russian language prove to be
fairly trivial." While granting the need to study Western theories of
management, Burlatsky warned, however, against "any attempts at
mechanical adoption of some particular organizational idea or
method without due consideration of our own experience, of the
differences in principle not only in the social but also in organizational structures, forms, and methods of management in socialist and
capitalist countries." [103] V. Shcherbitsky, First Secretary of the Ukraine
and Politburo member, voiced similar concerns in the Party's theoretical journal in April 1973. Several scholars working on problems of
management and decision theory, he contended, "sometimes try to
create certain abstract schemes that are supposedly universal in character but which have, in fact, been mechanically borrowed from
bourgeois concepts." [104] Strictures of this sort continuously punctuate
and steer the ongoing debate in the USSR over the use and misuse of
modern methods and Western models. They provide a continual reminder of the determination of the regime to preserve the primacy of
politics while trying to broaden somewhat the limits of administrative rationality in meeting the challenges of the modern age.

Efforts to remake the Soviet political process, therefore, involve
basically a "creative search" to develop and assimilate more advanced
methods of making and implementing policy that are compatible with
Russia's conditions, traditions, and underlying philosophy of government. "To *combine organically* the achievements of the scientific and
technological revolution with the advantages of the socialist economic
system, to unfold more broadly *our own, intrinsically socialist forms*
of fusing science with production"—such was the way Brezhnev himself
described at the Twenty-Fourth Party Congress the main task which
the political leaders face today.[105] Similarly in May 1973, the director
of the Economics Institute under the USSR Academy of Sciences out-
lined the main problems in the field of planning and management by
quoting Lenin: "Socialism must implement this movement forward in
its own way and by its own methods or, to put it more precisely, by
Soviet methods." [106]

While an evaluation of the future prospects of the current craze for
the systems approach in the USSR is beyond the scope of this essay, a
few general observations may be noted. Despite the claims of "hard
sell" technologists and management "medicine men" in the Kremlin,
computers and PPBS-type techniques alone are not likely to produce

radical improvements in decision making and administrative performance. Certainly the Western experience with management information
systems is not very reassuring in this respect, nor has PPBS proven to
be the godsend to decision makers that its initial champions sometimes
portrayed it to be. Today the Kremlin still feels the first flush of enthusiasm for computer technology and systems analysis. In time, however, this intoxication is likely to dissipate, as it has in the United
States, upon more intimate acquaintance with modern tools and systems methods. As has happened in the American federal bureaucracy,
PPBS in the Kremlin may prove to be largely a paper tiger and die a
quiet death.

The main problems in the area of decision making and science
policy in the Soviet Union, as elsewhere, are fundamentally political,
not technical. "They cannot be conjured away," one Western authority notes, "by 'technology assessment,' 'cost-benefit analysis,' 'social
engineering,' 'systems analysis,' or other social-science equivalents of
the 'technological fix.' " [107] While more sophisticated analytical tools
can aid in policy making, they cannot substitute for it. They cannot
usurp the place of the political process and group bargaining. Soviet
scholars are quick to point out that engineering methods alone cannot
resolve the contradictions of contemporary capitalist society. Nor are
such methods, it must be added, capable of solving the basic problems
of socialist societies. There are formidable obstacles that block any
rapid and easy progress.

In conclusion, the systems movement in the USSR seeks to work a
new balance between the center and the periphery, between hierarchy
and bargaining, which will enhance the Kremlin's capabilities to plan
and manage national policies and programs. As always, however, a
yawning gap will persist between the Kremlin's aspirations and re-
calcitrant reality. Conflicting tendencies and competing values will
continue to impose constraints and limits on the plans and actions of
decision makers.

# The Virgin Lands
since Khrushchev:
Choices and Decisions
in Soviet Policy Making

RICHARD M. MILLS

The virgin lands program initiated in 1954 was a grandiose and risky attempt to solve the perennial grain problem at a critical juncture. Much has been written in the West about the program's fate up to 1965, when it was widely assumed that the new lands either had been or were about to be abandoned because of the catastrophic crop failure there in 1963, dustbowl conditions, the recent removal of the program's indefatigable promoter, Khrushchev, the elimination in October 1965 of Tselinny krai (Virgin Lands Territory, established in 1960), and the virgin lands crop failure of 1965 which received less publicity but was more severe than the one in 1963.

The virgin lands of Kazakhstan have been the touchstone for evaluating the program's success up to 1964 in both the Soviet Union and the West.[1] There are no Western studies of the ensuing period which is so crucial for developing an understanding of how the post-Khrushchev leadership coped with the possibilities and limitations facing them in a critical decision-making area. This essay is a public policy analysis, a consideration of the factors impinging upon the formation, execution and evaluation of policy decisions. The role of the political leaders in decision making will therefore be considered in terms of the concrete issues that had to be taken into account in producing decisions.

A general picture of what has transpired on the new lands since 1964 emerges from the available official crop data on the six oblasts in Kazakhstan comprising the former Tselinny krai—Pavlodar, Kokchetav, Tselinograd, North Kazakhstan, Turgai, and Kustanai.[2] Obviously, the virgin lands were not abandoned despite the disasters of 1963 and 1965, and the decision to retain those lands was vindicated not only by the statistics for the virgin lands in 1966–1968 but also by those for Kazakhstan in 1969–1972 when the republic produced bumper crops, the largest ever in 1972, that otherwise catastrophic year in grain yields.[3]

## WHY THE VIRGIN LANDS WERE RETAINED

Western speculations about abandoning the virgin lands originated with a hedged statement by Khrushchev in early 1964 that some of the new lands might be returned to cattle farming after grain yields were increased elsewhere through greater use of fertilizers and irrigation.[4] But with a bumper crop maturing in the virgin lands later in the year, Khrushchev spoke no more about abandonment and in his remarks in *Pravda* on August 13, 1964, he assumed his normal posture as chief exponent of the virgin lands' virtues.

Following Khrushchev's removal the new leaders had to determine the function of the virgin lands in their total agricultural program to be announced by Brezhnev at the March 1965 plenum. The policy options were: (1) to abandon the virgin lands entirely, (2) to abandon them partially, (3) to continue Khrushchev's policies, or (4) to modify those policies.

The available evidence does not indicate that any major politician favored total abandonment even though it would have been easy to do so on the basis of the disturbing fact that grain yields in Tselinny krai had been declining steadily even before the failure in 1963 from 7.6 quintals per hectare in 1959 to 6.9 in 1960, 5.4 in 1961, and 5.1 in 1962.[5] Favoring abandonment would have been even easier since the state farms on the Kazakh virgin lands, the mainstay of production there, had sustained operating losses amounting to 1.5 billion rubles during the first ten years of their existence.[6]

On the other hand, the new leaders had hardly assumed office when the 1964 Tselinny krai bumper crop was brought in, dramatically reversing the decline in yields. The policy decision was therefore to be made in a new, more hopeful context.

Apart from these circumstantial factors, some political and ideologi-

TABLE 10.1   Virgin lands oblasts: grain production and state grain purchases (in millions of tons).

| Year | Grain production | State grain purchases |
|------|------------------|-----------------------|
| 1954 | 4.6 | 2.5 |
| 1955 | 3.1 | 1.7 |
| 1956 | 17.7 | 12.6 |
| 1957 | 6.7 | 3.0 |
| 1958 | 14.3 | 9.9 |
| 1959 | 13.8 | 8.7 |
| 1960 | 12.9 | 7.4 |
| 1961 | 10.3 | 5.5 |
| 1962 | 10.1 | 5.2 |
| 1963 | 4.9 [a] | — |
| 1964 | 16.0 [a] | — |
| 1965 | 4.3 | 1.2 |
| 1966 | 17.0 | 12.2 |
| 1967 | 10.3 | 6.2 |
| 1968 | 11.2 | 6.5 |
| 1969–1971 | — | — |
| 1972 | — | 12.4 |
| 1973 | — | 11.0 [b] |

Sources: Carl Zoerb, "The Virgin Lands Territory: Plans, Performance,
Prospects," in Roy D. Laird and Edward L. Crowley, eds., *Soviet Agriculture:
The Permanent Crisis* (New York: Praeger, 1965), pp. 29–44; *Narodnoe
khoziaistvo Kazakhstana v 1968* (Alma-Ata, Kazakhstan: 1970), pp. 116,
132 for 1965–1968; *Kazakhstanskaia pravda*, November 22, 1972, for 1972;
*Pravda*, October 23, 1973.
[a] Estimate.
[b] Preliminary data.

cal factors affected the decision. The new leadership was again trying
to solve the grain problem, the very one Khrushchev tried to overcome
when he formally proposed his virgin lands policy to the Party's
Presidium. In his memorandum of January 22, 1954, "Ways of Solving
the Grain Problem," Khrushchev had viewed the virgin lands as a
major source of more grain but indicated that there were still other
ones.[7] Particularly noteworthy about his list of sources was the absence of grain imports. In keeping with the time-hallowed policy of
seeking to achieve self-sufficiency in agricultural production it was
politically impossible to advocate that as an alternative.

Similarly, the post-Khrushchev leaders did not consider importing grain a permanent solution to the grain problem. As the Resolution of the March 1965 plenum was to show, the preferred solution was to increase yields. Future years would demonstrate that this preference was unrealizable and that grain of various kinds would have to be imported on a continuous basis. But the important point here is that in 1965 the leadership chose to remain true to the tradition of its predecessors in this question of fundamental policy, and the goal of autarky prevailed. Therefore, every internal resource had to be tapped.

The record of the Kazakh virgin lands up to and including 1964 now appeared in a more favorable light since they had contributed a healthy average of 9 percent of the total USSR grain purchases, the overwhelming portion of that being wheat.[8] While making this contribution the virgin lands state farms suffered the financial losses already noted, but those were tolerable to the state because the farms' produce helped fill out the government's none-too-large grain stocks, and they were tolerable to the farms because government subsidies eventually covered the farms' monetary losses.

The intractable fact was that, before the virgin lands could be abandoned, the Soviet leaders would have to provide for a sharp increase in grain yields in the older grain-growing regions, a policy not offering quick results and entailing considerable risks of its own in view of past performance in attempting to raise yields. The final unpleasant consequence of abandoning those lands would have been liquidation of a multibillion ruble investment already made in new state farms, grain elevators, railroads, and grain processing facilities.

Still, the leaders might well have abandoned everything and taken the losses with a stiff upper lip had it not been for the conviction among agricultural experts that these lands could be farmed efficiently and effectively if only a rational system of farming could be applied consistently. The elements of that system had been developed during the last years of Khrushchev's incumbency. But they were never put into practice because of his obstinate desire to squeeze the maximum short-term production from the virgin lands. That was in large part responsible for the decline in yields of the late 1950s and early 1960s and for the dustbowl conditions of the mid-1960s.[9]

A special session of the V. I. Lenin Academy of Agricultural Sciences on virgin lands agriculture held in Tselinograd provided good examples of the thinking which became prevalent under the new leadership.[10] In sum the session's recommendations were a compendium of the best advice advanced in the Soviet Union (especially by the experimental researcher A. Baraev) respecting dryland farming, the study of Canadian dryland farming techniques, and the lessons of eleven years of practical experience. If there was very little new in the recommendations, there seemed to be a refreshingly sincere commitment to put the total dryfarm system into effect as opposed to the only too obvious lip service paid to similar proposals during the last few years of the Khrushchev era.

Finally, there was a Kremlinological factor in the decision to continue the virgin lands program despite the imposing problems associated with it. Many key post-Khrushchev leaders had been associated closely with the Kazakh virgin lands. Brezhnev himself had spent two years in Kazakhstan as Second and then First Secretary during the critical early stages of the program from February 1954 to March 1956. V. V. Matskevich, reappointed Minister of Agriculture following Khrushchev's ouster, had been Chairman of the Tselinny Kraiispolkom in the early 1960s. And D. A. Kunaev, the Kazakh First Secretary deposed by Khrushchev in December 1962, was quickly reinstated in that post by Brezhnev in early December 1964.[11]

Brezhnev's attitude toward the virgin lands in late 1964 and early 1965 was of indubitable importance. The most revealing comment by him on that matter was his interruption of Kunaev's speech at the March 1965 plenum to note that while he (Brezhnev) was First Secretary in Kazakhstan, Khrushchev had prevented him from extending the fallowed area in the virgin lands.[12] The question of how large the fallowed area ought to be was the major policy issue respecting the virgin lands. Khrushchev favored fallowing the smallest possible proportion, others favored fallowing more in varying proportions to ensure higher per hectare yields.

Insofar as the virgin lands program was a policy issue, there is no evidence that Khrushchev's removal was occasioned to any extent by his opponents' desire to abandon the virgin lands. On the contrary, the policies adopted by the new leaders show clearly that they objected to the irrational way in which virgin lands agricultural policy was being formulated and administered. Khrushchev's successors chose the fourth of the policy alternatives noted previously.

Consequently, there was something old and something new in the successors' objectives in the virgin lands which were worked out before the March 1965 plenum. They were only briefly mentioned by Brezhnev at the plenum, but were specified in some detail by Kunaev in a speech he delivered in Kazakhstan in April.[13] Kunaev stated that not only was Kazakhstan to remain a major grain producer, especially of wheat, but what appeared to be a very high delivery target was set.

A *minimum* of 9.8 million tons of grain were to be sold to the state annually over the next six years (including 1965), while the annual average delivery of grain for the previous six years had been 9.6 million tons. The major share (7.2 million tons) was to come from what Kunaev now called "the former virgin lands regions." The role of the virgin lands was to be enhanced, whatever name one applied to them. Apparently the bumper crop of 1964 had raised hopes for future performance rather high—but not altogether unrealistically.

THE NEW LEADERSHIP AND SOME OLD PROBLEMS

The decision having been announced to retain the new lands, attention now focused on the many problems bequeathed by Khrushchev and other difficulties created by the very structural characteristics of the political and economic system. It proved easier to correct the difficulties attributable to Khrushchevian mismanagement than to overcome the problems peculiar to Soviet agricultural and industrial organization.

First there was the question of farming practices, which had been subjected to harmful political pressures under Khrushchev. It has often been noted that at best wheat farming on the virgin lands entails considerable risk. More accurately put, the *wrong* kind of farming maximizes risk, whereas appropriate techniques can result not only in minimizing risk but in relatively high yields as well. In the early 1960s Khrushchev began to throw caution to the winds and insist, against the advice of most agricultural experts, that either as little land as possible be left fallow each year (rather, various beans were to replace wheat periodically in a senseless crop rotation scheme), or that wheat be sown year after year in order to keep gross output from the new lands high.

The new leaders were also committed to high output, but they were unwilling to risk as much. From a dangerously low 5 percent of all plowland kept fallow in Tselinny krai in 1963 the fallows reached 16 percent in 1970 with the intention of increasing them finally to 22–25 percent.[14] Although even the latter proportion is still too low (under roughly analogous climatic conditions the farms in Canada's Saskatchewan province fallow about 40 percent of the land) a very important step was taken to rationalize farming. The one disadvantage to fallowing is that the fallows must be worked in order to collect as much moisture as possible and, if herbicides are not used widely, to kill weeds. Although fragmentary reports indicate that this has not always been done, the precise extent to which the fallows were worked cannot be determined; but where they were, the cost of production increased.[15] Yet that was a relatively small price to pay for achieving the greatest benefit of fallowing, the stabilization of yields. Wide fluctuations in yield entailed some substantial costs to be discussed further on.

Closely connected with considerations of cost is the problem of appropriate equipment. Because the overwhelming portion of the equipment used up to the mid-1960s was not designed for use in the unique conditions of dryland farming, large losses of crops and money (incalculable, but nonetheless large) were sustained. Almost all the tractors were crawler types, while more wheeled varieties were needed; specialized plows which do not break up the soil to a great extent and thus inhibit erosion were too little used; seeders performing several other operations simultaneously were in rare evidence; reapers capable of being adjusted to a variety of harvest conditions were not in general use, and neither were reapers with a broad swath; grain drying equipment was both in short supply and not powerful enough to handle the unusually moist grain. Moreover, the grain contained a great deal of foreign matter that needed sorting out. This catalog of complaints, abstracted here from a body of Soviet writing on the virgin lands in the late 1950s and early 1960s, was summarized by the high-ranking Kazakh Party agricultural administrator G. Mel'nik in an astonishingly frank article (*Pravda*, December 4, 1963) where he enumerated the equipment needed to farm the virgin lands more efficiently.

In the Khrushchev era requests for requisite types of machines produced few quick results for two reasons. One was the familiar difficulty of manufacturing new products, the other the desire to keep investment in the virgin lands somewhere near the minimum because of the capital investment shortage and also to be able to claim a large profit from those lands.[16]

The new leaders' attempts to alleviate the equipment problem were only partially successful. Improved plowing equipment was supplied to the extent that in four of the six virgin lands oblasts an average of 80 percent of the plowing was done with the proper equipment.[17] But in some areas improved equipment was unavailable up to 1974.[18]

Improved equipment has increased the efficiency of the farms in two critical periods, the sowing and harvesting, when an almost incredible volume of work has to be performed in a very short time and, in the case of the harvest, under most trying conditions since the usual rains during that period increase the demands upon the skill and stamina of the equipment operators.

The virgin lands have always been plagued with manpower problems whose nature has varied down through the years.[19] The rhythm of work on the new lands creates two peak periods of manpower utilization, a smaller one in spring, a very much larger one in late summer and early fall, and a period of substantial underemployment and unemployment in the winter months. The latter problem is difficult to resolve because wheat farming is so predominant that alternative employment is rarely available. The most complete study of this matter established that in the early 1960s the total number of workers (rabochie) employed on the state farms in Tselinny krai varied annually on the average from 302,000 in January to 505,000 in September, and that in January 1960, for example, 66,000 persons less than the annual average worked on those farms, while in September of the same year 157,000 more than that average were employed.[20]

There were three possible ways to alleviate this problem. The first, introducing more efficient equipment to diminish the number of personnel needed, has had some effect as already noted. The second, trying to keep as many workers as possible on the farms year-round, has not worked because winter unemployment more or less forces the workers to seek jobs in industry and then return to the farm only for the sowing and harvest, if at all. So the third alternative has been applied consistently in Khrushchev's day and since. Large numbers of equipment operators (tractor drivers, combine operators, and truck drivers) have been imported during the harvest from other regions of Kazakhstan and also from other republics in the Soviet Union, sometimes bringing their own equipment, particularly combines and trucks.

The magnitude of this phenomenon is only partially documentable from scattered data. In 1964, a bumper year following a disastrous year, the virgin lands regions lacked 127,000 equipment operators out of a shortage of 158,000 for all Kazakhstan.[21] In 1966 17,000 equipment operators came to the virgin lands from other republics; in 1968 12,000 combine operators came to help man the 60,800 combines on hand in the virgin lands oblasts; and in 1972 15,000 combine operators were brought in.[22] While there are no data on the over-all shortage of equipment operators in 1968, the deficit was so severe that a special massive training program was announced in Kazakhstan to produce more of them.[23]

Since the early 1960s such efforts, over and above the normal training programs, had been initiated about once every two years. The one announced for 1971 (Kazakhstanskaia pravda, December 17, 1970) for training 43,000 persons experienced the same problem as the earlier ones. Only about half the number of planned trainees actually took the courses. And on the basis of previous experience it was safe to anticipate that half the actual trainees would spend only one year in agriculture and then leave for the factories.

Another aspect of the personnel problem is the large turnover among what ought to be the permanent personnel on the state farms. Equipment operators quit the farms not only because oscillations in employment produce fluctuations in pay but also because of poor living conditions, especially the lack of satisfactory housing. The task of stabilizing the workforce is therefore connected with spending the large capital funds needed to overcome the causes of turnover, and there has been a shortage of such funds.

Finally, special efforts to supply personnel had to be made in the bumper years of 1972 and 1973, and that included utilizing military personnel and equipment—but on this matter we have no statistics.

The new leadership has not yet succeeded in resolving the personnel problem or even in reducing it to manageable size. The influx of so many temporary operators has had a destructive effect on the machinery they used so carelessly, the cost of transporting them has been high, and the fact that many were granted temporary leave from their jobs in industry must have had deleterious effects in that sphere as well. But the priorities here were in favor of agriculture rather than industry, quite the reverse of the usual situation.

More progress is to be noted in other areas since 1965. Of primary importance, many of the state farms were now able to make a profit. Especially after 1961, when state purchase prices were unrealistically lowered for virgin lands grain, it was extremely difficult for even the farms that had been profitable before to remain so.[24] Circumstances were reversed once purchase prices were increased in 1965 and when (only some years later for the virgin lands) premium prices were paid for grain purchases in excess of the planned amount.[25] This was done in connection with placing the state farms on full *khozraschet*, which meant eliminating the state subsidies that had gone to many farms regularly to cover the losses they had sustained.

In another area, the improved equipment aided, where available, in increasing the yield as did improved farming practices. In 1969 Kunaev enumerated rather completely the factors contributing toward the comparatively large and stable harvests since 1966, including greater utilization of the following: appropriate plowing equipment, clean and stubble fallow,* rational crop rotation patterns, adapted

---

* Clean fallow is tilled during the growing season to keep it free of weeds and to retain moisture. Stubble fallow remains untilled after the harvest so that the stubble will help retain snow, preventing it from being blown off the fields by strong winter winds.

seeds, herbicides, pesticides, fertilizer, anti-erosion techniques, more powerful tractors, broad-swath reapers and self-propelled combines.[26] To all that must be added the somewhat intangible but nonetheless real factor of the experience acquired over the years by the virgin landers who had in particular learned how not to be outwitted by the unstable weather at harvest time.

Inevitably, little could be done to overcome the periodic ravages of drought or, alternatively, the rains, as in 1967 when the grain was exceptionally wet, the harvest was hampered by unusually heavy concentrations of volunteer wheat,* and a less than average crop was brought in. The point is, however, that in the normally complex conditions during the harvest it is possible to minimize crop losses if only one has developed the expertise and is allowed to apply it. The new leaders have gone far in that direction.

RESULTS AND PROSPECTS

Dryland farming performance is usually rated by comparing average production over several periods of years. In the four years for which statistics are available since Khrushchev's dismissal (1965–1968) the average annual grain harvest in the virgin lands oblasts was 10.7 million tons, while in the 1961–1964 period it was 10.4 million tons, and in 1957–1960 it was 11.9 million tons. When the short-term effects of the droughts in 1963 and 1965 are taken into account (that is, dustbowl conditions) the 1965–1968 average looks impressive, and the subsequent harvests were far better.

In appraising the virgin lands it is necessary to remember that they produce mostly wheat, a crop whose significance to the Soviet economy cannot be overestimated. If in the drought year of 1965 Tselinny krai produced 4.6 percent of the USSR's total wheat crop, in the bumper crop year 1966 and the more normal years 1967 and 1968 the share of this region was 14.3 percent, 10.6 percent, and 10.5 percent, respectively.[27] But wheat purchases are the most telling statistic because of the inflated nature of grain production figures (see note 8). The Kazakh virgin lands' share of the Soviet Union's state wheat purchases was 5.4 percent in 1965, 12.5 percent in 1966, 13.7 percent in 1967 and 12.6 percent in 1968.[28] Even though there may be some doubt as to the quality of this grain, it is impossible to envisage the USSR doing without that quantity of wheat so long as the leadership refused to import large amounts of grain regularly.

---

* Volunteer wheat grows from seed lost in the previous year's harvesting operations and results in an excessively thick crop which is difficult to harvest.

On the other hand, virgin lands grain is very expensive. In 1959–1962 the cost of production of one quintal of grain was 3 rubles in the Ukraine, an average of 4.3 rubles throughout the Soviet Union and 5 rubles on the Kazakh virgin lands.[29] Over the period 1955–1968 the average cost of production per quintal of grain on those lands was 5.76 rubles, still the highest of the major grain-producing regions.[30] Hence the dilemma confronting the leaders: Virgin lands wheat may be indispensable, but it is bought at a high price.

Other aspects of that dilemma were addressed in Kunaev's speech announcing the targets for the current Five Year Plan.[31] Kazakhstan was to produce an annual average of 24 million tons of grain, 4 million (20 percent) over the annual average produced in the first four years of the preceding Five Year Plan. The minimum state grain purchases were to be 10.6 million tons annually, of which 8.74 million were to be wheat. Although Kunaev did not mention specific figures for the virgin lands as he had done in 1965 when it was necessary to publicize the fact that the virgin lands were not being abandoned, the new production targets clearly assumed heightened output from the virgin lands.

At the same time Kunaev envisaged a sharp increase in the construction of housing, hospitals, schools, kindergartens and production facilities on the Republic's state farms. As of the moment, Kunaev stated, only 38 percent of the total projected construction on the state farms had been completed, and the proportion was to reach 55–60 percent by the end of the current Five Year Plan. That was another way of saying that if even higher grain production is projected, higher investments are required to eliminate some causes of massive personnel turnover. Apparently, the new leadership either felt that it could now make those large investments or that it simply had to. Only time will tell what this commitment will produce, but the record of shortcomings in construction bodes ill.

In other areas as well much more remains to be done. The time is overdue to cut down to manageable size some problems of long standing. The desire to maximize gross production from the virgin lands led to cultivating marginal and less than marginal land, especially in Pavlodar oblast, and thus contributed to low per hectare yields and large losses exemplified by the steadily declining output per tractor. Removing such lands from production would allow considerable savings. Concomitantly, if fallows on the remaining lands were increased to about 40 percent, per hectare yields would be maximized on a significantly smaller area than has been sown each year heretofore. The farms would then not require so many workers and, most important, so much equipment inefficiently employed harvesting sparse grain on large tracts of land. Production costs would drop.

While eliminating some losses, the leaders would have to absorb others. Some state farms would have to be abandoned, and smaller harvests might have to be tolerated, at least until the fallowed lands can be brought to their full production potential. These are only some of the "reserves" for increasing yields.

These measures would increase the efficiency of farming and the per hectare yield on the virgin lands. Even so, it can be argued that they would not increase sufficiently the Soviet Union's total production of grain and especially wheat since continued population growth, the commitments to supply grain to foreign countries, the lack of new arable land (a fact noted by Brezhnev in his speech to the Central Committee plenum in July 1970), and the unstable climate indicate that the grain problem will be with the Soviet Union for a long time. Be this as it may, without the virgin lands' production the grain gap would be insurmountable. Moreover, with the growing population in the eastern regions it might prove valuable to retain a grain base there.

The leadership clearly intends to retain the virgin lands whatever the problems associated with farming them. The continued special personnel-training programs and particularly the large-scale construction programs announced by Kunaev are indications of long-term commitment to farming those lands. There are many problems in dryland farming, as the experience of Saskatchewan has shown. But if the virgin lands can approximate Saskatchewan's performance there is little reason for abandoning them. They have shown themselves productive when requisite precautions have been taken, and have been even essential in filling the USSR's grain needs.

Inevitably, the virgin lands will be subjected to drought in the future, but if the proper farm techniques continue to be applied, and if the temptation is resisted to plow up more marginal lands to increase gross production, the over-all performance of the virgin lands is likely to justify their continued utilization.

The virgin lands have presented the Soviet decision-makers with two major sets of problems. One is the difficulties unique to the virgin lands. The other has to do with deficiencies pandemic in and endemic to Soviet agriculture in general, the virgin lands included. The leadership has attacked both sets simultaneously in about as rational a fashion as was possible under the circumstances imposed by ideological and systemic limitations. Capital investment in agriculture was increased, the mixture of equipment was diversified, technical decisions were more often left to be made by specialists, and other steps were taken to avoid some of the earlier causes of stagnation in agriculture.

The cost of these improvements has been staggering and promises to remain high for the next fifteen years. A good example of what lies ahead is the decision announced in April 1974 to effect massive improvements in agriculture in the RSFSR's nonblack earth zone through a 35 billion ruble investment between 1976–1980.[32] The land reclamation and soil improvement aspects of this program are expected to continue until 1990.

In addition, rationalization has involved even more serious and costly steps. Some of the pressure has been taken off domestic agriculture through massive food grain purchases abroad following the Soviet crop failures in 1972 and 1975. And the policy of steady imports of feed grains may make it possible to stabilize the herd and ultimately to increase the protein component of the Soviet diet. These policies were, to be sure, adopted with great reluctance, but they do in any event have the force of easing the situation in Soviet agriculture.

It seems safe to assume that these measures were viewed by the leadership as necessary steps in strengthening Soviet agriculture to the point where autarky can at last be achieved. And the same can be said for the other major initiatives in agriculture, land reclamation and irrigation.

Yet the question remains: Will all these improvements, or even additional ones, be enough to compensate for the harsh and capricious climate, and will they be able to keep pace with the growth in population? Conversely, will population growth, a positive value in the eyes of the leadership, be inhibited by the size and variety of the food supply? In other words, can autarky be achieved? Perhaps not. But if not, then the policies being pursued by the current leadership will make the Soviet Union as nearly self-sufficient as possible in agriculture in the long run.

The Soviet agricultural dilemma must be viewed from two final perspectives. In the long run the problem may be one of the comparative advantage to the Soviet Union of spending unprecedented sums of money to conduct agriculture under adverse conditions as opposed to importing a portion of its grain, thereby saving some investment funds for other purposes. On the other hand, the long-range problem may be a world-wide food shortage, and under those conditions there would either be no grain available to import, or the price of the available grain would be prohibitively high.

Recent American studies project long-term changes in weather resulting in major, repeated droughts affecting Canada, China, India, and Kazakhstan, making it likely that the virgin lands will have to be abandoned.[33] To date the choices that the Soviet leaders have had to make in agricultural policy have been incomparably difficult. Under the conditions projected in these studies the Soviet Union, along with the rest of the world, may be forced to seek or develop nonconventional food supplies through, for example, chemistry or the sea's resources. If natural forces outdistance humanity's political, economic, and technological capabilities to cope with them, the virgin lands will no longer be a policy issue.

# PART FOUR

# Political Development and Social Change

# Socialism and Modernity: Education, Industrialization, and Social Change in the USSR

GAIL WARSHOFSKY LAPIDUS

11

One of the main thrusts of studies of the Soviet system in recent years, and indeed of Communist systems more broadly, has been an emphasis on the conflict between revolutionary and developmental goals. A growing array of studies interpret the evolution of Communist systems in terms of the tension between the conflicting imperatives of utopia and development, and trace the gradual erosion of initial commitments to a classless, egalitarian and democratic society in the face of pressures for system adaptation to the functional requisites of modernization.[1] While this perspective points to suggestive issues in the development of Communist systems, in important respects it obscures more than it clarifies. By establishing a conceptual dichotomy between "socialism" and "modernity" it risks the danger of reifying developmental imperatives and abstracting them from political values, processes and choices. Furthermore, this formulation ignores the degree to which the very meanings of socialism and modernity are entwined in Leninism. The crucial problems in the development of Communist systems involve less the conflict between socialism and modernity than conflicting elements in the definition of both.

The purpose of this paper is to illuminate the diverse orientations which underlay the Soviet effort to create a society at once socialist and modern, and the changing vision of this society at successive stages of Soviet development, by focusing upon the evolution of Soviet educational values and policies between 1917 and the mid-1930s.[2] For education was central to the revolutionary transformation of economic, political and social life. It was the key to the "cultural revolution" that would create a society at once socialist and modern. It would inculcate the broad scientific knowledge and technological skills that would help transform Russia from a backward agrarian society to a modern industrial order. It would serve as a channel of social mobility for previously disadvantaged groups in Russian society, altering the hierarchical and ascriptive features of pre-Revolutionary Russian society and facilitating the creation of a genuinely egalitarian social order. Finally, education would transform the very character of the Russian population, imbuing it with new values, attitudes, and styles of behavior appropriate to modern, socialist men and women.

Questions of who should be educated, what skills taught, and what values and behavior inculcated through the educational system touched upon fundamental issues of economic and social policy. The Soviet quest for a strategy of educational development which would serve as a vehicle for a broader transformation of society involved a complex confrontation of revolutionary values, institutional interests and environmental constraints which defy simple classification into the static dichotomies of socialism and modernity. An investigation of conflicting orientations toward educational policy in the early years of the Soviet regime, and of the major shifts of educational theory and practice which accompanied broader changes in the character of the Soviet regime, may therefore illuminate the complex interplay of utopian and developmental concerns in the evolution of the Soviet system. It will also serve to focus attention upon the central political forces which resulted in the successive redefinition of both.

TOWARD A NEW EDUCATIONAL THEORY

"Education," insisted Vladimir Ilyich Lenin, "cannot help but be connected with politics." [3] "A school outside of politics, outside of life, is a lie and a deception." [4] If the organization and values of the pre-Revolutionary educational system were repudiated by the leaders of the new Soviet state it was not in order to free education from politics but to turn it to new purposes. Education would serve as an important instrument of revolutionary transformation.

In outlining the contours of a future society at once socialist and modern, the Bolshevik party program framed in 1903 and revised in 1919 sketched in sparse yet bold strokes a vision of a new educational system, differing radically from its Tsarist predecessor in clientele, curricula and values. Its purpose was set forth in general terms in the 1919 program: to transform the school "from the weapon of bourgeois class domination into a weapon for the total destruction of class divisions within society, into a weapon for the Communist regeneration of society." [5]

However, no distinctively Marxian educational theory existed to shape the construction of such a system. Encouraged by Lenin to formulate such a theory, and fortified by her personal commitment to popular enlightenment, Nadezhda Krupskaya had composed in 1915 an essay entitled "Public Education and Democracy" whose basic outlines guided early Soviet efforts. The essay revealed the special impact of Tolstoyan educational philosophy upon Krupskaya's own development, but it drew heavily as well upon the contributions of Russian and foreign progressive educational theory.

Despite important differences of attitudes and priorities, the movement for educational reform in pre-Revolutionary Russia had shared several common, if broad, objectives.[6] It sought the democratization of the educational system and the guarantee of equal educational opportunities to children of all social classes. To this end, it urged a national, unified system of education, free and compulsory, with a single educational ladder along which students would move entirely on the basis of individual achievement. It advocated, further, the autonomy of education, its freedom from control by church and state alike, an education at once secular and de-politicized, in which extreme centralization would be replaced by local control. The scholasticism of the traditional curriculum, influenced as it was by classical literary culture and Orthodox doctrine, was considered unsuited to the scientific and technological needs of a modern society, although disagreement existed over just how these should be defined. Finally, it urged an educational system that would through its formal organization and its teaching methods eliminate the rigidly authoritarian ethos of the Tsarist schools and replace it with an atmosphere more supportive of intellectual independence and creativity, an atmosphere which would encourage the behavior appropriate to a self-governing and democratic society.

Drawing inspiration from the pedagogical radicalism of this broader movement for reform, Krupskaya, Lenin, and other Social-Democratic educational theorists added two additional and distinctive elements. First, they denied the very possibility of an autonomous educational system so central to the values of the liberal reformers. Convinced that education inevitably reflects the structure of power and values in any society, they sought not the freedom of education from politics but its utilization on behalf of revolutionary objectives.

From the very beginning of his revolutionary career Lenin had insisted upon the primacy of politics. Scornful of cultural missionaries
who, he scoffed, thought Russia would be saved through Committees
on Illiteracy, Lenin had insisted that political action and not popular
enlightenment would serve as the catalyst of social change.[7] Rather
than accept the view that Russia was unprepared for socialism, Lenin
urged that socialist revolution be used to achieve modernity.[8] Cultural
revolution would become the consequence of the Bolshevik seizure
of power rather than its prerequisite, in Lenin's fundamental reformulation of classical Marxist doctrine.

The other innovation introduced into Bolshevik educational
theory was the insistence that education be linked with productive
labor. If the fragmented individual of capitalist society was to be
supplanted by the fully-developed socialist man of the Marxian vision,
education must overcome the division of labor.[9] A modern and socialist educational system would avoid the academic formalism that
created an intellectual elite ignorant of economic and social realities,
while at the same time rejecting an excessively vocational training
that would produce narrow specialists rather than many-sided men.
The Labor School, elaborated in theory and practice by two former
Tolstoyans, S. T. Shatsky and P. P. Blonsky, would join children's
production to study and constitute the core of the new educational
system.

The vision of socialism underlying this broad educational program
was an amalgam of several distinct and partly conflicting elements. It
combined a libertarian and humanist ideal of the free, fully-developed, and creative individual with a commitment to the revolutionary mission of the proletariat as a class. These goals were uneasily
joined to a definition of modernity that emphasized scientific and
technological progress and took industrial, mechanized America to
be the image of the Russian future.[10] The tension between these
strands emerged into the open only after the Revolution, when the
leadership of the new Soviet state was obliged to transform a vague
revolutionary program into concrete policies. It was then that definitions of socialism and modernity moved from the realm of intellectual
speculation and became the subject of political struggle.

THE QUEST FOR A STRATEGY OF REVOLUTIONARY EDUCATION:
PRIORITIES AND CONSTRAINTS

The new Soviet government announced by Lenin in October 1917
included a Commissariat of Enlightenment (*Narkompros*), to which

was assigned the task of reorganizing both education and the arts to serve the needs of the nascent socialist society. Under the leadership of Anatoly Lunacharsky, a philosopher-poet and revolutionary enthusiast who once described himself as "an intellectual among Bolsheviks and a Bolshevik among intellectuals," Narkompros set out to create a new educational system. It confronted from its very birth a variety of contradictory orientations.

The conflicts centered about three broad sets of questions: Who should be educated? What knowledge and skills should be taught? What character traits and values should be developed in the new socialist man and woman through the educational process? In each case, broad agreement on principle concealed divergent values and priorities which led to very different practical strategies.[11] Moreover, conflicting orientations were found not only among the political and social groups which formed the diverse constituency of Narkompros, but among the Commissariat collegium itself.

The first set of problems, involving the clientele of the educational system, had a superficially simple answer on which all could agree. The new educational system would be an egalitarian one offering every child the opportunity to devolop his individual abilities to the fullest. However, in view of the fact that actual educational opportunities were limited, the real difficulties involved their distribution. What individuals or groups should receive preferential treatment, according to what criteria, and for what purposes? How would the vague objective of individual development be defined in practice, and harmonized with the social and economic needs of the new state? What weight should be given to the conflicting needs for fully developed individuals, emphasized in the humanist strain of socialism, to the compensatory treatment of previously disadvantaged groups, urged by the revolutionary left, and to the pressing need of the economy for skilled manpower?

This question was in turn closely connected with that of the objectives of education itself. Again there was broad agreement that education should serve some practical function, communicating the knowledge and skills suitable to an industrial and socialist society. Should labor and production training, however, require the transformation of the educational system into an adjunct of industrial enterprises, or did a distinct system of formal education serve a larger function? How were the immediate needs for skilled labor to be balanced against the long-term goal of producing men and women with a grasp of the fundamental principles underlying all science and technology? What priority ought to be given general education by comparison with vocational training, or for that matter with political socialization?

Thirdly, if it was generally agreed that the educational system had an important role to play in creating new values, attitudes and behavior, how should they be defined? In what way might the organization of the curriculum and of the school itself serve these purposes? Even more important, how could the school become the bearer of new values and a counterpoise to the conservatism of family and church, when staffed by teachers or professors with little enthusiasm for, if not outright hostility toward, revolutionary goals?

The answers that different individuals and groups would give to these questions were shaped in important ways by the larger economic and political environment and the possibilities and constraints for educational policy that it created. In the early years of the new regime, war and civil war gave primacy to military and economic needs, and generated an atmosphere inhospitable to substantial educational investments. The accumulated educational capital of prewar Russia was partly dissipated: school buildings had been destroyed or converted into barracks, while large numbers of teaching personnel were victims of war, famine, epidemic, or emigration. Discussions of how to procure firewood and rations vied with more lofty educational concerns at meetings of the Narkompros collegium. Moreover, the absence of an administrative network that could extend the authority of the new government into the countryside meant that educational policy was formulated in a vacuum, out of touch with local realities. The undefined character of Party-state relations created confusion over the allocation of responsibility, while the lack of sympathy that many teachers and educators felt for the new regime generated conflicts with Party and Komsomol representatives which were a continuing source of tension in educational institutions at all levels.

The ability of Narkompros to obtain the allocation of the economic resources and cadres needed to pursue its goals depended upon its ability to mobilize political support from among the major economic and political forces contending for influence in shaping the new society. Here too Narkompros was at a disadvantage. Its educational leaders, and Lunacharsky in particular, tended to be the romantics and idealists of pre-Revolutionary Bolshevism, more concerned with the spiritual and cultural mission of the Revolution than with the necessities of political struggle and economic construction. Few influential Party figures with political and administrative skills participated directly in its work. For despite the importance assigned to education in early Bolshevism, other priorities engaged the attention and resources of the new regime during its first decade. Indeed, the tasks of cultural revolution never assumed, in the Soviet context, the transcending importance which would be accorded them in the Chinese and Cuban revolutions, for outside of Narkompros cultural change was viewed as largely derivative, a function of the redefinition of economic, political and social domains.[12] In its efforts to press for a massive commitment of resources to the education of fully-rounded individuals, Narkompros found itself continually under attack from groups within the Party outraged by its political unorthodoxy and sheer irrelevance, and from an economic and technical lobby based in the trade unions and in the powerful economic commissariats who wished to see the educational system directly serve the pressing manpower needs of a war-ravaged economy.

TRANSFORMING EDUCATIONAL ACCESS:
THE SOCIAL COMPOSITION OF THE NEW SCHOOL

In the quest for educational strategies which would help to build a modern and socialist society, the problem of educational access came to the fore as a central and controversial issue. One of the first concerns of the new Commissariat was to lay the foundations of equal educational opportunity, which would in turn alter the pattern of social stratification in Russian society. A series of sweeping decrees which established the basic features of the new educational system provided for equal access in three ways.[13] First, they removed all legal impediments to equal access by abolishing restrictions based upon religion, race, or sex. Secondly, they provided that a uniform educational experience be offered to all schoolchildren by establishing a single type of institution, the Unified Labor School, with a nine-year educational program, which would be free, coeducational, and universal. Finally, they promised a vast expansion of the entire educational network at all levels to make even higher education universally available to all who desired it. "In principle," Lunacharsky announced, "every child of the Russian Republic enters a school of an identical type and has the same chances as every other to complete the higher education." [14] The abolition of all admission requirements and the adoption of open enrollment would make higher education freely available to everyone aged sixteen or over. New institutions would be created to accommodate the anticipated demand, while existing facilities were to be utilized more intensively.

Dramatic and far-reaching as these measures were for their time, the first two objectives could be accomplished largely by decree. The third, however, required an enormous investment of resources. In the immediate post-Revolutionary period, widespread popular enthusiasm for education and the pent-up demands of the wartime years resulted in a vast expansion of the number of educational institutions and student enrollments at all levels.[15] The Commissariat actively encouraged local initiative with little concern for the availability of resources. The number of primary schools and students increased rapidly between 1918 and 1921 while 278 institutions of higher education existed at least on paper in 1921, three times the 1914 figure.[16]

But the wish to make access to education universal proved utopian in the extreme. The scarcity of resources and the primacy of military and economic needs relegated educational claims on the central budget to low priority. The New Economic Policy of 1921 brought a massive economic retrenchment, and the severe contraction of the central budget shifted the burden of support for primary education back to local communities. The commitment of the regime to free public education was eroded by the reintroduction of fees at all levels of the system.[17] Educational expenditures per pupil fell below prewar levels, despite the lamentations of Lunacharsky and the protests of a succession of Komsomol Congresses, and a massive contraction of the educational system occurred. A gradual recovery began in the mid-1920s, but not until 1926–1927 were prewar levels once again reached.[18]

With educational opportunities limited by larger economic constraints, Narkompros was obliged to establish priorities in the allocation of educational opportunities. The underlying tension between the commitment to equal opportunity and the pressures for preferential treatment of children of workers became increasingly acute. The new constitution of the Unified Labor School promulgated in 1923 gave explicit recognition to the primacy of proletarianization. It continued to insist that in principle education was open to all, but added that in view of the limited spaces available priority would henceforth be given to children of toilers.

Statements of principle were not the only mechanism at the disposal of educational authorities in seeking to alter the social composition of the schools. A wide variety of additional measures were devised to alter the distribution of educational opportunities in favor of previously disadvantaged groups. Certain categories of people might be refused admission altogether to certain educational institutions, or, as in the social purging of the universities in 1924, they might be expelled after being admitted. Preferential admissions was, of course, a second widely used device. The practice of *komandirovanie* was adapted for educational purposes, with quotas established and places reserved for students of a designated social background, occupation, sex, or nationality, or for graduates of particular compensatory programs. The most significant of the measures to increase the proportion of proletarian students in higher educational institutions were the *rabfaks* (workers' faculties), special programs attached to higher educational institutions to give workers the rapid and rough equivalent of a secondary education to prepare them for further studies at a higher level. In 1925, for example, of the 18,000 places available for entering students at the university level, 8,000 were set aside for *rabfak* graduates, and the remainder distributed among various organizations and social groups: 25 percent for talented secondary school graduates, 10 percent for the working intelligentsia, and almost 50 percent to Party, Komsomol, and trade union organizations. By 1928 176 *rabfaks* were in existence, with some 37,000 students, and they were supplying almost one-third of all incoming students in higher educational institutions.[19]

Financial constraints or incentives also acted, both directly and indirectly, to shape the composition of the student body. The adjustment of fee schedules and scholarships could be utilized to favor certain categories of students over others. Further, central control over the types and ratios of schools established, and the jurisdiction to which they were assigned, could also alter the structure of opportunities. The retention of the academic 7- and 9-year schools, for example, favored the children of the urban middle class, while agricultural and technical schools attracted a larger peasant or worker clientele.

Similarly, curricula and standards affected the social composition of various programs and schools. The suspension of admission requirements and entrance examinations in favor of open enrollment, and the creation of crash programs such as the *rabfaks,* facilitated proletarianization in the short run, though the maintenance of high academic standards could result in extremely high drop-out rates for the psychologically and academically unprepared. Finally, the regime attempted to raise the educational aspirations of the wider population by emphasizing the supreme importance of knowledge and learning, and by identifying itself with efforts to widen access to them.

Ultimately the distribution of educational opportunities was a political matter. Even during the Civil War period the humanistic individualism represented by Lunacharsky had come under attack by the advocates of more radical proletarianization. Urging that education be considered a privilege of the working class, and that preferential treatment be given its members, this group sought to use the schools to secure the future political and social dominance of the working class. E. A. Preobrazhensky was the most politically influential advocate of the intensification of class war in educational institutions. Its main support came from within the trade union movement, the *rabfaks*, the Komsomol, and the lower ranks of the Party. The proletarianizers sought to perpetuate the atmosphere of crisis and of class struggle that had marked the Civil War period and to fight the implications of what they viewed as bourgeois restoration after 1921. The appointment of Preobrazhensky to head the department of Narkompros responsible for professional education in 1921 exacerbated the conflict. Conjuring up the spectre of class war, Preobrazhensky conveyed a characteristic alarm in warning:

The bourgeois and intellectual strata of the population are frantically trying to maintain themselves and their children at the level of education and social position reached in the pre-Revolutionary period. This, of course, is quite understandable. But the proletarian state will never allow the parents and children of the former privileged classes to decide the question of the numbers and social origins of the future specialists we train in our schools. At the moment there is a genuine class war at the doors of the higher school between the worker-peasant majority of the country, which wants to have specialists from among its own kin in its own state, and the governing classes and strata linked with them. The proletarian state openly takes the side of its own people.[20]

Other priorities, however, defended by powerful institutional groups, mitigated against the radical proletarianization of educational institutions. The very anxiety of Party militants is itself evidence of the degree to which Soviet policy after 1921 was committed to the conciliation of former bourgeois specialists. Lenin was a particular advocate of such a policy, urging that special efforts be made to attract and utilize them in the administration of the Soviet economy, albeit under close political control. Lenin's policies were continued after his death and received strong support from Bukharin and Rykov. A Central Committee resolution of 1925 removed remaining civic disabilities from the specialists, while even Stalin referred to them in laudatory terms in 1927 as the "laboring Soviet intelligentsia." [21]

The bourgeois specialists were rewarded for their cooperation by including their children among those progressive strata who would receive priority in admission to schools. The precise definition of the "progressive strata" who would receive favored treatment shifted in response to political and economic needs, but in 1926 and 1927 the statutes of educational institutions were revised to include children of specialists in the preferred categories.

Other priorities further inhibited radical proletarianization. The various economic commissariats, Gosplan, and above all Vesenkha (the Supreme Council of the National Economy) were all concerned with the training of a stream of specialists with high levels of skill, and resisted policies that might erode academic standards in higher educational institutions. They might advocate the expansion of middle level technical training, but so anxious were they about the decline in academic standards at the university level which accompanied the rise of worker representation that in 1925 Vesenkha requested that the Central Committee permit thousands of engineering students to study abroad, and in 1926 the Central Committee itself ordered a renewed emphasis on academic performance in admissions.

Further, the reliance on private financing of education also conflicted with efforts to increase the enrollment of disadvantaged children. While in 1917 educational expenditures were shared equally between the state budget and local communities, the share of the latter rose to over 70 percent of the total by 1927–1928. The reintroduction of fees for primary education was at first resisted; Krupskaya denounced their introduction as a "vulgar retreat from the Party program" in 1921.[22] But widespread practice stemming from financial necessity received official sanction at the end of 1922 and fees were introduced at all levels of the school system. Certain disadvantaged categories were exempted from payment, but the repeated requests of Narkompros for additional resources for this purpose were refused by higher authorities. Although its critics charged Narkompros with a lack of commitment to the needs of the disadvantaged, the full responsibility did not lie in its hands. Despite the formal commitment of Narkompros to a radical restructuring of educational opportunities, in practice it was obliged to balance the goals of proletarianization against competing economic and social priorities.

Statistical reports published by Narkompros in the late 1920s reveal its own anxiety over the extent to which these financial, political, and cultural constraints had foreclosed a major expansion of educational opportunities and inhibited a radical change in the social composition of educational institutions. Indeed the early 1920s saw a general diminution of educational opportunities. The over-all contraction of the educational network reduced both the numbers of pupils in school at various levels, and the amount of schooling offered. The proportion of rural schools offering only a minimal three years of schooling rose from 30 percent in 1923–1924 to 55 percent in 1925–

1926, while the proportion offering a four-year program dropped from 65 percent to 43 percent and a five-year program from 4.6 percent to 1.1 percent. The urban primary schools, in which a four-year program was the norm before the Revolution of 1917, suffered similar if less extreme setbacks, with the proportion offering five years of instruction falling from 18.7 percent to 8.3 percent.[23]

Rural children were severely disadvantaged by comparison with their urban counterparts. In the larger towns primary education was nearly universal, and the average length of schooling in 1928 was 3.1 years. In rural areas only half the age cohort attended primary schools, for an average of only 2.3 years.[24] The opportunities for secondary education were even more limited in rural areas, despite some expansion of the secondary network in the mid-1920s. While the ratio of secondary to primary pupils was almost 1:2 in the cities, in rural areas it was an infinitesimal 1:30.[25]

The limited access of rural children to anything beyond the primary level is further demonstrated by statistics which reveal that while 50 percent of urban school children were in grades 1 through 3, 30 percent in grades 4 and 5, and 20 percent in grades 6 through 9, the figures for rural children show 87 percent of the total in grades 1 through 3, 12 percent in grades 4 and 5, and 2.5 percent in grades 6 through 9.[26] Some commentators have pointed to the lower level of educational aspirations of peasant families as a partial explanation,[27] but there is some evidence to suggest that popular frustration with the inadequate resources provided for rural education was widespread, and was even expressed by the creation of schools outside the official network.

The government was forced to sanction the creation of these "contract schools," as they were called, but sought to impose conditions on their financing and clientele. Official misgivings about this expression of popular initiative were great. As one author warned:

The need of the peasantry in elementary education is so great, that they, irrespective of financial burdens, over the heads of the authorities, found new schools. We are in danger of letting loose the reins from our hands. The opening of the contract schools is a serious warning to us. The peasantry by opening their schools powerfully accelerate the tempo of the development of education, which seems to be too slow for them, and in this way they are correcting the Soviet system.[28]

Disparities of educational opportunity based on sex were by 1928 much less pronounced, the consequence of pre-Revolutionary tendencies encouraged by Bolshevik policy. The ratio of male to female pupils in urban areas was almost equal at both the primary and secondary levels by 1928, although disparities persisted in rural areas where the proportion of girls was one-third the total enrollment, and the average length of schooling 2.1 years compared to 2.4 years for boys. Women were also continuing their education in significant numbers, comprising 41.9 percent of the students at technicums and 29.3 percent at higher educational institutions.[29]

By the end of the decade, the leadership of Narkompros could enjoy only modest satisfaction with the results of its efforts to expand and democratize the educational system. Indeed, the statistics probably overstate the degree of proletarianization because of the numerous devices that enabled children of bourgeois families to conceal their true social origins. As table 11.1 reveals, the Soviet educational system was still, in 1928, a highly differentiated one. The four-year schools in rural areas served a predominantly peasant clientele, whose opportunities for further education were negligible. The urban seven- and nine-year schools, which continued to serve as the main channels to higher education, were disproportionately composed of children of white-collar families. The statistical materials reflect not only the differential distribution of formal opportunities but disparities of aspiration and achievement reflected in the close connection of drop-out rates and class affiliation. Only one-fourth of the children of working-class background completed their education, and one-third of the peasant children, but nine-tenths of the children of white-collar background.

Substantial disparities also persisted at higher educational institutions, where the social composition of entering classes varied directly with prevailing admissions policies; 25 percent of the student body was classified as workers, 25 percent as peasants, and 50 percent as white-collar workers.[30] The proportion of proletarian students was greatest in industrial-technical faculties and socioeconomic specialties where political affiliations weighed heavily, and they tended to be graduates of *rabfak* programs rather than of the seven- and nine-year schools, while students of peasant origins tended to concentrate in agricultural and pedagogical faculties, and children of white-collar or intelligentsia background gravitated toward the arts. The proportion of both workers *and* employees was rising during the mid- and late-1920s, largely at the expense of the peasant contingent. In the socioeconomic specialties which experienced a large influx of working-class and Party elements the proportion of employees declined.[31]

As late as 1928 a major gap continued to exist between the formal commitment of the regime to a radical redistribution of educational opportunities and the actual social composition of educational insti-

TABLE 11.1   Social composition of educational institutions, by level, RSFSR, 1926.

| Schools | Workers | Farm laborers | Peasants | White-collar employees | Other |
|---|---|---|---|---|---|
| Level I schools (4 years) | 8.4 | 1.7 | 78.9 | 5.5 | 3.5 |
| Seven-year schools | 35.3 | — | 25.8 [a] | 26.5 | 12.4 |
| Level II schools (5–9 years) | 13.6 | — | 30.7 [a] | 34.0 | 21.7 |
| Vocational schools | 28.3 | 1.0 | 32.2 | 27.9 | 10.6 |
| Technical schools | 20.8 | 0.9 | 33.6 | 34.7 | 10.0 |
| Workers' faculties | 53.4 | 3.5 | 35.3 | 5.4 | 2.4 |
| Higher education | 23.7 | 1.6 | 24.7 | 39.3 | 10.7 |
| Social classes in the working population as a whole less family members | 17.0 | — [b] | 64.4 | 12.3 | 6.3 |

Source: *Narodnoe prosveshchenie*, 1928, no. 12, pp. 72ff.

[a] Includes independent professionals, nonworking population, and craftsmen as well as those classified as "other" in *Narodnoe prosveshchenie*.

[b] Precise figures not available.

tutions. Yet the failure to transform the educational system into a major channel of social mobility for children of working-class and peasant origins reflects not so much the shortcomings of Narkompros as its effort to balance a variety of competing claims in educational policy. It succeeded in widening access to existing institutions, but not in radically transforming their role in social selection.

TRANSFORMING CURRICULA AND METHODS:
THE UNITY OF EDUCATION AND LABOR

The dilemmas that confronted educational leaders in altering the social composition of the schools were compounded by the problems of defining their educational goals. The knowledge and skills central to a socialist education were defined as variously as socialism itself. An emphasis on the social and political functions of education distinguished the Russian educational tradition from more individualistic Western orientations, but did not preclude a variety of different approaches. The Narkompros leadership gradually defined its own educational strategy in the course of lengthy struggles against a variety of alternative models.

In conflict with the cultural left, which repudiated the culture of the past as the class-bound superstructure of obsolete social organizations and sought the creation of a uniquely proletarian culture,[32] Lunacharsky and Lenin defended the view that culture had transcendent elements which represented the accumulated wisdom and enlightenment of centuries. As Lenin argued in his famous speech to the Third Komsomol Congress in 1920: ". . . you would make a great mistake if you draw the conclusion that it is possible to become a Communist without mastering the store of human knowledge." [33] Socialist culture, in his view, was the culmination of historical development rather than a totally new creation and the function of formal education was to communicate that "store of human knowledge" in an organized and disciplined fashion. He was critical of those who believed that it was sufficient to learn Communist slogans in order to arrive at socialism, urging less emphasis on political indoctrination and more on acquiring modern scientific and technical knowledge and skills.

Institutional as well as cultural conservatism was defended by Narkompros against radical Marxists, who viewed the schools as inherently elitist and divorced from labor and sought to abolish formal educational institutions altogether. Theorists like V. N. Shulgin and M. V. Krupenina gave formal expression to the instinctive attitude of radical Communists that educational institutions would "wither away" in a future Communist society where the environment itself would exercise an educative role.[34] Narkompros, by contrast, defended the preservation of traditional institutions while altering their curricula and methods to create closer links with the economic and social life of the wider community. At the same time, Narkompros rejected the traditionalist position which viewed the school as essentially academic and deplored the dilution of academic programs for a variety of irrelevant activities.

Pressures of yet another kind came from an alliance of technocratic interests and the economic left. Calling for greater emphasis on vocational training which would harness educational policy to the short term needs of the economy, the economic commissariats and even Vesenkha joined in the clamor for an immediate supply of skilled workers and technicians. It viewed the concern of Narkompros with providing a broad general education to all pupils as entirely misplaced. As Preobrazhensky put it:

Only that part of the national income can be spent on enlightenment which corresponds to the given level of development of socialist production. And that part which is spent must be distributed according to the importance of this or that branch of enlightenment for the whole economy of the country in general. In any case, higher education must be highly diminished in favor of lower; and, in lower education, the general branch must be enormously diminished in favor of what is urgently important for industry and agriculture.[35]

Numerous concessions were made to this position in practice. The creation of Glavprofobr (Glavnyi Komitet professional'no-tekhniche-skogo obrazovaniia) in 1920 to supervise technical and vocational schools was a serious incursion into the educational jurisdiction of Narkompros, while the views of its first chairman, O. Iu. Shmidt, were fundamentally opposed to those of Lunacharsky in the insistence that the educational system respond directly to the immediate economic needs of the new Soviet state. Bowing to necessity, Lunacharsky nevertheless continued to insist on the importance of broad enlightenment and to defend the principle of a general education at the secondary as well as primary level. He attacked the notion that it was an indefensible luxury at a time of crisis.[36] Short-term economic needs, he insisted, had to be balanced against other considerations of equally fundamental importance.

The curriculum that emerged from these struggles was intended to combine general education with socially productive labor and with polytechnical training, two key innovations in Soviet pedagogy designed to break down a class-based division of labor by unifying intellectual and manual work, and to replace the fragmented man of bourgeois society with the universal multicompetent man of Marx's vision. Polytechnicalism—a vaguely defined principle which was the source of endless controversy in subsequent decades—was designed to avoid the twin pitfalls of academic formalism at one extreme and narrow vocationalism at the other. It would prepare men for participation in a modern and changing industrial economy whose future shape was not fully known by equipping them with a broad understanding of modern industrial processes and the principles underlying all science and technology rather than encouraging specialization in one particular field. The Marxian image of the many-sided man alternating in a variety of roles remained the inspiration. The practice, however, came to encompass everything from workshops to laboratories to apprenticeship training, indeed, as one observer remarked, anything short of a lecture or text.[37]

The preoccupation of Narkompros with developing a curriculum which would achieve the elusive "close unity of education and socially productive work" which Lenin and Krupskaya had inscribed in the Party theses of 1918, inspired a wide range of experiments to end the isolation of the schools and encourage the participation of school-children in the economic and social and political affairs of the larger community. It also guided a variety of efforts to develop curricula that would replace the compartmentalized disciplines of traditional education with a synthetic project-oriented approach centering on the theme of labor and moving in concentric circles to an ever-widening appreciation of the complex interrelationships of the natural and social environment. The chaotic consequences of many of these experiments at the local level as well as the popular opposition they evoked, were eloquently described by a rural teacher:

In the beginning when the method of self-help was introduced everything was based on manual labor. We used to mend our desks, to wash the floors and walls. We did everything in order to provide for our needs ourselves . . . Lessons we had none. We were too tired. We had no time for lessons . . . Later the heuristic method was applied, then the active-labor method which may be called the laboratory method and which is closely connected with the method of excursions. After that followed the method of concentration. But we were unable to stop on the "Complex method" . . . The next was the Dalton Plan and everything was in working order, the children worked eagerly. But the peasants intervened and demanded that we should teach "properly" . . . At present . . . I work with all methods.
In other words, I am applying the pluralistic method . . . Children are developing and reason about everything . . . But they read very badly.[38]

By the end of the decade, then, the policies of Narkompros were under attack from a number of different sources for their approach to problems of labor and technical training, as they were for their handling of the question of social selection. At the primary level, in the view of many critics, an excessive and frivolous preoccupation with experimental methods had diverted attention from the teaching of basic skills, while at the secondary level the educational system had failed to create an optimal relationship between learning and production or to accelerate the training of technical specialists vitally needed for industrialization. In still a third area of vital concern to Narkompros—the effort to transform authority relationships within the school as a way of altering attitudes and behavior within the wider society—the dominant orientations of the educational leadership were also coming into increasing conflict with the emerging structure and ethos of the Soviet political system.

From its very origins, Russian Marxist pedagogy had envisioned a socialist educational system as more than a mechanism for altering patterns of social stratification and for inculcating scientific knowledge and technical skills. It was also viewed as a means through which the very character and values of the Russian population would be altered. "Socialism," wrote Krupskaya, "will be possible only when the psychology of people is radically changed. To change it is the task standing before us." [39]

The Tsarist educational system was identified in the minds of the Marxist reformers with an authoritarian form of discipline which destroyed precisely those qualities needed in the future socialist man. Regimentation and harsh discipline and the emphasis on rote learning stifled the energy and creativity of children and made them passive objects. What was required instead was an education that was child-centered, that encouraged activity, creativity, and inner discipline. The libertarian orientation of the new school was to be reflected both in its educational methods, which viewed education as a spontaneous process, the natural unfolding and maturation of the child, and in the democratic organization of the school itself, which was viewed as an embryonic social system in which children would gain the organizational and socializing experiences that would be carried into their dealing with the larger community.

Traditional methods of teaching that emphasized the role of the teacher as the source of knowledge, formal lectures, evaluation of individual achievement through examinations, were all swept away in favor of methods that emphasized the independent activity of the student in meeting flexible collective goals. Observation and discovery were encouraged on excursions and through laboratory methods. The Dalton Plan, which substituted long-term contracts for assignments, was seized upon as a way of permitting children to formulate their own educational goals and of encouraging rational planning and use of time; it was an approach to education congruent with the larger enthusiasm for Taylorism and for the rationalization movement in leading Soviet circles. Even at higher educational institutions efforts were made to replace formal lectures by laboratories and activity-oriented, collective methods of work.

The character of the school as a social system was also altered in support of the new values. The authoritarian discipline of the Tsarist school was replaced by the self-governing community of equals. Partly an effort of the new regime to undermine the authority of such bastions of conservatism as the family and teacher, and partly influenced by a syndicalist image of socialism as a free association of self-regulating communes, it reflected the particular faith of Krupskaya and Lunacharsky that the spontaneity and creativity of the masses were essential elements in the construction of a socialist community.

Here, too, contradictory visions lay just below the surface. In the earliest years of the new regime the influence of Lunacharsky's socialist humanism pervaded the official documents of Narkompros. The preamble of the Education Act of October 16, 1918 offers a classic statement of his views:

The personality shall remain as the highest value in the socialist culture. This personality, however, can develop its inclinations in all possible luxury only in a harmonious society of equals. We, the government, do not forget the right of an individual to his own peculiar development. It is not necessary for us to cut short a personality, to cheat it, to cast it into iron moulds, because the stability of the socialist community is based not on the uniformity of the barracks, not on artificial drill, not on religious and aesthetic deceptions, but on an actual solidarity of interests.[40]

But a very different image of socialist man emerges from the dramatic metaphors of a Trotsky, full of militant imagery of collective discipline, where the hammering and forging of a hardened national character contrasts sharply with the gentler reshaping of a malleable human nature envisioned by Lunacharsky.[41] Because an educational ethos concerned with the free development of personality was not readily reconcilable with the devotion to raising a class-conscious generation of fighters for Communist discipline, the revival of militant leftism in the late 1920s called into question the educational philosophy that guided the entire school system, and portended serious difficulties for Narkompros.

As a consequence of the succession struggles which dominated Soviet political life in the mid-1920s, the diverse orientations of the early post-Revolutionary years had crystallized around two competing economic and political programs. Each aggregated a variety of positions with respect to a broad range of economic, political and social issues. The dominant orientation was expressed in the New Economic Policy. It was defended by Sovnarkom (Council of People's Commissars) and an industrial lobby eager to facilitate the cooperation of bourgeois specialists in rebuilding the national economy and in educational affairs it involved a preoccupation with maintaining an adequate level of academic preparation. A concern for skills and standards mitigated against policies that went too far in undermining objective criteria of achievement. A more militant proletarian-revolutionary impulse hostile to the implications of NEP existed spontaneously at the local level and was taken up by the Party left and the Komsomol in particular, eager to heighten class contradictions, critical of the preservation of the academic features of the educational system, and impatient for more radical proletarianization. In its effort to steer a course which responded to pressures from each of these factions Narkompros had incurred the hostility of both.

## THE CULTURAL REVOLUTION AND ITS IMPACT: 1928-1931

The year 1928 marked a turning point in Soviet educational policy whose proportions have been neglected in conventional treatments. The new political and economic climate created by the attack on the Right Opposition and the inauguration of forced industrialization and agricultural collectivization dramatically altered the environment in which educational policy was shaped. Between 1928 and 1931 both the institutional structure and the ethos of the educational system created by Narkompros was radically transformed. Yet the reorientation which occurred during these years did not represent either a solution to the accumulating problems of the 1920s or the first steps in the direction which educational policy would take in subsequent years. It represented, rather, the secondary effects upon education of a shift to militant leftism shaped by the economic and political considerations of Party factional conflict, a shift which the "great retreat" of the mid-1930s was designed to undo.

The new policy was launched with sudden unexpectedness in the spring of 1928. Just a few months earlier, in December 1927, the Fifteenth Party Congress had dismissed the oppositionist alarm at an impending bourgeois attack on the cultural front, and had called for increased investments in education to meet the growing manpower needs envisioned in the Five Year Plan. Lunacharsky reported with satisfaction that the Party leadership had finally acknowledged the degree to which further economic advances were dependent upon educational and cultural progress.[42] To his added pleasure, pressures for the transfer of higher technical education to the economic com· missariats had been resisted.

Lunacharsky's satisfaction was to be short-lived. The arrest and trial of 55 engineers and technicians on charges of sabotage in the Shakhty affair touched off an assault on the bourgeois specialists, and ultimately a vast ideological campaign against class enemies. Cultural revolution was redefined to eliminate its association with gradualism and progressive enlightenment. The head of the Central Committee Agitprop department now warned that the most dangerous distortion of the Party line in cultural work sprang "from an opportunist, anti-revolutionary conception of cultural revolution as 'peaceful' cultural development . . . irrespective of class war and class contradictions." [43]

Stalin's assault on the Right Opposition appeared to give official sanction to the advocates of more radical proletarianization of educational institutions. It touched off a wave of purges of students and faculty which the Narkompros leadership tried in vain to halt.[44] Campaigns to increase the proletarian purity of higher educational institutions raised the representation of working-class students from 30 percent of the total in 1928–1929 to a high of 58 percent by 1932–1933.[45] Enrollments were massively increased at all levels of the system, although the failure to provide the resources for such expansion brought the entire educational system to a state of virtual collapse.

The new political climate altered the educational function of the schools as well as their social composition. Crash programs became the order of the day, and vocationalization the universal panacea. Higher educational institutions were broken into separate and narrowly-specialized fragments, and the authority of Narkompros was diluted by subordinating them to Vesenkha or to individual economic commissariats. By 1931–1932 just eleven universities remained of the twenty-one in existence in 1924–1925, while seventy new institutions had been formed offering by 1932 some 900 different specializations.[46] At lower levels of the system schools were transformed into workshops, or into mere adjuncts of local enterprises and collective farms. Shulgin's enthusiasm at the prospect of an imminent "withering away" of the schools offered an optimistic rationalization of educational chaos.

Yet the political turbulence and socio-economic upheaval of the times encouraged apocalyptic visions of a socialist utopia. The Third Revolution unleashed an unstable alliance of political militants and cultural visionaries, briefly joining the diverse critics of Narkompros in a common assault. But this wave of cultural radicalism had only a temporary utility; it was fundamentally incompatible with the new society emerging during these years. The cultural revolutionaries were useful accomplices in an assult upon the Narkompros leadership. But the replacement of Lunacharsky in the fall of 1929 by A. Bubnov, a former political commissar of the Red Army who brought to Narkompros the military style of the Civil War period, foreshadowed the ultimate outcome of the Third Revolution, the subordination of educational policy to more direct Party control.

## THE CONSOLIDATION OF THE EDUCATIONAL
## SYSTEM UNDER STALIN

The disintegration of the educational system during the initial phase of industrialization and cultural revolution was a secondary, and to some extent unintended consequence of the forces loosened by shifting political priorities and alliances at the center. With the initial breakthroughs accomplished, the Right Opposition defeated, and Party control over educational and cultural affairs firmly assured, the alliance with cultural radicalism had served its purpose. The Party leadership could now address a whole range of policy issues in substantive terms. Beginning in 1931 a series of Central Committee decrees [47] laid the foundation for the reorganization and stabilization of the educational system along lines which, aside from a brief departure under Khrushchev, have prevailed to this day.

The new orientation differed from that of the 1920s as well as that of the cultural revolution in its approach to the questions of who should be educated, with what skills, in what kind of social setting. Stalin's repudiation of "petty-bourgeois egalitarianism" signaled the end of admissions policies designed to give preferential treatment to children of working class or poor peasant background. The use of objective socioeconomic categories such as social origins as criteria for educational preferment was abandoned in favor of an emphasis on "social worth," a far more flexible criterion. The definition of social merit encouraged the reward of technical expertise as well as political loyalty, and would readily merge with a functionalist rationalization of inequality.

An emphasis on individual achievement was strengthened by the restoration of examinations and grades, and their use as criteria for promotion, indirectly reinforcing the link between advantaged family background and educational opportunity. The practice of compiling statistics on the social origins of students was abandoned by the late 1930s, but they reveal a sharp decline in the proportion of students of working-class background and a rise in the proportion of white

TABLE 11.2 Social composition of students in higher educational institutions, USSR, 1924–1938.

| Class | 1924–25 | 1926–27 | 1927–28 | 1928–29 | 1929–30 | 1930–31 | 1931–32 | 1932–33 | 1933–34 | 1934–35 | 1937–38 |
|---|---|---|---|---|---|---|---|---|---|---|---|
| Workers (%) | 17.8 | 24.2 | 25.4 | 30.3 | 35.2 | 46.4 | 58.0 | 50.3 | 47.9 | 45.0 | 33.9 |
| Peasants (%) | 23.1 | 23.3 | 23.9 | 22.4 | 20.9 | 19.3 | 14.1 | 16.9 | 14.6 | 16.2 | 21.6 |
| Nonmanual (%) | 59.1 | 52.5 | 50.7 | 47.3 | 43.9 | 34.3 | 27.9 | 32.8 | 37.5 | 38.8 | 44.5 |

Source: Nicholas DeWitt, *Education and Professional Employment in the USSR* (Washington, D.C.: National Science Foundation, p. 655).

collar categories. The image of socialism as an egalitarian proletarian democracy was supplanted by another image which equated socialism and meritocracy, albeit in a plebiscitarian framework.

The abandonment of a commitment to equal educational opportunity was also expressed in a more fundamental reorganization of the educational system that abandoned the elusive goal of a unified and uniform educational experience for all children and substituted a system of educational streaming. Two distinct and separate educational channels were created, one permitting a small proportion of students the opportunity of a complete academic education and the other channeling the majority into vocational instructional programs closely tied to industrial enterprises which offered little opportunity for rapid upward mobility. The educational foundation for a division of labor which early educational reformers had tried so hard to undo was recreated in new form.

This process was facilitated by a reorganization and stabilization of the curricula of all educational institutions along lines that differed from the combination of general with polytechnical education in the schools of the 1920s as well as from the extreme vocationalism of 1928–1932. It emphasized the formal and academic content of the programs of the general schools, adding a strong ideological component to the curricula, while transferring vocational functions for which the schools were poorly equipped to special programs closely linked to enterprises. The vision of a genuinely polytechnical education was essentially abandoned.

Finally, the reorientation brought with it a dramatic shift in the values and ethos of the entire educational system. The experimentalism and diversity which had been encouraged by the decentralization of educational administration in the 1920s ended, as the Party took an increasingly active role in shaping the fundamental orientation of the schools, while the emergence of more uniform policies was accelerated at higher levels of the system by the creation of a central State Committee for Higher Education.

The child-centered approach to education came under direct attack from the Central Committee. Its emphasis on environmental determinism was criticized as the quintessence of fatalism, at a time when dramatic departures in economic and social policy required energetic efforts to transform the environment. A preoccupation with natural laws of human and social development was replaced by an unlimited voluntarism.[48] Not maturation but training was henceforth to be the central concern of Soviet educators.

The libertarian ethos of an earlier epoch succumbed to an authoritarianism that stressed the disciplined subordination of hierarchical units rather than the automatic solidarity of collectives. The new ethos and values were elaborated in new textbooks whose images of socialism were dramatically different from those of the 1920s, and were communicated by means of an increasingly formal system of political indoctrination.

But despite the superficial resemblance of the Stalinist educational system to its Tsarist antecedent, the events of 1928–1931 had decisively and irrevocably altered the economic, political and social foundations of Soviet life. The reorientation of educational policy in the mid-1930s represented not a return to the staus quo ante but a new synthesis, a selective adaptation of traditional elements within a radically new context. It built upon the vast expansion of the educational network which had occurred between 1928 and 1932, and the decisive shift of emphasis toward engineering and technical programs. It drew upon the experience of these years in concluding that vocational education required a distinct institutional form, building upon but separated from the general educational network and under the close supervision of the economic ministries. And it elaborated still further the integration of education with economic planning by undertaking the development of manpower planning on a national scale.

The Stalinist amalgam drew upon several elements of the experience of the 1920s as well. It shared with Narkompros a recognition of the fundamental importance of a system of formal general education in communicating basic knowledge and skills to the broadest mass of the population, and the conviction that education was central to both economic development and political integration. It expanded educational access while emphasizing criteria of achievement. Yet it turned to more authoritarian antecedents in rejecting the experimentalism and libertarianism which were so crucial a part of the early revolutionary ethos. In this sense, Stalinism joined a radical transformation of the economic, political and social bases of Soviet society to a system of values which contained powerful traditionalist as well as authoritarian components, giving a very specific character to Soviet patterns of industrialization and modernization.

Stalinism, then, represented a redefinition of the meaning of both socialism and modernity rather than a shift from utopia to development. In their concern for equality of opportunity, a democratic structure of authority, cultural secularism, and effort to develop individual autonomy the educational policies of the 1920s were more congruent with present definitions of modernity than the orientations which emerged under Stalin. By the same token many aspects of Stalinism have been demonstrated to have been "dysfunctional" in recent scholarship both Western and Soviet.[49] The repudiation of earlier approaches to education, as well as to other areas of Soviet life, represented less the triumph of universal developmental laws than the destruction by Stalin of their political and institutional bases.

# Values and Aspirations
of Soviet Youth

## RUTH W. MOULY

# 12

Half the population of the USSR is under thirty; about 45 percent of
the people were born after World War II.[1] Thus, in treating Soviet
youth we are dealing with vast numbers constituting not a minority
but half the people of the world's third most populous country. This
study attempts to portray the values and goals of the under-thirty
population of the Soviet Union, some of whom will soon be running
the huge Soviet economy and bureaucracy, planning the military and
space programs and conducting relations with the rest of the world.
Their outlook on life, their aspirations and the degree to which they
are satisfied or frustrated are matters of concern to everyone interested
in the future of American-Soviet relations.

It is as difficult to generalize about Soviet youth as it is about youth
in any other modern society. Urban youth are different in their life
styles from young persons born and raised on collective farms; there
are great economic and social distinctions between the sons and
daughters of a successful and prosperous manager of a large enterprise and the offspring of one of the unskilled workers in the same
factory. Students in universities and colleges differ in attitudes and
perceptions from young people in the labor force. Even within the
student population there are differences between liberal arts students
and those in the physical sciences and between the political activists
and the rank and file who are indifferent to politics.

### PERSONAL GOALS AND ASPIRATIONS

In spite of the many differences that characterize the youth of the
USSR, there are some qualities, aspirations and values that appear

221

to be very widespread and can be considered typical of this particular generation.[2] One of the most widely shared aspirations of Soviet youth is the desire for material well-being. This is reported by nearly all foreign scholars who visit the Soviet Union and it is attested to by Soviet sources as well. Some of the opinion and attitude studies included in the new sociological research are a valuable source of information regarding the values of youth. A study of Short-Term Aspirations of Young People, involving a poll conducted in Leningrad of more than 2000 people, has been especially revealing, as table 12.1 indicates.

TABLE 12.1   Short-term aspirations of young people.[3]

| Ranking | Aspiration | Number choosing | Percentage of total respondents |
|---------|------------|-----------------|---------------------------------|
| 1 | To get an interesting and enjoyable job | 1,339 | 60.6 |
| 2 | To get a higher education | 1,316 | 59.7 |
| 3 | To visit other countries | 1,269 | 57.5 |
| 4 | To achieve material well-being | 1,209 | 54.9 |
| 5 | To acquire good housing | 1,202 | 54.6 |
| 6 | To raise professional qualifications | 965 | 43.7 |
| 7 | To find true friends | 951 | 43.2 |
| 8 | To raise children to be good human beings | 921 | 41.8 |
| 9 | To find one's true love | 916 | 41.5 |
| 10 | To marry | 705 | 32.0 |
| 11 | To have an automobile | 693 | 31.4 |
| 12 | To get a secondary education | 487 | 22.0 |
| 13 | To work on a construction project | 405 | 18.4 |
| 14 | Other | 148 | 6.7 |

The number of choices was not limited.

The achievement of material well-being was ranked as a major aspiration of 55 percent of the respondents. Furthermore, the three highest ranking choices are related to material welfare. As we will see, the kind of jobs young people aspire to are not only those that are interesting and enjoyable, but also lucrative, and acquiring a higher education is the most important stepping-stone toward the obtaining of such jobs. Traveling abroad requires financial means well beyond those of the average citizen.

The Komsomol distributed a questionnaire a few years ago on the goals of youth. One girl's frank answer—which probably reflected the feelings of many others as well—was that her goal was money. "With money," she declared, "you can have luxury, prosperity, love and happiness." [4] The Soviet press occasionally reveals the consternation of employers who are asked first of all by young job-seekers: how much do you pay? [5]

Newspaper articles also reveal disappointment in finding that sometimes the youth who volunteer to spend a summer (or a longer period) in the fields of Kazakhstan or working at a construction project in Siberia do so for material reasons rather than a selfless desire to participate in the country's progress. An American scholar knew students who frankly expressed this motive: "An acquaintance who had spent a summer working in the Virgin Lands did not mind the hardships he had endured. 'After all,' he said, 'I returned to Moscow with enough money to buy myself a new suit and a phonograph.' Another acquaintance informed me that he had requested the placement committee to assign him to the Far North. He admitted that life would be difficult there, but then he added: 'I will receive double pay. There is nothing to spend our wages on so I hope I have enough money to buy a car when my three year obligation ends.'" [6]

If the young person with extra rubles cannot afford a car, at least he will be able to purchase a few less costly luxuries and can occasionally live it up in expensive restaurants where he will be served by tuxedoed waiters who will ply him with caviar, champagne, and exotic delicacies, and he can dance to the tunes of a brassy jazz band. The high-priced restaurant-nightclubs are very popular and on weekends and holidays there are long queues waiting to be admitted. Many young people do not have money to patronize these places and remain on the outside, looking wistfully in, dreaming of the day when they will be able to afford these pleasures themselves.

A study of the consumer desires of a group of Moscow young people revealed that the most sought-after objects were, in the following order: tape recorder, guitar, motorcycle, movie camera, car, piano or accordion, and still camera.[7] This list does not mention some of the most popular possessions cherished by Soviet youth—Western consumer goods such as mod clothes, phonograph records, and tape recordings of rock music. Many visitors to the Soviet Union, including the author, have had the experience of being pursued by young people who plead with them to sell their shoes, suits, and above all, blue jeans to them.

An American exchange student reports having known a young Russian who made his living by selling Western phonograph records on the black market.[8] The recording of *Jesus Christ, Superstar* has been immensely popular among Soviet youth. A copy of it can bring as much as 100 rubles ($110), the monthly salary of a young worker.[9] A recent observer notes that rock music is *the* great unifier of Soviet youth from all strata of society: "A university student from a prominent foreign-traveling Moscow family is a world apart from a young factory worker in Ryazan . . . let alone the rough youth in the Far North or a Siberian village. The one language that comes closest to speaking to all of them is pop music." [10]

Professor Schwartz tells of meeting a fashionably dressed young man carrying a copy of *Newsweek* in a Moscow subway. He started a conversation with the man and learned that he worked in a factory and had bought his suit and the magazine from foreign tourists. Though he could not read a word of English, he carried the *Newsweek* as a status symbol. Another acquaintance told Dr. Schwartz that he always looked for foreign-made clothes in the shops and if he could not find them, he refused to buy Russian ones.[11] This kind of clothing is very expensive (jeans sell for as much as seventy-five to eighty rubles on the black market and foreign clothing sold legally is also very high priced) and the desire to acquire it is one reason for the striving of young people for good incomes.

There have been several explanations of why Soviet youth are so enthralled by Western products. Many letters in teachers' journals discuss the subject and some of them give the most obvious reason why youngsters clamor for Western clothes: "Because our industry makes no effort to provide them with attractive things of the sort they want." [12] If Soviet clothing manufacturers would provide jeans, fashionable shoes, well-fitting suits, wide ties, and pantsuits for girls, the black market in these items would disappear. Allen Kassof speculates that the fascination with foreign goods may be due to the present provision by the Soviet consumer-goods industry with "enough to whet appetites though not enough to satisfy them. The fact that the desired items are foreign also adds to their lustre. Real need does not seem to be a major factor." [13]

Some observers believe that defying the regime in one's dress, hair style, and musical preferences is one of the few ways that Soviet youth can express its independence and perhaps its hostility and resentment toward parents and toward the regime, both of which generally disapprove of these things. However, too much should not be made of the aping of Western styles in clothes or music as an expression of rebellion. Wearing jeans often has no significance other than snob value. They are worn by sons of the political elite as well as by offspring of Jewish dissidents. A young Russian told an American friend, "Just because we dig Jimi Hendrix [American rock singer] doesn't mean we are any less ready to fight for our country." [14]

It is the urgent desire for material comforts and the appeal of foreign consumer goods, combined with an almost complete lack of revolutionary zeal, which has led the Chinese Communist leaders to debunk the Soviet Union as bourgeois and "soft on capitalism." It was partly to prevent Chinese youth from going the same way as Soviet youth that Mao Tse-tung decided to unleash the Great Proletarian Cultural Revolution.

Another thwarted desire of Soviet youth is their wish to travel abroad. In the Soviet study of short-term aspirations of youth, "to visit other countries" was the third most popular goal of the respondents. A young Soviet student who defected to England while on a cultural exchange mission told a reporter that, of all things Soviet youth wanted, "above all, they long to travel and see the world." [15] Some young people are so eager to go abroad that they try to get into the Institute of International Affairs with the hope of becoming a member of a diplomatic team.[16]

CAREER PREFERENCES AND ATTITUDES TOWARD WORK

Intimately linked to youth's great thirst for more consumer goods is the desire to pursue careers in lucrative professions, and a disdain for lowly, poorly paying jobs. This interest in professional careers is not due solely to material considerations but to a mix of complex motives. Such careers not only make possible a higher material standard of living; they are also considered more creative, interesting, and fulfilling, and they offer greater status and prestige in society.

The preference of overwhelming numbers of youth for jobs that exist in only limited numbers, and their reluctance to take work in jobs where there is a great need for manpower, is a matter of increasing concern to Soviet educators, economic planners, and political leaders. When graduates of the technical institutes in Leningrad were questioned about their future plans it was found that four out of five of those polled wanted to go into research or creative design work. A research sociologist comments aptly regarding this situation: "Everybody, obviously, cannot become a research worker or a creative designer, and many of these young people are in for a big disappointment." [17]

A few years ago high school graduates of the Novosibirsk region were asked to estimate the attractiveness of seventy occupations in many different fields. The results were anything but encouraging for a regime that badly needs workers in the construction and service industries. Over half of the graduates wanted to become doctors, chemists, physicists, or engineers. The ten highest ranking professions were, in order of preference: physicist, engineer, medical scientist, geologist, mathematician, chemist, radio technician, aircraft pilot, chemical engineer, biologist. Careers in agriculture, construction, and service industries were far down on the list.[18] The Soviet reporters commented: "There is nothing wrong with that, but one may ask, who is to grow grain and bake bread, make shoes and cook dinners? . . . There is a contradiction between the fact that communal service jobs are unpopular with the young and that the trading and catering services now need four times as many young workers as agriculture and twice as many as industry." [19]

A letter sent to *Komsomolskaia pravda* by a young worker puts the problem of snobbery toward manual workers in touching human terms:

What brought on this letter was a recent meeting with my schoolteacher. We had not seen one another for twelve years since the time I graduated from the seven-year school. All these years I have kept my feelings of warmth and gratitude for her. And now I was glad to see her. There were the usual questions that people ask at such meetings, "How are you? What are you doing?"

How am I? Just fine. What am I doing? I'm a metal worker. I can feel my teacher's mood become gloomy. "But you had such great ability. You could have become an engineer." After this the conversation flagged. I don't hold it against her at all. But the encounter set me to thinking.

There are children playing in the small square and standing out among them is a group discussing their parents. One little boy with blond hair says proudly, "My father is a commanding officer." Another fellow says, "My daddy is a shop manager in a factory." A little girl pipes up, "My pappa is a pilot." A thin boy about six years old says nothing. I know his father. He works in the grocery store by the Nikitin Gate.

I get up from the bench and walk along the square. Several grandmothers are sitting at a table . . . I hear the following: "My daughter-in-law graduates from the institute this year." Another one says, "My grandson has entered the Moscow Aviation Institute. With luck he will get ahead in the world."

To get ahead in life. It seems to me that nowadays, for some people, this means only one thing—to get a college degree.

. . . I agree that it is a good thing when people take pride in the achievements of their loved ones, when youngsters are proud of their parents and grandmothers of their children and grandchildren. But why does that little boy say nothing, the one whose father works in the grocery store? And why isn't some grandmother quick to say with pride, "My grandson is a truck driver?" Why did the conversation with my teacher become painful for me?

At the end of high school some boys and girls, who have never done any manual work and never really examined their own desires, are motivated by the sole wish "to get ahead in the world" and try at all costs to get into an institute . . .

In many families the parents would not even dream of having their offspring go to work in a factory and wear a worker's overalls. Not under any circumstances! The only place for him is the university. They do not take into account either the abilities or the inclinations of the young people. And if, in spite of everything, their child does not get into college, the parents take it as a tragedy.

A person can find his place in life not only in an office and at a design board, but behind the wheel of a truck and in the cab of a turret crane as well, on the scaffolding of a new building and even at a shoemaker's bench. To get ahead in work, in my view, means primarily to win the respect of the society by the work you do and by your behavior.[20]

*Izvestia* has considered this problem serious enough to discuss it in its columns. In a recent article deploring the low regard in which service occupations are held, the case is given of a girl who became a successful hairdresser but was made to feel that this was not a really respected occupation. She was embarrassed when two of her former classmates saw her doing this work. Eventually she gives up an occupation she enjoyed and performed well and goes to a higher technical school to prepare herself for a more "honorable" profession.[21] A few months later *Izvestia* again raised this issue, pointing out that sociological research shows that most students (80 percent in some places) are far more eager to go to research or design institutes after graduation than they are to enter the productive labor force. They do not feel that they have been prepared for factory conditions. The article indicates that changes are presently being prepared in the educational system to correct this situation.[22] Educational journals contain frequent articles about the need for more vocational guidance in the schools. This has been a badly neglected field in the Soviet Union and may now be coming into its own.

Preference for professional careers is not new in the Soviet Union. It has been accelerating ever since the mid-1930s when, manual workers began to lose their preeminence, overshadowed by managers, engineers, and scientists. In 1956 the members of the editorial board of the Children's Publishing House were asked by an American scholar what they considered the most pressing problem of the new generation. Their reply is equally applicable today: "too many young people were refusing to take routine and relatively low-paying jobs." [23] Khrushchev altered the public school system in an effort to put more emphasis on manual work and discouraged the admission of students to colleges and universities until they had worked for at least two years. But none of these measures really worked because youth (encouraged by their families) naturally are eager to pursue careers that provide a decent livelihood and social status rather than labor that has neither prestige nor good pay, which is the case with most ordinary occupations in the Soviet economy. "The most salient fact brought out by all sociological studies of the attitudes and aspirations of today's Soviet younger generation is that, in the land of 'workers and peasants' very few among the youth aspire to be ordinary workers, much less peasants." [24]

Soviet leaders have been wrestling with the matter of how to instill into Soviet youth the old socialist virtues of love of physical labor and willingness to sacrifice one's personal interests for the common good. But the industrialization process has inexorably produced a reward system that vitiates these ideals. So while young people are indoctrinated in Party youth organizations with the belief that all work is honorable, their families often try to persuade them to "better themselves" by acquiring a "respectable" career and young people can clearly see that material advantages and social esteem go with professional occupations and not with manual labor. Either the regime will have to raise wages for lowlier jobs or find other means of compensating those in manual and service occupations if it is to satisfy the aspirations of its youth.

DESIRE FOR HIGHER EDUCATION

The pursuit of professional careers requires the right kind of educational training. In the study of aspirations of Soviet youth referred to earlier, the desire to obtain an interesting and enjoyable job was given first choice by the largest number of respondents and the goal of a higher education was the second choice of the largest number. Soviet sources indicate that the intense preoccupation of youth with securing higher education is a problem of major proportions. Surveys conducted at different times in five widely scattered areas, regarding the preference of high school graduates for immediately joining the work force versus acquiring a higher education, revealed that 80 percent wish to pursue full-time studies. Only 8 percent want to take a job, and 12 percent wish to combine work and study.[25]

A study of schools in the Sverdlovsk area revealed that the overwhelming majority of students wanted to enter higher educational institutions. In the schools of the region an average of 91 percent of the pupils, out of a total of 2000 upper grade students, intended to pursue higher education. In a few of the schools, 95 to 98 percent indicated that they planned to enter higher educational institutions.[26] In a recent survey of a tenth grade of a school in Moscow with thirty-two students from predominantly working class families, twenty-seven indicated their intention of going on to a university.[27]

In actuality, not more than 35 percent (and often less) of secondary school graduates enter higher educational institutions. This means that the plans of about two-thirds of these graduates remain unrealized. As Soviet writers point out, "This entails certain moral consequences, such as disillusionment, depression, insecurity. Switching from one goal to another is a difficult matter." [28]

The desire for higher education is prevalent among all social classes. Among children of the intelligentsia it is only slightly higher than among workers, peasants and noncollege white-collar families. In all cases it is more than 75 percent.[29]

Between 60 and 80 percent of the students graduating from secondary schools in Soviet cities try to enroll in some institution of higher learning. In the most prestigious universities as many as ten to fifteen applicants compete in tough entrance examinations for each vacancy. Admission to the University of Moscow is the most coveted of all and the most difficult to achieve. The natural science faculty in a typical year accepted only 1900 out of 13,000 applicants. The mechanics-mathematics faculty, the most popular at the University, accepted one out of eight applications.[30] Even in the more ordinary higher education institutions, only one out of three applicants can be accepted. The rest resort to study in a trade school or take a job that does not require higher education. Some wait and take the entrance examinations over again the following year.

There are complaints in the press from time to time that some secondary school graduates refuse to take ordinary employment when they are refused admission to a college or university. The authorities claim that these young people end up as "parasites," *stiliagi* ("mod dressers"), idlers, and even juvenile delinquents.[31] Others believe that the frustration of so many youth with regard to their educational and job aspirations is one of the factors that account for the high rate of alcoholism. Excessive drinking is by no means limited to young people whose desires for higher education have been thwarted—it is a serious problem among all age groups and all occupations—but a recent study suggests that alcoholism as well as delinquency and crime involves a disproportionate percentage of young people.[32]

The great struggle to obtain admission to higher educational institutions is possibly one of the reasons why Soviet students are politically more passive and less likely to carry on demonstrations and protests than students in many other countries. An American professor, probing reasons for lack of activism in the Soviet Union, asked many students why there are no student demonstrations in their country. He was told, "With the fierce competition to get in, is there any wonder that students will think a dozen times before doing anything that might get them expelled?" [33] Fear of political reprisals damaging career prospects is a very real concern of students.

The almost universal desire of Soviet youth to acquire a higher education stems in part from the previous efforts of the regime to encourage higher education, as well as from the need for a degree in order to obtain better paid, more satisfying jobs. From the mid-1930s to the early 1950s the rapidly industrializing economy required specialists with higher education, and the Party and Komsomol did much to stress the need for college-trained personnel and to promote the idea that young people should seek as much education as possible. Income policy under Stalin linked economic rewards to the amount and type of education the individual had attained.[34]

By the time Khrushchev came to power it was obvious that the rapid expansion of secondary school facilities and a shift in the skill requirements of the labor force resulted in many more high school graduates than were needed or could be accommodated in higher educational institutions. He tried to restore the prestige and dignity of manual labor and to discourage the growing elitism of the society. But not enough was done to bring social and financial rewards up to a level where manual jobs would offer attractions comparable with the professions. Some manual occupations are better paid than some professions—highly skilled tool-and-die makers, coal miners, first-class mechanics, for example, may earn more than the average doctor or teacher, but by and large the jobs requiring a college education are still much more desirable from both a status and an economic point of view. "Not surprisingly, both parents and children have balked at the shift in the official line, and the prospects for change in their attitudes do not seem bright. It is patently self-defeating for the Party to demand that the Komsomol alter young people's occupational and educational preferences, while simultaneously continuing distributive policies which helped generate those preferences in the first place." [35]

### ANTIPATHY TOWARD RURAL LIFE

Another problem which haunts the regime with regard to its youth is: How are you going to keep them down on the farm and on the construction projects of the remote northern and eastern areas where the plans call for extensive and continuous development? It is quite apparent that urban young people are extremely reluctant to leave the cities, and those on the farms are busily packing their bags to move to the cities. A survey in the Smolensk region showed that the number of Komsomol members working on state farms had been halved in a five-year period; on collective farms the decline was 58 percent.[36] (The exact five years is not mentioned in the original source.)

The city is the place to be, where there are luxury goods to look at and occasionally buy, there are theaters, restaurants, nightclubs, amusement parks and the excitement and bustle of crowds. By comparison, life in the boondocks is insufferably dull. We have noted that some young people volunteer for jobs in distant and inhospitable areas because the pay is higher, but most have no intention of remaining in these "primitive" places. Some go only so that they can later indulge more fully in the amenities of city life. Others invest a summer in Siberia or Kazakhstan in the hope of avoiding a longer assignment to such a place later on.

College and university students are expected to work after graduation for three years wherever their services are most needed, as a repayment to society for the free education that the student has received. Usually this involves employment in a remote and underdeveloped area where it is difficult to attract voluntary labor. American observers frequently report that their acquaintances in higher educational institutions were deeply worried about where they might be sent, and used considerable ingenuity in trying to avoid assignments in undesirable locations. Some evade their assignments by marrying a person who already has a job in a large city with permission to reside there. Soviet law provides that husbands and wives must be assigned to the same area. After the partner has found himself (or herself) a job in the city, a divorce often takes place. Others claim that they have a physical disability or that some member of their family is dependent on their physical presence. A common method is to cultivate contacts with influential persons and organizations who can put pressure on the labor distribution committee to assign one to a job in a large city.[37]

Many students either fail to appear at their designated jobs or desert their work assignments before the three-year term expires. Such problems have been frequently alluded to in the Soviet press.[38] An article in *Pravda* pointed out that in one year "only half of the teachers assigned to the Tadzhikistan schools by the Russian Republic universities went to these schools . . . Almost as many specialists as are sent to Kazakhstan leave that republic each year." [39] The Chairman of the Central Council of Trade Unions stated that "5000 doctors were assigned to permanent posts in rural areas . . . but about the same number left the rural social institutions. Therefore, many rural medical institutions do not have doctors." [40] A Moscow youth publication reported that in one year 30 percent of the graduating class of Yerevan State University and 60 percent of the graduates of the Yerevan Institute of Foreign Languages did not accept their assigned jobs.[41] Although the Komsomol encourages young people to remain and work in the countryside, the Komsomol secretary of the Moscow region indicated that only one out of the hundreds of youth from Moscow who had gone to work in the Virgin Lands had decided to stay there.[42] Out of 33,000 young men and women selected to work on farms in one year, only 1000 went through with their assignments.[43]

Scarcity of attractive consumer goods and lack of varied, lively, and interesting activities in the rural areas are important reasons why many youth do not want to remain on the farms. Youth are also leaving the villages in order to further their education, so they too can enter the race for prestigious and lucrative jobs. It is estimated that 75 percent of rural youth from the Orel and Kurgan regions want to leave the villages for cities in order to continue their education. Only 8 percent of pupils in the Sverdlovsk region planned to work in agriculture. This is far below the manpower requirements of collective and state farms.[44]

The leaders admit that they have not been able to do much about the situation. According to a Soviet authority, "The question of directing school graduates into agricultural production has not been solved yet. Last year 7,680 people finished rural middle schools in our region, but only 1,250 of them remained to work on the kolkhozes and sovkhozes." [45] The following year things were still bad. Not one of the 127 pupils who graduated in a particular district came to work on a collective or state farm even though there was a serious shortage of labor.[46]

## POLITICAL AND IDEOLOGICAL VIEWS

Nearly all observers of the Soviet scene comment on the lack of interest in politics and ideology among the present generation of Soviet youth. Dr. Taubman, who lived in a dormitory at Moscow University where he was a graduate student in the Juridical Faculty, was asked by some students what he was studying in the United States. When he told them that Communist ideology was one of his subjects, "They were aghast," and asked, "Why do you bother? We spend our time trying to avoid it." He says, "Many Russians made clear to me their contempt for Party history as an academic subject." [47]

Articles in the Soviet press point out that students attend lectures on the history of the Communist party, Marxism-Leninism, and on political economy only in order to be counted present. A few students, sometimes only one, take part in the discussion, not out of interest but on a cramming mission for the whole group. These conditions are obvious in the Minsk Medical Institute where the students in such courses pay no attention to the instructors with their lectures on "The Moral Code of the Builders of Communism." [48] Required courses on Party history and ideology have had the highest rate of absenteeism of any courses. A regional Komsomol newspaper, commenting on the situation in a local institute, noted that more than half of the first-year students are often absent from lectures on the history of the Communist party.[49]

If interest in ideological matters exists anywhere (except, of course, in Party circles) one would expect it among college students. But the most common attitude is a passive indifference on the part of the majority of the students. There are a few political activists, enthusiastic Komsomol leaders (though not all Komsomol leaders are really dedicated; some use leadership in the movement to further their careers) and at the other end of the spectrum there are a few rebels. Fainsod divided the latter into what he called "explorers" whose intellectual curiosity leads them into forbidden ideological paths; "westerners" who look for stimulation to bourgeois manners and morals, and the "inner emigrés" who retreat into a private mental world of their own.[50]

The Soviet press complains about the "nihilism," "skepticism," and "cynicism" of student youth, but much less often does one see reports about active student dissent. Students do not oppear to be an important element in the "Democratic Movement," composed of a group of Soviet citizens who are critical of various aspects of the system, especially the lack of meaningful civil liberties. Peter Reddaway's book, *Uncensored Russia,* indicates that one-half of the Democratic Movement's members are in academic positions; one-fourth are writers, artists or actors; one in eight is an engineer or technician; one in ten is in publishing, teaching, medicine, or law; one in twenty is a worker, and one in twenty is a student.[51]

Hedrick Smith of the *New York Times* says of Soviet students: "Cynicism there is. But rebellion, no. By world standards, Soviet youth is abnormally quiescent."[52] There are numerous reasons for this lack of active dissent on the part of students. They would not have been admitted to prestigious institutions, such as Moscow University, in the first place if there were any indications of lack of loyalty in their backgrounds. Soviet students realize that defense of dissenters or expression of unorthodox views of their own could result in expulsion and that this would endanger their whole future careers. If you are put out of one university you cannot get into another. As a Russian explained to Smith, "If someone loves biology or physics or history, he cannot take the risk of being thrown out of a university for any reason, because that means he is throwing away a lifetime. No wonder our students are conformists . . ."[53]

It should be noted that while rare, dissent is not nonexistent among student youth. The *Chronicle* of the Democratic Movement provides particulars from time to time about young people, including students, who have been arrested and subjected to various punishments for their political activities. Taubman reports that there was a protest meeting at the Philological Faculty of Moscow University regarding the trial of Sinyavsky and Daniel, and that those who took part were severely disciplined. In meetings which he attended he heard no one speak out against the verdict and very few students wanted to discuss the subject, even in private, though he was told by friends that hardly anyone at the university approved of the verdict. Many students read samizdat works but Taubman knew of none who belonged to any underground group.[54]

While students are turned off by stereotyped slogans and worn-out shibboleths from Party propagandists, they are basically loyal to the system. "I met no one at MGU (Moscow State University) who was losing sleep over the world revolution, the coming of 'full Communism' or the withering away of the state," says Taubman, "yet almost every student I met at MGU praised Soviet progress, which they spelled out as the industrial might, the achievements in space, free education and medical care, low-cost housing and transportation. They attributed that progress to the country's socialist system.[55] The same general impression is reported by other commentators. One recent observer says, "For all their grumbling, these students were still far from meeting the description of 'nihilists.' In fact, whenever I posed an alternative to the Soviet system, I could find none ready to reject it in favor of capitalism or anarchism or any other system." [56] The remark of one student seems typical of the views of many of his generation: "The great bulk of our young people respect the basic goals set by the Party. True, they are becoming more critical, but it is not in the sense of replacing the social system. They want to renovate and refresh it. They want an end to intellectual stagnation." [57]

Students reject tiresome and dogmatic lectures on Party history but they welcome discussions that permit lively give and take, and these interchanges are becoming more frequent, at least in Moscow and Leningrad. The formal classroom courses in Marxist ideology are still anathema, but there are many other lectures and discussions provided for students in which timely and controversial subjects are taken up. In the past when a Party official gave a lecture, no one dared to question anything he said, but in recent years if a Party speaker makes unfounded statements or repeats hackneyed slogans, students heckle, argue, and give him a generally bad time.

Several scholars who have spent considerable time at Moscow University report that while any organized political opposition is absolutely taboo, there is some freedom of inquiry and even of verbal dissent. The authorities now permit students to question subjects that a few years ago were considered sacrosanct. Students say, "We are now allowed to question and even to differ on the official Party line without being punished." [58] Taubman gives accounts of many meetings he attended at which students asked frank and sometimes embarrassing questions and did not seem in the least cowed by the presence of Party leaders. The Party today, he says, "does not equate all ideological nonconformity with criminal delinquency." [59]

In spite of this significant gain in freedom of expression, there are still many aspects of the system that are deeply resented. Students want to be left alone in their personal lives and resist pressures on them to volunteer for work projects—for a Sunday a month or for the whole summer. They do not want their private habits pried into and criticized at Komsomol meetings.

Many youth do not feel that the Party gives them the truth, and believe it often keeps important information from them altogether.

They are disgusted with doctored and phony explanations of failures and shortcomings in Party programs. They look to non-Soviet sources for answers in these cases, but they are stymied by the paucity of materials available from the West. There is enormous interest in other countries, especially the United States. One of the most popular journals among college youth is *Inostrannia literatura* ("Foreign Literature") which carries translations of certain Western authors. But American books and journals are unavailable except for those approved by the authorities and those which tourists bring into the country and leave behind. Nearly all Soviet students (and professors) have a keen desire to read more American magazines and newspapers, especially the much-prized *New York Times*.[60] They greatly envy Western students who can read whatever they wish. Russian students listen frequently and with much interest to Western radio broadcasts, especially the BBC and the Voice of America. They consider these broadcasts valuable sources of information either omitted or distorted in the Soviet media.

The cynical and critical attitudes of many college students is no more typical of all Soviet youth than are the attitudes of college students reflective of youth in general elsewhere. Outside the capital and the large universities, simple, often unquestioning patriotism is still common among many youth.[61]

YOUTH—PAST AND PRESENT: CONTINUITY AND CHANGE

Every young generation in a dynamic and rapidly changing society has had different life experiences than its elders and is thus bound to have differing views and attitudes. The Soviet Union, while it was poor and backward, struggling for survival, for industrial development and international prominence, made different demands on its citizens than the USSR of the late fifties, the sixties and the seventies, which has largely achieved its major goals. The years of struggle called for sacrifices, a high degree of patriotic fervor, the deferring of material comforts, a heroic figure to idolize and obey.

With no urgent need today to defer present pleasures, the great hero debunked, the homeland now one of the great world powers, the contemporary generation quite naturally has more concern for personal fulfillment than for massive social crusades. The goals and traits of Soviet youth discussed above—desire for material well-being, for higher education, for professional careers, preference for urban life, and demands for greater freedom—are probably inevitable concomitants of the direction in which Soviet society has been moving.

The characteristics of youth which we have explored, however, do not represent a sharp break in the value system of the regime. We have noted that the youth are basically loyal to the system and while they do not flaunt their patriotism, it is a deeply felt sentiment (except perhaps in some of the national minority areas—a subject in itself). Today's youth are more skeptical, pragmatic, and materialistic than their parents and grandparents, but in most vital respects they are the products of their parents' upbringing. Parents have shaped the most important values of their children. Over and over, for example, one reads about how mothers and fathers instill in their children a dread of manual labor, encourage them to study hard so they will be admitted to a good college or university, support them financially and morally if they are not admitted, and perpetuate the belief that the good life lies in the choice of a respected and well-paid profession.

In terms of the most cherished aspirations of youth there is a continuity with the older generation. Children may consider their parents old-fashioned fuddy-duddies or berate them for having had blind faith in Stalin, and parents may disapprove of jeans, long hair, and rock music. But these are minor disagreements compared with the shared values of the generations—love of country, commitment to socialism, and ambition to rise in the socioeconomic scale.

While the young generation does not question in general the socialist aspects of the system and would undoubtedly defend their country, they are still a far cry from the concept of the "New Soviet Man" who was supposed to emerge as a product of a socialist environment, an educational system that would instill the proper moral values, and media that would carry the message into every home. The ideal socialist youth was supposed to be willing to sacrifice his personal desires to the needs of the community, to care more about fulfilling the goals of the Party than realizing private ambitions, to be ideologically fervent, to regard hard physical labor as ennobling and to be eager to work wherever the Party needed him—and to do all these things in a comradely spirit with zest and enthusiasm. The third generation brought up under the Soviet system has few, if any, of these traits. There is no "New Soviet Man." The hardy young construction workers in Magnitogorsk and Dnepropetrovsk during the First and Second Five Year Plans came much closer to the image of the model Soviet man than the youth of today, hankering after Western gadgets and clothes, whose fondest dream is to own a private car and who have nothing but disdain for physical labor. The Soviets' own sociological studies have indicated that Soviet youth is lacking in nearly all the qualities that Soviet society was supposed to produce, and that they share many of the same characteristics and aspirations as their counterparts in the West. Thus, in perhaps the most fundamental aspect of all—the remolding of human character—the Soviet system has failed. It could hardly have done otherwise. An economic system putting its highest priorities on military and industrial power, rewarding engineers, physicists, industrial managers, and army generals with high social status and high incomes while relegating unskilled workers and peasants to the bottom of the heap could not produce a generation of selfless young zealots.

It seems quite clear that the present generation is going to accelerate the drive for prosperity and some degree of personal fulfillment in the previously Spartan-like Soviet society. The day of inordinate sacrifices for a distant goal is long past. Today's youth want to live for today and their offspring will imbibe to an even greater degree the values typical of a consumer-dominated economy and a more relaxed social environment. Socialism in the formal sense of public ownership of the means of production will continue to be the dominant feature of the economy, but the loftier dreams of the "Socialist fathers" about the transformation of human nature, have become less and less a reality as Soviet society has increased in power and wealth and its class distinctions have multiplied.

# Modernization, Generations, and the Uzbek Soviet Intelligentsia

DONALD S. CARLISLE

Communist rule in what was once Russian Turkestan and is now known as Soviet Central Asia offers the student of modernization abundant materials for the study of political development. This essay focuses on the Uzbek SSR, the leading republic of Soviet Central Asia. I will seek to probe the process of politically directed modernization in Uzbekistan, with special attention to the role of the Communist party, changing generations, and the emergence of an Uzbek Soviet intelligentsia. This rapid and telescoped transformation went into high gear during the 1930s, and the task was pursued simultaneously with the Communist regime's effort to eradicate "bourgeois nationalism" and to see that new locally-oriented primary loyalties did not emerge. Moscow imposed industrial secular patterns on a traditional Moslem society and unleashed a process of traumatic change without fully mobilizing Uzbek, Tadzhik, Kirghiz, or Turkmen nationalism; quite the contrary, for the independent nation-state was bypassed as the primary integrating framework.

It is true that only after 1925, when the Soviet regime subdivided Turkestan into several republics, did the Central Asian peoples find themselves in separate units formally defined and delimited by ethnic principles. Consequently, only under Soviet rule were these peoples provided with the territorial framework for national identity. But the Soviet leadership never hesitated in its opposition to "bourgeois nationalism." Instead it demanded identification with broader goals and symbols that transcended nationality as the primary loyalty and the nation-state as an independent unit: "Soviet patriotism" was projected as a more advanced allegiance and the multinational Soviet State was to be the integrating unit within which modernization would take place. Thus a series of key questions confront us: How did the Soviet regime accomplish the transformation while dispensing with Uzbek nationalism? More specifically one might ask: How did the Communist regime simultaneously master traditional society, contain the urge for independent statehood, and yet elicit the support and mobilize the talent necessary for a profound social and economic transformation?

In the following pages I attempt to sketch some partial answers to these questions. I emphasize two major forces that conditioned and promoted Soviet success in Uzbekistan: (1) the Communist party as the political agent for directed modernization, with particular emphasis on its changing internal composition; and (2) the Uzbek intelligentsia, with a focus on the issue of generational change. Special attention is given to the creation of a partially native, Soviet-oriented, technical intelligentsia, its recruitment into the Party, and its accelerated mobility after the 1937–1938 purge. The basic contention is that a major key to Communist success in mastering modernization can be found in the conjunction of these two factors: (1) the political victory by 1929 within the Uzbek Communist party of Moscow-oriented native Communists, and, subsequently, (2) the post-1938 emergence of a new local, secular intelligentsia with a vested interest in modern industrial patterns imposed "from above." By 1938 Stalin had destroyed the native political leadership that had ruled in the Uzbek SSR since 1925, and brought to power a new native generation and new Russian cadres. The Uzbek native elite found its interests, attitudes, and future success more closely linked to Moscow than to traditional Moslem society. This new social stratum that emerged in the course of industrialization and collectivization provided an important part of the technical talent and political cadres necessary to staff the rapidly multiplying posts in the emergent society. By providing the ambitious and upwardly mobile Uzbeks with entry to the technical age, the Soviet regime both created and then manipulated the quasi-technical elite's predisposition to identify with those who had sponsored its mobility and who commanded the avenues to power. The crucial phase in the conjunction referred to took place in the late 1930s and early 1940s. For after the "cleansing" of the Party by the Purge and Terror, the new Uzbek Soviet intelligentsia, as well as some non-elite strata, were recruited into Party ranks.

In his classic study of Smolensk, Professor Fainsod drew attention to a process similar to the one highlighted here, one that helped explain Bolshevik success. He underlined the "capacity of the regime to manipulate and discipline the new social forces which its grandiose experiment in social engineering released." [1] Fainsod stressed the "Creation of a New Class of Beneficiaries," in the course of which "a formidable combination of vested interests had become involved in one way or another in the regime's survival," and he observed:

Industrialization and collectivization exacted a high price in suffering and deprivation from the mass of the population. But it is sometimes forgotten that the accent on growth in the Five Year Plans also spelled expanding vistas for many members of the younger generation and fresh opportunities for those who grasped them. The rush of young people to the universities and technical institutes finds graphic exemplification in the Smolensk Archive, and the same processes were at work on an all-Soviet scale. Industrialization unleashed an almost insatiable demand for factory managers, engineers, technicians, foremen, and skilled workers. On a smaller scale, collectivization inspired a similar need for managers and skilled specialists to serve the machine—tractor stations, state farms, and kolkhozes. Those who qualified themselves to discharge the new managerial and technical tasks were appropriately rewarded; industrialization and collectivization created a whole new class of beneficiaries of the regime's largesse. Essential to the regime, they nevertheless remained dependent on it for their privileges and perquisites.[2]

The Central Asia experience confirms the fact that indeed "the same processes were at work on an all-Soviet scale." But creating a new Soviet intelligentsia in Tashkent, Frunze, or Ashkhabad exposed a political dimension and imposed special difficulties not present in Moscow, Leningrad, or even Smolensk: the nationality or ethnic issue compounded the technical problems of educating workers and peasants and promoting them to new responsibilities. The following key question loomed over the Central Asian modernization process: would the emergent technical intelligentsia and leading political cadres be truly "native," composed of Uzbek, Tadzhik, Kazakh, Turkmen, and Kirghiz personnel, or would the new Soviet elite consist mainly of Russians or Ukrainians recruited from the local Slav population or imported from European Russia? The answer to this question not only provides insight into the past character of modernization, but also provides some perspective on the present situation and perhaps clues to the future course of the nationality question in Uzbekistan.

## BOLSHEVIK RULE AND NATIVE LEADERS: CHANGING GENERATIONS

The task of mobilizing local support and creating reliable organizations under backward Uzbek conditions produced gigantic problems for the Bolsheviks. These problems persisted after the Revolution, during the NEP, and in a somewhat transformed guise, throughout the era of the Five Year Plans. A key issue under the Leninist dispensation has always been that of leadership and the quality of political cadres. Where then was Moscow to find reliable and qualified individuals to direct the Uzbek Party and state? It is possible to identify three active or operative leadership circles to which Moscow could turn in the post-Revolutionary period in order to give it the necessary cadres and a support base in the local milieu. In addition, there was another yet still potential source of cadres that would emerge only in the future. These separate leadership pools can be distinguished from one another on ethnic grounds, by their assumed relative degrees of loyalty to the Soviet regime, and by their susceptibility to Russian chauvinism or local nationalism. First, of course, there was the small but strategically placed local Russian population, supplemented by other indigenous or imported "Europeans" raised to positions of command and responsibility. However, earlier experience, especially that of the Tashkent soviet during the Revolution and Civil War, provided vivid evidence of the native population's resistance to such Russian domination. The thrust of NEP policy with its effort to root the regime in the local milieu eliminated the possibility of sole reliance on this Russian personnel pool.

Moscow had few illusions about the traditional Moslem elite, that is, the mullahs and bais, who were the least reliable and yet the strongest of the local sources of leadership and close linkage with the native masses. Vivid memories of the *Basmachi,* the anti-Soviet, native partisan movement of the Civil War years, reinforced the Bolshevik bias against the traditional social order. But if the active support of the traditional leaders could not be elicited their tolerance and acquiescence were required. A few did win Communist approval and rose to important positions within the new Soviet order. The more backward the region and the closer the particular organization to the masses, the more tolerant were the Bolsheviks during the NEP of those native leaders contaminated by the old ways. After 1925 when the important land-water reforms were launched in the Uzbek

SSR, the more progressive of the clergy, the so-called "Red mullahs," were drawn into the campaign to propagate a liberal and even radical interpretation of the Koran in support of Soviet policy.

Stability and native acceptance of the Soviet regime was a paramount concern during the 1920s. Consequently, Moscow avoided both of the extremes I have discussed in its search for an adequate local leadership attuned to the times. It turned instead to a third leadership source with a heavier native complexion than the first group and a stronger nationalist and secular orientation than the second. Reference is to the native national intelligentsia rooted in the pre-Revolutionary Turkestan *dzhadidist* ("new method" or reform) movement that had sought to update and modernize Islam. Many *dzhadids* had emigrated, been killed, or been compromised by participation in anti-Soviet organizations during the Civil War. Those who remained or who had joined the Bolshevik cause were hungry for power and for some form of modernization and the opportunity to serve their people. Some from the more radical wing of the dzhadidist movement had allied themselves with the Bolsheviks in 1919–1920. Moscow's sponsorship of the *Musbyuro* (Moslem Bureau) at that time and the Eastern orientation of the Comintern had drawn these radical dzhadidists to the Soviet cause. But the Moslem national intelligentsia was a weak, thin stratum; its roots did not reach deeply into native soil, nor had its reformist program struck a responsive chord among the Moslem masses of Turkestan who remained under the influence of the traditional leaders. Experience indicated to the Bolsheviks that this young radical wing of the intelligentsia could be manipulated and even trusted to implement a reform policy that, while serving Moscow's interest, also overlapped with its own modernizing aspirations. The traditional Moslem elite had earlier rejected the secular dzhadidists, and the latter found themselves in an insoluble dilemma: their modernizing design was either rejected or ignored by those they sought to serve and to whom they were related by blood, language, and culture, while their aims were supported by an alien power with whom they shared none of these deep-seated emotional ties. This disturbing division within the Moslem elite provided Moscow during the 1920s with the opportunity to court the native modernizers while circumscribing their nationalist tendencies. Thus, by playing on the wounds within the native community, the Bolsheviks could turn the alliance with the local nationalists into an instrument for acquiring and sustaining their indirect rule. The stakes were high but the Communists held many trumps, and, if the cards were played shrewdly and with restraint, the outcome seemed secure. The sympathetic pro-Soviet natives and collaborationists could be used as a shield from and as a transmission belt to the masses, while Russians would be placed in strategic positions so as to direct and check on the "national Communists." Consequently, Moscow could avoid blundering into the trap that undermined tsarism among the minorities, reliance on traditional imperial-colonial patterns, while not actually delivering on Lenin's initial promise of full national self-determination and independent statehood.

Lastly among political generations was the group referred to previously as only a *potential* source of leadership; these were the amorphous Uzbek "toiling" native strata, to whom the Bolsheviks claimed to be ideologically committed. I refer here to the transitional natives or "newcomers" to city and factory: those marginal men and women who were former artisans or semi-peasants, orphans, the uprooted of the countryside, the newly liberated Moslem women, and the unemployed and unskilled of the cities. While this group was unlikely during the NEP to produce leading trustworthy and trained personnel, it was to these Uzbeks that Moscow and the radical native Communists looked for the new generation of Soviet man. It was on them that the main long-turn gamble was to be made for successors to the suspect native "bourgeois" intelligentsia. While such cadres were not as numerous or reliable in the 1920s as the regime would have liked, their ranks would be augmented, especially after 1928, when the process of drastic change unleashed by industrialization and collectivization uprooted the traditional Moslem order and produced many more "atomized" native recruits. Those who did appear on the political scene earlier were taken under the wings of the Party and were prepared for the time when they would rise swiftly to hold the multiplying positions created by the Five Year Plans and to fill the yawning gaps subsequently created by the 1937–1938 Purge.

THE PURGE AND THE "CLASS OF '38": UZBEK STALINISTS

Throughout the 1920s and most of the 1930s, Moscow depended on Uzbek Communists who had their roots in the dzhadidist movement, educated in the pre-Revolutionary period, and some of whom had exhibited Pan-Turkic or Pan-Islamic tendencies. This first generation of native Uzbek Communists was best illustrated by Faizulla Khodzhaev, Chairman of the Uzbek *Sovnarkom*, and his rival Akmal Ikramov, First Secretary of the Uzbek Communist party. Notwithstanding their political origins and early experience, they appeared politically reliable and responsive to Moscow's directives throughout this period.

Faizulla Khodzhaev was born in 1896, the son of one of Bukhara's wealthiest merchants.[3] As was customary, he studied in a Moslem *maktab* and his education also included two years' special study of the Koran in a Bukharan *medresse*. In 1907 he journeyed with his father to Moscow where he apparently remained for five years. His father died in 1912 and Faizulla soon returned to Bukhara. There he became associated with the dzhadidist cause and was instrumental in the founding of the "Young Bukharans," the radical wing of the reformist movement. After a futile effort in 1917 to force the Bukharan Emir to transform and liberalize his regime, Faizulla and his associates fled Bukhara for Tashkent.

Here they began the practice of calling on the Russians to supplement their meager strength, a process that eventually was to result in virtual dependence on Moscow. In September 1920 with the aid of the Red Army, the Young Bukharans overthrew the Emir and Faizulla Khodzhaev became head of the government of the quasi-independent new Bukharan state. In 1924–1925, when Russian Turkestan under Soviet auspices was subdivided into a number of republics, Faizulla was elevated to the post of Chairman of the Council of Peoples' Commissars (*Sovnarkom*) of the Uzbek Union Republic, a position he was to hold until his arrest in 1937.

Akmal Ikramov was born in 1898 at Tashkent, the son of a Moslem religious teacher. While at first he was educated in traditional Moslem fashion, he apparently became associated with the dzhadidist movement. Ikramov turned to teaching and sought to acquire the necessary credentials as a Moslem intellectual by trying his hand at poetry. He entered the Communist party in February 1918 at a time when the local Soviet regime temporarily tolerated an attempt to fuse Islam and Communism. In 1920 he served as a Party Secretary in Ferghana and was soon promoted to a more important Party post at Tashkent. In 1922 he left Turkestan for Moscow where he studied for two years. While apparently loyal to Bolshevism, he must have taken an unorthodox position at the 1923 conference called to condemn Sultan Galiev, for Stalin himself responded to Ikramov's charges:

Comrade Khodzhanov spoke well, in my opinion, and Comrade Ikramov also did not speak badly. But I must mention a point in the speeches of these comrades which gives food for thought. They both said that there is no difference between present-day Turkestan and tsarist Turkestan, that only the signboard has been changed, that Turkestan has remained as it was under the tsar. Comrades, if this is not a slip, if this is a considered speech and was said deliberately, it must be said that the Basmachi are right and we are wrong. If Turkestan is really a colony, as it was under tsarism, then the Basmachi are right, and it is not we who should be trying Sultan-Galiev, but Sultan-Galiev who should be trying us for tolerating the existence of a colony under the Soviet government. If this is so, I fail to understand why you have not gone over to the Basmachi yourselves. Evidently, Comrades Khodzhanov and Ikramov have not thought over this passage in their speeches, for they cannot help knowing that present-day Turkestan radically differs from tsarist Turkestan . . .

I take upon myself certain of the charges brought by Comrade Ikramov against the work of the Central Committee to the effect that we are not always attentive and did not always succeed in raising in time the practical questions dictated by the situation in the Eastern Republics and regions . . .[4]

In 1925, after returning to Uzbekistan, Ikramov became a Secretary of the Uzbek Central Committee. By late 1929 he had become Uzbek First Secretary as well as a candidate member of the All-Union Central Committee of the Communist Party. In 1934 he was chosen a full member of the Central Committee, a position allotted to only seventy-one others. This was however a debatable honor, given the subsequent fate of the 1934 Central Committee, for of the 139 members and candidates of that body, 98 were arrested and shot (mostly in 1937–1938).

The summer and early fall of 1937 was the turning point in the careers of Khodzhaev and Ikramov. During the Seventh Kurultai (Congress) of the Uzbek Party in June 1937, a sudden and vicious attack was launched against Faizulla Khodzhaev. At the conclusion of the Congress he was not elected to any leading Party bodies, and soon afterwards he was stripped of his governmental posts as well.[5] He disappeared from the political scene except to make a brief appearance in the dock and to give an abject confession along with Bukharin, Rykov, and the others at the March 1938 Moscow show trial.[6] One cannot be sure about Ikramov's role in the attack on Khodzhaev at the Seventh Party Congress in 1937; he did emerge from the Congress still a viable political figure. However the attacks, removals, and general hysteria gathered momentum during the summer of 1937. In September 1937 Ikramov too was removed and arrested on the personal order of Stalin. Like Khodzhaev, Ikramov was a defendant at the March 1938 trial and was sentenced to death.[7] In 1937–1938 not only Khodzhaev and Ikramov but virtually all their associates were eliminated. Apparently, in Stalin's eyes, they were indeed compromised by their origins and their early political experience, as well as by the false sense of security he believed followed from too long a tenure in office. The extent of the destruction of this political generation is reflected in the following figures on the turnover in membership of the Uzbek Central Committee: only 46 percent of that body chosen in June 1937, before the full impact of the Purge, were new, but of the 1938 Central Committee 94 percent were elected for the first time.[8]

The key figures in the post-Purge leadership were Usman Yusupov, the First Secretary of the Uzbek Party, and Abduzhabar Abdurakhmanov, the Chairman of the *Sovnarkom*. They represented the new generation of Uzbek Soviet man and their rise marked a distinct break with the dzhadidist generation. They were members of "the class of '38" so to speak—prototypes or models of the Uzbek Stalinist. In 1938 Yusupov was thirty-eight and Abdurakhmanov only thirty-one years of age.

Yusupov was born in 1900 in the Ferghana valley, the main cotton-producing region of Turkestan and later Uzbekistan. The son of a peasant and from a large family, he early took up the life of a wandering poor peasant and sharecropper. He was later to work in a cotton-cleaning factory and it was not until 1926 that he entered the Communist party. In 1927 Yusupov was elevated to the important post of a Secretary in the Tashkent Party organization. In 1929 he suddenly reached the political heights, for he was then appointed Third Secretary of the Uzbek Party, serving under, and perhaps even posing a threat to, Ikramov. In 1931 Yusupov was relieved of this key post, and "kicked upstairs," probably with an assist from Ikramov, to the largely formal position of head of the Central Asian Trade Union organization. In 1934 he was sent to Moscow for studies in Marxism-Leninism, thus undertaking his first formal education. Returning to Uzbekistan late in 1936, Yusupov was chosen as Uzbek First Secretary in October 1937 after Ikramov's fall.[9] Abdurakhmanov represents, both chronologically and politically, a clearer case of a new man of a new generation. Born in 1907 at Tashkent, he quite early began factory employment, and then entered the Party in 1928. He left Uzbekistan and studied at the Ivanov Industrial Institute between 1935 and 1938.[10] In the latter year in the wake of the worst of the Purge and back in the Uzbek SSR, he became Secretary of the Bukhara *obkom*. In July 1938 he was appointed Chairman of the Uzbek Sovnarkom after his predecessor, Sultan Segizbaev, was unmasked as an "enemy of the people." Abdurakhmanov held this post until 1950, when he was removed.[11]

The new accent on youth was reflected in the age as well as the limited political experience of other Uzbeks promoted in the wake of the Purge and Terror. Neither Yusupov nor Abdurakhmanov were connected in education or in political experience with the dzhadidist movement, although Yusupov had a brief period of political prominence in the early 1930s. In both cases, and there were many more instances, their taste for power was whetted in the course of "socialist construction" and their mobility was accelerated by the destruction of their Uzbek predecessors. Neither the Revolution nor the Civil War marked their entry into politics. Consequently, unlike Khodzhaev and Ikramov, they had not begun political activity when Russian rule was disintegrating; nor had they sensed, even so briefly, as Khodzhaev and Ikramov must have, that their dependence on Moscow was tempered at first by the Center's mutual dependence on them. Wholly dependent on Moscow and naturally beholden to Stalin (and perhaps Kaganovich in particular) for their elevation to political heights, these new men were also implicated in his crimes as the beneficiaries of the elimination of those natives who had previously held their posts. They were indeed men of the class of '38, graduates of a tough political school, surely conscious that they were continually being tested and that their degree could be revoked at any time. "Produce or perish" was the compelling norm, though success in the production realm did not guarantee survival, as the experience of Khodzhaev and Ikramov had clearly shown. Fainsod wrote that the Uzbek elite "was privileged, but it lived in perpetual fear and in perpetual motion." [12]

While Yusupov and Abdurakhmanov were the most prominent of the new men, they were not alone. Many natives stepped into the positions made available to the ambitious through the impact of the 1937–1938 Purge. Still other young Uzbeks climbed onto the lower rungs of the political ladder to begin the rapid upward mobility which in the course of World War II or soon thereafter would bring them near to the political summit. It was however while Khodzhaev and Ikramov still ruled in Uzbekistan that this group acquired its initial education and in some cases a semblance of training for the new responsibilities that it was so soon and so unexpectedly to assume. The creation of the class of 1938 consequently must be sought in the telescoped socioeconomic transformation launched during the Five Year Plans. It is to this process and the post-Purge entry of this group into Party ranks that I now turn.

MODERNIZATION AND "NATIVIZATION"

A German visitor to Central Asia in the early 1930s reported the following remarks by a Russian leather expert on his way to the area:

All that these Uzbeks and Tadzhiks know about Karl Marx is that streets are named for him; all they know about Lenin is his statue. And people like that are allowed to govern themselves! Letters have reached our trust signed by the chairman and secretary of a Regional Soviet, that ended with the flourish: "May Allah bless the comrades Marx, Engels, Lenin and Stalin and may He give them strength to guide our revered Communist Party along the paths of glory, to which end we daily bow in prayer! . . ."

Much time . . . is being lost. Before giving the former colonies their freedom, they should have been dealt with all the more firmly because of their very subjection. All the mosques and all the Koran schools should have been closed. All the beys, all the mullahs, all the old functionaries should have been arrested and deported. The wearing of the veil should have been prohibited and every infringement punished without mercy. The soil should have been parceled out immediately and the planting of cotton made obligatory. Every case of bribery should have been punished with death, and the children, girls and boys alike, should have been driven to school by the police. Ten years of such a regime, and the country would have been so modernized that one could have said to its native sons: "There you are! Now carry on for yourselves."[13]

This Russian leather expert expressed the persisting viewpoint of the Russian imperialist, or as the Soviet regime was to label it, that of the "Great Russian chauvinist." The colonial or imperialist mentality, which Lenin had warned against, must have been fairly widespread in the bureaucracies in the Uzbek SSR. Changing the bureaucrat's label from "Tsarist" to "Soviet" was no magic formula for eradicating prejudice and a condescending attitude toward the Moslems. The Soviet version of the "White Man's Burden" trampled on native sensitivities and fueled national resentment just as much as its West European counterpart in other parts of the globe. During the 1920s the Soviet leadership stressed the need for *korenizatsia* or "rooting" the new state and Party organizations in native soil in order to broaden the support base of the Soviet regime. In areas such as Uzbekistan, this entailed increasing the percentage of natives in bureaucracies, schools, and the economic realm. It also called for transferring state administration to the native languages as well as to native hands. There were practical difficulties that stood in the way of educating, training, and promoting Moslems but the task was further complicated by local Russian prejudice against the natives. *Korenizatsia* ("nativization" or "Uzbekization," however it was labeled) was thus hampered by more than just language differences and a dearth of textbooks and technical institutes. In addition to many natives' attitude of general indifference, there were political and personal factors that threw massive roadblocks in the path of the announced Soviet policy during NEP of "nationalizing" the bureaucracies. These difficulties stemmed partly from the reluctance of Russian bureaucrats to complicate their lives by engaging in social experiments that many considered foolish, ill-timed, and doomed from the start. Whether traced to bureaucratic conservatism, ethnic differences, or political motives, tension between the Russians and the natives was evident in the 1920s and 1930s. In fact it permeated multiple facets of local life and gave a special character to what was a difficult enough task without the addition of this fundamental complication: modernizing an economically backward area in a short period and at a rapid tempo.

The limited success as of the late 1920s in "nativization" of the Uzbek state administrative system is apparent from the data presented in table 13.1. They show that among the almost 1,200 employed at the highest echelon of the Uzbek state apparatus, the republic level, there were only 138 natives. Further down the hierarchy the role of the natives increases, but not substantially. Even at the lowest major administrative level, that of the *raion,* which was in close proximity to the Moslem population, only 41.6 percent of the posts were in native hands. The information presented in the table on the administrators' competence in the local language is also illuminating. Clearly the nonnatives were not inclined to learn the local languages. A similar situation with regard to the role of natives existed in the Party bureaucracy. Indeed, as of January 1929, Uzbeks made up only 47 percent of the membership of the Uzbek Communist party as a whole, although it is estimated by Soviet sources that Uzbeks comprised 76.19 percent of the Uzbek SSR's population.[14] In many ways the accelerated tempos of development after 1928 compounded the difficulties and sharpened the dilemmas associated with training and promoting native cadres. The Five Year Plan and the sharply increased obligatory cotton quotas for the Uzbek SSR made it certain that henceforth the republic's internal development had to be calculated as a subset of over-all Soviet economic development and Uzbek domestic programs undertaken only at Moscow's directives. Increasingly those directives came to encompass almost every aspect of the republic's life. The key issue posed for Uzbekistan by the Five Year Plans was the immediate and intermediate consequences of these events for Uzbek national development. Did the impact of *socialist* industrialization necessarily undercut the possibility of authentic *Uzbek* modernization? Were the two processes, socialist industrialization and genuine Uzbek national development, complementary or contradictory? Were the accelerating economic demands of one in-

TABLE 13.1   Native representation in the Uzbek state apparatus, 1928.

| Administrative level | Total personnel | Natives (%) | Others (%) | Competent in Local Language | | |
| --- | --- | --- | --- | --- | --- | --- |
| | | | | Yes | No | Unknown |
| Republic | 1,199 | 138 (11.5%) | 1,061 (85.5%) | 312 | 857 | 30 |
| Okrug | 3,497 | 639 (18.3%) | 2,858 (81.7%) | 1,353 | 2,023 | 121 |
| Raion | 1,060 | 441 (41.6%) | 619 (58.4%) | 797 | 244 | 19 |

Source: Kommunisticheskaya Akademiya, *National''naya politika VKP (6) v Tsifrakh* (Moscow: Izdatel'stvo Kommunisticheskoi Akademii, 1930), pp. 238–239.

compatible with the cultural requirements of the other? The answer to these questions was largely embedded in the specific character of the development process, the inclination of those outside the republic who would shape that process, and the ethnic composition of the cadres who would control and administer modernization within Uzbekistan. Would Russian directives, talent, and cadres play these roles exclusively, or would these burdens and opportunities fall predominately to native personnel? This choice and the "mix" between foreign and native ingredients would have an overpowering impact on the outcome. Whatever the expressed long-range goals, it was the actual native weight in controlling the modernization process itself that would determine whether the outcome would be authentic Uzbek national development or something quite different. The danger expressed by a student of Soviet politics in another context was equally present here: the "means might devour the ends."

The Five Year Plan gave a new impetus to the program of producing leading cadres for the economic and political realm from the lower classes. In Uzbekistan, it raised with special vigor the problem of nativization. Never before or after were "workers, poor peasants, and *batraks*" to enjoy as formally a privileged position in the Soviet state or in its rhetoric. The attempt to ride the wave of mass enthusiasm for egalitarianism and "building socialism" did produce some economic gains but also societal and political difficulties. Uzbekistan, as well as other minority areas, responded to Moscow's baton; but achieving "proletarian hegemony," the main theme of this period, had direct and perhaps ominous implications for the treatment of the nationality problem. The meager size of the Uzbek working class sharply contrasted with the more numerous local Russian proletariat which was constantly augmented by others imported from European Russia. It appeared that in the Uzbek SSR the inevitable consequence of highlighting the proletarian dimension of the development endeavor was to downgrade the natives and concomitantly to elevate Russians or Slavs. Two developments, however, could divert the process in a less ominous direction evaluated from the Uzbek national perspective: first, if there were a simultaneous rapid expansion of the native working class, and second, if special attention were paid to recruiting, educating, and training "rural proletarians" who were of course Moslems. Should events have unfolded in that manner, there was a reasonable chance that a sufficient native base would have emerged in the not too distant future to counter Russian monopoly of working-class privilege and proletarian identification.

In the late 1920s the Uzbek social structure and the predominant

Russian role in industrial occupations provided a less than optimum point of departure for such an outcome. Indeed the obstacles in the way of creating a native working class and a new Soviet Uzbek intelligentsia were not simply economic backwardness and the resistance of traditional society. There was evidence of a lack of enthusiasm on the part of "Europeans" or local Slavs to preoccupation with uplifting the native community. Some apparently thought that building socialism "from above" with reliance on Russians and recently imported cadres was a simpler and less painful solution; consequently, evidence of "Great Russian chauvinism" surfaced again and again.

Nevertheless modernization in the Uzbek SSR went forward, and especially after 1930 there were substantial efforts led by the native Communist leaders to move Moslems into new economic sectors, to train them for new roles, and to advance them to new positions. Both Akmal Ikramov and Faizulla Khodzhaev apparently took the lead in promoting the renewed emphasis on korenizatsia that followed the collectivization catastrophe of early 1930 and the directives of the Sixteenth Party Congress. Nativization and "cultural construction" in the Uzbek SSR between 1930 and 1934 produced the following general results. In 1930 there were seven vuz's (universities) with a student body of 2,900. By 1934 the vuz's had increased to sixteen and the number of students to 8,700.[15] In 1930 there were seventy-seven *tekhnikums* (technical institutes) where 16,000 studied. By 1934 these figures had contracted to sixty-two tekhnikums with a total student body of 12,900.[16] Table 13.2 shows the percentage of Uzbeks as of October 1933 in vuz's and tekhnikums broken down by area of specialization. At the university level the results of the nativization campaign were far from impressive, although Uzbeks were preeminent in the field of medicine and substantially present in the area of potential educators. Aside from these two sectors, the data indicated that a future native presence in key positions demanding advanced training and university attendance was unlikely to be in accord wth the Uzbeks' proportion of the republic's population. However, the tekhnikums' role in producing middle-range specialists and some top-level personnel should not be underrated. With tekhnikum entrance requirements less demanding, the Uzbek share of the student body was more impressive, although according to table 13.2 native preparation for assuming roles in the industrial-transport sector again left something to be desired.

We can gain perspective on emerging trends in the cadres-specialist preparatory process by examining the national composition of students entering vuz's and tekhnikums in the spring of 1934. Uzbeks com-

TABLE 13.2   Uzbeks in vuz's and tekhnikums of Uzbek SSR (October 1, 1933).

| Specialization | Vuz's | | | Tekhnikums | | |
|---|---|---|---|---|---|---|
| | All students | Total | Uzbeks (%) | All students | Total | Uzbeks (%) |
| Industry and transport | 2,070 | 1,102 | 184 (16.7%) | 4,871 | 3,472 | 1,216 (35.1%) |
| Agriculture | 2,037 | — | — | 6,188 | 1,054 | 636 (60.3%) |
| Social-economic | 2,157 | 961 | 247 (25.7%) | 1,487 | 532 | 396 (74.4%) |
| Education | 2,735 | 1,681 | 639 (38.0%) | 7,490 | 1,953 | 1,154 (59.1%) |
| Medicine | 1,602 | 427 | 295 (69.6%) | 1,066 | 941 | 607 (64.5%) |

Source: Gosplana SSSR, *Kul'turnoe stroitel'stvo SSSR v Tsifrakh ot VT k VII S''ezdu Sovetov (1930–1934)* (Moscow, 1935), **p**. 53.

prised 47 percent and Russians 20 percent of the vuz entering class.[17] They were 42 percent and 56 percent respectively of those entering in the field of education and medicine. Of a total of 2,638 entering tekhnikums, 1,864 (or 76 percent) were Uzbeks, a rather impressive accomplishment given the earlier general preconditions.[18] As noted, the difficulties confronted in training and advancing natives were not simply technical. The Uzbek republic press in the years 1931 to 1933 was filled with horror stories. Russians opposed the advancement of Uzbeks and grumbled about the latters' inferior capacities. Epithets such as "stupid" and "lazy," hurled at the natives, had to be censured in the press. In this phase of official attacks on "Great Russian chauvinism," the press recounted stories of malicious tricks played on the natives. Russian officials and teachers sometimes ignored the training of the natives and some even refused to work with them.[19]

The period of intensive emphasis on korenizatsia or "Uzbekization" and full-scale preoccupation with native advancement began in the fall of 1930. Apparently by late 1933, higher authorities concluded that overenthusiastic stress on nativization in the Uzbek SSR had come into conflict with other priorities and perhaps interfered with the imperatives of production. The korenizatsia campaign had created such confusion and disenchantment among the Russians that a slow-down seemed necessary, and the offensive was terminated. Attacks on "Great Russian chauvinism" that had filled the Uzbek press ended. After 1933 there was virtually no attention devoted to this matter or to korenizatsia, a subject which for three years had competed with cotton production for the attention of the reader. Authoritative approval for future inattention or "benign neglect" was clearly implied in the treatment of the nationality question at the Seventeenth Party Congress in 1934.[20]

Economic development in Uzbekistan went forward during the Second Five Year Plan. Industrial and urban change continued at a rapid rate. But this continued growth of the working class did not necessarily signify the transformation of the rural native populace, for by 1937 only 36.5 percent of industrial workers were Uzbeks. Although industrial, transport, and construction workers rose from 6 percent to almost 14 percent of the urban population, local nationals comprised only 30 percent of the construction labor. In the key realm of engineering-technical personnel, local nationals also made up only 20 percent.[21]

The growing number of schools and the expansion of the training network during the period was impressive. But the problem of pedagogical cadres and languages was pressing and central to the task of creating a native Soviet intelligentsia. Many of the teachers were Slavs, too many of whom did not know the native language, and they were also precluded by the teaching materials, mainly in Russian, from transmitting skills to even the most earnestly aspiring native. These and similar issues were surely the essential but not exclusive backdrop for the decision in the late 1930s to introduce a modified Cyrillic alphabet as a substitute for the Latin alphabet which had replaced the traditional Arabic script in the late 1920s. Another element in an emerging pattern of "Russification" was the decision in 1938 to make the study of Russian compulsory even in Uzbek primary schools.

The Soviet boast that by January 1937 there were 10,869 specialists with completed higher education in the Uzbek SSR must be approached with caution since no nationality breakdown has been given for this figure. Many Russians, Ukrainians, and Tatars had entered the Uzbek SSR in the 1930s, and they surely must have comprised a significant proportion of this total number. Some illumination is thrown on the general situation by the fact that of the 1,113 students graduating from Samarkand University in 1938 only thirty-five were Uzbeks. The number of natives in schools producing skilled agricultural cadres was little more impressive. In 1937 the total local national contingent at Samarkand Agricultural Institute was only 33.7 percent, while in its counterpart institution at Tashkent, the total native group amounted to only 13.2 percent of the student body.[22]

## THE UZBEK COMMUNIST PARTY AND THE CLASS OF '38

The Party's recruitment policy provides a revealing index of the regime's effort to walk the tightrope between the isolation from local elements that would compel reliance on rule by force, and the opposite pitfall of being swamped by needed but unreliable recruits who might drag the Party into the morass of local ways, submerging it in the traditional environment that it sought to master. The Party's changing internal composition before 1938 reveals that Moscow was adept at recruiting those it could use in one policy phase and ejecting them subsequently when their usefulness came to an end. It underlines the leadership's ability to adjust the Party's size and composition, by discarding those not considered "steeled Bolsheviks" as it moved to confront new tasks and to reshape the social and economic environment through a "socialist transformation." The Party's accordian-like movement, expanding and contracting, illustrates the dual technique of enlisting social classes and categories and subsequent "trimming" as the system moves to a new breakthrough. Thus through recruitment and ejection ("purging" or "cleansing" the ranks), the Party's internal composition was broadened or narrowed and the nature of its societal support adjusted.

Stalin had once observed: "from time to time, the master must without fail go through the ranks of the party with a broom in his hands." [23] From 1933 through 1938 the master made a clean sweep of the Party. As a result of the mass purge, Party size contracted, dropping from a high point of over 3,500,000 in 1933 to somewhat over 1,500,000 in 1938.[24] One of the major consequences of this "cleansing" of Party ranks was to open channels for the upwardly mobile young Communists and the emerging new Soviet intelligentsia. During the 1930s the Party was purged of many whose life experiences and political activity reached back to pre-Revolutionary times. Into the positions left unfilled by their exit and multiplied by industrial expansion flowed the young technical-scientific elite, the new "Soviet intelligentsia." It consisted of people "employed professionally in mental labor (students, teachers, engineers, writers, artists, agronomists, a large part of the employees, etc.)." [25] who, it was contended, did not make up a separate class but represented a social stratum serving the toiling masses. After the 1939 change in Party admission rules at the Eighteenth Party Congress, this group no longer faced discrimination in gaining entry; on the contrary, it was to be accorded the preferential status in Party ranks commensurate with its special and leading position in Soviet society.

Some perspective on the development process in the Uzbek SSR, including the emergence of the class of '38 and the Uzbek Soviet intelligentsia, is provided by an examination of the changing size and composition of the Uzbek Communist Party. Table 13.3 shows the growth pattern of the Uzbek Party. There was a phenomenal increase between 1929 and 1933, followed by an equally striking numerical decrease in Party size between 1933 and 1937. The table then shows a sudden meteoric increase in Party size between 1938 and 1941. The earlier growth phase had been linked to two waves of recruitment, the second of which (as the growing percentage of Uzbeks documents) brought a substantial number of natives into the Party. The numerical decline between 1933 and 1937 was of course the reflection on the Uzbek scene of the "continuous Purge" and Terror. The post-1938 recruitment phase brought in the new Uzbek Soviet intelligentsia and gave the Party an essentially elite white-collar or "employee" center of gravity (in terms of social origins) different from the largely worker-peasant mass base which had crystallized during the First Five Year Plan. This crucial shift is illustrated in figure 13.1. Projecting the

TABLE 13.3  Changing composition of the Uzbek Communist Party, 1929–1941.

| Year | Members and candidates | Nationality | | Social background | | |
|---|---|---|---|---|---|---|
| | | Uzbeks (%) | Russians (%) | Workers (%) | Peasants (%) | Employees and others (%) |
| 1929 | 36,093 | 47.3 | —[a] | 49.8 | 25.9 | 25.2 |
| 1931 | 54,583 | 52.1 | 28.8 | 56.3 | 28.5 | 15.2 |
| 1932 | 68,495 | 56.9 | 22.8 | 54.5 | 33.2 | 12.3 |
| 1933 | 81,612 | 60.9 | 20.1 | 50.5 | 39.3 | 10.2 |
| 1934 | 56,702 | 63.8 | 16.8 | 43.2 | 44.5 | 12.3 |
| 1935 | 33,834 | 60.6 | 23.9 | 39.4 | 43.2 | 17.4 |
| 1936 | 28,458 | 58.1 | 21.2 | 40.9 | 41.4 | 17.7 |
| 1937 | 29,934 | 52.2 | 25.5 | 44.91 | 34.6 | 20.5 |
| 1938 | 30,233 | 48.6 | 25.7 | 45.6 | 35.0 | 19.4 |
| 1939 | 35,087 | 47.0 | 26.8 | 43.4 | 33.7 | 22.9 |
| 1940 | 63,847 | 50.1 | 23.8 | 29.0 | 32.8 | 38.2 |
| 1941 | 72,068 | 48.8 | 24.6 | 28.1 | 32.1 | 39.8 |

Source: *Kommunisticheskaya partiya Uzbekistana v Tsifrakh (sbornik statisticheskikh materialov 1924–1964)* (Tashkent, 1964).

[a] No separate listing of Russians or Slavs was presented. For the category Europeans the figure listed was 42.8 percent. A separate listing for Russians was first submitted in 1931.

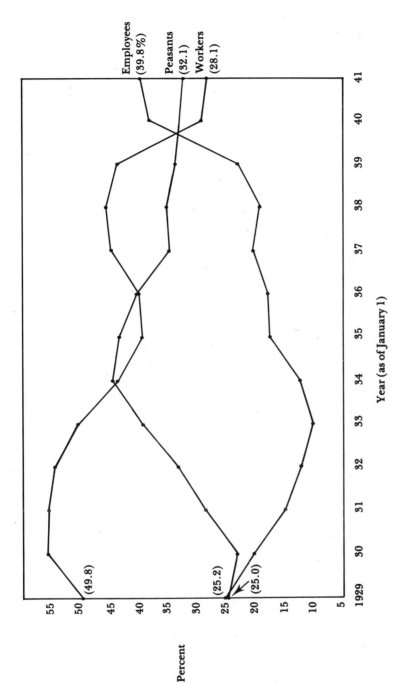

FIGURE 13.1 Social background of Uzbek party members, 1929–1941.

259

data on social background or social-class origins of Party members, it shows that recruitment from the employee class or stratum was a post-1938 phenomenon. As of 1941, virtually 40 percent of the Uzbek Party was "employee" with regard to social origin. In fact, if one considers the social class profile in 1941 on the criterion of actual present *occupation*, 53 percent of the Uzbek Party were listed as employees rather than workers or peasants. Table 13.3 also presents the changing nationality profile of the Uzbek organization. The highpoint in "Uzbekization," as the high tide of korenizatsia discussed earlier, was between 1931 and 1933. The percentage of Uzbeks continued to decline from 1934 to 1939, when an upturn began that continued until World War II.

A probe of the data for the Uzbek Party as a whole reveals something like the ascent of the class of 1938 and the emergence of a new Uzbek technical intelligentsia in the post-1938 recruitment pattern. For the Party as a whole, in contrast to the Party leadership, it was the class of 1939 that deserves most attention, for it was in this year that massive recruitment took place. In January 1939 the Uzbek Party totalled only 35,087. By January 1940 its size had jumped to 63,847 and by January 1941 it reached 72,068. The increase in the year 1939 alone was 28,760.[26] Who were these new recruits? What were the social, ethnic, and educational characteristics of this new central core of a refashioned Uzbek Party?

The startling jump in the percentage of the Party whose social background was "employee" points clearly in the direction of white-collar personnel and the Soviet technical intelligentsia. The educational profile of the Party produced as a result of the new recruitment also draws attention to the entrance of this new elite group into the ranks.[27] The change in generational focus that has been suggested in the discussion of the Yusupov-Abdurakhmanov leadership can be statistically documented for the Party as a whole with regard to these new recruits. Those who entered the Party in 1939 to 1940 can be analyzed by age group, revealing a youthful profile. Of the 28,760 who entered in 1939, almost 11,000 were between the ages of twenty-five and thirty.[28] This was almost ten times the figure for those in the same age interval recruited in the previous year. For the composite category of twenty-one to thirty years of age, the total recruited in 1939 was over 15,000. In addition, the figure for the age interval thirty-one to forty was over 10,000 entering the Party in 1939.[29]

This absorption of youth resulted by 1940 in the Uzbek Party based on a new generation from both a chronological and a political perspective. By January 1940, almost 75 percent of the Party was between the ages of twenty-five and forty. Indeed, that the Party sought its anchor in youth is testified to by the fact that 65 percent of the Uzbek organization were below the age of thirty-five. By January 1941, 82 percent of the Uzbek Party were forty years old or less.[30] But what of the ethnic profile of these youthful newcomers? Of the 1939–1940 total recruits, 15,453 were Uzbeks and 5,803 were Russians; unfortunately, there is no ethnic breakdown of the specific age groups or social classes. It seems a fair assumption, however, that many of the "employee" group were Slavs, but natives also must have constituted an important share of this total, especially in middle-range positions.[31]

In trying to understand the hold of Moscow over Uzbekistan and the means used to carry out modernization, it is not sufficient to point to force, coercion, and terror. Although they were an essential part of the story, one must also explore the more positive grounds capable of generating support from various native sectors for the Soviet regime. The alliance between the Uzbek dzhadids and Moscow, which served both sides' interests for a time, has been noted. But the main thrust of our argument has been to highlight the new "alliance" forged by Stalin with the post-1938 generation of the emergent Soviet Uzbek elite. Merle Fainsod's general conclusion regarding the Soviet system as a whole thus has a special relevance for Uzbekistan:

Revolutions begin with the defeat and elimination of an established ruling group. But they also create fresh opportunities for social categories that had previously been suppressed and inert. They make it possible for the abler and more ambitious members of the newly activated groups to rise in the social scale and to attain previously undreamed of heights of authority and influence. In a fundamental sense a revolution only begins to consolidate itself when it calls forth new energy from below to defend its conquests.

In many respects the Bolshevik Revolution followed this classic pattern. It dethroned an established ruling caste and set a profound social revolution in motion. It tapped fresh talent from the lower depths of society and harnessed it to the revolutionary chariot. It gradually welded together a new governing apparatus, drawn substantially from social elements that had previously been political ciphers. It built its own network of revolutionary beneficiaries with vested interests in the perpetuation of the new order.[32]

FATHERS, SONS, AND "ELDER BROTHERS"

The key role played by nonnatives and "outsiders" in Uzbekistan's development is striking. The Russians have coined the expression "elder brothers" to describe their special role. Today in the ranks of the Party and the intelligentsia in the Uzbek SSR, Russians continue to play a large and key role out of proportion to their share of the republic's population.

On the basis of the 1970 census we know that Russians make up 12.5 percent and Uzbeks 64 percent of the Uzbek SSR's population. However, as of 1967 Russians made up 21.5 percent and Uzbeks 53.3 percent of the total membership of the Uzbek Communist Party. Indeed the weight of the Russians increases as one moves closer to the key centers of power. In 1949 Russians constituted 39 percent of the Uzbek Central Committee; in 1952 the figure dropped to 36 percent, and by 1961 it had declined to 28 percent. By 1966 it had risen again to 31 percent. Of the members of the Uzbek Central Committee chosen at the 1971 Uzbek Party Congress, 34 percent were Russians or other Slavs. However, on the Central Committee chosen at the Nineteenth Congress in February 1976, the nonnative contingent had dropped to about 30 percent. The most important decision-making center of the Communist Party, and of the Uzbek Republic, is the Bureau of the Central Committee. In 1949 of its fourteen full members nine were Russians and five were Uzbeks. On the 1971 Uzbek Central Committee Bureau there were six Russians and five Uzbeks. However, on the Bureau chosen in February 1976, the balance had shifted: the full membership was made up of five Russians and six Uzbeks.[33] A characterization of this situation as "Russian imperialism" might seem to some as not far off the mark, but this is not a fully accurate description. It does not encompass the full power configuration including the native component; nor does it provide sufficient insight into the likely future political dynamics. Russians do not rule alone, and, although Moscow has a grip on key political posts, the local native intelligentsia has risen in the political and economic realm to occupy many important positions. The key question concerns the local elite's attitudes and the likelihood of the native intelligentsia rising to full control of its own republic.

This Soviet Uzbek intelligentsia, as Richard Pipes has written, possesses "many of the characteristics which distinguish the Soviet intelligentsia as a whole," but it also displays "certain traits engendered by special conditions prevailing in Central Asia." Regarding this special condition, he adds: "by origin, language, culture and family ties, it is connected to the Muslim population: by training, work and much of its world outlook, it is identified with the Soviet regime. It thus belongs fully to neither of the two groups, constituting something of a third element which functions as a connecting link between the Russian-dominated regime and the native population." [34] An analysis keyed solely to social class will tend to highlight the intelligentsia's integration within the broader framework of Soviet society; but this may be a deceptive guide to attitudes and perhaps understates the emergence of national and ethnic loyalties in a new guise. The new elite's search for renewed native roots could take the form of "localism" and Uzbek patriotism. Having created an Uzbek Soviet intelligentsia in order to bypass nationalism and to cement All-Union integration, Moscow may yet find that it has created the basis for a series of new ethnic tensions.

This phenomenon may be linked to generational differences. As the second or perhaps the third generation of the Soviet Uzbek intelligentsia emerges, it may find itself less beholden to Moscow and more confident of its local status. One may even find it contemplating the "colonial tie" as it seeks out its own cultural past and perhaps begins to shape its own political future. There may also appear, as evidence already suggests, a search by the native elite for symbols linking it with the Uzbek masses, and with its pre-Russian past, and further differentiating it from other branches of the Soviet intelligentsia.[35] The new generation accepts the Soviet societal framework, but takes Moscow's largesse for granted. Broad industrial forces tend almost automatically to socialize the engineers and techniques to accept integration within a multinational Soviet system. But industrial society also breeds its own problems. To what degree, for instance, will ethnic tension unfold as more and more Uzbeks emerge from the schools armed with skills but confronted with Russians and Ukrainians blocking the channels for mobility and occupying key positions? The dynamics of national loyalty are far from charted and the grip of ethnic ties is often strong even though submerged. These attachments often emerge in unexpected fashion, cutting their own paths and channels, often eroding seemingly monolithic structures, and returning to plague colonial rulers. Of course this is a hypothetical projection, laden with all the dangers of such constructs. It would be just as foolish to view the Soviet experience through the prism of the fate of the Tsarist system as it would be to project the future course of the USSR in a descending line on the pattern of the West European overseas imperial ventures. However this historical epoch has dealt cruelly with imperial systems and supranational experiments; and there is no special character to socialist ventures making them immune to similar problems and crises. Just as Western imperialism had its "White Man's Burden," so Moscow's modernization rationale revolved, implicitly if not always explicitly, around a similar "Bolshevik Burden." In the past the dominance of Slavs in Central Asia could be justified to some degree on a technical, nonpolitical basis, since the natives lacked the wherewithal to create and manage an industrializing society. But skill and education is no longer the monopoly of the Europeans, and a perception of colonialism may well become the common currency explaining Russian dominance in elite positions in the Uzbek SSR as well as providing the incentive to probe past Russian and Soviet indiscretions toward the native community. In the future, Moscow may yet be confronted with the dilemma of either granting full power to the Uzbek elite, or, if not, then running the risk of stimulating a growing native alienation and discontent. The very visible Russian presence and continued monopoly of key positions might serve as a concrete focus for local unrest.

It would be a mistake to imagine that such serious difficulties lie in the immediate future. There is no evidence of seething unrest ready to break into the open in Uzbekistan.[36] But neither need one project such a scenario very far beyond the present and emerging Uzbek generation. Much depends on how the Russian political elite responds to what will be key national or ethnic questions: some of these issues will seem cultural in character, some will appear to be historical in form, and still others will involve political and economic equity. Whether Moscow will prove more adept than its Western European counterparts in managing the transition from the Stalinist "Russification" solution of the problems of Uzbek modernization to something more equitable and better rooted in Uzbek soil is an open question. Indeed it is worth calling to mind Fainsod's observations regarding the conservative, aging Soviet leaders:

Like Stalin before them, they remain determined to make their revolution the last revolution and to preserve the Party monolith as the repository of ideological "truth." They have still to face what E. E. Zamyatin (one of the talented writers whom the Soviet regime muzzled) once observed, that "There is no such thing as the last revolution; the number of revolutions is infinite." [37]

# Modernization and National Policy in Soviet Central Asia: Problems and Prospects

GREGORY J. MASSELL

Soviet politics and government have had, since the Revolution's inception, an unparalleled fascination for Western students of politics. The Soviet political system has been perceived, first and foremost, as novel, if not totally unprecedented. The novelty had to do primarily with the system's well-nigh extraordinary effectiveness, pervasiveness, stability, and longevity against very great odds. It had to do, specifically, with the regime's ability to *modernize* while *maintaining order*—in what was largely a tradition-bound milieu entering a period of severe psycho-cultural disorientation, economic dislocation, and social upheaval.

Of course, when compared with such a record, the performance of other newly emerging states could not seem very inspiring. Not illogically, therefore, the appeals of Communism have come to be seen as importantly linked with the appeals of the Soviet developmental model for impatient revolutionary modernizers, especially in traditional, underdeveloped milieus emerging from colonial or semicolonial dependency and striving toward sovereign self-assertion as nation-states. The appeals of the Soviet model have come to be related not so much to its ideology or economics as to its combination of mobilization and organization as the main routes to Party strength and effective authority. The most recent (and forceful) expression of this view may be found in Samuel Huntington's work on political development.[1]

What is remarkable about this view is that it emphasizes one dimension of Soviet political performance at the expense of others, leaving conspicuous lacunae in our understanding of the complexities involved here. It alerts us to the thrust of mobilizational imperatives and organizational arrangements, but it tells us little about actual institutional performance and human behavior at the operational level—that is, about the strategies and problems of applying new norms and forms at the grassroots of society. It tells us even less about an issue that is likely to be crucial from the point of view of nationalist reformers and revolutionaries aspiring to independent statehood on all continents. This issue concerns the capacity of the Soviet system to reconcile the building of a new unitary order with the full-fledged participation of all national minorities in that order—and its capacity, as well, to reconcile comprehensive modernization with the political development of all of its component nationalities.

It is surely reasonable to suggest that, in order to test the relevance of the Soviet developmental model for the new nations of Asia and Africa, one would need to know not just about the evolution of such a model for the Union as a whole, but about the conditions of its application in sociocultural milieus most closely approximating Asian and African realities. It would seem that Soviet Central Asia is ideal for this purpose.[2]

There are some very obvious reasons for this choice. For one thing, at a high level of generality, the region's ecology, social structures, ethno-cultural configurations, religious traditions, and patterns of political evolution (including colonization by a major imperial power, Tsarist Russia) share a number of important features with large parts of what we regard as the underdeveloped, traditional world, and especially with Chinese Sinkiang, South Asia, the Middle East, and North Africa. Central Asia comprises a cluster of relatively intact Islamic societies, the largest such traditional element to come under Soviet rule. Thus the region offers a unique opportunity for research on revolution and modernization, as well as multinational integration, as consciously induced and managed processes. Specifically, it offers an opportunity to study in detail the confrontation between highly developed, radical, determined, authoritarian Communist forces and a cluster of Turko-Iranian traditional Moslem societies based on kinship, custom, and religion.

It goes without saying that the study of the nuances of such a confrontation should help to enhance our understanding of the strategies, problems, and costs of deliberate, holistic social engineering under-taken under authoritarian auspices on a vast scale. Of course, while we have a long way to go before arriving at an all-inclusive paradigm of directed social change,[3] most Marxist-Leninists (especially in es-tablished Communist systems) would tend, and probably need, to deny or deemphasize complexities and doubts concerning such a task. Yet even a cursory study of the Communist developmental model, especially in Central Asia, alerts us to the fact that we are dealing here not with a coherent strategy of social engineering in action, but with a feverish, protracted, and far from conclusive quest for (and experimentation with) a variety of strategic approaches to engineered social revolution and multinational integration.[4] In fact, after decades of bland insistence that Central Asia constitutes a perfect example of the Communist Party's inherent capacity to effect the transition from a "feudal-patriarchal mode of life" directly to "socialism"—thus "by-passing the agonies of the capitalist developmental stage"—All-Union and Central Asian academies of science were instructed in 1965 (!) to "study the experience" of Soviet Central Asia. They were to do so with a view of producing (ex-post-facto, as it were) a rationalized and com-prehensive—and presumably comprehensible—model that would be applicable to the development of new nations, especially in Asia and Africa.[5] So far, a decade later, no report of a model, scientific or other-wise, has come to light.

Thus, let it be quite clear at the outset: no magic wand for social change is to be found in Central Asia, and no easily applicable model for the benefit of impatient revolutionary modernizers elsewhere. Nonetheless, in spite of scarce data, Central Asia's revolutionary ex-perience does permit us to pose some preliminary questions that are central to comparative politics in a world of new nations pursuing unprecedented goals. To wit: How, and to what extent, may political power be used in simultaneously modernizing and integrating a cul-turally and ethnically heterogeneous milieu? Specifically, to what ex-tent are the aims and means of Soviet-sponsored modernization in Central Asia congruent or incongruent with those of stable multi-national integration as defined by Soviet nationality policy?

In posing this question as the main issue to be considered in this essay, I base my argument on two assumptions. First, it seems reason-able to assume that the *optimization of the modernizing process* (through rapid social mobilization and economic development) and the *maximization of control* (in part through advancing multinational integration) are among the central operational objectives of the Soviet regime. Second, given the nature of the tasks implicit in these objectives, it seems safe to say that the patterns and problems of modernization in the Soviet multinational system, perhaps especially in Central Asia, are *necessarily interdependent* with the patterns and problems of Soviet nationality policy.

Proceeding from these assumptions, and considering their implications in real life, it seems justifiable to suggest that simultaneous Soviet commitments to optimal modernization and to maximum control in a multinational context are not necessarily congruent. By the same token, Soviet modernization policies and nationality policy are not necessarily consistent and mutually reinforcing. In fact, it may be said that the two policy strands have been markedly contradictory in their effect, *reinforcing* and *stabilizing* the overarching political system while, at the same time, *negating* and *destabilizing* it. Let me explain what I consider especially important in this basically incongruent policy interaction, and let me do so in the context of a simple analytical framework consisting of two brief catalogues: the catalogue, respectively, of stabilizing and destabilizing factors in Soviet modernization and nationality policies, with special reference to Central Asia.[6]

THE IMPACT OF MODERNIZATION AND NATIONALITY POLICY:
STABILIZING FACTORS

### The Functions of Tactical Nation-States

As I have suggested elsewhere,[7] the establishment of formal ethnocultural units in the Soviet Union—as a prime expression of Soviet nationality policy—may be visualized as the formation of what might be called *tactical nation-states*. These denote units designed largely exogenously, that is at the initiative and under the control of outside powers, to serve as temporary and expedient means toward larger ends. There can be little doubt that the structure and functions of these states (presently Soviet constituent republics) were viewed as purely instrumental in character and were intended to be ultimately self-liquidating in nature.

As such, the tactical nation-states may be said to have been predicated on striking a balance between positive and negative incentives in consolidating the Soviet system: incentives designed to optimize local participation and performance and minimize alienation and resistance on the part of minority nationalities. We know that the *positive* incentives included, *inter alia*, formal differentiation of ethno-cultural groups into well-defined units with a national-territorial base and an elaborate symbol-system of statehood, as well as equal representation of these units in the super-state's formal legislative bodies in Moscow (even if the latter were themselves merely democratic facades). It is safe to assume that in Central Asia, perhaps more than elsewhere in the Soviet Union, such features tended to generate a sense of effectiveness and pride, at least in the ranks of the new secular intelligentsia—given the relative novelty of nationality and statehood in the region. These features provided what were, in effect, surrogate forms of local group-identity and self-determination. To this extent they tended to be stabilizing factors in Central Asia, legitimizing to some extent the Soviet system itself and mitigating the tensions caused by Russian presence.

From a *negative* perspective, the new units, while structured to endow a social and territorial universe with features of a nation-state, were specifically designed to keep those features sufficiently impotent or selective to forestall the emergence of a real national consciousness and the formation of a real nation. However, it is probably safe to say that as long as the Soviet regime dealt with representatives of new native elites who were politically inexperienced as well as personally dependent on the regime—in that they owed their positions of real or apparent authority directly to Moscow—the tactical nature of the new nation-states was bound to remain a relatively muted issue.

### The Functions of Totalitarian Equality

The term "totalitarian equality," coined by Barrington Moore, has been unjustifiably neglected. When applied in the context of Soviet modernization and nationality policies, it assumes especially great significance as a merit principle, "whereby people and groups receive their status in accordance with their contribution to the power of the ruler, while those who resist are excluded from the society or destroyed." [8] While we know that even such equality has never been absolute in the Soviet system, the usefulness of the concept itself seems self-evident. Merle Fainsod unquestionably had this in mind when he emphasized one corollary of Moore's notion, thus emphasizing one element, among others, with a potentially stabilizing effect in Soviet politics. He did this by emphasizing the universality and pervasiveness of the totalitarian experience in the USSR as a prime factor in the horizontal stratification process that cuts across ethnic solidarities,[9] and thus hinders the consolidation of cohesive (and self-assertive) ethnic collectivities.

At the same time, it is safe to assume that some aspects of Soviet

modernization policies and totalitarian equality have meant reasonably egalitarian allocation of life-opportunities, especially material
goods, to all Soviet nationalities. This could not but serve to mitigate
incipient tensions, thus lending a measure of stability to society and
politics—perhaps especially in Central Asia, where material scarcities
as well as rank inequality vis-à-vis the Russian rulers had been
especially pronounced before the advent of the Soviet regime.

## The Implications of Authentic vis-à-vis Inauthentic Politics

While this distinction is well known in sociology and political science,
it has recently been developed by Harry Eckstein and Amitai Etzioni
in terms that are especially relevant to the issues under review.[10] As
defined by Etzioni, for example, an inauthentic political system is one
wherein "(1) the appearance of give-and-take masks a 'take' but, no,
or only a token, 'give'; (2) participation is manipulated and is not a
genuine sharing in the decision-making process; and (3) the political
superstructure does not represent the societal bases, though it tries to
appear as if it does." [11] We can indeed say that the Soviet political
system has been characterized not only by an inordinate emphasis on
manipulative and instrumental considerations, but also by a very high
investment in structures and arrangements that would give the system an elaborate appearance of responsiveness to human needs. Surely
Soviet-sponsored modernization was intended to endow men not with
rights, but with responsibilities and duties, and to liberate not their
personalities but their energies. An authoritarian system could not
afford to encourage genuinely egalitarian and libertarian dispositions.

Yet, in spite of what Etzioni, for example, would expect of an inauthentic political system—widespread alienation, mobilizational paralysis, inherent instability—the Soviet regime has so far evidently
succeeded in maintaining a significant degree of cohesion as well as a
significant momentum in modernization. One obvious reason for this,
I suggest, is that the Soviet system has never been "purely" inauthentic and totalitarian in nature (although it has approached such a
threshold very closely more than once), and that the Soviet regime
has been less than omniscient and omnipotent in manipulating its
subjects, and less than totally determined to emphasize manipulation
and repression exclusively for the sake of self-preservation. To put it
in a somewhat different perspective, the system's monism has been (as
George Fischer sees it) decidedly "limited" in kind, although this has
in no way involved a movement towards genuine pluralism.[12]

More specifically, what needs to be stressed here is the *extent* to which the regime has gone to develop structures indicative of its responsiveness and authenticity. For example, it has encouraged the mass development of talents and application of energies among all nationalities, and has gradually expanded the provision of significant roles in society on a large scale. Moreover, in ways especially important in the Central Asian milieu, it has tolerated or allowed (after some coercive, and disastrous, experiments) a number of social sectors to retain elements of traditional authenticity. These sectors include some dimensions of family, village, and clan life, as well as some local customs and religious traditions.

At the same time, while some aspects of Soviet authority patterns—such as centralization and bureaucracy—certainly contradict traditional Central Asian patterns, others may be said to have been both congruent and consonant [13] with antecedent local relationships. I have in mind especially aspects of Soviet authoritarian and paternalistic leadership styles, and group rather than individual-focused social orientations and actions. The same may be said about the elaborate Soviet pattern of social recognition: previously underprivileged native strata are enmeshed in the kind of ritualized public acknowledgment and praise (for requisite performance and behavior) and in a network of ceremonial mass-participation that are certain to evoke, at least among those directly affected, a sense of belonging, approval, and gratitude. Thus, it is perhaps especially in Central Asia —where paternalism, collective involvement, and ceremonial recognition have been traditionally appreciated in a special way—that some of the regime's patterns of rule may have done much to keep popular anxiety and alienation within manageable bounds and thereby contribute to over-all stabilization.

## The Significance of Modernization

Whatever else may be said about the Soviet system, one thing is surely beyond question—namely, Soviet commitment to modernization, albeit in a special sense. I suggest that, in essence, a Leninist modernizing disposition involves an interventionist, manipulative, and instrumental approach to nature, society, and politics. It is, in effect, an activistic disposition to travel an unprecedented developmental distance on routes that are autonomously chosen, in a deliberately telescoped period of time, and hence at a pace and toward objectives that are forcibly imposed from above. By the same token, such a disposition involves a conscious, constant, and largely pragmatic quest for optimum techniques and instruments useful in the mobilization of human energies and material resources—albeit for purposes envisioned by the regime.

How does this relate to the stabilizing effect of modernization on inter-ethnic relationships in the USSR? Basically Soviet operational norms make no fundamental distinctions between the human talents and energies that must go into the process of modernization. To put it bluntly, from the Soviet point of view one man's sweat is as good as another's. Thus, the maximum contribution of *all* men is not only encouraged, but expected and demanded. Hence, at least in this sense, racial, national, and ethno-cultural discrimination in the context of modernizational tasks would stand in direct contradiction to Soviet objectives. At the same time, Soviet operational commitments do include a society's dynamic secular development and speedy, high-level material achievement, accompanied by relatively egalitarian distribution of such achievements among all nationalities within the system.

In sum, it may be said that an unusual, if not unique, combination of definite ideological commitments, intense modernizing dispositions, and political expediency has impelled the regime toward modernizing initiatives of a kind and on a scale that mitigate, to a considerable extent, the rigor of controls and the inauthenticity of the political system. While expediency as a factor of political performance is, of course, commonplace, ideological and operational commitments to modernization are not. In my judgment, it is precisely this aspect of Soviet commitments—operative, as it is, not only in the metropolis (the Russian "mother country") but in all ethno-cultural components of the Soviet super-state—that distinguishes the Soviet system most clearly from classical colonial empires.

It should be apparent that, while analytically distinguishable from each other, the four sets of stabilizing factors—pertaining to the positive functions of tactical nation-states, totalitarian equality, political authenticity, and modernization—overlap in many ways and are interdependent as well as mutually reinforcing. They also illustrate some of the ways in which Soviet-sponsored modernization and nationality policy can interact and enhance each other's impact, both in mobilizing ethnic groups for overarching state-wide purposes and in maximizing the state's capacity to control societies in the process of mobilization.

Given such a balance of forces at work (augmented, as they are, by a constant threat of force and a highly refined machinery of surveillance) it is surely difficult to question the potency and pervasiveness of Soviet integrative efforts. It is precisely such reasoning that prompts Cyril Black to argue—largely on the basis of the modernizational and integrative experience of the United Kingdom—that "the near future is . . . likely to see a further absorption of the various minority peoples of the Soviet Union into its dominant Russian culture. *It is a natural process* that is probably encouraged but does not need to be enforced." [14]

But, as we shall see, the forces at work in this realm are not uniformly unidirectional, and not necessarily consistent with each other.

THE IMPACT OF MODERNIZATION AND
NATIONALITY POLICY: DESTABILIZING FACTORS

*Problems in the Functioning of Tactical Nation-States*

There are reasons to suppose that Soviet national republics can be, or become, destabilizing factors in the Soviet system. For one thing, the Soviet regime may not be totally in control over some consequences of its own actions in this realm. While the national idea itself gained currency in Central Asia shortly before the Bolshevik Revolution, the actual national republics were created and delimited under the aegis of the new regime. The basic criteria and rationalizations in this case—including linguistic, territorial, and to some extent cultural and administrative autonomy—were provided by none other than the Soviet regime, and expressed in ideological as well as constitutional terms. Thus, even though we know that the republics had been created as tactical devices, merely to play a designated temporary role and then disappear, it cannot be all too easy for Moscow to discard them by mere sleight of hand. Through a series of historical coincidences, the Soviet union republics have become, together with the Communist Party, the official ideology, the soviets, and the like, a characteristic institutional expression of the Soviet system as such.

This has entailed a fundamental dilemma. Most obviously, the dominant value system of Soviet political culture has involved a definite and coterminous commitment to the equalized and fullest possible development *and* to the speediest possible dissolution of ethnic collectivities. It has involved both the need to encourage the formation of nationalities as active, thriving, self-conscious macro-cohesive units; and the need as well to discourage at all cost the emergence of minority nationalism. It has turned out to be of fundamental importance that the imperatives of undermining ethno-cultural solidarities could not easily be reconciled with the imperatives of mobilizing and using these solidarities as bases for sustained and committed mass-effort benefiting the purposes of the state. From the Soviet point of view, to lean too far in one direction was to risk the crystallization of nationalist orientations by default (or even with the regime's active help); yet to move with all might and speed against any and all manifestations of ethno-cultural identity was to risk the alienation of entire national groups from the Soviet system and its works.

It would be foolhardy to maintain that the Soviet regime has some-how "solved" this problem.[15] For that matter, it is probably safe to say that, at this point, both internal *and* international considerations [16] would make the jettisoning of national republics, together with the principles they embody, highly problematic. This brings us to the crux of the matter. It would seem that what had been intended as purely tactical institutional arrangements actually acquired a certain status and momentum of their own. They may have little in common with genuinely sovereign national collectivities; yet some of their built-in functions, no matter how carefully circumscribed, demon-strably serve as highly important catalysts in the crystallization of a national or ethno-cultural awareness that is largely unprecedented in Central Asia. In a nutshell: by emphasizing the principles of over-arching ethnicity and nationality, including especially language, his-tory, and territory—thus transcending, as it were, the worlds of local dialects, regions, communities, and sects—republican structures un-questionably accelerate the breakdown of traditional social solidarities. In effect, they tend to pull older Central Asian loyalties and identifica-tion patterns upward: from a *communocentric* to an *ethnocentric* focus; from the level of kin, village, and tribe to the level of ethnicity and nation.

Tactical nation-states had, of course, been created, at least in part, for this very purpose: to serve as vehicles of modernization and in-struments of social engineering; to undermine the roots and hence stability of the traditional order, and redirect human orientations and commitments as efficiently as possible toward Soviet beliefs, institu-tions, and tasks. Yet in the process of doing just that, the new struc-tures may prove to be relatively independent variables, as it were, and affect the equilibrium of the Soviet system itself. And this is, of course, precisely what Richard Pipes, among others, would expect, though he might argue his case differently.[17] But, as we shall see, this is a necessary, though not quite sufficient, factor in the process of building self-assertive national communities, and not one that would, in and of itself, automatically affect Soviet political development.

*Problems of Political Authenticity and Totalitarian Equality*

While Soviet modernization and nationality policies could indeed promote the indicators of the system's authenticity and egalitarianism, they could do so only to the extent that the regime actually adhered to its own ideal norms. Yet it would be misleading to say that the regime's demonstrable, "objective" departure from these norms—surely the rule rather than the exception in Soviet history—has necessarily, automatically called into question among Soviet citizens and nationalities the system as a whole. This seems axiomatic: it is not so much *objective reality* as the *perceptual capacity* of people affected by Soviet policies that is likely to matter here. What seems decisive is the readiness and capacity of individuals to perceive themselves as a separate, distinct as well as deprived group—as a community based on shared experience, purpose, and action. In other words, what is likely to matter most are the conditions and stimuli that would especially sensitize particular groups of people to the inauthenticity and inequalities of the system of which they are a part; that would both make them sharply aware of the issues at stake and dispose them to interpret their situation in a new way; and that would, ultimately, compel them to act as a community in accordance with their new self-image and vision of the outer world. As Wallerstein has put it, "any 'ethnic' group exists only to the extent that it is *asserted* to exist at any given point in time by the group itself and by the larger social network of which it is a part." [18]

There is growing, albeit scattered, evidence that Central Asians are indeed beginning to perceive the realities of their existence in unaccustomed ways, as they respond to completely new or gradually maturing circumstances. [19] It would seem that the sharpening of perceptions, in this case, became especially manifest in the crucible of two basically conflicting tendencies in the Soviet Union after Stalin's death. Both of these tendencies impinged directly on the functions of tactical nation-states as expressions of political authenticity and ethnocultural equality.

One of the tendencies, connected with the post-Stalin "thaw" in politics, society, and culture—as well as in foreign policy—provided a powerful impetus for a veritable cultural renaissance in Central Asia, especially when seen against the background of the cultural wasteland prevailing there in the later Stalinist years. The momentum of this revival was compounded by a simultaneous opening of cultural contacts—encouraged by Khrushchev's regime for diverse political reasons —with Asians, Africans, and Arabs. Yet, even as this trend was gathering momentum, a countervailing tendency asserted itself with grow-ing force, especially in the later years of the Khrushchev era. It em-bodied a basically conservative mood in Moscow, a renewed proclivity for regimentation and retrenchment, including a multifaceted at-tempt to set in motion a new phase in multinational integration. The latter found expression in a series of officially sponsored initiatives, including political, literary, academic, and "scientific" conferences on problems of nationality. These were concerned with refining the rationale and optimal stages for minority nationalities, together with their languages, literatures, and cultural institutions, to "converge" and ultimately "merge"—that is, dissolve in a greater, homogeneous, "Soviet" nation. Official insistence on Russia's role as the most "ad-vanced" nation, as the guide, model, as well as "elder brother" to all other nationalities, left little to the imagination: the projected new national amalgam, even though still without precisely delineated character and time scale, would have decidedly supranational (Soviet) as well as Russian features.

At the same time, yet another pervasive trend materialized, whose incongruity has presumably not passed unnoticed in Central Asia. It has to do with the emergence of a subtly expressed pecking order of ethnic groups in the USSR—directly or indirectly manifested in official policies or informal practices—in effect, a graded scale of ethnic reliability, trustworthiness, and intrinsic value. Aside from what is perhaps a special case of the Jews, it is no exaggeration to say that the subtle gradations in the regime's attitudes towards nationalities are probably most clearly apparent in the Central Asian situation. Aside from the explicitly leading role assigned to Russians, there have been signs that Ukrainians, for example, are considered more reliable in authoritative political positions outside the Ukraine than other non-Russian groups. Armenians and Georgians are considered more trustworthy than Central Asians—both in Armenia and Georgia, re-spectively, and in Central Asia. Some Soviet Moslems, such as the Uzbeks, are viewed as more important and reliable than others, espe-cially the Crimean Tatars, most of whom are now living in Central Asia and are considered expendable. Some nationalities—mainly the smaller and weaker ones, such as the Tadzhiks—are viewed as candi-dates for absorption by others—in this case, the Uzbeks—thus contrib-uting to what is clearly envisaged as a relentless process of widening the circles of regional associations which would themselves be merely transitional steps towards a single Soviet nationality.[20]

In these circumstances, what were surely, from a minority's point of view, the most and least authentic, and the most and least egalitarian, elements of the Soviet system came to the fore almost simultaneously. While launched—or permitted to develop—essentially on parallel lines, these elements were bound to enter a collision course. Accordingly, Central Asian cultural aspirations, revived and encouraged during one phase of Soviet policy, were bound to encounter, in the overlapping second phase, growing frustrations. Not surprisingly, then, Central Asian sensibilities came to be marked by both defensive and assertive qualities. While far from reckless, their expression showed a sense of pride and a degree of confidence that had been missing in the region since the early 1920s. In fact, we have here the manifestations of a lively, complex, self-conscious, increasingly resourceful, and sophisticated quest for ways to preserve and deepen the richness of a newly-found cultural autonomy and identity—hopefully without coming into head-on collision with the strictures of the Soviet regime.

The following set of orientations, necessarily presented in summary fashion, is but a small indication of the range of developing interests, concerns, and grievances among educated men and women (especially academics and students in the humanities and social sciences, as well as artists, writers, and poets) of the region:

(a) Personalistic and romantic, including mystic and visionary, involvement with the immediate environment—with what is, in effect, "any piece of town or terrain with which an individual is linked by ties of kinship or affection . . . "[21]; concurrent concern with the exploration of personal relationships, including especially the problems of personal identity, love, and trust.[22]

(b) Preoccupation with what can only be characterized as the golden past—of a particular local culture, or ethnic group, or titular nationality, or overarching Turko-Iranian and Islamic civilization—including exploration and idealization of a group's mythical origins as well as special features, glories, and achievements. Parallel preoccupation with restoring the region's folk memory, emphasizing the virtues of land, village, tribe, and custom in the formation of a "home" and a "homeland" (separate and apart from the Soviet Union), a repository of loyalty and love, a cradle of valued heritage and enduring group identity and links. Preoccupation, as well, with restoring the legitimate stature of ancient folk heroes, including tribal and other traditional leaders as well as reformers, artists, and poets who had been under a cloud of official Soviet opprobrium.[23]

(c) Defensive or assertive concern for legitimizing ethno-cultural features and achievements in a comparative perspective, including more or less circumspect emphasis on the equality or even superiority

—certainly the uniqueness—of the region's linguistic, literary, esthetic, scientific, and broadly historic heritage relative to the achievements of alien civilizations.[24]

(d) Explicit or implicit attempts to defend the intrinsic validity and political legitimacy of the original autonomist arrangements in Soviet nationality policy—concerning language, literature, and culture and, by implication, territory and administration as well. Systematic reference, on this account, to the writings and actions of Lenin and of other Revolutionary and pre-Revolutionary *Russian* figures who had expressed a concern for the preservation of the autonomy and vitality of Asian cultures against the encroachments of "Great Russian chauvinism." [25]

(e) Implicit or indirect assertion of the need to rectify what is still a decided underrepresentation of Central Asians in higher and specialized education, and in technical, managerial, and other authoritative roles in the region—and, conversely, the gross overrepresentation of Slavs and other nonnatives in such roles, as well as the overrepresentation of natives in rural, underemployed, and unskilled sectors of society, economy, and labor.[26]

Significantly, the Soviet leadership has shown marked restraint in dealing with the revival of ethno-cultural concerns in Central Asia. There has been, so far, no draconic crackdown on expressions of this revival. Aside from complex domestic considerations in this case (having to do with the character and style of the post-Stalin central leadership as well as with the new realities in Central Asia), at least two other reasons for this hesitation should be mentioned here, primarily because of the built-in quality of their effect on Soviet choices and commitments.

It would seem that we are dealing here with what may be viewed as positive and negative incentives for restraint. In positive terms, there is the continued need, expressly bequeathed by Lenin, to present the cultural, political, and economic development of Central Asian republics as a showcase, model, and beacon for other developing nations—in effect, a model of the success of Soviet-sponsored modernization and nationality policy in a formerly "backward," colonial milieu. As a reflection of this need, Central Asia has become, since the late 1950s, a beehive of representational activity, wherein a steadily growing stream of invited, feted, and guided delegations from Asia, Africa, and the Middle East is also beginning to be balanced with a trickle of Central Asian representatives—particularly intellectuals and artists—going abroad on good-will missions. The negative incentives in this case have to do with the intensifying competition between the USSR and China in Asia. This has gone hand in hand not only with Chinese irredentist demands involving Central Asia, but also with appeals from both sides to each other's Turkic minorities, accompanied by mutual accusations of imperialist, discriminatory, assimilationist, and generally destructive nationality policies.

There can be little doubt that the combination of such incentives has helped to inhibit overly crude, regimenting, and repressive policies in Central Asia, all the more so since such policies would directly impinge on the value and validity of Moscow's prime exhibit in the region: the "many-sided flowering" of local nationalities and cultures. By the same token, relative Soviet permissiveness in dealing with some of the new ethno-cultural concerns in the region has probably done much to encourage the development (and even public airing) of these concerns. On the other hand, though, while the newly articulated interests and grievances are an important barometer of growing self-consciousness and potential alienation, they still seem to be quite disparate and inchoate expressions on the part of separate, most likely isolated and groping individuals or, at best, small, fluid, unconnected groups. They do not seem to be expressions of conscious, purposive, large-scale collectivities. In this sense, they are, again, necessary but insufficient factors in the formation of a coherent, cohesive, and assertive ethnic or cultural identity, one that would seriously influence the course of Soviet politics.

### Problems of Modernization: Points of Incongruity and Tension

As noted earlier, to the extent that it is operative, totalitarian equality can be a stabilizing political factor. But we also know that totalitarian equality is an abstraction; it is not a static and consistent condition. In fact, it is violated precisely because of the tensions generated not only within but also between Soviet policies of modernization and nationality policy. It is violated because the imperatives of modernization are not necessarily reconcilable with the imperatives of Soviet nationality policy.

As we have seen, the main points of tension, in this case, are viewed by Pipes (as well as Allworth, Conquest, and others) as determined by the very nature of the national republics, whose special constitutional features tend to generate a new national consciousness in the region which in time will make itself felt in the arena of Soviet politics. Bennigsen and Lemercier-Quelquejay add to the complexity and persuasiveness of this argument. Essentially, their view is predicated on what they see as the confluence of two processes, which may be summarized as follows: (a) The evolution of the traditional Moslem family in Central Asia toward nuclear forms has coincided with the erosion of clan and tribal structures and of other particularistic solidarities which had "inhibited the birth of national consciousness in [local] traditional societies . . . Now that the individual is isolated in a numerically restricted family, his need to attach himself to a larger group remains unsatisfied . . . All that remains to him is attachment to a national group—the only large collective entity that survives in the Soviet Muslim world." (b) In spite of their coercive features, Soviet modernizing and administrative policies have led, in effect for the first time in local history, to the emergence of an "elite capable of ruling," as a new secular intelligentsia received training for technical as well as managerial roles in circumstances demanding self-conscious, efficient, and large-scale organizational performance. In addition, growing contacts with Asians and Africans abroad, and a greater sense of its own historical and intellectual antecedents in Russia and Central Asia, have spurred this elite toward an awareness of its own role and goals that is more solid and confident than ever. "In this sense, the nationalism of the Muslims of the USSR is certainly stronger now than in 1917, and it places in their hands weapons which are more effective in resisting Russian pressure than ancient Muslim traditionalism." [27]

This argument raises several issues of principle. First, why should the individual's loyalties, presumably released from a traditional, kin-oriented matrix, necessarily focus on a national rather than on a still larger, supranational Soviet collectivity—when so many of the regime's efforts have gone into attracting and moving him, precisely, in the latter direction? In other words, why should a new overarching aggregative process, itself a result of an increasingly successful social mobilization, stop at one rather than another level? Second, why should the new secular intelligentsia choose to focus on a national (and highly dangerous) identity—when it has been the regime's consistently declared policy to attract and co-opt members of this group into the supranational Soviet fold, including the power structure? Finally, how can these two parallel mobilizational trends lead toward a new, coherent national collectivity without some new, compelling stimuli to solidarity between the mobile masses and elites—the potential followers and leaders?

The arguments proposed by Bennigsen and others, do not grapple fully with these issues. They tend to assume a certain degree of automaticity in sociopolitical correlations—a virtually automatic effect of language, territory, and other formal attributes of ethnicity on national consciousness, as well as an equally automatic effect of eroding traditionalism and new elite-capabilities on specifically national mobilization and integration. I find it difficult to assume such direct cause-and-effect relationships. There is a need to consider some intervening variables in this case, special catalysts that would sharpen the relevance of a new national consciousness in Central Asia. In other words, it is important to pinpoint factors that would spur local receptivity to the new idea and make the new consciousness personally important—important, in this case, to Moslems and Turks as individuals and groups—rather than advancing yet another abstraction. Let me suggest, very briefly, one way to tie in many of the preceding arguments, and to visualize a denouement wherein many of the incipient issues and problems we have discussed so far may indeed come to a head.

In the simplest terms, it is possible to visualize Soviet modernization and nationality policies as inducing in Central Asia two mutually contradictory processes. On the one hand, we have here the fairly recent crystallization of a broad range of life-opportunities in a secular, urbanizing, industrial world. We have here also the emergence, and in some sectors the well-nigh meteoric rise, of native specialist elites. This is, of course, merely one reflection of a very much broader process of social mobilization (by means of a rapidly growing educational system, and in other ways).[28] In this process, masses of men and women are encouraged to shed traditional mores, ties, and orientations, to acquire new capacities and skills, and to fill the myriad of roles and positions opened up by systematic social engineering and its main concomitant, comprehensive modernization.

The opposing development, a long-term reflection of Soviet administrative and nationality policy, is a massive (and in part officially sponsored) influx of European, and especially Slavic, settlers and professional personnel. They have come to Central Asia to staff the local apparatuses of development and control, as a rule including the most specialized and complex roles, the highest ranks, and the authoritative as well as strategic positions in all sectors of society, anchored especially in the region's cities and towns. We can, therefore, speak of two growing streams of people arriving simultaneously to fill the new system of roles and opportunities.[29] This situation is further complicated by the fact that, since the 1960s, the birthrate among Russia's Moslems has been far higher than among Slavs, making it all but a certainty that Moslem pressure on available positions will be strongly augmented.

In and of itself this need not be of special significance; competition for valued roles is, after all, a universal phenomenon in most of the world's complex societies. But if present circumstances in Russia's Moslem borderlands remain unaltered, it is quite reasonable to expect that the volume and pressure of the two massive human streams—one rising from native grassroots, the other arriving from outside—may soon outstrip the system's capacity to absorb them. This, in turn, could lead to what would be, in effect, a saturation of role-opportunities and status-positions in Central Asia—a development fraught with potentially grave tensions. One of the results of such a saturation may well be a condition of profound role-strain among Central Asia's newly rising secular elites, that is, a condition of growing frustration on the part of people who are trained for and led to expect specific life opportunities yet find such opportunities unreal or unobtainable. The frustration is likely to sharpen to the extent that it involves an increasingly specific perception of incongruence among native elites— a perception of palpable discrepancies between their role-expectation and role-fulfillment in the economy; between their formally equal public recognition and their actual differentiation and depreciation as minorities; between their honorific participation and genuine representation in the system; between their status in the prestige hierarchy and status in the executive and political hierarchy; in short, between ceremonial and substantive authority. As Merle Fainsod saw this succinctly more than two decades ago, a highly trained and increasingly self-confident native intelligentsia, "hav[ing] been educated for administrative and other responsibilities . . . [may be expected to] aspire to real as well as formal authority . . . "[30]

There is reason to assume that both natives and outsiders in Central Asia are beginning to be aware of the possibility and consequences of just such a role-saturation, and that Moscow may not be able to postpone dealing with this issue much longer. This leads us to the fourth (and last) element in the analysis of factors likely to compound the destabilizing effects of observed trends.

## The Function of Heretical Models

In perceiving discrepancies between role-expectation and role-fulfillment, people may feel deprived; they may experience a sense of grievance and threat; yet they may be unable to understand the meaning and visualize the consequences of their condition. Moreover, even people who understand the roots of their deprivation may not be able to formulate appropriate demands and visualize ways to take spe-

cific action. It is a truism that such people need models with which to
identify and associate. This is surely all the more relevant in societies
where it has been inherently difficult to conceive of alternative patterns of perception and action—in part because of long isolation from
a changing outside world, in part because significant alternatives to
prevailing orientations could be viewed as profoundly heretical in a
traditional Islamic milieu. (It is but one indication of this problem
that, at the time of the onset of Soviet rule in Central Asia, there
were remarkably few native Moslem writings dealing with the outside
world and with the newly raised issues of the time, including modernization, self-determination, and ethno-cultural identity.) Hence, again,
we see the need for models that would tangibly, even dramatically,
demonstrate the meaning and implications of locally perceived conditions.[31]

It should be useful to assess this problem by juxtaposing (albeit
very briefly) two sets of models that I assume to be operative here:
exogenous and endogenous. It would seem self-evident that the processes impinging on a large-scale multinational aggregate cannot be
adequately understood unless one considers them in the context of
what is (in Hansen's terms)[32] a dynamic interaction between an internal regional dialectic and changing international environmental
pressures.[33]

*Exogenous models.* It is undeniable that some such models became
available to Central Asians in the 1950s and 1960s from abroad—for
example, through the national renaissance of the Afro-Asian world,
through the rise of revisionism and polycentrism in the international
Communist movement, and through the rise, as well, of Communist
China as a major (and self-consciously Asian) power willing and able
to challenge the legitimacy of Soviet rule and nationality policy as
well as Soviet Russian hegemony in Asia and elsewhere.[34] While these
developments have certainly limited Soviet freedom of action in Central Asia, their influence on local societies has been essentially indirect
rather than direct. Moreover, it is probably safe to say that these
models, while potentially important, were so far too distant, too alien,
or too abstract to be easily assimilated and followed in Central Asia.
In any event, their association specifically with the issues of local
ethno-cultural identity and autonomy seems to have been tenuous
at best.

As it happens, though, the emergence of these potential exogenous
influences largely coincided with the rise in the Central Asian world of
new forces that were much closer to home, geographically as well as

culturally and spiritually. I have in mind the newly emerging, and quite extraordinary, role of the Crimean Tatars in Central Asia.

*Endogenous models.* I suggest that the Crimean Tatars are potentially among the most important models (and possibly agents) of change in Central Asia, perhaps especially in the realm of ethno-cultural identity and national as well as human rights. They may be said to represent, to Central Asians, five highly significant elements: (a) People who have been historic allies, close cultural relatives, as well as ethnic kinsmen of Central Asians. (In these societies where distrust of new ideas was often directly related to the distrust of strangers who were exponents of these ideas, Tatars have been the only major group of outsiders who were, as a rule, not viewed as strangers.) (b) People who have been among the most important agents of religious reform, secular modernity, and national renaissance in Central Asia, especially between the time of Tsarist Russian arrival in the region (circa mid-nineteenth century) and the Russian Revolution and Civil War. (c) People who are in the process of losing (or have already lost) their national homeland, after having been forcibly deported to Central Asia. (d) People who, having been decimated by years of hounding and hunger in the course of deportation, now live in uneasy exile in Central Asia, thus constituting a living example, a palpable reminder, an especially potent demonstration of what can happen to Central Asians. (e) People whose own new political consciousness closely paralleled the rise of the Human Rights Movement in European Russia in the 1950s and 1960s—indeed, whose fate and resistance have themselves been important catalysts of the democratic movement in Russia, and who have emerged as the standard-bearers of dissent (including samizdat) in Central Asia in the 1960s and early 1970s. These are thus people who are now in a position to be highly persuasive mediators in Central Asia of the most explosive message to emanate from Russian cities since the October Revolution: the idea of ethno-cultural equality, national self-determination, and human rights as values that are intimately connected, indeed interdependent.

It is in this sense that the Tatars can be critically important heretical models in Central Asia, models of attitudes and behavior that, while largely unprecedented and involving unaccustomed risks, may become acceptable precisely because they are expounded by Tatars. Under what circumstances are the Tatars most likely to play such a role? I suggest they can do so especially in a context I have mentioned earlier: the growing saturation of role-opportunities in Central Asia and the implementation of some forceful Soviet measures in dealing with the new situation.

## SOVIET OPTIONS IN DEALING WITH NEW REALITIES: IMPLICATIONS AND PROSPECTS

What can Moscow do about the problems of potential role-saturation and a new cultural and political consciousness in Central Asia? How can it defuse such a potential tinderbox? Let me group some of the available options ranging in emphasis within a spectrum from typically permissive, unconditional, and open-ended to constraining, conditional, and closed-ended choices.

First, some typically permissive options: (1) Admit all qualified aspirants to positions of responsibility and authority in the social system of status and roles and in the political power structure—both in national-republican and in supranational institutions—irrespective of race, ethnicity, and national origin. (2) Encourage uninterrupted, dynamic economic growth at a pace and of a kind that would readily accommodate all comers, thus either augmenting the capacity of the sociopolitical system to absorb all relevant claimants or at least providing acceptable alternatives to scarce roles. (3) Reduce or reverse the influx of Slavs into Central Asia, thus reducing the pressure on available positions and enacting in reality one of the oldest and most dramatic formal Soviet commitments: the "nativization" of local republican apparatuses of modernization and control, not only on a "functional" but also on a "proportional" basis, leading to genuine self-determination for indigenous majorities in each republic.

Second, some typically constraining options: (1) Curtail the access of qualified Central Asian cadres to some positions of skill, responsibility, and authority, especially in sectors that are heavily weighted with Slavic incumbents and are considered too sensitive on security grounds to accommodate all comers. Concurrently, limit the access of indigenous young generations to the system of higher and specialized education, thus reducing at the source subsequent native demand for high-achievement roles. (2) Reduce the pace of economic growth— or especially limit the modes of industrial development—in Central Asia, in ways that would discourage and reduce the pace of native social mobility and migration to the region's cities, thus also reducing the likelihood of interethnic encounters, competition, and tensions.[35] (3) Systematically disperse the mobilized segments of the Central Asian population, beginning with native specialist elites, throughout the Soviet Union, preferably to the least populated and most manpower-hungry areas, such as Siberia as well as central and northern Russia. Concomitantly, co-opt qualified natives to Russia's multinational consortium of specialized cadres, but largely at the price of dispersal. Concurrently, disperse Central Asia's supply of semiskilled, including rural, labor throughout the USSR, thus accomplishing two things: reducing the potentially embarrassing heavy native concentration in the region's semiskilled, underemployed, and rural sectors, and also reducing potentially troublesome native pressure on the land.[36] This would ensure the supply, for industry in Siberia and European Russia of what is becoming an increasingly scarce commodity in the Soviet Union—a semiskilled workforce suitable for filling the lowest rungs of industrial production and urban services.[37]

These, as I see it, are the six main Soviet options relevant to this case.[38] There is a basic reason for grouping them in this fashion. Paradoxically, while the prime imperatives of Soviet modernization and nationality policy have been to turn the USSR into a homogeneous, continental system, predicated on the gradual absorption and assimilation of minorities into the supranational Soviet fold, some very different dispositions have also been at work here. These dispositions have been competing directly with formally enunciated values, and may thus entail decidedly dysfunctional effects for the political system. The implications may be dysfunctional because the regime's commitments and actions have not been unidirectional.

Specifically, as long as the reservoir of available positions was large, and the volume and quality of native cadres for these positions remained low, the advancement of these cadres up the mobilizational ladder (say, from the 1920s to the early 1960s) was fairly swift. But even then two phenomena were clearly manifest. First, as already noted, there was an official tendency within the confines of each republic to assign native cadres to positions of public esteem rather than managerial responsibility and political power. Second, there was an even more pronounced tendency to exclude Moslems almost completely from all decision-making bodies at the apex of the power structure in Moscow and throughout the all-Union apparatus, most notably from the Politburo and the nomenklatura. To paraphrase Seweryn Bialer, while most rewards of the system were distributed in accordance with universalistic criteria, some, notably those pertaining to membership in the power elite, were distributed on the basis of an individual's ethnic identity.[39] Nowhere has this been more true than in Central Asia.

It may be said, therefore, that while some dimensions of Soviet initiatives stressed integration and assimilation, others emphasized segregation and exclusion. In other words, at a certain critical junction of the political system, at least in Central Asia, the high-pressure, purposively assimilative process has tended to go hand in hand with a deliberate freeze in the process of assimilation. Attraction has gone hand in hand with repulsion, as it were. Accordingly, the rate of social mobilization in the region could not but exceed to a growing extent, perhaps by far, the rate of effective assimilation. Having been mobilized from a particular traditional and ethnic matrix, Central Asian specialist elites and political cadres, instead of being designated for full membership in the ruling stratum, were in effect relegated to what could come to be perceived as precarious interstitiality in politics and culture. Instead of becoming full-fledged political actors in their own right, they were designated as political and cultural brokers in their own societies—to act on behalf of forces beyond their control, and to be neither fully a part of their own native milieu nor a fully integrated part of the world of their Soviet Russian sponsors.

Given the pervasive ambivalence on the part of the Soviet power elite toward Central Asians as full-fledged citizens and fully equal partners, and at the same time the continued Soviet commitment to dynamic modernization, it would seem that we have here the makings of a classic dilemma. Generally speaking, unless new rules are devised for mobilizing and integrating the Asian nationalities, a high and growing rate of modernization and social mobilization in the region probably cannot be sustained without straining Soviet capacity to control the process as a whole. On the other hand, a deliberate reduction in the scope and tempo of modernization in Central Asia (including a massive reduction in native social mobility) would be equally likely to have a deeply destabilizing effect. In short, in the eyes of the Soviet ruling stratum, the distaste for implementing some of the permissive options is probably matched by the grave risks implicit in implementing the constraining options. To wit, emphasis on permissive choices would not only contradict some of the basic operational principles of the Soviet state; it would entail the danger of antagonizing the Europeans—the dominant, favored, strongly entrenched group in Central Asia—as well as the danger of a gradually growing interest, on the part of Central Asians, in meaningful forms of group identity and autonomy. Emphasis on constraining choices, while probably more palatable to the European and Bolshevik core of the Soviet political apparatus, would run counter to the regime's most solemnly articulated commitments and norms, and would surely entail all the greater dangers of rapid and massive native disaffection in Central Asia.

Specifically, this latter, coercive course of action would help to accomplish precisely that which the regime has tried hard to avoid: the tendency of Moslem mobilization to focus on local culture, ethnicity, and nationality rather than move men from a traditional fold directly to the supranational level. In fact, it is all the more likely to lead to the reinforcement rather than erosion of national consciousness here because the obstacles to assimilative integration are due not only to the resistance of those subject to such integration but also to the ambivalence of those who sponsor it. As has been noted since the mid-1950s, new perceptions of internal and external realities on the part of the Central Asian elites have heightened (though to an as yet unknown extent) their self-conscious ethnocentric sensibilities. Imprudent, sharply constraining Soviet actions would certainly exacerbate these sensibilities. Nothing is likely to do so more surely than the perception of crisis by these elites, wherein a latent sense of relative deprivation is confirmed by indifference, neglect, dispersal, or repression, and wherein the discrepancy between their new role-expectations and their actual role-fulfillment is more apparent than ever before.[40] Similarly, nothing is likely to exacerbate the sensibilities of Central Asia's rural masses and semiskilled town dwellers more than a coercive attempt to make them leave their ancestral lands for the distant, alien, impersonal, and physically inhospitable world of Siberia and European Russia.[41] In such a crisis the threat to a man's status on the basis of his ethnicity may well be seen as coincidental with a threat to his sense of self-worth and ego-identity.

As Wallerstein would visualize such a denouement, in a broader context: "Ethnic consciousness is eternally latent everywhere. But it is only realized when groups feel either threatened with a loss of previously acquired privilege or conversely feel that it is an opportune moment politically to overcome long-standing denial of privilege." [42] It is in this sense that group self-consciousness and ethnic self-consciousness of native elites may come to coincide. Under such circumstances, even those who would have preferred to associate themselves with the dominant Soviet-Russian culture, but find themselves suspended between a world they had left and one that does not fully accept them, may feel compelled to reestablish ties with their original ethnicity and culture. They may feel compelled to do so even though it is bound to be extremely difficult for them to decide which components of Turko-Iranian ethnicity, Central Asian traditions, and Islamic religious civilization are meaningful and viable enough—indeed, "authentic" enough—under the new circumstances to constitute foci for renewed attachments. Under such circumstances, also, the region's secular elites may find it both necessary and possible to re-establish ties with the masses of their compatriots in villages and towns—who, in turn, may be more amenable to the renewed relationship precisely because of the shared sense of deprivation and neglect.

It is in such a situation, then, that the latent resentments and frictions in the region could become both cumulative and manifest, just as the long-term causes of the problem and the short-term precipitants would tend to coalesce. Indeed, in these circumstances, the Central Asians may be driven (by Moscow's possible insensitivity or intransigence, as well as by their own new self-image) toward ever sharper and more hostile self-differentiation on ethnic grounds. For that matter, their hostility may be compounded by an all too possible equation of the status of a separate ethnic group with that of a relatively deprived social class; ethnic consciousness and class consciousness may thus indeed intertwine.[43] And, as has often happened before in such situations, hostility may prove to be the most readily mobilizable of human emotions. By the same token, religion, culture, ethnicity, nationality, and race—all of them bases for sacred solidarities evoking highly charged affective commitment—may prove to be the most congenial collective vehicles for the expression of new group interests as well as of hostility and self-differentiation.

To be sure, the Soviet regime has often shown astuteness in controlling or adjusting to tensions and demands, and a great deal of sobriety and pragmatism—perhaps especially in the case of Asian nationalities—in adapting to complex or unfavorable realities. But Moscow has also frequently shown a disposition to evade or "encapsulate" fundamental issues and conflicts,[44] at times to dispose of them by resorting to rigid prescriptions and draconic repressions.

It is in the latter instance, at a time of passionately perceived crisis that might be mismanaged by Moscow, that Central Asians, even if unable to respond in a cohesive and organized way, may assert themselves in heedless expressions of frustration—as they have done before on other grounds.[45] They may do so on purely expressive rather than instrumental grounds—that is, regardless of punishment and losses, and without clear reference to the practical relevance and feasibility of their effort. However, to the extent that their self-assertion may be *other* than purely expressive, it will not need to (and, given the intricacy and pervasiveness of Soviet controls, probably could not) proceed along secessionist lines in order to be effective.[46] It would more likely take the form of increasingly specific and self-conscious, as well as more aggressive, even militant, demands on the system and its center: demands for more genuine ethnic participation in the system's roles and rewards, for broader and more meaningful jurisdiction in the management of the local milieu, and, perhaps most subtly, for recognition of the intrinsic value and validity of some customary, ethical, and esthetic components of local cultures and life-styles.

Paradoxically, perhaps, significant repercussions are likely in either case: if the Soviet regime finds it possible to grant the minorities an institutionalized capacity to express demands and overcome inequalities, the system itself will be markedly, albeit gradually, transformed; if, on the other hand, the present trends are allowed to continue, ethnicity and nationality may well become the most explosive, chronically destabilizing factors in Soviet politics.[47]

PART FIVE

# Continuity and Change in Foreign Policy

# Peaceful Coexistence:
# From Heresy to Orthodoxy

PAUL MARANTZ

# 15

In the days and months following the Bolshevik Revolution of 1917, the Soviet leaders were convinced that capitalist rule was doomed to rapid extinction. While Lenin, the most pragmatic of the Bolsheviks, recognized that expediency was often the inescapable fate of the weak, he shared with his corevolutionaries a deeply ingrained hostility to cooperation with the imperialist powers. Coexistence—peaceful or not so peaceful—was dismissed, both because capitalism was seen as a transient phenomenon destined to disappear shortly and because close ties with the imperialist enemy were viewed as a violation of revolutionary principle.

Yet despite these expectations and predilections, capitalism and Communism have managed a precarious coexistence for more than half a century. Moreover, in the past two decades, no concept has been more frequently and fervently championed by the Soviet Union than that of peaceful coexistence. Peaceful coexistence eventually became enshrined as one of the most basic tenets of Soviet doctrine. Over the years outright hostility gradually shaded into grudging tolerance which, in turn, ultimately gave way to energetic advocacy. This essay traces the emergence and evolution of the Soviet doctrine of peaceful coexistence.

The relationship between the overt doctrine and the actual, operational views of the Soviet leadership is complex and uncertain. One rarely encounters an exact, one-to-one correspondence between public declarations and private beliefs in any political system, Communist or non-Communist. Nonetheless, if the self-justifying functions of the official doctrine are taken into account, and if this doctrine is traced step by step as it evolved and unfolded over a period of several decades, a great deal can be learned concerning changing Soviet perceptions and expectations. There may be few startling revelations, but new evidence does emerge, evidence that must be taken into account in any attempt to formulate a sound and comprehensive explanation of Soviet conduct.

LENINIST ORIGINS

Claims to ideological continuity with the founding fathers of Bolshevism constitute one of the most prized legitimizing devices of the Soviet regime. Consequently, as soon as Khrushchev's report to the Twentieth Party Congress proclaimed peaceful coexistence a basic tenet of Soviet doctrine, it became incumbent upon the Party's ideologues to demonstrate that it was none other than Lenin who originated, developed, and expounded a carefully elaborated concept of peaceful coexistence. Few jobs could be more demanding. Although Lenin's speeches and writings fill more than fifty solid volumes, his direct remarks on peaceful coexistence are barely enough to comprise a single page. It appears that Lenin used the term peaceful coexistence on only five different occasions.[1] On none of these occasions was Lenin's reference to peaceful coexistence anything more than a passing comment of insignificant importance. For example, in February 1920 Lenin responded to a question concerning Soviet plans for Asia by stating: "They are the same as in Europe: peaceful coexistence with all peoples; with the workers and peasants of all nations awakening to a new life—a life without exploiters, without landowners, without capitalists, without merchants." [2] Two years later, during an interview with an English journalist, Lenin remarked:

The League of Nations bears so many marks of its world war origin, it is so intimately bound up with the Versailles Treaty and is so marked by the absence of anything resembling the establishment of the real equality of rights between nations, anything resembling a real chance of their peaceful coexistence, that I think our negative attitude to the League can be appreciated and does not stand in need of further comment.[3]

Furthermore, in four of the five instances when Lenin alluded to peaceful coexistence, he was directing his remarks to visiting journalists from abroad. On those occasions, he had an obvious interest in presenting himself as a man of moderation and good will whatever his private views on the possibility or desirability of peaceful co-existence. In the unending stream of speeches, articles, and letters that Lenin addressed to his Party comrades, only once did he even so much as refer to coexistence: In a letter written in April 1921 to the Communists of the various Caucasian republics, Lenin urged these republics to expand their trade and commercial dealings with the West. In passing he noted: "The Caucasus can adjust its 'coexistence' and trade with the capitalist West more quickly and with greater ease [than Russia]." [4] Needless to say, this hardly constitutes a discussion of major theoretical or doctrinal significance. To the Party faithful these terse comments may serve as "proof" of the Leninist origins of the concept of peaceful coexistence, but to the outside observer they are much less convincing.[5]

Lenin's colleagues mentioned peaceful coexistence, but their references to this concept were only slightly more frequent and certainly no more significant. Ironically, it appears that Trotsky, who staunchly opposed accommodation with the capitalist world, was the first Bolshevik to use the term coexistence publicly.[6] On November 21, 1917, in a speech to the Central Executive Committee, he said that he looked forward to Russia's "fraternal coexistence with the neighboring peoples of Western Europe." [7] On the following day he stated: "We want the most rapid peace on the basis of the honorable coexistence and cooperation of peoples." [8] Yet the very next sentence indicates just what Trotsky thought were the preconditions that must *precede* coexistence: "We want the most rapid overthrow of the rule of capitalism." [9]

In calling for coexistence, Trotsky was not advocating peaceful relations between Soviet Russia and capitalist Europe. On the contrary, at this time he was an avid supporter of a revolutionary crusade against Germany. He was simply reflecting the basic Marxist-Leninist belief that the destruction of capitalism would bring permanent peace to the peoples of the world. He advocated the destruction of capitalist *governments* as a prelude to the peaceful coexistence of *peoples*. It is clear that during the immediate post-Revolutionary period peaceful coexistence was a very minor element in the Soviet approach to international politics.

STALINIST NEGLECT

During the early 1920s, the phrase peaceful coexistence had not yet taken on a well-defined meaning in the lexicon of diplomacy and foreign policy. Soviet spokesmen casually used the term peaceful coexistence to characterize both the Soviet Union's tense relations with capitalist nations and the uniquely harmonious relations that were said to flourish among the fraternal peoples of the Soviet Union. On those occasions in 1921–1924 when Stalin mentioned coexistence, it was solely in reference to the nationality problem within the Soviet Union. For example, in December 1922 he stated: "In the camp of capitalism there are imperialist wars, national strife, oppression, colonial slavery and chauvinism. In the camp of the Soviets, the camp of socialism, there are on the contrary, mutual confidence, national equality of rights, and the peaceful co-existence and fraternal cooperation of peoples." [10] This was a common formulation, and even the first Constitution of the USSR, ratified in January 1924, hailed the "peaceful coexistence and fraternal collaboration" of the peoples of the Soviet Union.[11]

It was not until December 1925 that Stalin first applied the term peaceful coexistence to a discussion of international politics. At the Fourteenth Party Congress, Stalin noted: "What we at one time regarded as a brief respite after the war has become a whole period of respite. Hence a certain equilibrium of forces and a certain period of 'peaceful co-existence' between the bourgeois world and the proletarian world." [12]

Peaceful coexistence first played a significant role in Soviet diplomacy in 1927, at the World Economic Conference in Geneva. At this conference the Soviet delegation launched a sustained effort to secure international recognition for the principle of peaceful coexistence as a means of improving the Soviet Union's international image and securing better access to trade and credits.[13] Some success was achieved. Although the Western nations cautiously shied away from an acceptance of Soviet terminology, they were willing to endorse the general principle of economic cooperation between the two systems.[14]

The progress of the Geneva conference was followed with some care in the Soviet press, and the advocacy of peaceful coexistence by the Soviet delegation was duly noted. Conceivably the conference could have provided the opportunity for the development and exposition of a well-defined concept of peaceful coexistence as a means of transforming a vague slogan into a major element in Soviet discourse and thinking on international politics. However, this did not occur. Before the year was over, the Soviet Union withdrew into isolation, and Stalin declared that *"the period of 'peaceful co-existence' is receding into the past,* giving place to a period of imperialist assaults and preparation for intervention against the USSR." [15] This unequivocal pronouncement ruled out any meaningful discussion of peaceful coexistence, and within a short time even passing references to the term became exceedingly rare.

The lack of interest in the concept of peaceful coexistence continued for more than two decades. Even during the relative thaws in East-West relations (for example, the Popular Front period of the mid-1930s and the Grand Alliance of World War II), Soviet commentators made only sporadic reference to peaceful coexistence, and the concept was never examined in any detail. In fact, Soviet identification with peaceful coexistence was so weak that advocacy of it by Earl Browder (then head of the American Communist Party) could be cited as evidence of a reformist, antirevolutionary orientation by Jacques Duclos of the French Communist Party in early 1945! [16]

Stalin can hardly be termed an enthusiastic champion of peaceful coexistence. After 1927 he never again used the term in his public speeches. At neither the Party congresses in 1930, 1934, 1939, and 1952 nor at any other official function did he ever so much as utter the words peaceful coexistence. In fact, in the following *quarter of a century* (1928–1953) Stalin apparently referred to peaceful coexistence on only three occasions. In each case, Stalin's remarks were clearly directed at a foreign audience: an interview in 1936 with the correspondent Roy Howard, a reply in May 1948 to a letter from Henry Wallace, and a statement of 1952 responding to the questions of a group of American newspaper editors.[17] In contrast, it was not uncommon for Khrushchev to refer to peaceful coexistence half a dozen times in a single speech. This itself indicates how little importance Stalin attached to peaceful coexistence.

Although the Soviet Union advocated peaceful coexistence at Geneva in 1927, it was not until 1949 that the first major peaceful coexistence campaign in Soviet history can be said to have begun. Never before had peaceful coexistence been given such prominence. Malenkov devoted much of one of his statements in December 1949 to its exposition.[18] In March 1950 *Pravda* published a lengthy article on peaceful coexistence citing Lenin's and Stalin's statements of support for it.[19] The campaign intensified in April when *Pravda* and *Bolshevik* published for the first time the texts of two interviews that Lenin had in February 1920 with foreign correspondents.[20] Lenin's answers were rather unexceptional and were full of those expressions of diffuse good will that befitted a communication destined for publication abroad. However, the publication of these documents in April 1950 became the occasion for an avalanche of references to peaceful coexistence, and Lenin's statements were continually cited during the next few years.

The Soviet Union was endorsing peaceful coexistence during this period to lend support to the pro-Soviet peace movement in the West and to expose the supposedly reactionary nature of capitalist foreign policy. Malenkov's opening salvo in the peaceful coexistence campaign reflects this orientation:

> Unmasked in their adventurous designs, the warmongers desire to deceive simple people by the false assertion that the Communists allegedly consider the peaceful co-existence of socialist countries and capitalist countries to be impossible. They desire to screen their criminal actions in preparing for a further war by slandering the honest peace policy followed by the Communists.[21]

Discussions of peaceful coexistence did not involve an exploration of possible common ground for East and West. They served solely as a backdrop to highlight Soviet appeals to the masses of the capitalist nations to compel their governments to abandon their reactionary, anti-Soviet policies.

Thus the campaign on behalf of peaceful coexistence in 1949–1953 can be appraised from two perspectives. If the period before World War II is taken as a point of reference, the declarations of 1949–1953 stand out against a background of almost total neglect. But if the period beginning with the Twentieth Party Congress serves as the standard for comparison, it can be seen (as the following section notes) that this early endorsement of peaceful coexistence sprang from different sources, served different purposes, and was barely related to the doctrinal innovations which were yet to come.[22]

KHRUSHCHEVIAN ADVOCACY

When Khrushchev began his tireless advocacy of peaceful coexistence in the mid-1950s, there was a good deal of suspicion in the West. Many scholars argued that this was simply a repetition of past tactics: whenever pressures have forced the Soviet Union's rulers to seek a temporary lull, they have been quick to speak up in favor of peaceful coexistence. Peaceful coexistence, in this view, is an old Communist Trojan horse which is trotted out whenever the Soviet leaders are forced to accept a temporary respite in their continuing campaign to subvert the West.[23]

Yet this view is not entirely accurate. Even though it is true that tactical considerations have often caused the Soviet Union to launch peace campaigns, the important point here is that, with the exception of the late 1940s, these campaigns have not been closely tied to support for peaceful coexistence. The period of 1953–1954 is a case in point.

Upon Stalin's death, the new leadership quickly sought to improve relations with the West. As part of the new look in Soviet diplomacy, calls for "a relaxation of international tension," "mutual understanding," and "peace" abounded. But considering the Soviet Union's strong desire for a détente, it is significant that peaceful coexistence was *not* elevated to a central position in Soviet peace appeals, and it was mentioned in the press probably only slightly more frequently than it had been in Stalin's last years.

During the two-year period in which Malenkov headed the Soviet government, he delivered two foreign policy speeches of special significance—his August 8, 1953, address to the Supreme Soviet and his March 1954 election speech. It is significant that even though the Supreme Soviet speech was very conciliatory toward the United States, peaceful coexistence was mentioned only in passing; and the election speech, which created a stir both in the Soviet Union and abroad for its unprecedented acknowledgment that nuclear war would mean not just the demise of capitalism but the "ruin of world civilization," does not even refer to peaceful coexistence.[24] As in the early 1920s and the mid-1930s, so too in 1953 and 1954, the Soviet Union's efforts to improve its relations with the West were not intimately related to the advocacy of peaceful coexistence.[25]

It was not until 1955, following Khrushchev's successful assault on the power of Malenkov and Molotov, that peaceful coexistence began to play a major role in Soviet pronouncements on foreign policy. The May Day slogans for 1955 provide a clear indication of this change. These slogans extend back to the early days of the Revolution, but it was not until 1955 that peaceful coexistence was deemed worthy of mention in the slogans—for the very first time in Soviet history.[26] The year 1955 also witnessed the publication of two pamphlets on peaceful coexistence. This in itself might not have been of paramount importance except for the fact that this was also a major break with past practice. It apparently was the first time that a book on peaceful coexistence had ever been published in the Soviet Union. A year-by-year examination of the titles listed in *Ezhegodnik Knigi SSSR (Yearbook of Books of the USSR)* for 1945–1954 indicates that not a single book or pamphlet on peaceful coexistence was published in that period. Although only a spot check could be made of earlier years, all the evidence strongly indicates that the same is true for 1917–1944.[27]

While 1955 witnessed increased publicity for peaceful coexistence,

1956 saw a major effort to give a new, expanded meaning to this traditional concept. Khrushchev's report to the Twentieth Party Congress on February 14, 1956, was a landmark in the development of the Soviet doctrine of peaceful coexistence. Never before had peaceful coexistence been discussed at length and in such glowing terms at a Party congress. Unlike Stalin, Khrushchev did not limit himself to a grudging acceptance of the possibility of peaceful coexistence. He went well beyond this and boldly proclaimed that peaceful coexistence was nothing less than "the general line of our country's foreign policy." [28] Khrushchev's speech set in motion a thoroughgoing process of doctrinal adaptation and change which within the space of the next few years destroyed all similarity between the Stalinist and Khrushchevian conceptions of peaceful coexistence.

For the purposes of ideological continuity and domestic legitimization, Khrushchev used the traditional and time-honored phrase "peaceful coexistence." But it was clear that his grandiose conception of peaceful coexistence had little in common with Stalin's very limited view. In speaking of the "possibility of prolonged coexistence" between the two systems, Stalin's spokesmen were conceding little. They were simply asserting that if, somehow, the inherently aggressive nature of imperialism was temporarily bridled, then capitalism and socialism could precariously exist side by side without war.

Stalin's conception of peaceful coexistence may be said to be characterized by five features. (1) It was *situational:* it referred to a condition or situation in world politics, not to a policy pursued by the Soviet Union. (2) It was *nondirective:* this situation was said to exist when the capitalist powers refrained from hostile acts. Adherence to peaceful coexistence did not necessitate a Soviet commitment to specific policies or principles. (3) It was *pessimistic:* peaceful coexistence was deemed inoperative unless the Western powers genuinely abandoned their "aggressive intentions," a precondition which not only might be absent, but which—given Stalinist assumptions concerning the dynamics of world politics—could scarcely ever be expected to be met. (4) It was *propagandistic:* pronouncements on peaceful coexistence were designed primarily for foreign consumption, and no attempt was made to harmonize these statements with fundamental tenets of Soviet doctrine. (5) It was *circumscribed:* peaceful coexistence referred only to the absence of war and not to any significant form of political or economic cooperation between the two camps.

At the Twentieth Party Congress, Khrushchev put forth a new framework for the conceptualization of peaceful coexistence. The Khrushchevian conception of peaceful coexistence was *normative, optimistic, conceptual,* and *open-ended.* In view of the extent to which he was breaking with the past, it is not surprising that it was months, and in some cases years, before all the implications of this new conception were elaborated and the nuances and fine points were fully sketched. But this speech pointed the way and adumbrated the general outlines of the structure that was to follow.

Khrushchev did not speak of a prolonged condition of peaceful coexistence, but of the Leninist *policy* of peaceful coexistence and of the *principles* of peaceful coexistence. This meant that he was claiming that there were certain basic principles and norms of international conduct which were binding on all states—Communist and non-Communist. Under Stalin there was a pervasive vagueness as to what specific principles—if any—could transcend class differences and govern relations between capitalist and Communist countries. Of course, even in Stalin's day the Soviet Union was said to be interested in peace. But this is very different from an explicit endorsement of, for example, nonintervention or territorial integrity, since in Marxist-Leninist thought even an unprovoked war initiated unilaterally by the Soviet Union is seen as a progressive contribution to eventual world peace. Although there is still room for ambiguity and self-serving definition, a commitment to specific principles of peaceful coexistence, rather than a general endorsement of peace in the abstract, is potentially much more binding, and opens the door to a reasoned discussion of the concrete ground rules that must be observed by all countries regardless of social system if there is to be a modicum of international stability.

From the Soviet perspective, the task of specifying the norms of international conduct that transcend class lines is obviously fraught with acute problems of both empirical political analysis and doctrinal justification. For this reason, it is understandable that Khrushchev's speech was rather vague on this question. Nonetheless, basing himself on the Five Principles agreed to by China and India in 1954, he provided a starting point for subsequent analyses by Soviet writers. In his speech to the Twentieth Party Congress he said that all nations were bound by such principles as: "mutual respect for territorial integrity and sovereignty, non-aggression, non-interference in each other's domestic affairs, equality and mutual advantage, peaceful coexistence and economic cooperation." [29]

In another major innovation, Stalin's pessimism was replaced by typical Khrushchevian optimism. Whereas Stalinist foreign policy strongly implied that capitalist ruling circles could not possibly make the radical break with past policy that was a prerequisite for the creation of a stable condition of peaceful coexistence, under Khrushchev just the reverse was argued. Peaceful coexistence was seen not as a purely theoretical possibility, but as necessary, and even inevitable! The correlation of forces was said to have shifted so decisively against the capitalist camp that its leading politicians were forced to stifle their anti-Communist sentiments and engage in practical and honest cooperation with the Soviet Union.

Here, too, this new approach to coexistence, which was to become so prevalent in future years, was hinted at, but not fully elaborated in Khrushchev's speech: "The principle of peaceful co-existence is gaining ever wider international recognition . . . And this is natural, for there is no other way in present-day conditions." [30] In the same vein, earlier in the speech he notes that "symptoms of a certain sobering up are appearing among influential Western circles" and declares that it is not "fortuitous that prominent leaders of bourgeois countries frankly admit with increasing frequency that 'there will be no victor' in a war in which atomic weapons are used." [31] Stalin's spokesmen had argued that peaceful coexistence was not really possible given the predatory nature of capitalist foreign policy; Khrushchev's ideologues contended that peaceful coexistence was inevitable given capitalism's forced acceptance of the realities of the nuclear age.

Although Soviet spokesmen have found it difficult to specify the precise nature of the mutual interests shared by the two systems, it is clear that the Khrushchevian view of peaceful coexistence is much less restricted than Stalin's. In what may actually have been a tacit criticism of the Stalinist view, Khrushchev declared: "We believe that countries with differing social systems can do more than exist side by side. It is necessary to proceed further, to improve relations, strengthen confidence between countries, and co-operate." [32] Far from being circumscribed, Khrushchev's definition of peaceful coexistence was open-ended virtually without limit. It gave the regime an ideological carte blanche, and in the subsequent years almost any policy—from disarmament to a Soviet-American rapprochement—could be sanctioned by reference to peaceful coexistence.

During the late 1950s and early 1960s, the majority of Western foreign policy analysts emphasized the elements of continuity in the Soviet conception of peaceful coexistence, and they attached little importance to the subtle shifts that were taking place.[33] There were sound reasons for this skepticism: first, the West had been misled by Soviet protestations of peace and friendship before; second, the Soviet endorsement of peaceful coexistence was far from unambiguous and failed to dispel doubts that this might be no more than a replay of the 1949–1950 campaign; third, it was clear that there were compelling political factors that gave the Soviet Union an immediate interest in presenting a benign face to the West. A peaceful Soviet demeanor would tend to undermine the unity of the NATO alliance, encourage domestic opposition to large Western military expenditures, and attract the support of neutralists in Asia and Africa.

Clearly Khrushchev was well aware of the benefits that a verbal espousal of peaceful coexistence would bring. However, I would contend that under Khrushchev, peaceful coexistence acquired a new significance that went well beyond its previous propagandistic function. Following Stalin's death there was a need for a new *conceptual framework* for comprehending international politics. Perhaps the single most striking characteristic of Stalinist foreign policy doctrine is its rigidity. In the quarter of a century of Stalin's rule, it hardly changed at all. If one were to remove the identifying date, a reader would find it difficult to distinguish a 1952 *Pravda* article on foreign policy from one of the late 1920s. The world was still being viewed in terms of capitalist encirclement, inevitable war, just wars, and unrelenting imperialist intrigues. Stalin's successors had to work their way out of these doctrinal confines. With the proliferation of nuclear weapons, skewed perceptions were a luxury they could no longer afford. The elaboration of a new, expanded conception of peaceful coexistence was part of this effort to adjust to the political realities that Stalin had so long ignored.

At the same time, peaceful coexistence took on added importance because it dovetailed with and reinforced this new conceptual framework for viewing international politics. Under Khrushchev, the Leninist belief in the inevitability of capitalist wars was declared invalid, the final victory of socialism in the Soviet Union was proclaimed, and capitalist encirclement was said to belong to the dead past. But Khrushchev went even further. He also repudiated the traditional belief that meaningful disarmament must await capitalism's final demise. Instead the argument was put forth that changes in the structure of capitalism meant that genuine disarmament could be achieved here and now. Similarly, Khrushchev also rejected the pessimistic and deterministic view that since a country's foreign policy was defined by its domestic economic system, capitalist states were inextricably wedded to imperialistic, anti-Soviet policies. With typical optimism and voluntarism, Khrushchev argued that within the United States and other capitalist countries two opposing forces were contending—the "warmongers" and the "sober" forces. Should the latter triumph—and they were said to be gaining in strength—a new era in

East-West cooperation was deemed fully possible.[34] Given his abandonment of Stalinist assumptions concerning the workings of international politics, Khrushchev had as much reason to view peaceful coexistence as a serious goal for the Soviet Union as Stalin did for perceiving it as a temporary and not terribly significant interlude before the next violent confrontation.

In addition to its conceptual role allowing the Soviet leadership to comprehend better international politics, Khrushchev's newly expanded doctrine of peaceful coexistence served a second major internal function—that of *legitimizing* a more moderate policy toward the Western powers. After years of unrelenting hostility toward the West, it was necessary to meet the objections of those in the Communist movement who questioned the wisdom of a policy of cooperation, no matter how limited, with the imperialist enemy. Under Khrushchev, Soviet pronouncements on peaceful coexistence were not meant just to beguile the West, as many foreign observers feared, but were part of a major campaign to establish peaceful coexistence as a legitimate and duly sanctified part of the Marxist-Leninist doctrinal corpus.

It is for this reason that peaceful coexistence was expounded not just in forums that would be readily noticed in the West, but also in communications meant primarily for a domestic audience. New Lenin documents were unearthed to convince the Party faithful of peaceful coexistence's orthodox pedigree; Party propagandists were urged to devote lectures to the subject; the official slogans for May Day and the Anniversary of the Revolution endorsed peaceful coexistence; innumerable mass circulation pamphlets on this theme were published; and the two official texts that contain the most authoritative presentation of the Party line, the *History of the CPSU* and the *Fundamentals of Marxism-Leninism,* embraced peaceful coexistence in the strongest possible terms.

Khrushchev's steadfast determination to win acceptance for peaceful coexistence within the Communist movement is further illustrated by the unusual treatment accorded his defeated political rivals.

In June 1957 Khrushchev succeeded in routing his opponents within the Party. The opposition group, headed by Malenkov and Molotov, was stripped of all power and vehemently denounced as being "anti-Party." At this point Khrushchev, with his power to prevent divergent views from appearing in the press, had a vast amount of leeway in choosing the political sins to be attributed to his rivals. The history of past succession struggles indicates that the victor need not be constrained by historical accuracy in selecting the particular allegations that he believes would afford him the greatest political benefit.

In all previous power conflicts, the defeated contender was denounced for being insufficiently resolute in the struggle against imperialism. Stalinist historiography condemned Trotsky as a man of the Right, as a purveyor of Menshevik ideology, not as the advocate of an overly aggressive policy. Similarly, Beria was variously portrayed as a British agent and a capitulator on the German question, while Malenkov was alleged to be insufficiently militant in his neglect of heavy industry. Yet Khrushchev's opponents were castigated for opposing peaceful coexistence, the easing of international tension, and improved relations with the capitalist world!

In a speech of July 6, 1957, Khrushchev charged: "In the field of foreign policy this group, and Comrade Molotov especially, in every way impeded the implementation of measures for the relaxation of international tension and for the strengthening of world peace. They preferred the policy of 'tightening all screws,' which contradicts the wise Leninist policy of peaceful coexistence of the socialist and capitalist systems." [35] These same accusations were spelled out in greater detail in the official "Resolution of the Central Committee of the CPSU on the Anti-Party Group," and in numerous articles that appeared in *Kommunist* and other journals.[36]

This meant that henceforth peaceful coexistence was to be considered a fundamental and indisputable part of official Marxist-Leninist doctrine. Notice was being served that any questioning of peaceful coexistence with the capitalist world could be regarded as nothing less than treasonous, anti-Party activity. Similarly, in subsequent years when Soviet advocacy of peaceful coexistence became a major factor exacerbating the Sino-Soviet dispute, Khrushchev refused to modify his position that support for peaceful coexistence was one of the most important elements in Soviet foreign policy.

DEVELOPMENTS SINCE KHRUSHCHEV

Khrushchev was a man of dramatic gestures and grandiose goals. A policy aimed at the slow, patient accumulation of day-to-day gains had little attraction for him. Time and again he boldly launched a new initiative (such as the planting of corn, de-Stalinization, the rapprochement with Yugoslavia) only to reverse course equally suddenly as unrealistic expectations were disappointed and unanticipated problems were created. His policies toward the West were equally erratic. At times his goal appeared to be nothing less than Communism's "world-historical victory over capitalism," while at other times he seemed to set himself the equally ambitious, if somewhat less defined, goal of "an end to the Cold War" and the establishment of a joint Soviet-American partnership to manage the world. Hoping somehow both to win the Cold War and to negotiate its end, Khrushchev was able to achieve neither objective.

The successors to Khrushchev have shown themselves to be very different men. Whereas Khrushchev was impulsive, unpredictable, and flamboyant, Brezhnev and Kosygin are cautious, deliberate, and pragmatic. Their policies cannot be neatly characterized as "conservative" or "liberal." Rather the common thread running through their policies is that of hard-headed realism and a careful attention to the basic interests—military, economic, and ideological—of the regime.

Brezhnev and Kosygin have patiently sought a middle path which would be responsive to a wide range of concerns and problems such as the maintenance of Soviet hegemony in Eastern Europe, the containment of the conflict with China, the rapid increase of Soviet military might, the overcoming of persistent economic difficulties, and the suppression of domestic dissent. None of these problems has an easy solution, and the current leadership is painfully aware that progress in one area may intensify difficulties in another. (A high level of military spending retards economic progress; détente with the West promotes domestic dissent, and so forth.) Only a cautious policy which carefully anticipates and weighs possible costs and benefits holds out any promise of success.

One sees this same pragmatism and search for a middle path in the post-1964 treatment of the doctrine of peaceful coexistence. Khrushchev's successors have been unwilling either to endorse his more extravagant claims on behalf of peaceful coexistence or to tamper with such a useful doctrine. The compromise solution is to leave the basic doctrine intact, but to deemphasize it somewhat by mentioning it less in official pronouncements and by stressing other important guiding principles of Soviet foreign policy such as proletarian internationalism.

Under Khrushchev there was a clear tendency to regard peaceful coexistence not just as a major principle of Soviet foreign policy, but as *the* determining principle dwarfing all others. It was not uncommon for Khrushchev and his supporters to refer to peaceful coexistence as nothing less than "the general line" (that is, the central goal) of Soviet foreign policy.[37] By the same token, when Khrushchev enumerated the foreign policy tasks of the Party in his speech to the Twentieth Party Congress, the need to strengthen the socialist camp and to support the neutral nations occupied second and third place respectively, while the very first task was said to be: "To pursue steadfastly the Leninist policy of peaceful co-existence between different states irrespective of their social system." [38]

All this changed with Khrushchev's downfall. Peaceful coexistence was no longer referred to as the general line, and veiled criticisms of its overestimation appeared in the Soviet press.[39] Brezhnev's official ranking of policy priorities differed sharply from Khrushchev's. Peaceful coexistence quickly sank to fourth position behind the goals of building Communism, consolidating the Socialist camp, and supporting the National Liberation movement.[40] In the West, Khrushchev's enthusiastic espousal of peaceful coexistence was regarded with much mistrust as a political ploy to conceal more menacing Soviet designs. In the Soviet Union, on the other hand, it would appear that there was concern that Khrushchev took peaceful coexistence much too far and that in his pursuit of the elusive goal of improved East-West relations, he was neglecting other, more fundamental, Soviet foreign policy interests.

In the years since 1964, peaceful coexistence continued to be championed by Soviet spokesmen, but it was now done in a more balanced and restrained manner. The continued value attached to peaceful coexistence is illustrated by its inclusion in the joint declaration of "Basic Principles" signed by Nixon and Brezhnev in May 1972.[41] The Soviet leadership was elated over obtaining this first official acceptance by the United States of the principle of peaceful coexistence. Yet there was also a note of cautious restraint and a careful avoidance of the exaggerated rhetoric of the Khrushchev years. In a sober fashion Soviet commentators called not for the banishment of all East-West differences, but for continued progress in those areas where the interests of the two camps paralleled one another.[42]

In this essay it has been suggested that Khrushchev's creation of a ramified doctrine of peaceful coexistence to fill the void left by Lenin and Stalin was an event of major importance. It signified a heightened awareness of both the durability of the capitalist world and of the possibility of meaningful, long-term cooperation between the two systems. Yet, paradoxically, the partial downgrading of the doctrine of peaceful coexistence after Khrushchev was not without its positive side. In the short run it suggested an abandonment of Khrushchev's infatuation with the unrealistic and potentially dangerous idea of a Soviet-American duopoly.[43] And over the long term, it meant that Khrushchev's erratic lunging from grand design to grand design, from the Spirit of Camp David to the Cuban missile crisis, was replaced by a cautious policy which sought a gradual improvement of East-West relations within the context of careful attention to the full range of Soviet interests. If one believes that in a world of nation-states, peace can only come from the patient accommodation of disparate national interests, then the Soviet acceptance of a concept of peaceful coexistence that is neither as limited as Stalin's nor as grandoise as Khrushchev's offers some ground for optimism.

In pursuing a policy of détente, the current leadership has made it clear that there are two core interests which they will not sacrifice: Soviet hegemony in Eastern Europe and the maintenance of one-party rule at home. Expressing this position in doctrinal terms, they have reiterated with special force the traditional, orthodox position: (a) that peaceful coexistence is a principle that applies to relations between socialist and capitalist states, not to relations among socialist states (which are said to be guided by the higher principle of proletarian internationalism which allows such "fraternal aid" as that extended to Czechoslovakia in 1968); [44] (b) that while substantial progress is possible in state-to-state relations and in the spheres of economics and politics, ideological struggle continues and "ideological coexistence" is impossible.

There is, of course, nothing new in these reservations. They were an integral part of Khrushchev's view of coexistence as well. Only now that significant progress in East-West relations has materialized, the lack of movement in these other areas has become all the more obvious and painful. If this were an ideal world, one might wish to improve relations with the Soviet leaders while simultaneously working for a relaxation within the Soviet Union and Eastern Europe. Forced to choose between these objectives, Western leaders have decided not to demand the radical transformation of the Soviet system as a precondition for East-West détente. Whether the realms of domestic and foreign policy can successfully be insulated from one another, only time will reveal.

# Global Power Relationships in the Seventies: The View from the Kremlin

ROBERT H. DONALDSON

16

The frenetic pace of great-power diplomacy in the opening years of the 1970s evoked from Western journalists and scholars much speculation concerning the evolution of the international system. With the apparent waning of the Cold War, the growing political and economic competitiveness among the United States and its alliance partners, and the continuing diplomatic, ideological, and military clashes within the Communist world, a number of observers in the West began to call into question the continued utility of the "loose bipolarity" model for the world of the 1970s.

Some perceived developing international relationships as a neo-Orwellian triangular pattern among the U.S., the USSR, and China.[1] Others, including the American president, spoke in terms of a future world dominated by five major actors—with Japan and the expanded European community joining the three mentioned above in a pentagonal competition.[2] Still others, recognizing the emerging diplomatic multipolarity or "polycentrism" stemming from the loosening of the Cold War blocs, yet emphasizing the continuing strategic dominance of the two superpowers, preferred to speak in terms of a multilevel international system.[3]

My purpose here is not to take sides in this debate, but rather to add another perspective to it, by analyzing the *Soviet* assessment of changing global relationships in the early 1970s. This was a period that witnessed four bilateral summits between the United States and the

Soviet Union in a period of only thirty months—in contrast to only seven meetings involving the leaders of the two countries in the preceding four decades of their relationship. More significantly, it was a period in which the two leading rivals of the USSR—the United States and China—were recasting their policies toward the world and shaping new approaches toward each other. My present objective is to examine Soviet perceptions and behavior in the midst of this new and more fluid situation. After first sketching the broad outlines of the prevailing Soviet assessment, I proceed to a more detailed analysis of the unfolding Soviet approach to three interconnected issues: bilateral Soviet-American relations, the construction of an Asian security system in the post-Vietnam era, and the future of East-West relations in Europe.

### THE DOMESTIC POLITICAL CONTEXT

To speak of a "Soviet assessment" necessarily risks oversimplification. The phrase ascribes a uniformity of vision to a sizeable number of individuals who participate both in the making of Soviet foreign policy and in the process of communicating it in the official media. To be sure, public pronouncements emanating from the USSR do suggest a much greater apparent and real uniformity of perception and policy than exists among the participants in the foreign policy process in pluralist societies. But even the Kremlin's "official" sources can reveal to the student attentive to the nuances of expression characteristic of "esoteric communication" an occasional divergence of opinion. Both in these instances, and in those more numerous cases in which the surface harmony is unblemished, a process of private debate among competing interests and policy alternatives occurs behind the public Soviet facade. In its broad contours, this process is not entirely dissimilar to the more obvious pulling and hauling within "open" systems.

Soviet foreign policy, rather than being simply the product of the perceptions and calculations of a monolithic decision-making elite, is thus more accurately perceived as the product of the interaction of decision makers representing a variety of personal and institutional perspectives and involved in the simultaneous resolution of a number of internal and external issues. Ideally, explanations of Soviet policy choices should identify not only the particular interests in contention, but also the broad range of issues competing for the attention of the elite and the resources of the society. In fact, severe limitations on data compel toilers in this field to accept results far short of the ideal.

For the present inquiry, limitations on both space and information necessitate merely a brief mention both of the major institutional perspectives of the elite and of the domestic problems confronting Soviet decision makers at the beginning of the decade.

Vernon Aspaturian has recently identified six major "demand sectors" in Soviet society: (1) ideological, (2) security, (3) producer, (4) consumer, (5) agricultural, and (6) public service and welfare.[4] The first three sectors, those consisting of a variety of structures including the police and armed forces, ministries and enterprises producing defense and heavy-industrial materials, and the wing of the Party apparatus devoted to the preservation of ideological purity and the dissemination of propaganda, comprise the Soviet equivalent of the "military-industrial complex." The latter sectors include elements of the Party and state bureaucracies involved with agricultural and light-industrial production or concerned with upgrading the consumption standards of the Soviet population. These two groupings tend to be on opposite sides in their perceptions of the international arena and, specifically, the degree of danger to Soviet security interests and opportunity for expansion of Soviet influence and their view of the competition for budgetary resources.

Long accustomed under Stalin to a predominant share of Soviet resources and to a policy stance favorable to its perceptions, the "military-industrial complex" suffered briefly in Khrushchev's later years because of his efforts to orient the international position of the USSR so that a greater share of the budget could be diverted to "consumptionist" ends. Khrushchev's successors, having capitalized on the dissatisfaction of the offended "lobbies" in achieving the ouster of their patron, appeared to be restoring the former emphasis on defense and heavy-industry spending (while not entirely abandoning their predecessor's experiments with "détente").

Numerous signs show, however, that there is a continuing debate and indecision within the Soviet leadership on the "guns or butter" issue. The long delays associated both with the formal publication of the 1971–1975 Five-Year Plan and with the decision to enter into the SALT negotiations with the United States are two examples. There are other signs that the Soviet economy has not had the capacity to provide satisfactory amounts of *both* guns and butter—as the dominant centrists in the Politburo promised. Dramatic failures in agricultural production have persisted despite relatively larger investments in this sector. And growth in industrial output and labor productivity has been disappointing despite efforts at providing both material (Liberman-style) and "moral" (Shelepin-style) incentives. If the much-ballyhooed (and probably overstated) emphasis of the leadership on improvement in the standard of living is to be translated into concrete results, the regime will undoubtedly have to make some very difficult choices. Equally thorny and not unrelated problems continue to plague the regime in the noneconomic sphere. Three of these are the festering intellectual dissent, the unrest among minority nationalities, and the continuing uncertainty concerning the relative role of Party and state bureaucracies.

DECEPTIONS OF THE GLOBAL BALANCE

Khrushchev's exuberant claims in the late fifties and early sixties concerning a decisive shift in the world balance of forces in favor of socialism, and the globalist policy he based on those assertions, had by the end of his rule collided with a number of contrary developments. The first was the massive American strategical and conventional military buildup, provoked in part by Khrushchev's own bluster. The Cuban confrontation brought home in unmistakable terms the marked degree to which the Soviet strategic position was inferior to that of the United States. Moreover, America's global capability was increasingly evidenced through its involvement in "third world" areas in opposition to nascent "revolutionary situations" that Khrushchev favored. The second major development was the sharpening conflict with China, which posed a challenge not only to Soviet security and diplomatic interests in Asia, but Moscow's ideological and organizational authority in the international Communist movement. The third was the continuing ferment in Moscow's East European sphere matched against the growing economic and political strength of a West Europe seemingly resistant to Soviet efforts to achieve recognition of the postwar division of the continent. Khrushchev had failed to achieve his goal of dislodging the West from Berlin and encouraging the spread of neutralism among America's allies; his successors faced a Western counteroffensive aimed at encouraging further dissolution in the Eastern bloc through a policy of "bridge-building."

The colorless bureaucrats of the successor coalition—hesitant, cautious, and methodical in contrast to Khrushchev's impulsive and "adventurist" style—preferred a policy of the "low profile" because it was more in keeping with the USSR's limited capabilities. They continued to espouse the latter-day Khrushchev line of affirming that the main *internationalist* duty of the USSR was the building of Communism at home, but at the same time the new leaders turned over to the "military-industrial complex" the task of remedying Soviet strategic in-feriority.

By the end of the 1960s, with the U.S. consciously drawing back from the arms race and waiting for the Soviets to catch up, the strategic gap had greatly narrowed. Soviet global capability, both strategic and conventional, was increasing. The United States was mired in Vietnam and undergoing a domestic debate from which a continuation of American globalism was unlikely to emerge. The Chinese were undergoing a severe internal crisis which put a virtual halt to their own foreign activity. The Soviet leaders could therefore enter the 1970s with a new, more self-assured perspective.[5] In the opinion of the authoritative observer A. Sovetov (presumably a pseudonym), international relations were at a turning point. The global structure was radically altered and the balance had changed in favor of socialism, though further improvements would come only through struggle. Recent events had shown that the imperialist alliance was no longer the moving force; the initiative had been "completely and forever grasped from the hands" of the imperialists. True, U.S. imperialism had seized on the theory of the "so-called balance of forces" in an effort to bolster its weakened position, and it was actively resorting to "maneuvering and entering into blocs with different forces, including those which it but yesterday called its adversaries." But this theory would fail to hold water, because it placed all states "on the same plane," ignoring the class factor. Thus, Sovetov indicated that he did not expect any permanent equilibrium to result from this new arrangement. Rather, he perceived the international milieu as a dynamic arena, with the Soviets holding the historical initiative.[6]

This relative strengthening of the socialist camp, entailing a decisive and "irreversible" change in the correlation of forces in the world arena, was one of a number of "objective factors" cited by Soviet analysts that underlay the new Soviet-American relationship. Another prominent factor was said to be the increasing success of the "national-liberation" and labor movements, best exemplified in the "victory" of the "Vietnam patriots." The defeat of American aggression in Indo-china most clearly demonstrated the bankruptcy of the U.S. posture of "world policeman," a policy by which Washington had sought to halt sociopolitical change in the world. In addition, successive international currency crises and the erosion of America's trade position evidenced the exacerbation of competition among the capitalist powers. Together with this shift in the nature of the U.S. relationship with other capitalist countries had come a positive change in Soviet relations with these same states. And finally, Soviet writers pointed to the continuing domestic social and economic crises in the United States and to the "unprecedented rivalry" between foreign and domestic expenditures, which strained the U.S. budget to the breaking point.[7]

A change in American strategy, however, would require that "objective forces" first be perceived and comprehended by the ruling class. This process began in the U.S., according to V. M. Berezhkov, only with President Nixon's accession to the White House. American politicians had thus been "compelled" by these factors to conduct an "agonizing reappraisal" of their policies, leading to a "more realistic" approach toward the pursuit of American interests abroad. At first, Soviet analysts seemed reluctant to take at face value the new president's announced switch from a policy of confrontation to one of negotiation. Thus, V. Nikolaev, writing in the Soviet journal *International Affairs* early in 1972 on "U.S. Foreign Policy: Real or Imagined Changes?" argued that the changes to date had been only technical, failing to alter the essence of the policy. Though American leaders made fewer direct threats and used greater discretion in international conflicts, it was premature to speak of a renunciation of "gunboat diplomacy." Having failed by force or ruse to impose its solutions, Washington continued to engage in "tricks" and "maneuvers" in pursuit of the old aggressive aims. A prominent example was the "quick rapprochement" between the U.S. and China, which proceeded not from "realistic and constructive" positions, but from an attempt to use Peking's "anti-Sovietism" to American advantage. The Americans were holding to a "positions of strength" policy, and in most "key issues" of American-Soviet relations, they were failing to take constructive positions.[8]

## SOVIET-AMERICAN DÉTENTE

Only after the two U.S.-Soviet summits of 1972 and 1973 did the Soviets seem to gain confidence in the genuineness of the Nixon administration's new approach. Again, the explanations sought to go beyond "subjective" factors. The class basis for the American shift was seen in the increased influence of a group of American "monopolies" whose orientation was toward foreign export markets. These more "sober" representatives of the bourgeoisie, who realized that the pursuit of the arms race and of foreign adventures was damaging the competitive position of the American economy, had overcome the pressures of the "military-industrial complex." [9] Partly because of the personal efforts of Comrade Brezhnev, broader strata of the U.S. public had been mobilized behind business and political interests on behalf of the new policy, which was increasingly becoming a "two-party course." [10] This policy was assessed by Anatolii Gromyko and A. Kokoshkin in the summer of 1973 as "more cautious," based on a "saner" perception of America's international interests, and characterized by a comparative diminution of military means, increased concern for America's competitive position in the capitalist world, and a reorganization of U.S. relations with developing nations.[11]

Although the Soviets cited a growing network of common interests as a "considerable obstacle" to any reversion by Washington to a Cold War position, they stressed the existence of a determined coalition of "right-wing forces," led by the "military-industrial complex" and "Zionist" interests, who were struggling to discredit the new American orientation. Among the tactics allegedly employed by the opponents of peaceful coexistence were suggestions that the United States align itself with Peking's anti-Soviet strategy, hints about the weakness of the Soviet economy, and efforts to tie normalization of relations to changes in internal Soviet policies. Some writers even hinted that the Watergate scandal was being manipulated in an effort to discredit the Nixon Administration's foreign policy course.

It was clear that through the promotion of his own "peace program," Brezhnev had built up a certain stake in President Nixon and the American leader's new foreign policy. And when Nixon announced his resignation in August 1974, some Soviet commentators observed that he had been unfairly "hounded" from office.[12] But Moscow was quick to reaffirm its intention to maintain a policy of further improvement in U.S.-Soviet relations, and to restate the "need to observe agreements unswervingly and to fulfill pledges." Although the change of president was said to be an "internal affair" of the Americans, "it makes a lot of difference to the international public just how the U.S. foreign policy and Soviet-American relations will be developed." [13] But while Brezhnev moved quickly to establish a personal relationship with President Ford, the Soviets appeared to be increasingly disturbed over the intrusion of domestic American political controversy into such areas as Soviet-American arms and trade agreements.

Still, the transition in Soviet-American relations "from the Cold War to relations of genuine peaceful coexistence" was believed by the Soviets to have "historic significance." In Georgii Arbatov's view, though these relations remained competitive, the change in form signified that the political and economic competition could proceed without constant crises and the attendant danger to world peace. The Soviet Union, he said, consistently had shown a willingness to pursue such relations since the time of Lenin, though it was only with the changing American assessment that it became possible. But now there existed a wide framework of parallel interests, primarily an interest in the prevention of nuclear war, but also including interests in arms limitation and "mutually beneficial cooperation" in the economic and scientific-technological fields.[14] By the summer of 1973, almost twenty concrete agreements had issued from this new bilateral relationship, including the Agreement on Prevention of Nuclear War, which the leading Soviet journal of American studies termed "one of the most important documents in the history of international relations." [15]

In the opinion of the Soviets, the summit meetings represented a favorable beginning toward U.S.-Soviet normalization. Their effect spilled beyond the bilateral relationship itself to foster improvements in other spheres of international relations as well. But it was too soon to count on this relationship as a "permanent factor" in world politics, and much remained to be done before the détente could be stabilized and consolidated. The most important precondition of further progress, in the words of the joint Politburo-government statement of June 29, 1973, was the "consistent and steady fulfillment by both states of the commitments they have assumed." [16]

But even if further progress in the spheres of "parallel interests" is registered—an eventuality cast in doubt by the Middle East conflict of 1973 and the controversy over trade and emigration in 1974—the Soviets have at no time failed to perceive the limits to détente. As Arbatov put it in July 1973, "these relations will never become relations of an alliance between 'two superpowers who have divided up the world,' as some opponents of normalization and détente try to assert." [17] Relations of peaceful coexistence, in the Soviet sense of the term, are reserved for ties between states with different social systems, and are thus undergirded by contradiction and struggle. Even under the best of inter-state relations there would inevitably be "principled ideological struggle" and economic-scientific competition. As Arbatov has written, these relations "no matter how successful the process of normalization and détente is, in the historical sense will remain relations of struggle." The *form* of the struggle—more or less violent, more or less dangerous—is not unimportant, but the fact of struggle itself is "historically inevitable." [18]

In the face of charges from the Chinese (and probably from internal factions as well) that the policy of normalization of relations with the U.S. amounted to a superpower condominium, entailing a sell-out of

Soviet commitments to socialist allies and fighters for national liberation, the dominant coalition in Moscow issued effusive assurances
that such commitments would not be abandoned. The Soviet government would continue to rebuff the aggressive intrigues of imperialist
forces and would double its vigilance against those who sought to
undermine its principled socialist positions—and most especially
against those who sought to utilize détente as a weapon for the prop-
agation of bourgeois ideology and like forms of interference with
Soviet domestic affairs.[19]

That Brezhnev's internal critics in 1973 were continuing to question
whether positive results had been reaped from the new Soviet-American relationship was evident in an *Izvestia* commentary in April,
which chided certain "incorrigible skeptics who are asking in smart-
aleck tones: Where is the tangible proof that favorable changes have
actually taken place in the international situation?"[20]

Still, the dominant Soviet assessment came down on the side of
"sobriety" and the continuation of mutually advantageous relations.
In his 1973 speech to the Indian parliament, Brezhnev praised the
American leadership for displaying "political realism, foresight, and
understanding of the requirements of the times." He waxed poetic in
rejecting the path of "cold war" which "like a gloomy whirlwind
. . . drew into its orbit even those who would like to remain aloof"
and "threw a somber shadow on the entire situation on our planet."
The alternative path, "gradually becoming a reality," called for eliminating hotbeds of war and tension, establishing normal relations between states, and developing extensive and equal cooperation. This,
in turn, would "create more favorable conditions for the accomplishment of many other important tasks—national liberation, social progress, overcoming the scandalous inequality between various countries."[21]

Arbatov, too, saw continuing opportunities for progress in Soviet-
American détente. His reading of the results of the 1972 Moscow summit included an attack on those "foolish" persons (unnamed, but
probably present in both the U.S. and the USSR) who sought to determine "who won" and "who lost" at the summit. In an eloquent
and explicit call for a rejection of zero-sum imagery, Arbatov wrote:
"The unsoundness of this approach is self-evident. Big politics is not
like reckless gambling, in which one player wins the same amount
the other player loses. Completely different situations are possible
here, *situations in which all sides are winners.* As a matter of fact,
this is the only realistic situation for true world politics."[22] On the
whole, Arbatov's writings picture the international arena as one

in which the U.S. will continue to be a superpower, though her global interventionism will be largely deterred by Soviet strategic might. Thus, for the present, the United States and the Soviet Union, in a state of acknowledged parity, will dominate the strategic sphere, existing in a limited-adversary relationship in which agreements promising mutual advantage will be possible.

Indeed, the conclusion at the 1972 Moscow summit of the first-stage SALT agreements, setting limits on further quantitative developments of strategic weapons, did appear to signify a choice by the Soviet leadership *not* for the present to attempt the achievement of strategic superiority vis à vis the United States. As Thomas Wolfe has pointed out, this choice seems to have been deferred as long as possible.[23] Justifying the decision, V. Viktorov stressed that—based as they are on the principle of "equal security"—the arms agreements do not harm either party, but rather "help each to strengthen its national security in full conformity with its national interests." Moreover, by preventing the pouring of resources into deployment of additional offensive or defensive missiles, the agreements are "bound to benefit the peaceful economic development of both states." [24]

It was evident from press comment on the first Moscow summit agreements that some participants in the Soviet decision-making process—for reasons of "trust" or otherwise—had been dissatisfied with the SALT accords. Thus, prior to the summit, Prof. V. Sobakin, in defending Soviet efforts to achieve partial arms accords as well as "general and complete disarmament," had written that "There must be resolute rejection of all claims that only struggle for maximum measures is worthwhile, that partial agreements constitute an abandonment of this main objective and are 'concessions to imperialism' . . . precisely, rejection of the day-to-day struggle for partial agreement constitutes a concession to the forces of imperialism and war." [25] Another sign of attack on the agreements appeared shortly after the summit, when Yurii Chernov, describing the "fruitful results" of the negotiations as almost unmatched in the history of international relations, felt compelled to add: "Negotiations conducted from principled positions and with reasonable tactical compromises fully in accord with these positions are not a sign of weakness or softness but are an obligation for all those who are guided in their deeds by the genuine interests of peace and socialism, not by 'revolutionary' phrases . . ." [26]

As the prospects for success in the second-stage SALT negotiations, seeking a permanent limitation on offensive strategic weapons, appeared to dim in 1974, Brezhnev continued to defend the search for arms control. In his June election speech, he declared: "The supporters of the arms race cite the argument that limiting arms, and all the more so reducing them, means taking a risk. In actual fact, there is immeasurably more risk in continuing the unrestrained accumulation of arms." [27]

Other Soviet voices, prominently including some in the military, were more pessimistic. Thus, whereas *Pravda* had asserted in July 1973 that "the dark clouds of military danger . . . are dispersing," [28] the military's newspaper editorialized a year later that "the clouds of military danger still darken the sky above our planet." [29] Less frequent than such clear contradictions were distinct differences of emphasis among certain spokesmen. Marshal Grechko, for example, declared in February 1974 that "the world has changed but the aggressive, misanthropic nature of imperialism has remained unchanged." [30] The previous month, Arbatov had stated substantially the same premise with considerably different emphasis: while the "class nature" of imperialists has not and could not change, "what has changed is the world in which they have to live and operate . . . they have been compelled to adapt their policy to these changes and to the objective realities of the international situation." [31]

In the wake of the failure of the 1974 Moscow summit to conclude a new offensive arms agreement, the contending factions in the U.S. and USSR continued to debate the trustworthiness of the other side. A charge by U.S. Senator James Buckley of Soviet violations of the SALT agreement called forth an indignant denial by the chief of Soviet rocket forces, General Tolubko, who declared: "in all its history the Soviet Union has never violated obligations which it has assumed." [32] For their part, the Soviets accused the Pentagon of contradicting the spirit of détente by searching for ways of making "limited" use of nuclear weapons. The civilian authors of this complaint concluded with an observation ostensibly directed toward the Pentagon, but conceivably meant to apply to their own military planners as well:

Considerable progress in further improvements of basic missile systems, by improving the quantity and yield of warheads in conjunction with improving accuracy, can give rise to fear . . . of attempts to acquire capability for a neutralizing counterforce strike. This, even before the capability is acquired, will call forth a corresponding reaction, giving a new impetus to the arms race . . . [and by engendering] new suspicions regarding the other side's intentions, will affect the over-all political situation. [33]

Despite such foreboding, an agreement was reached at the November Ford-Brezhnev summit on provisions to serve as the basis for a new temporary SALT treaty to cover the period through 1985. The agreement would entitle both sides to have 2400 strategic delivery vehicles, including 1320 "MIRV'ed" launchers, and it provided for further negotiations on limitations and possible reductions by 1980. Moreover, the Soviet and American leaders agreed to continue "without a loss in momentum, to expand the scale and intensity of their cooperative efforts in all spheres." [34] The summit agreements were hailed by *Izvestia* as representing "undoubted progress, progress which inspires hope, progress which enables us to look with greater confidence in the future." And, in light of the earlier Soviet debate on the subject, it is interesting to note *Izvestia*'s conclusion: "a very hard blow has been struck against the view that nuclear war is a fatal inevitability and that curbing the arms race is impossible." [35]

In view of the Soviets' choice after some debate, to accept for the immediate future a limited-adversary relationship with the United States based on strategic parity, two additional points should be made explicit. First—as argued in some detail further on—this choice by no means relegates the Soviets to foreign policy "quietism" or to a position as a "satisfied power." Though their policy could hardly be described as "revolutionary global expansionism," the Soviets will yet be capable of engaging in "fishing operations" on the Eurasian continent, in Africa, and in the Middle East. In the course of such efforts they may fully expect their new-found status of nuclear equality—in a world in which "imperialism" is perceived as a declining force—to bring political advantages in crisis-bargaining situations. A world of parity is not necessarily a world in which risk-taking is foresworn.

To put it in another way, the Soviets expect that their rivalry with the United States will continue, even though the summits may have established some important ground rules for the conduct of the rivalry. Buttressing this expectation are quite concrete needs of the Soviet leadership stemming from its ideological commitments and from the continuing necessity to utilize the struggle with the imperialist enemy as a justification for its policy choices—and its very rule—at home. As evidence of this tendency we might note Suslov's exhortation following the 1972 Moscow summit against relaxation of the struggle against "bourgeois ideology." As the futility of attempts at military, economic and political pressure become more apparent, he argued, "the struggle precisely in the field of ideology, the field where there cannot be any peaceful coexistence, has sharpened considerably." [36] Two weeks later, a *Pravda* editorial on ideological work noted similarly that peaceful coexistence "signifies not the cessation of class struggle between the two systems, but only the disavowal of the use of military methods in this struggle." [37]

In June 1974, another important *Pravda* editorial voiced a new—and yet quite venerable—assessment of the prospects for revolutionary advance in an age of détente. The alleviation of international tensions, it said, *together with* "the intensification of the political and economic instability of capitalism," influenced the deployment of class forces by opening up "unprecedented opportunities" to the workers' movement in capitalist countries.[38] Developing this theme four months later at a speech to a meeting of European communist parties in Warsaw, Boris Ponomarev cited the "conditions of détente" and "the general crisis of capitalism" as presenting particular opportunities for leftist forces in Portugal, Spain, Greece, Italy, and France. "At this time, we believe, the communist parties have greater opportunities and resources than ever before for influencing the course of events in Europe." [39]

The second point concerning this new relationship involves the nature of a "limited adversary" situation in a world that is no longer strictly bipolar. It is quite correct to point out, as Arbatov did, that the absence of a zero-sum situation may allow both parties to make gains (or to suffer losses). Yet the Soviets are also quite aware that the burgeoning presence of a *third* major party to the relationship complicates the question of relative gains and losses even further. It is to the Soviet perception of the role of that "intruder"—the People's Republic of China—that we now turn.

## SOVIET-CHINESE RELATIONS

After an initial and unsuccessful attempt to patch up the dispute with China, Khrushchev's successors had vigorously renewed the "principled" defense of their ideological and organizational interests in the international communist environment. Recent Soviet polemics, aimed at proving that despite Soviet efforts at "normalization" China had finally forfeited all pretense of following a socialist policy, suggested a revived Soviet effort to strip the Chinese regime of its Marxist-Leninist credentials in international communist circles. An article by I. Aleksandrov in *Pravda* in 1973 accused Peking's leaders of having made "a full break with Marxism-Leninism" and of becoming "more and more frequently the immediate ally of the most reactionary imperialist circles." [40] The following year, the Soviets began to refer to Peking's policy as "anti-communist." [41] Maoism, argued Moscow, is not socialism but "a hodgepodge of Confucian postulates, preaching obedience for the masses and deifying the supreme ruler, of feudal arrogance, petty-bourgeois chauvinism, Trotskyite 'left-wing' radicalism, and downright ignorance." [42]

But the clash, of course, has gone far beyond mere polemics. Thus, the Soviet leaders were by no means unmindful of China as they took steps to expand the USSR's military capabilities; Soviet forces on the Sino-Soviet border were increased threefold between 1968 and 1971. And though relations between the two parties have improved since the low point of 1969, both Soviet and Chinese decision makers still consider the other side to be a major security threat.

The Soviet side's judgment of the unlikelihood of any imminent return of Sino-Soviet relations to a "fraternal" basis was evidenced by Brezhnev's remarks to the Soviet trade unions' congress in March, 1972. At that time he accepted the possibility of conducting relations between the two socialist states under a formula at which the Soviets had recoiled in horror when the Albanians had suggested it as a basis for their own relations with Moscow a decade earlier:

Official Chinese representatives tell us that relations between the USSR and the CPR should be based on the principle of peace. Well, if Peking does not deem it possible to go any farther than this in relations with a socialist state, we are now prepared to construct Soviet-Chinese relations on this basis . . . we not only proclaim our readiness to do so but also translate it into the language of fully concrete and constructive proposals on nonaggression, on the settlement of border questions and on the improvement of relations on a mutually advantageous basis. These proposals have long been known to the Chinese leaders. The next move is China's.[43]

By autumn 1974, the Soviets seemed resigned to the notion that prospects for improved relations would come only with the departure of the Maoist leadership of China. Thus Brezhnev, reaffirming the Soviet commitment to continued efforts at normalization of state relations and restoration of fraternal party ties, declared: "We are convinced that such an unnatural state of affairs cannot last indefinitely. This grim page . . . will inevitably be turned by the Chinese people themselves." [44]

The Chinese, of course, have not been inactive of late in the conduct of their own diplomacy, and it is that fact which has brought the dispute more squarely into the international arena and made life even more complicated for the Soviet leaders in past years. I have already alluded to Moscow's judgment of the Sino-American talks as amounting to imperialist exploitation of China's "anti-Sovietism."

Brezhnev himself expressed skepticism in the March 1972 speech that the U.S.-Chinese dialogue was limited to matters of bilateral relations. Earlier, an article in *International Affairs* had suggested that China's "anti-Soviet" policy was compensation to the Western states for their aid in developing China's economy and "turning China into a state capable of realizing its territorial claims on the Soviet Union, and of bringing under its influence the neighboring states in East and Southeast Asia." Mao, who had covertly sought to improve relations with the U.S. since 1964–1965, was acting as the "Trojan horse of imperialism in the international revolutionary movement, thus forming the essence of the intensified diplomatic flirtation" between Washington and Peking.[45] This line was repeated in an article published after Nixon's Moscow and Peking summits, in which it was contended that Peking's divisive activity constituted a "permanent line," made "still more dangerous" by its "more adroit tactics." [46]

THE NEW TRIANGLE

Because their interests are more directly and concretely in conflict, it is the Soviet and Chinese leaders who must most fear being "odd man out." They perceive the triangular relationship between Washington, Peking, and Moscow as a struggle on two fronts. But, to borrow Michel Tatu's framework, China sees the USSR as "adversary number one" and undertakes to reduce its own antagonism to the U.S. in order to struggle more effectively against the Soviets. This in turn alarms the Soviets and causes them also to appeal to the Americans. Or, in Tatu's more general terms: (1) the existence of "adversary number one" leads to objective collusion with "number two"; (2) each of the three parties aims to reduce collusion between the others to a minimum; (3) it is in the interest of each to bluff its chief adversary by threatening collusion with the other; (4) the surest way for any party to provoke the other two into collusion is to display undue aggressiveness.[47]

Tatu's framework helps us to see what is new in this situation. So long as the Chinese and Americans were simply not in contact, the Soviets occupied the advantageous position. Far from having to offer concessions to the West in return for cooperation, they were able to use the Chinese "threat" as a lever with which to attempt to exact concessions *from* the West. Thus, in their campaign to achieve a "collective security" system and recognition of the status quo in Europe, the Soviets took no pains to deny the impression that such a "quieting of the Western front" was in the common interests of both

East and West in Europe, since it would allow the Soviets more effectively to defend the alleged interests of Western civilization against the "Chinese menace." In fact, as Tatu suggests, the reverse was actually the case: the Soviets had consciously moved at the end of 1969 to ease tensions on the Sino-Soviet border in order to pursue a more active policy in the West.

In 1971, however, the continued sorry state of their own relations with Peking, together with their fears that the Americans and Chinese were teaming up in anti-Soviet maneuvers, seemed to put the Soviets in a more disadvantageous position in this triangular relationship. Indeed, it was the United States that seemed to hold the favored position, if one accepts Brzezinski's aphorism: "it is advantageous to have better relations with the other two parties than they have with each other." [48]

In the wake of the Moscow summit, though they continued to charge Peking with collusion as the Trojan horse of imperialism, it became increasingly difficult for the Soviets to reconcile the notion of a Nixon-Mao "anti-Soviet axis" with the further development of Soviet-American détente. The resulting Soviet reassessment produced a new line more congruent with the Western analysts' version of "triangular politics." Indeed, V. P. Lukin, in a February 1973 article on Sino-American relations, seemed to acknowledge that in a three-way competition, it is completely understandable that each party will be concerned with the health of its relationship with the other two, so that no power has a monopoly in its dealings with the others. Conceding that most "serious and influential" American scholars were aware of the extreme danger in an anti-Soviet axis, Lukin argued that "In the framework of its current 'triangular' tactics, Washington is seeking to create a system of parallel and mutually conditioned relations with our country and with the C.P.R. In all spheres where this is possible, the United States is trying to create a situation of the C.P.R.'s 'active participation,' which would mean that a permanent 'alternative' exists." [49]

Lukin's response to this design of the American policy makers serves as a graphic illustration of Tatu's scenario. Lukin wrote that while Moscow could not object to a normalization in U.S. Chinese relations, the U.S. should not get caught up in the fiction that China is a great power. "The Maoists are as yet unable to exert an influence on major political events" in Asia "that is effective enough to satisfy the needs of the creators of 'triangular' combinations." [50] The notion that American contacts with Peking should be symmetrical and of an equal intensity to its ties with Moscow was "absurd." China could not possibly offer the U.S. as much as the Soviets could. Chinese-American trade would never develop to match the potential volume of Soviet-American trade. China does not have the equivalent of Soviet military power. The United States should not pursue the Chinese "alternative" to the point of missing the opportunity Moscow was offering. And above all, the U.S. must not be tempted to intervene in the Sino-Soviet dispute.

THE SOVIET TACTICS: CAMPAIGNS FOR "COLLECTIVE SECURITY"

While the new international relationships may thus have complicated the situation, they apparently did not alter the Soviet purpose. Having won recognition as the military and negotiating equal of the United States, they continued to seek containment of China, the protection of their East European "commonwealth," and the expansion of their own influence into Western Europe. Most prominent among the tactics for the achievement of the latter goals were high-geared Soviet campaigns for the establishment of new "systems of security" in both Asia and Europe.

The Soviet proposal for collective security in Asia [51] originated in May 1969 with the publication in *Izvestia* of an article by V. V. Matveyev entitled, "A Filled 'Vacuum.' " Pointing to the greedy looks being cast by American, Japanese, and Chinese leaders amidst talk of a "vacuum" in Asia following British withdrawal from east of Suez, Matveyev predicted that in fact there would be no "vacuum" to fill. Already India, Afghanistan, Pakistan, and other independent states were making efforts to consolidate their sovereignty, though they could best resist interference from foreign powers by setting up "the foundations of collective security in this region." [52]

Matveyev's article commanded little foreign notice at this time. But a little more than a week after its publication, Brezhnev, speaking to the Moscow Meeting of Communist and Workers' Parties, declared toward the very end of his lengthy address: "We are of the opinion that the course of events is also putting on the agenda the task of creating a system of collective security in Asia." [53] Foreign diplomats and journalists who inquired of Soviet officials about this single cryptic statement were directed by them to Matveyev's article.[54]

But the *Izvestia* piece had been no more specific than Brezhnev on what the Soviets meant by a "collective security" system. Were they in fact proposing to sponsor an Asian military and political pact aimed at the containment of China? This was certainly the interpretation offered by the Chinese, who identified themselves as the target of this "sinister" plan picked up by the Soviets "from the garbage heap of the notorious warmonger Dulles." According to Peking, India and Japan were to serve as the linchpins of this projected security system in which the revisionists and imperialists were collaborating.[55]

On balance, the Soviets could not have been overly encouraged by the cool Indian, Indonesian, and Japanese reactions to the Brezhnev proposal. On the other hand, given the purposeful ambiguity with which the whole Soviet "plan" was shrouded, it must be concluded that since they had ventured so little, they could not have expected much to be either lost or gained. Brezhnev's cryptic comment had probably been intended as no more than a trial balloon. And the Soviets took pains in the six months following the speech to keep the idea alive, frequently alluding to its intent but without ever committing themselves to more details.

The probable reason for this studied ambiguity lies in the variety of purposes that the proposal could serve. On a very modest level, the proposal was an effective way of reminding the world that the Soviet Union considers itself an *Asian* as well as a European power, and that it intends to play a more active role in Asian security matters. This, of course, was one of the themes which had been emphasized by Kosygin's role in mediating between India and Pakistan at Tashkent.

A second possible purpose of Brezhnev's proposal was to serve notice that the Soviets were aware of the potential change in the military balance in Asia as Britain began to withdraw from "east of Suez." It would alert smaller Asian states to the danger of allowing American or Japanese "imperialism" to take up the British role, as well as suggest that alternative arrangements could gain Soviet support. Even if no Soviet-sponsored "collective security system" were to result, by promoting the erosion of existing security arrangements and forestalling the construction of new Western-backed pacts, the Soviets could have achieved a net gain.

Despite their loud protestations against the theory of "filling the vacuum," the behavior of the Soviets—especially in the Middle East and the Indian Ocean—has indicated that they are indeed sensitive to such opportunities. Since the spring of 1968, from six to fifteen Soviet warships have been present in the Indian Ocean, calling at some twenty ports in fourteen different countries from India to East Africa. With the reopening of the Suez Canal, the ability to link up this fleet with the more formidable force in the Mediterranean represents the fulfillment of an ambition even greater than that of which the Tsars once dreamed. The Soviets can already calculate an increased political impact from the present limited naval force.

If the United States continues to follow the British in reducing its

Asian commitments, the leaders of South Asia may well be left to feel that a "collective security system" under Soviet guarantee is a viable alternative. The Brezhnev initiative, then, may be seen as an invitation to the states of the area to discuss with the Soviet Union, collectively or individually, cooperative defense arrangements for the post-Vietnam era.

The Russians' denials of an interest in "filling the imperialist vacuum" in Asia have doubtful credibility in light of their military and political behavior. But their protests that the collective security proposal had nothing to do with an anti-Chinese grouping also ring hollow. Brezhnev's speech followed by only three months the bloodiest and most far-reaching clash of Soviet and Chinese troops on their common border, and rumors of an impending full-scale Sino-Soviet war were at the time very much in the air.

In the context of "collective security" against the Chinese the Soviet-Indian treaty of August 1971 acquires special significance. Negotiations for the treaty, which had begun fully two years before, and were resumed in the wake of the Pakistani civil war, were spurred by the announcement of Nixon's impending trip to China. This visit of the American president to the capital of India's "adversary number two" had been facilitated through the cooperation of her "enemy number one," and this fact seriously concerned Mrs. Gandhi as she faced the prospect of yet another war with Pakistan.

Almost immediately after the signing of the treaty, the Soviets revived the long-dormant notion of a "system of collective security in Asia." An article in *New Times* in September 1971 quoted approvingly the view of a left-wing Indian newspaper that the treaty could become the first step toward establishment of such a system.[56] Brezhnev himself returned to the idea in his speech of March 1972. Noting the Soviet-Indian treaty and the subsequent strengthening of Soviet relations on the subcontinent, he then praised the recent "turn for the better in our relations with Japan." Gromyko in January had made his first visit to Tokyo in six years. His trip—obviously timed to exploit Japanese disillusionment with the United States and to divert Tokyo from following the American lead in conducting talks with China—had won from the Japanese the promise of a resumption of talks on a Moscow-Tokyo peace treaty. It was thus in the context of Soviet relations with Tokyo and New Delhi that Brezhnev went on to say:

The idea of guaranteeing security in Asia on a collective basis is arousing increasing interest in many Asian countries. It is becoming increasingly clearer that the real path to security in Asia is not the path of military blocs and groupings but the path of good-neighbor cooperation among all the states interested in this. Collective security in Asia must, in our view, be based on such principles as renunciation of the use of force in relations between states, respect for sovereignty and the inviolability of borders, non-interference in internal affairs and the broad development of economic and other cooperation on the basis of full equality and mutual advantage. We . . . are ready to cooperate with all states with a view to the implementation of this idea.[57]

A new wave of articles in the Soviet press echoed Brezhnev's idea. Prominent among them was a piece appearing in June in *Pravda* by Viktor Mayevsky, entitled, "Collective Security in Asia is an Urgent Problem." [58] Why the sense of "urgency" in Moscow about this long-standing notion? One probable reason was the increasing evidence that an Indochina peace arrangement was imminent. Rather than allow this area to slip under Chinese influence following an American withdrawal, Moscow may well have wanted to include it as part of a larger Soviet-sponsored security system in Asia. The other, perhaps stronger, reason for urgency was Soviet concern at the increasing pace of Peking's diplomatic activity; the Chinese were simply refusing to be "contained." To prevent Tokyo—and even New Delhi —from becoming ensnared in Peking's active net, the Soviets were offering to these and other Asian countries the alternative prospect of their own security grouping—which was not, of course, "directed against any other country." Mayevsky argued, in fact, that objections to the Soviet proposal were being voiced precisely in unnamed "countries" that had made territorial claims against others. In this connection, he raised a fascinating parallel with the "security" situation in Europe in the aftermath of the German treaties: creation of security systems in Asia that, "among other things, would confirm the inviolability of borders and the non-use of force clearly does not suit certain circles in various countries . . . It might be recalled that in Europe the border problem found a realistic solution that is registered in well-known international treaties and that this is of paramount importance in strengthening European security." [59]

In this context, another interesting facet of the recent Soviet talk of Asian security was the alacrity with which Moscow propagandists seized on the report of Congressmen Boggs and Ford implying that Chou En-lai had expressed reluctance to see a complete American withdrawal from Asia. The Soviets linked this "evidence" of Sino-American collusion to similar charges that Peking was conspiring with the U.S. and the capitalists of Europe for the purposes of retaining an American presence in Europe, "knocking on the door" of the Common Market, and wrecking Soviet plans for a European Security Conference. Thus, O. Ivanov wrote in September 1972 that alleged Chinese plans to spur on the integration of capitalist Europe and "torpedo" the "socialist countries' program of easing tension and strengthening security" was further evidence that Mao's "chauvinist, great-power line" had led him to collude with the imperialists.[60]

Soviet "security" campaigns in Asia and Europe were linked not only by Peking's "wrecking activities" with respect to both, but also by the fact that the stated "principles" on which each of the proposed security plans would be based were virtually identical. Both proposals called for a system of guarantees and obligations based on: (1) respect for the inviolability of borders and exclusion of territorial claims; (2) renunciation of the use of force in relations among states; (3) development of relations on the basis of equality and noninterference in internal affairs; and (4) broad development of diverse, mutually-advantageous economic and other ties between states.[61] Though the precise form (bilateral or multilateral) of the system of obligations was left ambiguous in Soviet statements, the Soviets have in both settings called for the new "system" to replace existing regional "blocs."

The Soviet campaign for a Conference on Security and Cooperation in Europe—which was the chief tactic in Moscow's drive for "normalization" in Europe—was both longer and better publicized than its Asian counterpart. The Soviet proposal had actually undergone a number of stages, beginning with a draft All-European Treaty on Collective Security, tabled by Molotov at the Berlin conference of foreign ministers in 1954. The following year, at the Geneva summit, the Soviets called for the simultaneous dissolution of NATO and the new Warsaw Treaty Organization, and for the negotiation of an All-European Treaty on Renunciation of Armed Force. Three years later, the Warsaw Pact countries proposed a nonaggression pact between themselves and the NATO countries.

All of these earlier initiatives were closely linked to the German problem, as the Soviets sought to forestall the Federal Republic's integration into the Western alliance system and to overcome the isolation of the GDR. When the all-European conference plan was revived in January 1965 (while official Washington was absorbed in major policy deliberations on Southeast Asia), it again called for a nonaggression pact and a German peace settlement based on the recognition of two German states pledged to forego nuclear armaments. Appearing in the wake of the ill-fated American attempt to create a multilateral force for NATO, the Warsaw Pact initiative seemed designed to capitalize on tensions within the Western alliance as well as to prevent the acquisition of nuclear weapons in any form by the "West German revanchists." As Gromyko made clear the following year, an additional target of the proposal was the "influence wielded by a large non-European power" which at the time was evidently not on the Soviet guest list.

With certain modifications of tone and emphasis, the proposal for an all-European security conference resurfaced at a conference of Warsaw Treaty members held in Bucharest in July 1966 (when the possibility was raised of the mutual disbandment of NATO and the Warsaw Pact), at a meeting of European communist parties in Karlovy Vary in April 1967, as well as—with renewed urgency—at meetings of the Warsaw Pact's Political Consultative Committee held in Budapest in March 1969, in Prague in October of that year, and in June 1970 in Budapest.

A "concrete program of action" to create a system of European security was detailed in June 1969 in the final communiqué of the Moscow international conference. Though citing the existence of only "imperialist-imposed" military blocs and bases as the obstacle to peaceful cooperation, the document repeated the call for the "simultaneous dissolution of NATO and the Warsaw Treaty." As stated in Moscow, the concrete goals of this initiative were to secure the inviolability of existing frontiers in Europe, especially along the Oder-Neisse and between the Western and Eastern parts of Germany. It would hopefully achieve the international legal recognition of the GDR, prevent the Bonn government from obtaining atomic weapons, and win from that government renunciation of its claim to represent the whole of Germany, while in general curbing "neo-Nazi" and "revanchist" forces in the Federal Republic. While thus dealing with the German issue, the Warsaw Pact proposal would at the same time guarantee to the peoples of Europe "their sovereign right to be masters of their continent without interference from the USA" and would facilitate mutually beneficial economic, scientific and technical cooperation between East and West.

By 1969, in the aftermath of the invasion of Czechoslovakia and its unintended galvanization of NATO, the Soviets were pursuing the idea of a conference with renewed emphasis on its defensive purposes: to achieve recognition of the East European status quo, and to combat the Kiesinger version of *Ostpolitik* which was threatening the further isolation of the GDR. With the subsequent "normalization" in Prague, and especially with the advent of the Brandt government in

Bonn late in 1969, the conference proposal receded temporarily into the background.

Within a year, Brandt had negotiated treaties with Moscow and Warsaw which brought, on a *bilateral* basis, a recognition of much of what the Soviets had originally sought to achieve with a conference. In the authoritative opinion of N. Inozemtsev, head of the Academy of Sciences' institute dealing with international relations, the treaties "above all signify recognition of the fixity and inviolability of the borders in Europe, including the Western border of Poland along the Oder-Neisse and the border between the FRG and the GDR; it signifies the renunciation of all territorial claims whatsoever and the obligation to respect the territorial integrity of all the states in Europe." [62]

The ratification of the German treaties, and the related Four-Power Agreement on Berlin indeed went far toward "normalization" of the status quo in Central Europe. The achievement of these agreements, together with Moscow's assent to the holding of negotiations on reduction of troops and arms in Europe "parallel" to an all-European conference, fulfilled the major American and NATO preconditions for the convening of the conference itself. Though without apparent enthusiasm, the Nixon administration formally agreed at the 1972 Moscow summit that preparations for the European Security Conference should proceed.

The Soviets continued to see certain benefits to be derived both from their continuing noisy campaign on behalf of the conference initiative, and from the holding of the conference itself. The propaganda benefits from the campaign itself had already been considerable. The Soviets had communicated to audiences in both neutral and NATO countries in Western Europe the image of the "socialist" countries as the major initiators and proponents of peace and stability on the continent, along with the image of assorted "NATO leaders," "European capitalist circles," and "revanchists" (meaning primarily the German opposition parties) as the opponents of these same laudable goals.

The perceived benefits of the conference itself were several: (1) recognition, on a multilateral basis, of the "inviolability" of borders of the GDR and other East European states; (2) achievement of full recognition of the GDR by virtue of its participation in the conference; (3) a lessening of American military presence and political influence, and a reemphasis on an "all-European" rather than an "Atlantic" Europe; (4) accentuation of divisions among NATO member-states and of the unwillingness in some NATO countries to support continued heavy defense expenditures; and (5) reversal of the trend toward tighter integration of the European Economic Community, and the expansion of trade ties—on the basis of "equality" and "non-discrimination"—between the Common Market and the recently-upgraded Council for Mutual Economic Assistance.

When the Soviets advocate, in the Conference on Security and Co-operation in Europe and the parallel talks on mutual force reductions in Central Europe, the "abolition of blocs" and "ending the division of Europe," they are giving these phrases a special meaning. In the words of Vikenti Matveyev, "the division of Europe into military-political groupings is one thing, and the existence of states with different social systems is another." [63] The Warsaw Pact and its military organization, which was from the beginning "purely defensive and open," can be disbanded simultaneously with NATO. But the division of Europe *"on social and political lines"* is a "natural result" of the advancement along the road of social progress, and it is "historically irreversible." Such division can and will be overcome "in the long term," but only as the result of the transformation to socialism in the West. Only then will there "be true grounds to speak of a united Europe, in the broadest and fullest sense of the word." [64]

It was evident throughout 1974 that a thirty-five nation summit capping the work of the Conference on Security and Cooperation in Europe was high on the agenda of the Soviet leadership. Such a meeting, the Soviets felt, by affirming the general principles of security and cooperation in Europe (in very vague terms), would provide a fitting climax to a diplomatic and propaganda campaign they and their allies had waged for almost a decade. But a major stumbling block to such a meeting was the radically different Eastern and Western conceptions of the meaning of what the NATO group terms the "freer movement of people and ideas between East and West." Soviet spokesmen characterized the Western proposals in this realm as an effort to interfere in the internal affairs of the socialist states. As Gromyko insisted in his 1973 speech to the United Nations: "internal procedures and internal laws are the devil at every state's gate in front of which other people should stop." [65]

In the Soviet view, the solution to specific problems in this area— the "broad development of cultural ties and solution of human problems"—was possible only if the threat of war had first been eliminated. The "key problem" was to develop a preamble elaborating the general principles on which cooperation in this field would be based. Prominent among these should be sovereign equality and noninterference in internal affairs, and respect for differences among social systems and originality of constitutional and legal systems, national traditions, laws, and customs. Anything less would open the way for "ideological subversion" of socialist systems by Western propagandists. By the time the Helsinki summit was convened in July 1975, the Soviets had achieved a compromise which essentially fulfilled Moscow's conditions.

Thus, in both its larger conception of peaceful coexistence and its particular strategy regarding the future security of Europe, the USSR perceived détente as inextricably linked with a continuing ideological and political struggle on behalf of "social progress." New revolutionary opportunities were seen as presenting themselves in the wake of the relaxation of international tensions and the exacerbation of the "crisis of capitalism." And in this context, the conferences in Geneva-Helsinki and in Vienna were viewed in Moscow not as ends in themselves, capable of overcoming the division of Europe, but as new "starting points" in an ongoing struggle to unite the continent on the basis of a universal transformation to socialism.

An essay that ranges over such broad terrain as this defies easy summary. Having noted the prevailing Soviet perspectives regarding the "balance of forces" in the unfolding international arena, I have dwelt in some greater detail on Soviet assessments of the bilateral Soviet-American relationship, on the Sino-Soviet rivalry and the problem of Asian security, and on the long-standing Soviet campaign for a European Security Conference. This emphasis does not imply that the Soviets will restrict their activity only to these issues on the Eurasian continent. Soviet diplomatic and economic dealings with the governments of Africa and Latin America—as well as with the communist and "revolutionary-democratic" parties in those areas—will continue, but with a lower priority and less expectation of immediate gain than was evidenced in the Khrushchev era. And the considerable Soviet presence and influence in the Middle East (an area not dealt with here but certainly closely linked to continental security issues) is not likely to soon fade away—as the 1973 war in that area again demonstrated. Rather, the essay's focus on Soviet security concerns on the Eurasian continent reflects a judgment that this focus is likely to remain a primary one for Soviet foreign-policy decision makers throughout the 1970s.

# PART SIX

Some Reflections

# Soviet Politics:
# From the Future
# to the Past?

ZBIGNIEW BRZEZINSKI

Soviet politics cannot be separated from Russian history. This history has shaped a political tradition and a political culture that have deeply influenced the manner in which Marxism was assimilated to the Russian tradition, the way in which Lenin adapted that doctrine to the political circumstances of the moment, and the means which Stalin employed to reshape society to fulfill certain political and ideological purposes. Revolutionary doctrine and a revolutionary elite, to be sure, produced a new political style but, with the passage of time, the elements of historical discontinuity in the Soviet political experience have become less dominant, while more enduring patterns of Russian political culture have begun to surface with growing clarity and have been impinging more directly on the Soviet future.

The central and significant reality of Russian politics has been its predominantly autocratic character. Unlike its western European neighbors, Russia had not experienced a prolonged feudal phase. The overthrow of the Tartar yoke gave rise to an increasingly assertive and dominant autocracy. Property and people were the possessions of the state, personalized by the Autocrat (designated as such explicitly and proudly). The obligation of well-nigh complete subordination of any individual to the personalized symbol of the state was expressly asserted.[1] Control over society—including the church by the state—among other means, through a census mechanism adopted centuries ahead of any corresponding European device, was reminiscent of Oriental despotisms and in fact was derived directly from that historical experience.[2] The result has been to establish a relationship of state supremacy over society, of politics over social affairs, of the functionary over the citizen (or subject), to a degree not matched in Europe; and differences of degree do become differences of kind.

This historical tradition can be neither ignored nor underestimated. It has been a living one, reinforced through time by legal codes, thereby solidifying that relationship of supremacy. Indeed, some of the expressly assertive codification of that relationship of domination of the society by the state took place during the nineteenth century, when the rest of Europe was moving toward more liberal conceptions of social order and more pluralistic concepts of political organization. Revisions in the Russian criminal code, undertaken in 1846, and then again extended in 1881, gave the government unprecedented powers of arrest, not only for acts against the state, but even for alleged intentions to commit such acts. Moreover, the right to exile a citizen as "untrustworthy" became the prerogative of local police, a situation which has endured beyond the Tsarist era.

The autocratic character of the Russian political tradition has gone hand in hand with a somewhat ambivalent attitude towards the West —an attitude that oscillated between periods of fascination and imitation on the one hand and conservative rejection and mystical superiority on the other, with the two sometimes combining. This self-consciousness has tended to express itself periodically through phases of sustained competitive imitation of the more tangible aspects of the Western way of life, be it through Peter's reforms or Stalin's social engineering, or recently through the obsessive competition with America. The effect has been to give Russian history a repetitive pattern of "fits and starts," as E. H. Carr has noted, with the state periodically initiating "revolutions from above," thereby reasserting its dominant relationship over society. This process has also had the effect of transforming "institutions and social groups deriving directly from imitation of Western models into something alien to the West and distinctively national." [3]

The adaptation of Marxism to Russia accordingly took place in a context that was bound to emphasize the authoritarian and dogmatic aspects of Marxism. That it took place at a time of accelerating social change in Russia, of the first pangs of the industrial revolution, and of increased political suppression, which came in the wake of unsuccessful populist terrorism, further tended to prompt more Manichaean, simplistic, and autocratic expressions among those who dedicated themselves to destroy the old for the sake of the new.*

## THE MEANING OF REVOLUTION

Leninism in its political style and organizational form thus became—for all of its sincere revolutionary content and obvious revolutionary social significance—a continuation of the dominant tradition rather than its termination. In terms of political tradition, the Duma-based Provisional Government was *more revolutionary* than Lenin's—though, to repeat, on the plane of social relations, property relations, and the role of classes, Leninism obviously meant a more profound and significant change. But on the level of politics, the Provisional Government, because of its democratic character, involved a sharper break with the past, a deeper discontinuity, than did Leninism.

Moreover, Lenin and Leninism set in motion an organizational dynamic that tipped the internal balances within the ruling class in favor of a leadership that concentrated effectively on maintaining political supremacy over societal affairs, without becoming diverted prematurely into external or domestic adventures. Awareness of the centrality of the power factor—so instinctively appreciated by Lenin and so deliberately inculcated by him among his supporters—worked to Stalin's advantage in the struggle for power.[4] Capitalizing on the instinctive desire for consolidation of power, and yet also for some ideological fulfillment, Stalin gave the new elite satisfaction on both the level of self-interest and self-esteem. (This appeal of Stalinism to the young and relatively ideologically crude apparatchiki emerges extremely well from Khrushchev's memoirs.) Leninism thus loaded the historical dice in Stalin's favor and made Stalinism an extension—rather than an aberration—of what immediately preceded.

Stalin further revitalized the autocratic tradition—though he gave it a qualitatively new character. Through acts not only of unprecedented terror but of unprecedented social engineering he undertook yet another revolution from above. Its political effect was to reassert, to

* Another aspect of the problem pertains to what Samuel P. Huntington has defined as the "bifurcated society." He has argued that "A one-party system is, in effect, the product of the efforts of a political elite to organize and to legitimate rule by one social force over another in a bifurcated society . . . One-party systems, in short, arise from pronounced bifurcations that cannot be resolved by secession and territorial separation" (*Authoritarian Politics in Modern Society: The Dynamics of Established One-Party Systems* [New York: Basic Books, 1970], pp. 11–12) .

an extreme degree, the domination of the political system over society
—but with the added features of ideological motivation and techno-
logically more advanced coercion. It is because of this experience, and
its institutional and procedural legacies that have continued to this
day, that one is justified in asserting that on the plane of politics the
Bolshevik seizure of power marked not the end but the renewal and
extension of a tradition deeply rooted in the Russian past.

That tradition has been marked by: (1) concentration of power in
the political organism as distinct from the social organism; (2) concentration of power in an extremely narrow circle of decision makers,
frequently a single individual; (3) insistence on the primacy of the
official truth over any other version or interpretation of reality; (4)
identification of the state with divinity or history; (5) subordination of
other groups—be they boyars or managers and/or intellectuals—to the
state; (6) domination by the state of property relationships and particularly of the rural masses; (7) periodic phases of social engineering
or "revolutions from above"; (8) insistence that political opposition
equals treason and hence the subordination of civil rights to political
interests. With only extraordinarily brief periods of time as exceptions,
the above has been true of the pre-, as well as the post-, Revolutionary
Russian experience.

That in turn justifies perhaps an even more radical assertion: the
Bolshevik revolution not only was not a break from the predominant
political tradition, but was, in historical perspective, an act of revitalized Restoration. The late Romanov period was a period of decay, of
the gradual weakening of the hold of the state over society. This was
produced by the combined influence of social change (urbanization
and industrialization, which also prompted the appearance of a more
assertive bourgeoisie and intelligentsia and finally working masses)
and of internal loss of vitality within the top elite, not to speak of the
autocrat's own personal weaknesses. The overthrow of that ruling
elite brought to power a new group, much more vital, much more
assertive, and imbued with a new sense of historical mission. The
political result of the Bolshevik revolution was thus revitalized restoration of long dominant patterns.*

---

* Indeed, it might be intriguing to examine other revolutions from this standpoint. To what extent have most revolutions involved revitalization of the dominant
social-political patterns and traditions in a slightly new guise and to what extent
do they really mark a fundamental break? More generally, continuity tends to be
the rule in political systems, as suggested recently by Ted Robert Gurr, "Persistence
and Change in Political Systems, 1800–1971," *American Political Science Review*,
68 (December 1974), pp. 1482–1504.

## THE QUESTION OF LABELS OR CONCEPTS

To postulate the above is not to slight the depth and the extent of the social revolution that Communism brought to Russia. That revolution was a revolution. It created a new society based on new structures and new social patterns. That society, however, does not have as yet a qualitatively new relationship with the political system, and the future, as will be shortly argued, may thus involve again some familiar dilemmas.

It is important to remind ourselves, in the context of this argument, that the relationship between the political system and society, even when falling within a certain general and established pattern, tends to be changing and dynamic. This change also creates problems of definition and confusion about labels, including more recently about the term totalitarianism.

To debate anew the relevance or utility of that political term might not be productive, but some observations are pertinent to the case developed here. The appearance of movements committed to a comprehensive social reconstruction, and the availability to these movements of means of social control commensurate to the monumental tasks undertaken, is a new phenomenon. This does not mean that totalitarianism comes into being and persists from the moment that power is taken by such a movement. Rather, the term—or some other term, if the word "totalitarianism" evokes too much passion*—is meant to define a particular phase in the system/society relationship in which that society is in almost complete subordination to the state. That phase may or may not persist for too long, depending on circumstances, but in itself it does involve significant expansion in the dimension of politics and it therefore commands analytical recognition as a qualitatively distinct phenomenon.

Speaking more specifically of the Soviet experience, the above might be clarified if the following stages are differentiated: (1) the appearance and formation of a movement, dedicated to a radical and extensive social reconstruction, 1902–1917; (2) seizure of power by that movement in the context of political disintegration and social inertia, 1917–1920; (3) consolidation of power by that movement and the beginnings of social mobilization, 1921–1928; (4) transformation of society from above by political means, including very heavy reliance on

* However, the argument that the word "totalitarianism" is a Cold War invention is not really an intellectual argument; those who allege this open themselves to the charge that they themselves may be politically motivated in rejecting it, and hence the argument becomes futile.

violence, 1929–1939; (5) following the end of the war (which prompted social mobilization reinforced by political means and by patriotism), consolidation of coercive social control by the political system, 1945–1956; (6) limited retraction of political control over society and the surfacing of some societal pressures from below, since 1956.

What has at times been called totalitarianism thus emerged in the Soviet setting in stage 4 and it was consolidated in stage 5. (For other systems some of these stages might be shorter or longer or simply telescoped.) It does not matter how these stages are labeled, but if one is concerned with understanding the scope of politics and the essence of politics in a given historical moment then one should not ignore the specific character of the system/society relationship and not obscure it by use of concepts that apply to other phases as well or that are meant to embrace at once several different kinds of authoritarian regimes.

Stalinism involved creating a system. In contrast, the historical essence of the Khrushchev era was perceived by his opponents as representing "objectively" an effort, mounted from within the political system, to weaken or even to break down its Leninist-Stalinist character. (Khrushchev, to be sure, thought he was revitalizing it and making it more "Leninist.") But that system, institutionally entrenched, proved resilient, especially since the relationship between the political system and society under Stalin already had become less revolutionary and more dominant (that is, the difference between phase 4 and phase 5).

As a result, by the mid-seventies the Soviet system had become in some respects more akin to traditional authoritarian regimes, but with an enormous and increasingly dysfunctional totalitarian residue, inherent in the doctrinal and political system of controls still bureaucratically, ritualistically, and occasionally coercively imposed on society. The contemporary Soviet system thus combines residual elements of revolutionary totalitarianism with features reminiscent of the more traditional autocracy.*

* I have argued elsewhere that *"This has made for a relationship between the political system and society which is ideologically ritualistic, defensive in character, and—very important—increasingly dysfunctional to the requirements of scientific and intellectual innovation in a relatively developed industrial society.* The political system itself is still totalitarian in its organizational and ideological modes in the sense that it monopolizes effective power and programmatic thinking, and suppresses information of alternative political groupings and programs. But with the political system no longer exacting from society total obedience on behalf of doc-

Given that context, the recently debated issue of pluralism and degeneration takes on a somewhat different meaning.[5] Institutional pluralism ceases to be an alternative view of what is, since a condition of Stalinist total control no longer prevails; rather it is an elaboration of what one aspect of the political reality has become, namely, a condition akin to the more familiar traditional authoritarian pattern within which limited institutional pluralism, coordinated from above on the basis of a shared and essentially conservative orthodoxy, is tolerable and normal. That being the case, the concept of institutional pluralism represents neither a definitional challenge nor a political prognosis. It does not challenge the over-all interpretation, but reinforces it. And by itself it does not tell us a great deal about the future, for an institutionally pluralistic authoritarianism might still revert to a more centralized form (a new revitalized revolution from above?) or, in time prompt—through more overt policy and power conflicts—a new and more fundamental challenge to the autocratic pattern as a whole.

THE QUESTION OF SOCIAL CHANGE

Perhaps a better guide to the future can be provided by analysis of social change in the Soviet Union. It can be argued, and it has been argued, that urbanization and industrialization produce a much more complex society, and that in time such evolution tends to be reflected also in changes within the political system.

The argument is certainly a potent one, and on the social level evidence for it is overwhelming. Soviet society has changed dramatically. A new relationship among the classes has emerged after fifty years of Soviet rule and the substance of class structure and class identity has similarly been dramatically altered. There is a new pattern of differentiation in Soviet society, the urban element has become increasingly dominant, and industrial values have been superimposed over the older rural tradition. The enormous extension of the educational system has similarly introduced profound changes in the subjective consciousness of the Soviet population, and that necessarily affects the system/society relationship.

This social change has led some of the more optimistic observers

---

trinally defined goals, the relationship between the political system and society is becoming gradually more interacting, more instrumental and less ideological" (Z. Brzezinski, "Dysfunctional Totalitarianism," in Klaus von Beyme, ed., *Theory and Politics* (The Hague, 1972), p. 379.

of the Soviet scene—especially Marxists like Roy Medvedev—to argue that change in the Soviet Union has already allowed a variety of groups to contest the ideological influence and authority both of Marxism-Leninism and of the Party. In Medvedev's words:

In the last few years these various moods among the masses have provided the ground for the appearance of several explicit political trends and groups, in what is now a continuing process. As a general rule, they proceed from a socialist viewpoint but try to interpret socialism and communism in their own way. For the most part they exist and are evolving *outside* the Party, though they have their supporters inside it as well. Their development is largely independent of Marxism-Leninism, although some of them do not reject many of its most important propositions. Nearly all of them are oppositional in character, but on the whole it is a question of loyal opposition involving only ideas and convictions.[6]

A central question, however, is whether such social change is capable of altering, or has in fact already altered in a significant fashion the underlying character of Soviet politics. That character, as I have argued, has been shaped largely by political traditions derived from the specifics of Russian/Soviet history, and it is deeply embedded in the operational style and institutions of the existing Soviet system. The ability of that system to resist de-Stalinization seems to indicate a considerable degree of resilience on the part of the dominant mode of politics in the Soviet context. It suggests, at the very least, that political changes are produced very slowly through social change, and that one must wait for at least several generations before social change begins to be significantly reflected in the political sphere.

This argument is reinforced by the contemporary experience of Eastern Europe. Eastern Europe has undergone social change in many ways similar to that of the Soviet Union. The make-up of social classes and the nature of class relations have been altered on the basis of a pattern derived largely from the Soviet experience, in the context of political systems that were initially almost carbon copies of the Soviet. However, the last decade and a half has seen the emergence of remarkably diverse patterns of political behavior in the various East European countries. The character of their political systems seems to be quite different *in spite of* the similarity of social change within them. The spread in the political style and procedures among East Germany, Rumania, Poland, Hungary, and Yugoslavia is quite remarkable and it does point to the conclusion that similarity in social change does not dictate identity of political behavior. It suggests on the contrary, that political processes have a viability of their own. If not independent, they are at least not rapidly affected by the patterns of social change.

A more fertile approach to the political consequences of social change might involve analysis based on generational change. But that itself implies that change will be slow, with politically significant effects felt only gradually after a prolonged passage of time. Moreover, even here one must be careful not to assume that a generational change means automatically political change. Transfer of values and of procedures from one generation to another is likely to be more effective in a closed and highly bureaucratized system than in more open, pluralistic conditions. In any case, it is unlikely that the effects of the entrance into the upper levels of the Soviet political leadership of the first genuinely post-Stalinist generation would be felt before the late seventies, and even then the generation immediately to follow might be more conservative or restorative.*

All this is not to deny the argument that alterations in social structure create conditions which affect the scope of the political process and which can moderate the extremes of politics, but it does appear that the process is an extremely tenuous and slow one. Here, too, the contrasting experience of Poland and East Germany in the last two decades is suggestive, since in one case it has involved a relatively stable modus vivendi between the ruling party, a powerful Catholic church, and a relatively free and large agricultural sector and in the other the further consolidation of what has emerged as the most successful modern and centrally controlled Communist state.

The foregoing would indicate in turn that economic change is not the decisive variable in inducing political change as occasionally has been argued. Varying political systems may coexist with similar economic systems and vice versa; they have done so in the past and they are likely to do so in the future. That being the case, increased economic sophistication in the Soviet Union need not dictate any particular political form, for it can be adjusted to a more centralized or to a more decentralized political framework. Thus in evaluating the prospects of change, the ability of the Russian political tradition to continue itself through the institutions and procedures of Soviet politics should not be underestimated.

* In a discussion of Soviet political generations presented by Professor Seweryn Bialer to my seminar at Columbia University, the following scheme for political generations was developed: (1) the conspiratorial—1902–1917; (2) the civil war—1917–1927; (3) the revolution from above/Stalinist—1929–1939; (4) the war-time—1941–1945; (5) the latter-day Stalinist—1945–1953; (6) the post-Stalin turbulence—1956–1964; (7) the bureaucratic restoration—1965–1975.

In this connection, one must also take into account the coercive capabilities of the state. That state does have at its disposal extensive means of controls and coercion—and these means are not restrained by legal checks. The following list is a mere summary of the means already available now to the Soviet elite for the enforcement of political compliance: (1) wiretapping of conversations; (2) mail surveillance; (3) informer networks; (4) control on movement and residence; (5) personal registration; (6) computerized data banks; (7) electronic surveillance, voiceprint detection devices, and so forth; (8) exile (internal or abroad); (9) imprisonment in labor camps; (10) confinement in an insane asylum; (11) chemical and psychological treatment; (12) imposition of the death penalty.

With increasing technological, especially electronic, sophistication, the ability of the state to control its citizens will grow—unless legal restraints are deliberately adopted. Since the means of coercion are designed to protect that elite's power and privilege, it seems prudent not to expect too soon the Soviet KGB or MVD to find themselves checked by legal restraints or mass media exposure. These considerations tend to reinforce Medvedev's rather pessimistic conclusion—reached despite his Marxist-Leninist optimism about the effects of social change—that "We see that the movement toward 'tightening of the screws' still seems a more likely prospect than a systematic development of social democracy." [7]

THE QUESTION OF DEGENERATION

If it can be argued that social change by itself is not a reliable indicator of the future, then what might be said concerning the future evolution of the Soviet system? [8] Present trends are certainly ambiguous enough. It is here that it might be useful to consider again the argument for degeneration. The Tsarist system, given its own historical patterns (the standards for degeneration for a Western type of social-political system would necessarily differ), was degenerating as a political system because—to put it in rather broad terms:

(1) It was losing control over social change, and that social change was acquiring external political manifestations contradictory to the values and effective operations of the system;

(2) The ability of the political system to make basic policy choices was becoming narrowed by an internal paralysis stemming from increased institutional pluralism;

(3) Its elite was beginning to question its own values and was be-

coming increasingly susceptible to values hitherto perceived as inimical to its interests;

(4) The routinization and bureaucratization of elite recruitment was prompting the supremacy of mediocrity over talent, with the latter increasingly forced outside of politics;

(5) The authority of the system was becoming questionable both on the grounds of legitimacy and efficiency.

The present Soviet system manifests to a degree some of the above symptoms—perhaps least so with regard to the third and the last. Admittedly, to assert this is not the same thing as to prove it. Alas, in political science what is more easily "proven" tends to be also more trivial.[9] More significant propositions concerning the historical processes or even the quality of decision makers necessarily tend to be elusive of the reassuring precision of the statistical method, and require somewhat impressionistic and therefore also controversial judgments. Since controversy is also a tool of thought, let us run this risk, in the knowledge that what follows cannot be fully "proven" but also in the hope that argument will help us see more clearly the larger picture.

Insofar as the first aspect of degeneration is concerned, recent years have seen relatively little social experimentation from above. The Soviet government has introduced policies designed to narrow somewhat the income gaps, but it has not undertaken to promote any far-reaching social change. Khrushchev's agricultural reforms as well as his administrative reform schemes were perhaps the only recent, but abortive, efforts involving significant change from above. Scholars have been debating the question of whether social differentiation is or is not widening in Soviet society, but there is in any case evidence of considerable inegalitarianism in access to higher education [10] and in life-styles. Aspirations for more consumption and for more leisure do clash with official values, but these contradictions generally would appear to be less acute than in the later Romanov days.

To the extent that Soviet political institutions and some social ones have now acquired institutional cohesion of the kind lacking under Stalin, it would follow that the ability of the top rulers to make grand choices tends to be narrowed. Incremental decision making becomes more the rule, with bureaucratic bargaining more the normal process. This condition interacts with the first, by gradually increasing the narrow scope for more autonomous social change.

With regard to the morale and motivation of the ruling elite, it does appear that cynicism is widespread—if the testimony of recent emigrés is to be credited. This cynicism evokes lip-service to the official ideology and much passion in the pursuit of privilege and in the preservation of official positions. In that sense, the erosion of revolutionary and ideological fervor is a symptom of degeneration. Moreover, but on a very narrow front, there have been known cases of actual rejection of orthodoxy and of official ideology and its replacement by alternative views. The histories of Sakharov and Medvedev—precisely because both claim to be still Marxists and both have been members of the elite—are in that sense more relevant here than dissidents like Solzhenitsyn. Given the political tradition, given the official and unofficial pressures on behalf of general social orthodoxy, it is a safe—but again unprovable—assumption that cases like Sakharov's stand out not as isolated exceptions but more likely as tips of an iceberg.

To be sure, Sakharov is primarily a scholar. Accordingly, one should also note the larger ideological significance of the remarkable case of Khrushchev. Apart from what his memoirs reveal about the evolution of his own thinking, the fact that he ultimately dictated portions of his memoirs in the knowledge that they would appear in the West—published by the ideological enemy—does signal a degree of ideological revisionism that is objectively inimical to the interests of the established orthodoxy. Shelest's apparent susceptibility to some form of Ukrainian nationalism, which he combined with high ideological orthodoxy, provides another example of ideological vulnerability even at the highest elite level.

That Soviet elite recruitment has become highly routinized and bureaucratized cannot be disputed. That it attracts less talent to the top cannot be conclusively demonstrated. The top Soviet leadership is doubtless better educated and trained than its predecessors and, given its key role in running the system (probably without parallel elsewhere), this is presumably an improvement. The Central Committee, similarly, has a higher quotient of degrees in technology and has a more widely experienced membership than used to be the case. It has also been co-opting the better trained and more successful individuals outside of the Party system, though this could have the effect of diluting the values of the political elite. Moreover, technical or professional expertise does not in itself mean the same thing as political creativity, imagination, responsiveness to change and to new ideas —all of which the Soviet bureaucratic context tends to confine.

It is pertinent to note here that the offspring of the top Soviet elite, young people in a better position than most of their contemporaries to make a free choice of the most fulfilling occupation, tend on the whole not to choose politics, thus telling us something about the attractiveness of Soviet politics.* Reports of American students who have studied in Soviet universities—confirmed again by recent emigrés —indicate that generally the Komsomol attracts the less creative, the more careerist, and the rather opportunistic elements in schools of higher learning. With subsequent advancement dependent on—and shaped entirely by—a rigid bureaucratic process, one is justified in hypothesizing that conformity and collusion, rather than creativity and initiative, provide the keys to political elevation.

Finally, with regard to the legitimacy and efficiency of this system, the social situation appears to be somewhat mixed. The efficiency of the system in satisfying daily needs probably is not gaining in public esteem, especially given increasing opportunity of comparison with Eastern Europe and even with the West. But, with the periodic exception of the harvest, neither has it dropped dramatically. The legitimacy of the system also does not appear to be widely questioned, especially among the urban masses, though there are indicators suggesting that increasing (but difficult to estimate) numbers of non-Russians are beginning to press more overtly for national rights—a development that in time could make less legitimate the system for a significant proportion of the Soviet population.

THE PAST IN THE FUTURE?

Cumulatively, the preceding discussion suggests the conclusion that a process of degeneration has set in, but also that it has not reached critical proportions. That other political systems, for similar or different reasons depending on circumstances, may be undergoing a similar process (an argument sometimes raised in rejoinder to such a proposition) is neither here nor there, especially since the above by itself casts no light on the adaptability to change of various political systems. In the Soviet case, adaptability appears to be narrowly circumscribed by the institutional weight and vested interests of the existing system, by its ideological legacies, and by the cumulative effects of political tradition on behavior and thought. Recent efforts to promote a deliberate break with the autocratic past, as Khru-

---

* In some East European countries, notably Poland and Czechoslovakia, initial "depoliticization" of the offspring of the upper political elite led rapidly to a "counterpoliticization," which expressed itself both in the Prague "spring" and in the Polish events of March 1968. However, in the Soviet case there has so far been less evidence of such rapid progression from "depoliticization" to "counterpoliticization."

shchev's anti-Stalinism campaign has shown, were effectively resisted and defeated. That experience as well as earlier Tsarist cases of aborted liberalizations suggest that obstacles to a true liberalizing evolution may be difficult to overcome without some dramatic internal or external catalyst. Perhaps such a catalyst might come to the Soviet Union from the cultural crisis of the urban-technological society that is likely to reach it by the end of this decade from the West, but it does not follow that internal turbulence, *which is to be expected,* will necessarily promote a liberal-pluralistic evolution.

Rather, we may witness a period of confusion, even of some political breakdown, made all the more severe by the rapid injection into the political arena of internal national tensions. The national question inherently complicates any prognosis based on a straight-line projection of Soviet domestic liberalization. The experience of the last several decades has shown that communism intensifies nationalism by stimulating mass popular political awareness. The East European countries and China are today more nationalistically self-conscious— in depth of feeling and in scope of social-class-national awareness— than at any point in their histories. This is also true of the Great Russians in the Soviet Union. And if that is the case, then it is also likely that the non-Russians of the Soviet Union will become steadily more and more nationally self-aware. In fact, there is considerable evidence that this is the case already.

This national self-awareness of the non-Russian nations of the Soviet Union—denigrated deliberately to the level of Soviet nationalities (a Soviet term which Western scholars need not adopt) —is still often Soviet in content; but increasingly non-Russians wonder why their nations should not have more autonomy or even formally independent status—like communist-ruled Hungary or even Mongolia— rather than be ruled from Moscow by a largely Great Russian elite. These sentiments, if tolerated and accommodated, are likely to grow; if suppressed, they are likely to grow, too, unless the suppression becomes massive and sustained (which then would have systemic consequences as a whole).

In either case, the national problem in the Soviet Union bears directly on the problem of change in the Soviet Union. The Great Russian elite knows that an adaptive evolutionary pattern, leading to a more pluralistic system, inevitably means more autonomy and freedom for the non-Russians. This, for nationalistic, big-nation reasons, reinforced by the territorial imperative (especially in regard to the riches of Siberia), they will not tolerate. The national question, therefore, creates a major block to gradual evolution. More than that, it could prove itself to be the fatal contradiction in Soviet political evolution.

The national question also has the effect of strengthening the importance of the Party as the coordinating organ, or if the Party should weaken, of the military. Some keen observers have already noted the intensifying "militarization of the Soviet social ethos" (in Seweryn Bialer's apt phrase) and that process has obvious political implications. It is noteworthy that Soviet military publications have been taking a noticeably harder line against tendencies that could imply a liberal evolution, and it is reasonable to assume that in internal bureaucratic conflicts the top Soviet military have been backing the more nationalistic, centralizing, and ideologically orthodox elements.[11] The shift in national goals from a world revolution to world military preeminence also inherently enhances the domestic importance of the military. The military is thus increasingly becoming the major repository of the state tradition and an alternative unifying symbol.

If political change in the Soviet Union should gradually begin to threaten the autocratic tradition, either through an evolution towards a significantly more pluralistic system, or if such change should involve a dangerous decay in the Party's ability to integrate the system as a whole or to cope effectively with the social turbulence that might even by the end of this decade spread from the West to the more advanced portions of the Soviet Union, then the military would become the force most likely to respond—with new vigor—in keeping with the imperatives defined by long-enduring traditions. It is certainly no exaggeration to say that today the military are in a more symbiotic relationship with the ruling party, and are thus more directly influential on policy matters, than at any point in Soviet political history.

A dictatorship fusing some of the Party and some of the more politicized top military hence becomes a scenario for the future to be taken quite seriously. There is no other elite group in the Soviet Union capable either of supporting the Party in the event of a major crisis, or of replacing the Party in the event the crisis should get out of hand. The managerial elite has neither the coherence nor the ethos. However, even if a Soviet marshal in full uniform were at some future Party congress to mount the podium as the Party's new Secretary General, his appearance should not be hailed as indicating a sharp discontinuity nor even as marking the end of the period ushered in by 1917. Rather, it would again signal the shaping of the Russian future by the living past.

NOTES

CONTRIBUTORS

INDEX

# Notes

---

2  POLITICAL LEADERSHIP IN SOVIET HISTORIOGRAPHY
*Nancy Whittier Heer*

1. See Nancy Whittier Heer, *Politics and History in the Soviet Union* (Cambridge, Mass.: MIT Press, 1971), ch. 1.

2. The confusion and differing interpretations of Stalin in the Soviet press since Khrushchev opened the issue in 1956 have been documented by Jane P. Shapiro, "The Soviet Press and the Problem of Stalin," *Studies in Comparative Communism* (July–October 1971), pp. 179–209. See also Heer, *Politics and History*, ch. 9.

3. *Istoriia kommunisticheskoi partii sovetskogo soiuza,* vol. 5, bk. 1 (Moscow: Political Literature Publishing House, 1970), p. 557.

4. Ibid., p. 655.

5. A. M. Nekrich, *1941, 22 iiunia* (Moscow: Nauka, 1965). See also Heer, *Politics and History,* pp. 253–257.

6. *Istoriia,* p. 153.

7. "Chitateli obsuzhdaiut knigu," *Voprosy istorii KPSS,* no. 2 (1966), pp. 154–157.

8. *Istoriia,* **p.** 24.

9. See Dina Spechler, "Permitted Dissent in the Decade after Stalin," in this volume, p. 49.

10. Roy A. Medvedev, *Let History Judge* (New York: Alfred A. Knopf, 1972).

11. Aleksandr I. Solzhenitsyn, *The First Circle* (New York: Harper & Row, 1968), pp. 85–116.

12. Medvedev, *Let History Judge,* p. 359.

13. Ibid., p. 360.

14. Ibid., p. 362.

15. Ibid., p. 565.

16. Ibid., p. 146.

17. Ibid., p. 365.

18. Nekrich, as quoted in "The Personality Cult," *Survey,* April 1967, p. 179.

19. Kulish, as quoted in ibid., p. 177.

20. Medvedev, *Let History Judge,* pp. 69–70.

21. E. N. Burdzhalov, "O taktike bolshevikov v marte-aprele 1917," *Voprosy istorii,* no. 4 (1956), pp. 38–56; "Esche o taktike bolshevikov v marte-aprele 1917," *Voprosy istorii,* no. 8 (1956), pp. 109–114. See also Merle Fainsod, "Soviet Russian Historians," *Encounter,* 18 (1962), 82–89.

22. N. V. Cherepenin, "Nauchnaia konferentsiia po istoriografii Oktiabr'skoi revoliutsii," *Voprosy istorii KPSS,* no. 2 (1972), pp. 142, 144.

23. M. P. Kim, "Razvitie V. I. Leninym marksistskogo ucheniia o klassakh i partiiakh," *Voprosy istorii,* no. 11 (1969), pp. 3–27.

24. K. V. Gusev, "V. V. Komin: Bankrotstvo burzhuaznykh i melko-burzhuaznykh partii Rossii v period podgotovki i pobedy Velikoi Oktiabr-skoi sotsialisticheskoi revoliutsii," *Voprosy istorii,* no. 1 (1967), p. 138.

25. See Gusev, "Komin"; see also Gusev and Kh. A. Yeritsian, "Ot soglashatel'stva k kontrrevoliutsii," *Voprosy istorii,* no. 6 (1970), pp. 136–138; A. L. Litvin and R. I. Nafigov, "Krakh levykh eserov byl neizhezhen," *Voprosy istorii KPSS,* no. 4 (1972), pp. 135–136; F. A. Guseinov, "O bol'shevistskikh fraksiakh v Sovetakh v 1917g.," *Voprosy istorii KPSS,* no. 10 (1968), pp. 112–122; E. G. Gimpelson, "Iz istorii obrazovanniia odno-par-tiinoi sistemy v SSSR," *Voprosy istorii,* no. 11 (1965), pp. 16–30.

26. T. N. Shipelina, "Razgrom kaledinshchinyi," *Voprosy istorii,* no. 10 (1970), pp. 19–21.

27. K. I. Varlamov, "Novye issledovaniia o bor'be kommunisticheskoi partii protiv Trotskizma," *Voprosy istorii,* no. 9 (1971), pp. 138–146.

28. M. I. Stishkov, "Raspad melkoburzhuaznykh partii v sovetskoi rossii," *Voprosy istorii,* no. 2 (1968), pp. 58–74.

29. Guseinov, "O bol'shevistskikh."

30. Gimpelson, "Iz istorii obrazovanniia."

31. V. Zh. Kelle, V. V. Denisov, and Ye. G. Plimak, eds., *Leninizm i dialektika obshchestvennogo razvitiia* (Moscow: Science Publishing House, 1970). It might be well to note that this is not the first time that sensitive historical issues have been ventilated outside that profession's academic territory. The best example is probably Khrushchev's encouragement of authors and literary journals—notably *Novy mir*—to open the question of the labor camps in 1962.

32. G. Ye. Glezerman, M. T. Iovchuk, and I. F. Petrov, "Leninizm i dialektika obshchestvennogo razvitiia," *Voprosy filosofii,* no. 10 (1970), p. 129.

33. Ibid., p. 130.

34. Ibid., quotation from Kelle, p. 236.
35. Ibid.
36. Kelle, Denisov, and Plimak, *Leninizm*, p. 247.
37. Quotation from ibid., p. 252.
38. Ibid., pp. 130–131.
39. L. I. Grekov and V. S. Markov, "Metodologiia leninizma i dialektika obshchestvenno razvitiia," *Voprosy filosofii*, no. 11 (1970), p. 171.
40. I. I. Ivanov, "O Leninskikh normakh partiinoi zhizni i printsipakh partiinogo rukovodstva," *Voprosy istorii KPSS*, no. 6 (1969), p. 114.
41. "Vazhnie zadachi istoricheskoi nauki," *Voprosy istorii KPSS*, no. 5 (1973), p. 15.
42. Ibid., p. 10. See also "O merakh po uluchsheniiu podgotovki partiinykh i sovetskikh kadrov v vysshei partiinoi shkole pri TsK KPSS," *Kommunist*, no. 16 (1972), pp. 3–5.

3   PERMITTED DISSENT IN THE DECADE AFTER STALIN
*Dina Spechler*

1. For the testimony of a Soviet writer to this effect see Nikolai Gavrilov, "Letter from a Soviet Writer," *The New Leader*, December 9, 1963, p. 14.
2. The man primarily responsible for a more liberal policy toward literature and the publication of a number of works on the terror in 1962 was reputedly "a certain Lebedev, allegedly chief of Khrushchev's personal cabinet." (Philip Ben, "The New Freedom and Its Limits," *The New Republic*, June 27, 1964, p. 16. See also Michel Tatu, *Power in the Kremlin* [London: Wm. Collins Sons & Co., 1969], p. 248.)
3. "Dissent" is understood in this essay to mean expressions of disapproval of or exposure of serious faults in: (1) important institutions, the way they function, or the individuals who hold power in them; (2) important policies, the way in which they are implemented or individuals who make, state, or enforce them; or (3) elements of Marxist-Leninist ideology, official interpretation of that ideology, or individuals who make those interpretations. Disapproval, rejection, or violation of cultural norms and restrictions derived from ideology are also considered dissent.

It is difficult to draw a completely satisfying distinction between dissent and that constructive self-criticism that has abounded in the press of the post-Stalin era. In this essay it is assumed that dissent has a number of distinguishing characteristics. What is criticized is not a minor, but a very important part of the apparatus of government or of its stated goals, claims, or policies. The problem cited is a serious one: many people are or were affected; there is/was much unhappiness or suffering as a result. The author is not responsible for the phenomenon attacked. He does not express basic approval or agreement with the institution, policy, or ideological formulation in question. The problem is presented not as exceptional, but as widespread and recurrent. The author is angry, alarmed, or embittered (not merely annoyed or displeased). Either he thinks the problem insoluble, or he seems to think its solution would require major changes in institutions, policies, or ideology; or for some other reason he thinks nothing is likely to be done about the problem. Not all these things are always true in a given instance of dissent, nor are they always true only of dissent, but they seemed to be possible guidelines for deciding which works should form the basis for this study. Some of the protest considered in this essay was encouraged by high officials. That was no reason to refuse to call it dissent. It was treated as dissent which the regime, for its own reasons, not merely tolerated, but promoted.

4. For a more complete discussion of the Zhdanovite criteria and other topics in this essay see my Ph.D. dissertation, "Permitted Dissent in the USSR: *Novy mir* as an Organ of Social and Political Criticism, 1953–1966," Harvard University, 1973.

5. The most important of these were the following: Vladimir Dudintsev, "Na svoem meste," no. 6 (1953), pp. 3–58; Tikhon Zhuravlev, "Kombainery," no. 7 (1953), pp. 3–91; G. Troepolskii, "Iz zapisok agronoma," no. 8 (1953), pp. 42–99; no. 1 (1954), pp. 99–122; idem, "Sosedi," no. 4 (1954), pp. 80–99; Valentin Ovechkin and Gennadii Fish, "Narodnyi akademik," no. 10 (1953), pp. 3–42; V. Tendriakov, "Padenie Ivana Chuprova," no. 11 (1953), pp. 104–134; idem, "Nenaste," no. 2 (1954), pp. 66–85; Anatolii Zlobin, "Uralskie vstrechi," no. 12 (1953), pp. 189–198; Valentin Ovechkin, "V tom zhe raione," no. 3 (1954), pp. 8–49; A. Bek and N. Loiko, "Molodye liudi," no. 7 (1954), pp. 3–73; no. 8 (1954), pp. 57–124; no. 9 (1954), pp. 63–121; S. Zalygin, "Vesnoi nyneshnego goda," no. 8 (1954), pp. 3–55.

6. *Literaturnaia gazeta* (hereafter cited as *Lit.gaz.*), August 18, 1953, p. 3; *Pravda*, November 18, 1953, p. 3; *Izvestiia*, April 20, 1954, p. 3; November 23, 1954, p. 2; *Soviet Literature*, no. 3 (1956), p. 186.

7. The March 6, 1954, Central Committee resolution on grain production and Khrushchev's speech on the subject, for example, acknowledged many of the shortcomings in economic administration cited by the *Novy mir* authors. (*Pravda*, March 5, 1954, pp. 1–4; March 21, 1954, pp. 1–5.)

8. Vladimir Pomerantsev, "Ob iskrennosti v literature," no. 12 (1953), pp. 218–245; Mikh. Lifshits, "Dnevnik Marietty Shaginian," no. 2 (1954), pp. 206–231; Fedor Abramov, "Lioudi kolkhoznoi derevni v poslevoennoi proze," no. 4 (1954), pp. 210–231; Mark Shcheglov, "*Russkii les* Leonida Leonova," no. 5 (1954), pp. 220–241.

9. In chapter 5 of "Za daliu – dal," *Novy mir*, no. 6 (1953), pp. 72–83.

10. See note 8 above.

11. Pomerantsev, "Ob iskrennosti," pp. 237–238.

12. *Lit.gaz.*, January 30, 1954, p. 3; *Pravda*, May 25, 1954, p. 3; June 3, 1954, p. 4; *Lit.gaz.*, June 5, 1954, p. 1; *Komsomolskaia pravda*, June 6, 1954, p. 2; *Lit.gaz.*, June 15, 1954, pp. 1–2; *Kommunist*, no. 9 (1954), p. 25; *Ok-*

*tiabr*, no. 7 (1954), pp. 141–147; *Lit.gaz.*, August 12, 1954, p. 1; August 17, 1954, p. 3.

13. On the failure of Writers' Union officials to let *Novy mir* editors know what rules they must observe, see remarks by S. Antonov and S. Sutotskii, *Lit.gaz.*, August 17, 1954, p. 3. Tvardovsky insisted on printing the dissenting works although other editors objected. (*Lit.gaz.*, August 17, 1954, p. 3.)

14. Since we rarely know when a given work was written, submitted to, or accepted by *Novy mir*, assertions about events to which the authors and editors responded are somewhat problematical. However, we do know when each issue was sent to the printer and when it was approved for publication by the censor (usually about thirty to forty days later). We can assume that the editors' final decision on the contents of an issue was usually taken a few days before it was sent to the printer. We know that the editors were perturbed by the fact that *Novy mir* almost always appeared late (the January issue was distributed in February or March, the February issue in March or April, and so forth). Thus they would have been unlikely to delay the typesetting and censorship processes. When Party or literary authorities intervened to prevent or hold up the publication of an issue, they did so after it was set in print, sometimes even after it was passed by the censor.

15. Konstantin Simonov, "Literaturnye zametki," no. 12 (1956), pp. 239–257; A. Metchenko, "Istorizm i dogma," no. 12 (1956), pp. 223–238.

16. Paruir Sevak, "Nelegkii razgovor," no. 6 (1956), pp. 121–132, Semen Kirsanov, "Sem dnei nedeli," no. 9 (1956), pp. 16–32; L. Denisova and V. Zhdanov, "Modernizatsiia i proizvol v osveshchenii proshlogo," no. 8 (1956), pp. 237–249; S. Zalygin, "Svideteli," no. 7 (1956), pp. 67–71; Vladimir Lugovskii, "V selskoi shkole," no. 8 (1956), p. 23; Liubov Kabo, "V trudnom podkhode," no. 11 (1956), pp. 105–206; no. 12 (1956), pp. 82–189.

17. D. Granin, "Sobstvennoe mnenie," no. 8 (1956), p. 130. Translation from Hugh McLean and Walter N. Vickery, *Year of Protest, 1956* (New York: Alfred A. Knopf, 1961), p. 256.

18. Ibid., p. 135.

19. Vladimir Dudintsev, "Ne khlebom edinym," no. 8 (1956), pp. 31–118; no. 9 (1956), pp. 37–118; no. 10 (1956), pp. 21–98.

20. Ibid., no. 8 (1956), pp. 39–40, 65; no. 9 (1956), pp. 41, 47, 71, 84.

21. *Lit.gaz.*, January 15, 1957, pp. 1, 3; May 16, 1957, pp. 1–2; *Pravda*, May 17, 1957, p. 3; *Partinaia zhizn*, no. 24 (December 1956), pp. 62–63; *Lit.gaz.*, November 24, 1956, pp. 2–3; *Izvestiia*, December 2, 1956, pp. 2–3; *Soviet Literature*, no. 5 (1957), pp. 165–166.

22. Ilya Ehrenburg, "Perechityvaia Chekhova," no. 5 (1959), pp. 193–208; no. 6 (1959), pp. 174–196; Nina Ivanter, "Snova avgust," no. 8 (1959), pp. 7–82; no. 9 (1959), pp. 3–72.

23. The leadership of the Russian Republic Writers' Union was securely in conservative hands, but that of the more powerful USSR Writers' Union was not. By the end of the period liberals had taken over the Moscow

writers' organization and the Central Committee bureau in charge of propagandizing artistic literature. In addition to *Novy mir, Tarusskie stranitsy* and *Iunost* (until December 1961) were headed by liberals. The editor of *Literaturnaia gazeta* was mildly liberal, and the heads of *Znamia* and *Teatr* welcomed unorthodox and experimental works, notable for their disregard of the Zhdanovite criteria. Conservative strongholds were *Oktiabr, Moskva, Neva, Literatura i zhizn, Ogonek,* and *Zvezda.*

24. Efim Dorosh, "Chetyre vremeni goda," no. 7 (1960), pp. 3-79; idem, "Sukhoe leto," no. 7 (1961), pp. 3-51; idem, "Raigorod v fevrale," no. 10 (1962), pp. 9-46; Aleksandr Yashin, "Vologodskaia svadba," no. 12 (1962), pp. 3-26; Aleksei Nekrasov, "Stariki Kirsanovy," no. 9 (1962), pp. 74-109; S. Zalygin, "Tropy Altaia," no. 1 (1962), pp. 3-77; no. 2 (1962), pp. 63-131; no. 3 (1962), pp. 49-129; V. Kaverin, "Kusok stekla," no. 8 (1960), pp. 3-20; Nikolai Dubov, "Zhestkaia proba," no. 9 (1960), pp. 43-84; no. 10 (1960), pp. 54-109; E. Rzhevskaia, "Zemnoe pritiazhenie," no. 6 (1962), pp. 3-95.

25. Ilya Ehrenburg, "Liudi, gody, zhizn," no. 9 (1961), pp. 113-114. See also ibid., no. 8 (1960), p. 24; no. 2 (1961), pp. 110-112; Vladimir Fomenko, "Pamiat zemli," no. 6 (1961), pp. 8-65; no. 7 (1961), pp. 84-124; no. 8 (1961), pp. 102-158; V. Tendriakov, "Sud," no. 3 (1961), pp. 15-60.

26. Ehrenburg, "Liudi, gody, zhizn," no. 9 (1960), pp. 87-136; no. 1 (1961), pp. 91-152; no. 2 (1961), pp. 75-121; no. 9 (1961), pp. 88-152; no. 4 (1962), pp. 9-63; G. Kozintsev, "Glubokii ekran," no. 3 (1961), pp. 141-172; A. Gladkov, "Meierkhol'd govorit," no. 8 (1961), pp. 213-235; S. Bondarin, "Eduard Bagritskii," no. 4 (1960), pp. 130-143; L. Yanovskaia, "Tri knigi ob Ilfe i Petrove," no. 1 (1962), pp. 256-260; A. Kamenskii, "O Sariane," no. 1 (1962), pp. 182-208.

27. Ehrenburg, "Liudi, gody, zhizn," no. 9 (1960), pp. 89, 109-110; no. 1 (1961), pp. 99-100, 102, 114, 116-117; no. 2 (1961), pp. 77-78, 81-83, 89, 92, 102-104, 111-112; no. 9 (1961), pp. 142-145; no. 10 (1961), p. 135; no. 4 (1962), p. 28; Gladkov, "Meierkhold govorit," pp. 230, 235; Viktor Nekrasov, "Po obe storony okeana," no. 11 (1962), p. 131; V. Maksimovoi, "Iz literaturnogo naslediia N. K. Krupskoi," no. 10 (1962), pp. 271-274.

28. Aleksandr Tvardovsky, "Za daliu-dal," no. 5 (1960), pp. 3-22.

29. Ehrenburg, "Liudi, gody, zhizn," no. 8 (1960), p. 28; no. 6 (1962), pp. 145-146; Tvardovsky, "Za daliu," no. 5 (1960), pp. 9-11, 13-14; M. Simashko, "Iskushenie Fragi," no. 9 (1960), pp. 137-154; V. Lakshin, "Doverie," no. 11 (1962), pp. 229-241.

30. Dorosh, "Raigorod," pp. 30, 36, 38-39; E. Gerasimov, "Shelkovyi gorod," no. 8 (1962), p. 18; Vasilii Rosliakov, "Odin iz nas," no. 2 (1962), pp. 18-19; Viktor Nekrasov, "Kira Georgievna," no. 6 (1961), pp. 70-126; Ehrenburg (on Stalin's treatment of the creative intelligentsia), "Liudi, gody, zhizn," no. 1 (1961), pp. 101-102, 144, 149; no. 2 (1961), pp. 81-82, 84, 107; no. 9 (1961), pp. 142-143, 152; no. 4 (1962), pp. 14-15, 28-29, 60; Gladkov, "Meierkhold govorit," pp. 226, 235; A. Solzhenitsyn, "Odin den Ivana Deni-

sovicha," no. 11 (1962), pp. 8–74; Iurii Bondarev (on the terror), "Tishina," no. 3 (1962), pp. 3–45; no. 4 (1962), pp. 64–135; M. Popovskii, "Selektsionery," no. 8 (1961), p. 202; Ehrenburg (on the terror), "Liudi, gody, zhizn," no. 8 (1960), pp. 24, 42, 53; no. 1 (1961), pp. 140, 146; no. 5 (1962), pp. 99, 110, 112, 123, 126, 140, 143, 150–152; no. 6 (1962), pp. 114, 128–129, 138, 146, 150; Ehrenburg (on Stalin's foreign policy), "Liudi, gody, zhizn," no. 4 (1962), p. 20; no. 5 (1962), pp. 101, 106–107; no. 6 (1962), pp. 130, 132, 146–147, 149; Veniamin Kaverin, "Sem par nechistykh," no. 2 (1962), p. 154; Bondarev (on Stalin's war policies), "Tishina," no. 3 (1962), p. 39; Ehrenburg (on Stalin's war policies), "Liudi, gody, zhizn," no. 6 (1962), p. 146; Tvardovsky, "Za daliu," no. 5 (1960), pp. 12–13; Ehrenburg (on Stalin's nationality policy), "Liudi, gody, zhizn," no. 1 (1961), pp. 120, 132, 134; no. 9 (1961), pp. 141–143; no. 6 (1962), p. 146.

31. Khrushchev claimed to have much trouble persuading the rest of the Presidium to allow· publication of "One Day in the Life of Ivan Denisovich," Solzhenitsyn's novel on life in one of Stalin's prison camps. Michel Tatu cites a report that Suslov and Kozlov were opposed and asserts that "some dissent was almost certainly voiced." *Power in the Kremlin* (London: Collins, 1969), p. 248. The editor of the journal *Oktiabr*, Vsevolod Kochetov, was an outspoken critic of anti-Stalin literature. (See *The Ershov Brothers* [1958], *The Obkom Secretary* [1961], and *What Is It You Want?* [1969].) Kochetov was known as a protégé of Suslov.

The opposition of certain powerful men in the leadership to exposure and condemnation of Stalin's crimes seems highly likely, in view of the fact that this treatment of the Stalin era ceased to be tolerated soon after Khrushchev's removal.

32. For Khrushchev's insistence on a "division of labor" between the Party and Soviet writers see N. S. Khrushchev, "Za tesnuiu sviaz literatury i iskusstva s zhizniu naroda," *Novy mir*, no. 9 (1957), pp. 3–22; idem, "Sluzhenie narodu—vysokoe prizvanie sovetskikh pisatelei," *Pravda*, May 24, 1959, pp. 1–3.

33. Tvardovsky's poem and Solzhenitsyn's story were, on the contrary, effusively praised and in 1961 Ehrenburg was awarded an Order of Lenin for his "services to the development of Soviet literature."

34. See notes 24 and 25 above.

35. Attacks on Ehrenburg for violating Zhdanovite criteria: *Kommunist*, no. 10 (1962), pp. 32–40; *Izvestiia*, January 30, 1963, pp. 3–4; February 16, 1963, p. 4; *Pravda*, March 9, 1963, p. 2; March 10, 1963, pp. 2–4; *Komsomolskaia pravda*, March 22, 1963, p. 2; on Nekrasov: *Pravda*, March 10, 1963, pp. 1–2; *Komsomolskaia pravda*, March 22, 1963, p. 2: *Pravda Ukrainy*, April 10, 1963, pp. 1–2; on Solzhenitsyn: *Moskovskaia Pravda*, December 8, 1962; *Literaturnaia Rossiia*, January 11, 1963; *Oktiabr*, no. 4 (1963), pp. 198–207; *Kazakhstanskaia Pravda*, October 6, 1963, p. 4; *Izvestiia*, December 29, 1963, p. 4; *Lit.gaz.*, January 11, 1964, p. 3; on Bondarev: *Oktiabr*, no. 9 (1962), pp. 212–213; *Zvezda*, September 1962, pp. 209–211.

4    TOWARD A THEORY OF SOVIET LEADERSHIP
MAINTENANCE
*Teresa Rakowska-Harmstone*

1. Melvin Croan, "Five Years After Khrushchev," *Survey*, 72 (Summer 1969), pp. 42–43.
2. As defined in Zbigniew Brzezinski and Samuel P. Huntington, *Political Power: USA/USSR* (New York: Viking Press, 1964), ch. 2.
3. As defined in Merle Fainsod, *How Russia Is Ruled*, rev. ed. (Cambridge, Mass.: Harvard University Press, 1953), pp. 180–184.
4. In this section I am indebted to my colleague Willard Mullins for constructive criticism and suggestions.
5. Carl Joachim Friedrich, *Man and His Government: An Empirical Theory of Politics* (New York: McGraw-Hill, 1963), p. 241.
6. Max Weber, *The Theory of Social and Economic Organization*, trans. A. M. Henderson and Talcott Parsons (New York: Free Press, 1964), pp. 328ff.
7. Ibid., pp. 363ff.
8. Robert V. Daniels, "Lenin and the Russian Revolutionary Tradition," *Harvard Slavic Studies*, 4 (1957), 339–353. See also Robert Tucker, *Stalin as Revolutionary, 1879–1929: A Study in History and Personality* (New York: Norton, 1973), chs. 1 and 2.
9. See Tibor Szamuely, "Five Years after Khrushchev," *Survey*, 72 (Summer 1969), 51–69.
10. For the discussion of the concept see Friedrich, *Man and His Government*, pp. 96–101.
11. For an illuminating discussion of Stalin's quest for legitimacy (as distinct from his pursuit of power mechanics), see Tucker, *Stalin*, ch. 8.
12. Weber, *Social and Economic Organization*, p. 369. " . . . One of the decisive motives underlying all cases of the routinization of charisma is naturally the striving for security. This means legitimization, on the one hand, of positions of authority and social prestige, on the other hand, of the economic advantages enjoyed by the followers and sympathizers of the leader. Another important motive, however, lies in the objective necessity of adaptation of the patterns of order and of the organization of the administrative staff to the normal, everyday needs and conditions of carrying on administration. In this connection, in particular, there are always points at which traditions of administrative practice and of judicial decision can take hold; since these are needed both by the normal administrative staff and by those subject to its authority. It is further necessary that there should be some definite order introduced into the organization of the administrative staff itself. Finally . . . it is necessary for the administrative staff and all its administrative practices to be adapted to everyday economic conditions" (pp. 370–371).
13. Ibid., p. 66 (Introduction).
14. Ibid.

15. The latest illustration of this is that Soviet linguists have apparently begun work on a five-volume dictionary of the language used by Lenin, to contain "every word and phrase known to have been used by Russia's most revered revolutionary during more than thirty-five years of political activity." See the *Christian Science Monitor,* January 22, 1975.

16. As defined in Secretary Brezhnev's report to the Twenty-Fourth Party Congress, April 1971: "The main thing in the activity of the Communist Party is the elaboration of the general prospects for the development of society and a correct political line, and the organization of the working people for the purpose of implementing this line. All our reality testifies to the fact that the C.P.S.U. is honorably fulfilling the role of political leader of the working class and of all the working people and is leading the Soviet people along the correct road, along the Leninist course." (*Current Soviet Policies,* VI, *The Documentary Record of the 24th Congress of the Communist Party of the Soviet Union,* p. 34.) Compare also the following definition: "The question of the hegemony of the working class and of the leading role of the Party in the revolutionary transformation of society today has become a central point of struggle between Marxist-Leninists and representatives of various forms of revisionism." (From a lecture to historians, *Pravda,* October 13, 1972, quoted in *Current Digest of the Soviet Press* [*CDSP*], vol. 24, no. 41, p. 25.

17. Such as the campaigns in 1956–1964 (see Erik P. Hoffman, "Ideological Administration under Khrushchev: A Study of Intra-Party Communications," *Canadian Slavonic Papers,* 4 [1970], 736–766) and other numerous campaigns later, such as the anniversary campaign to commemorate the fiftieth anniversary of the Soviet state (see *CDSP,* 1964–1974). In 1973 intensive campaigns began that were directed at the socialization of the intelligentsia, and a major new campaign of "moral rearmament" was reported in the *Christian Science Monitor,* October 31, 1974.

18. Richard Lowenthal, "The Return of Stalin's Mustache on a Higher Level," *New York Times Magazine,* March 28, 1971, p. 109.

19. Cf. the legal arguments used, as quoted in *Problems of Communism,* "In Quest of Justice," part I (July–August 1968) and part II (September–October 1968).

20. See Fainsod, *How Russia Is Ruled,* ch. 11.

21. See Teresa Rakowska-Harmstone, "The Dialectics of Nationalism in the USSR," *Problems of Communism,* 23 (May–June 1974), 1–22. It is interesting to compare the situation in Communist Eastern Europe. There the ideological legitimacy of communist systems, doubtful to begin with, has eroded far more significantly than in the Soviet Union. The leaders compensate through explicit identification with national desiderata, and in the search for popular sanction and popular approval, particularly in the satisfaction of economic needs. Nationalism has become more important than Marxism-Leninism as the legitimating authority, and in at least one case (Ceaucescu), the ultimate ideological mission of the Party has been redefined in national terms.

22. Brzezinski and Huntington, *Political Power*, ch. 3.

23. Zbigniew Brzezinski, "The Soviet Political System: Transformation or Degeneration," *Problems of Communism*, 15 (January–February 1966), p. 2.

24. Most important of these affected the theory of state ("the state of all the people" and the conditions of its withering away), the theory of national relations ("rapprochement-merger" theory), and the theory of relations with the capitalist world ("war is no longer inevitable").

25. See his collected works as well as the reports at the Twenty-Fourth and Twenty-Fifth Party Congresses.

26. According to Tatu, Brezhnev's first efforts to build up his personal image (his wartime exploits) date to 1965. (Michel Tatu, *Power in the Kremlin from Khrushchev to Kosygin*, trans. Helen Katel [New York: Viking Press, 1970], p. 516.) By 1974 four volumes of his collected works appeared— the last one reviewed in *Partiinaia Zhizn*, no. 13 (July 1974). Suslov's first volume of collected works was published in October 1972 (*Pravda*, November 1, 1972), and Kosygin's first volume— in September 1974 (ibid., September 20, 1974). As far as is known no other Politburo member published collected works, although some authored other books. Shelest's book on the Ukraine was severely criticized after his downfall (*CDSP*, vol. 25, no. 25, p. 22). A review of issues of *Partiinaia Zhizn* for 1973–1974 revealed ten major items by or about Brezhnev, and only one by another Politburo member, Suslov.

27. The *Christian Science Monitor* reported rapid growth in Brezhnev's personality cult, inclusive of a major TV build-up in 1973–1974. In Central Asia he was referred to as "Dear Father" (December 6, 1973). Electoral speeches of Politburo members which preceded the USSR Supreme Soviet summer 1974 elections revealed a high level of praise for Brezhnev, and the degree of this praise was higher among the general secretary's known clients, such as Kazakhstan's first secretary Kunaev, than among his rivals. (*CDSP*, vol. 26.)

28. See *Pravda*, February 26–March 5, 1976.

29. See note 31.

30. Weber, *Social and Economic Organization*, p. 65.

31. There is now a consensus among most students of Soviet politics that, despite systemic constraints that prevent formal incorporation, interest groups exist in the Soviet Union and exert varying degrees of influence depending on how close they are to the Party's decision-making structure. They can basically be defined as an "institutional" rather than an "associational" variety of interest groups. (See Gabriel A. Almond and James S. Coleman, eds., *The Politics of the Developing Areas* [Princeton: Princeton University Press, 1960], pp. 33–34.) But within and across institutional/occupational lines, interest coalitions form around an issue, a policy, or a demand, in a dynamic pattern pressing for advantage through access to decision makers. Extensive literature exists both on the subject in general and on specific groups, by authors such as H. Gordon Skilling, Franklyn Griffiths, Jerry

Hough, Sidney Ploss, Philip Stewart, Roman Kolkowicz, and others. There is no effort here, therefore, to cite authorities in support of the subsequent discussion except for specific citation.

32. The federal principle was explicitly rejected as the basis of the Party organization by the 1919 statutes; the Party's unitary character has since been reemphasized by Frol Kozlov (reporting to the Twenty-Second Congress on the Statutes [*Current Soviet Policies*, IV, 205]) and Secretary Brezhnev in a speech at the Fiftieth Anniversary of the Soviet Federation on December 30, 1972 (*CDSP*, vol. 24, no. 51, p. 9).

33. Identified here to include full-time professional officials in the Party in standing executive bodies (secretariats of territorial committees) at all levels down to and including districts and towns.

34. Leonard Schapiro, "Keynote—Compromise," *Problems of Communism*, 20 (July–August, 1971), 4. See also George Fischer, "The Number of Soviet Party Executives; A Research Note," *Soviet Studies*, January 1965, pp. 330–333.

35. Territorial Party committees include everybody who is anybody politically, that is, key Party posts, key state and managerial posts, plus a few social cultural activists and a token Stakhanovite worker or a dairy maid; the bureaus always include top Party and state administrators.

36. The problem of "substitute management" *(podmena)*, while present in the Stalinist period came to the fore in the wake of Khrushchev's bifurcation reform of 1962 (see below), which placed Party cadres directly in industrial and agricultural management. Criticism of the measure centered on resulting inefficiency and duplication of function as well as on the weakening of the leading role (see Tatu, *Power in the Kremlin*, pp. 440ff). In 1974 there was a controversy in which Party and state spokesmen blamed one another for excessive red tape in local management. (Christian Duevel, "Sverdlovsk First Party Secretary Takes Exception to Podgorny's Statements," *Radio Liberty*, 212/74 (July 10, 1974).

37. Carl G. Jacobsen, "The Role of the Military in Society" (unpublished manuscript), p. 5, and *Soviet Strategy, Soviet Foreign Policy*, 2nd ed. (Glasgow, 1974), ch. 8.

38. At the time of Beria's removal in 1953, and in Khrushchev's victory over the "anti-Party group" in the summer of 1957. In 1957 the army was rewarded with a seat in the Politburo for Marshal Zhukov.

39. See F. R. Kozlov Report, *Current Soviet Policies*, IV, 204. Turnover was established at 25 percent of the Central Committee and Presidium (with "escape clause" for elder statesmen), 33 percent of province/republican committees, and 50 percent at lower levels. Tenure of first secretaries was limited to three terms (two in primary party organizations).

40. Tatu, *Power in the Kremlin*, pp. 515–516.

41. The Statutes. *Current Soviet Policies*, V, 159.

42. From 5–6 percent annual growth rate in 1957–1965 to 2–3.5 percent annual growth rate in 1965–1971. Darrell P. Hammer, "The Dilemma of Party Growth," *Problems of Communism*, 20 (July–August 1971), 17.

43. The return to the old pattern took almost a year because of the opposition from the newly entrenched regional interests ("localism"). For the debate between the central authorities and the regional apparati see Tatu, *Power in the Kremlin,* pp. 444–446.

44. With four Central Committee secretaries in the Politburo in November 1964 it was impossible for Brezhnev, or anyone, to "pack" the Central Committee. This is reflected in lower membership turnover between congresses than was the case in Khrushchev's time. (Jerry F. Hough, "The Soviet System: Petrification or Pluralism," *Problems of Communism,* 21 [March–April 1972], 32.)

45. Podgorny's temporary ascendancy in control of Party cadres was reflected in the eclipse of Shcherbitsky, member of Brezhnev's Dnepropetrovsk faction, who was removed as candidate member of the Politburo in October 1964, only to return at the December 1965 plenum.

46. For the history of the commission see Grey Hodnett, "Khrushchev and Party-State Control," in A. Dallin and A. F. Westin, eds., *Politics in the Soviet Union: Seven Cases* (New York: Harcourt Brace Jovanovich, 1966), pp. 113–164.

47. V. Ye. Semichastny, Shelepin's protégé from the days when the latter headed the KGB was replaced at the same time by Yuri Andropov, as chairman of the KGB. Andropov became candidate member of the Politburo at the Twenty-Fourth Party Congress.

48. Suslov is the most durable Politburo member, the only one whose membership dates to pre-Khrushchev days (1955). By all accounts he enjoys a high degree of respect among party cadres. He is, however, seventy-two years old.

49. See "Politicheskii Dnevnik," AS1011, no. 67 (4170), *Sobranie Dokumentov Samizdata,* vol. 20, AS1001–AS1012 (December 1964–September 1970) (Columbus, Ohio); Jacobsen, *Soviet Strategy,* pp. 210, 215.

50. Voronov was a rival for control of the RSFSR machine and there were policy differences. Shelest, first secretary of the Ukrainian Party and member of a rival faction there, lost out over foreign policy disagreements and advocacy of Ukrainian autonomy. It has been reported that his removal was sealed when he appealed differences to the Central Committee over the heads of the Politburo. This is considered a cardinal sin against the "rules of the game." As reported by Dimitri Simes, a recent emigré from the Soviet Union and one-time employee of the Institute of World Economics in Moscow, at a lecture at the University of Toronto, February 8, 1974.

51. While the move may be interpreted as recognition that agriculture is a crisis area, it placed Polyansky in an unfavorable institutional and policy position. Moreover, in 1974 he was a target of criticism emanating from the Central Committee Secretariat. (See Christian Duevel, "High Level Party Criticism of the USSR Ministry of Agriculture," *Radio Liberty,* 214/74 [July 15, 1974].)

52. See Paul Wohl, "A Toughening in the Kremlin," *Christian Science Monitor,* January 24, 1975, and reports of major Western newspapers for the period.

53. Ibid., January 16 and 17, 1975.

54. Suslov and Ghechko (see Wohl, "Toughening in the Kremlin"); Shelepin, Kulakov, Kirilenko (Victor Zorza, "After Brezhnev," *Manchester Guardian Weekly,* January 25, 1975); a general discussion mentioning the various possibilities (Michel Tatu, "The Succession in Moscow," *Le Monde,* English Section, ibid.).

55. *Christian Science Monitor,* February 14, 1975; *Manchester Guardian,* February 22, 1975; *New York Times,* March 19, 1975.

56. Clearly, a sacrifice of agricultural failures. Polyansky remained a member of the Central Committee, but on March 16, 1976, lost his post as Minister of Agriculture.

57. Politburo members who were elevated by Brezhnev: Central Committee Secretaries: Kirilenko, Kulakov, Ustinov; Pelshe (Party Control Commission); functional representatives: Grechko, Andropov, and Gromyko; regional representatives: Shcherbitsky (Ukraine), Kunaev (Kazakhstan), Grishin (Moscow), Romanov (Leningrad). Politburo candidate members: Masherov (Belorussia), Solomentsev (RSFSR), Aliev (Azerbaijan). Of the remaining members of the Politburo, apart from the three ex-rivals, all of whom are elderly, there is only Mazurov, who is currently Kosygin's deputy, and was rumored in the past to have been associated with an anti-Brezhnev faction. Of the three pre-Brezhnev candidate members, Rashidov (Uzbekistan) and Demichev (culture) appear to support the General Secretary; Ponomarev has been closely associated with Suslov. In terms of Party appointments, Kirilenko is generally regarded as Brezhnev's alter ego. At the date of this writing (March 1976) it was not possible to analyze the newly elected Central Committee.

58. Inclusive of voting and candidate members: July 1953, 12 members, 2 Party, 9 State, 1 TU; June 1957, 24 members, 17 Party, 7 State; April 1966, 19 members, 12 Party, 6 State, 1 TU; April 1971, 21 members, 13 Party, 7 State, 1 TU; April 1973, 23 members, 14 Party, 8 State, 1 TU; March 1976, 22 members, 14 Party, 8 State, 0 TU. The power of the Party was also strengthened by additional control powers given primary party organizations in state agencies and institutions by the 1971 Statutes. (*Current Soviet Policies,* VI, 184.)

59. See Donald Graves, "Stability for the Cadres: A Promise Kept," *Analysis of the USSR's 24th Party Congress and 9th Five-Year Plan,* ed. Norton T. Dodge (Mechanicsville, Md., 1971), p. 89. The proportion of Party officials among voting members of the Central Committee declined steadily between 1956–1971 (50 percent in 1956, 46 percent in 1961, 42 percent in 1966 and 39 percent in 1971) (Hough, p. 35).

60. As pointed out by many Western observers, such as Hough, Brzezinski, Tatu, and others.

61. In terms of improved upward flow of objective data and relevant information and also in terms of encouragement of discussion of relative merits and demerits of alternative solutions, *providing* such a discussion does not question basic policy/doctrinal assumptions.

62. The latter tactic may occasionally succeed if personal power sup-

port in a parent body has previously been built. The case in point is Khrushchev's 1957 victory over the "anti-Party group" through his appeal to the Central Committee. He was unable, however, to repeat the feat in 1964; others, it is rumored, tried and failed. In each case, the subjective factor, that is, the individual's personal power ties to the Central Committee membership, is crucial. Speculations that a Politburo appeal to the Central Committee may be on the way toward institutionalization, appear, therefore, at best premature.

63. This has been too well documented to require footnoting here.

64. From the communiqué in *Pravda* (October 17, 1964) following the ouster. (Tatu, *Power in the Kremlin,* p. 422.)

65. For details see Keith Bush, "The Reforms: A Balance Sheet," *Problems of Communism,* 16 (July–August 1967), 30–41; "Resource Allocation Policy: Capital Investment," in John P. Hardt, ed., *Soviet Economic Prospects for the Seventies,* Compendium of Papers submitted to the Joint Economic Committee, Congress of the United States (Washington, D.C., June 1973), pp. 39–44; Gertrude E. Shroeder, "Soviet Economic Reform at an Impasse," *Problems of Communism,* 20 (July–August 1970), 36–46.

66. Tatu, *Power in the Kremlin,* p. 439.

67. Bush, in *Soviet Economic Prospects.* It may be noted here that consumer goods production is augmented by group A industries producing some consumer goods as a sideline. At the same time, however, allocations for social services remain low.

68. Roy D. Laird, "Prospects for Soviet Agriculture," *Problems of Communism,* 20 (September–October 1971), pp. 31–40; also Keith Bush, "Soviet Agriculture: Ten Years under New Management," Radio Liberty Research Paper, August 21, 1974. Bush reports that in 1969 the leadership apparently made a decision to switch funds from agriculture to defense, as spelled out in *Finansy SSSR,* no. 3 (1969), p. 16.

69. Karl-Eugen Wadekin, "The Countryside," *Problems of Communism,* 18 (May–June 1969), 12–20; *Christian Science Monitor,* December 18, 1973; "Moldavia's Agricultural Reorganization," *CDSP,* vol. 26, no. 6, pp. 1–5; "Brezhnev Speaks Out on Farm Policy, ibid., no. 11, pp. 1–7.

70. See Rakowska-Harmstone, "Dialectics," pp. 17–25. A new constitution, promised for the Twenty-Fifth Congress did not materialize; the federal question is crucial in any constitutional changes.

71. See reports on speeches by Grechko, Gromyko, and Suslov in *Radio Liberty* reports: *RL* 180/74 (June 1974); 200/74 (July 1974); *Christian Science Monitor,* December 10, 1973; January 2, 7, 10, 1974, October 23, 1974.

72. See, for example, *Manchester Guardian Weekly* (with *Le Monde*) January 25, 1975, on the setback to détente of Soviet policy moves in January 1975.

73. Western press, February 17–18, 1975.

74. See T. Rakowska-Harmstone, "Socialist Internationalism: A 'New Stage' in the Development of Eastern Europe," *Survey,* 22 (Spring 1976), 98.

75. Vernon Aspaturian, (Moscow's Options in a Changing World," *Problems of Communism*, 21 (July–August 1972), 1–20.

76. Roy Medvedev, *On Socialist Democracy*, (Amsterdam-Paris, 1972); Sergei Razumnyi, "Rasstanovka politicheskikh sil v KPSS," 1969, AS570; *Arkhiv Samizdata*, vol. 8. See also *Politicheskii Dnevnik*.

77. Brezhnev gradually squeezed out his numerous rivals in foreign policy (notably Kosygin but also Podgorny) and appears in full control, although Suslov continues to play an important role in relations with the world Communist movement.

78. Tatu contends that the power of individual leaders within the Politburo has been severely circumscribed since 1964. None can make a decision without first securing a support of the majority, and each can be overruled; none can alter the team's composition without his colleagues' approval; and each can be dismissed at a moment's notice by a hostile coalition. (Tatu, *Power in the Kremlin*, p. 528.)

79. "The decisive feature (of the oligarchic model) is the incapacity of any individual to prevent the adoption of policies to which he may be opposed." (Myron Rush, "Brezhnev and the Succession Issue," *Problems of Communism*, 20 [July–August 1971], 9.)

80. As developed by H. Gordon Skilling and Franklyn Griffiths, eds., *Interest Groups in Soviet Politics* (Princeton: Princeton University Press, 1971); Philip Stewart, "Soviet Interest Groups and Policy Process," *World Politics* (October 1969), and others.

81. Defined as the system in which "major policies *cannot* be adopted against the will of the leader." (Rush, "Brezhnev," p. 10.)

5    OFFICE–HOLDING AND ELITE STATUS
*Robert V. Daniels*

1. See especially Michael P. Gehlen and Michael McBride, "The Soviet Central Committee: An Elite Analysis," *American Political Science Review*, 62 (1968), 1232–1241; Robert H. Donaldson and Derek J. Waller, "The 1956 Central Committees of the Chinese and Soviet Communist Parties: A Comparative Analysis of Elite Composition and Change," paper delivered at the American Political Science Association, Los Angeles, September 1970, p. 2.

2. See, for example, Robert H. Donaldson, "The 1971 Soviet Central Committee: An Assessment of the New Elite," *World Politics*, April 1972; Frederick Fleron, "Representation of Career Types in Soviet Political Leadership," in R. Barry Farrell, ed., *Political Leadership in Eastern Europe and the Soviet Union* (Chicago: Aldine, 1970); Michael P. Gehlen, "The Soviet apparatchiki," ibid.; Vincent E. McHale and Joseph H. Mastro, "The Central Committee of the CPSU: Analysis of Composition and Long-Term Trends," paper delivered to the American Political Science Association, Los Angeles, September 1970.

3. See, for example, ibid., p. 19; Frederick Fleron, "Towards a Recon-

ceptualization of Political Change in the Soviet Union," in F. Fleron, ed., *Communist Studies and the Soviet Sciences* (Chicago: Rand McNally, 1969), p. 235; Robert Conquest, *Power and Policy in the USSR* (London: Macmillan, 1961), p. 35; Donaldson and Waller, "Central Committees," p. 2; Zbigniew Brzezinski and Samuel P. Huntington, "Cincinnatus and the Apparatchik," *World Politics*, 6 (October 1963), 52–78.

4. A major exception is the analyses prepared for Radio Liberty by Christian Deuvel and his associates. See, for example, "Who Has the 'Right' to Election to the Leading Organs of the Party at the 24th Congress of the CPSU?" *Radio Liberty Research Bulletin*, February 25, 1971. ("The right to a seat in the central organs is given by definite offices . . . ") See also Darrell P. Hammer, *USSR: The Politics of Oligarchy* (Hinsdale, Ill.: Holt, Rinehart and Winston, 1974), p. 190. (" . . . Members of the Central Committee . . . in current practice . . . are chosen on the basis of the positions they hold.")

5. Evidence of these rules of demotion is developed in Peter D. Coburn, "The Central Committee of the Communist Party of the Soviet Union: Patterns and Politics, 1952 to 1971," M. A. Thesis, University of Vermont, 1975, pp. 25–30.

6. Contrary to McHale and Mastro, "Central Committee," p. 5, it is not election to the Central Committee that confers elite status, but appointment to the Central-Committee-level job with its assurance of subsequent election.

7. There is good reason to believe that the same principles of job-slot composition and status representation operate down through the entire system of Party committees at the republic, provincial, and local levels. See Hammer, *USSR*, p. 154.

8. The status of Moscow, deducible from Central Committee ranking practices, is indicative of both the fine sense of status involved in Central Committee membership, and the analytical value of the status concept. As of 1971, the first secretary of Moscow City (V. V. Grishin) was a member of the Politburo; the first secretary of the province (V. I. Konofop), a mere Central Committee member. The second secretary of the province (V. S. Paputin), merely a candidate member. The third and fourth secretaries of the city, R. F. Demetieva (incidentally, representing women) and V. M. Yagodkin, were candidate members; the third secretary of the province had no Central Committee status at all. It follows that the Party administration of the city could not be subordinate to that of the province, but in fact had an independent and higher status. In Leningrad, by contrast, though its representation was consistent with its status as the second-most important center in the country, the assignment of seats made it clear that the city was secondary to the province (first and second secretaries of the province on the Central Committee but only the first secretary of the city; second secretary of the city merely on the Central Auditing Commission). It may further be noted that the Leningrad province, subsuming the city, had more status (two full Central Committee memberships) than the Moscow province excluding the capital city (only one full membership).

9. There is an intriguing, if loose analogy here with the Tsarist "Chin" system equating rank and bureaucratic job—cf. Helju Bennett, "The Chin System and the Raznochintsy in the Government of Alexander III, 1881–1894" (Ph.D. dissertation, University of California at Berkeley, 1971), especially pp. 57–58, 79–80. For jobs below the three Central Committee ranks the Soviet practice of nomenklatura (specifying the level at which the Party exercises supervision over appointments to particular positions) perpetuates, so to speak, the *chin* system. Cf. Hammer, *USSR*, p. 197; D. Pospielovsky, "Programs of the Democratic Opposition." Radio Liberty Research Paper, no. 38 (New York, 1970).

10. These were the Departments of Agriculture (Kulakov, Politburo, head; Karlow, Central Committee candidate, first deputy); Cadres (head vacant; Bogoliubov, CAC, first deputy), and Relations with Communist Parties of Socialist Countries (Rusakov, Central Committee, head; Rakhmanin, CAC, first deputy). Another CAC member, Gostev, is listed as first deputy head of the Department of "Planning and Financial Organs," with no known head. (*Sostav Rukovodiashchikh Organov KPSS*, Radio Liberty [Munich, 1971].)

6   THE PROBLEM OF SUCCESSION
*John H. Hodgson*

1. Alfred G. Meyer, *The Soviet Political System: An Interpretation* (New York: Random House, 1965), p. 178, n. 10.

2. Philip E. Mosely, "Khrushchev at 70—Who Is Next?" *New York Times Magazine*, April 12, 1964, p. 96.

3. Robert Conquest, "Stalin's Successors," *Foreign Affairs*, 48 (April 1970), 512. See also Myron Rush, "Brezhnev and the Succession Issue," *Problems of Communism*, 20 (July–August 1971), 9–15; Frederick C. Barghoorn, *Politics in the USSR* (Boston: Little, Brown, 1966), p. 199.

4. See Grey Hodnett, "Succession Contingencies in the Soviet Union," *Problems of Communism*, 24 (March–April 1975), 5, n. 20.

5. *Osnovy Marksizma-Leninizma*, 2nd ed. (Moscow: Gospolitizdat, 1962), p. 554–555.

6. Jerry F. Hough, "The Soviet Concept of the Relationship between the Lower Party Organs and the State Administration," *Slavic Review*, 24 (June 1965), 218.

7. Some might argue that the chairman of the presidium of the Supreme Soviet of the USSR is as important and powerful, perhaps even more so, than the prime minister. The dominance of the prime minister can be demonstrated, however, through an analysis of the membership of the Supreme Soviet of the USSR. The Council of the Union is without question the more important of the two chambers in the Supreme Soviet, and it is significant if not conclusive that the fifteen Union-Republic prime ministers have in at least the last four elections been substantially better represented in the Council of the Union than have the fifteen chairmen of Union-Re-

public Supreme Soviet presidia. Furthermore, the results of these four elections also show that chairmen of Autonomous-Republic Supreme Soviet presidia are only rarely represented in either chamber of the Supreme Soviet of the USSR, whereas most or all Autonomous-Republic prime ministers have been elected to one or the other chamber. In short, to be a prime minister rather than a Supreme Soviet presidium chairman is to have more power.

8. See the *New York Times*, November 19, 1966, p. 7. It was not until 1971, however, that Zhivkov vacated the prime ministership in a move that elevated him to the post of chairman of the newly created State Council.

9. See Carl A. Linden, *Khrushchev and the Soviet Leadership, 1957–1964* (Baltimore: Johns Hopkins University Press, 1966), pp. 4, 23, 179, for a discussion of the "supreme ruler" concept. See also the reference by Zbigniew Brzezinski and Samuel P. Huntington, *Political Power: USA/USSR* (New York: Viking Press, 1964), p. 237, to "a Hobbesian war of all against all until a new Leviathan has emerged."

10. In 1953 Beria sought unsuccessfully to challenge the preeminence of the Great Russians. See Myron Rush, *Political Succession in the USSR* (New York: Columbia University Press, 1965), p. 59.

11. See Seweryn Bialer, "How Russians Rule Russia," *Problems of Communism*, 13 (September–October 1964), 47, 51.

12. See Yaroslav Bilinsky, "The Rulers and the Ruled," *Problems of Communism*, 16 (September–October 1967), 24–25.

13. John A. Armstrong, "The Ethnic Scene in the Soviet Union: The View of the Dictatorship," in Erich Goldhagen, ed., *Ethnic Minorities in the Soviet Union* (New York: Praeger, 1968), pp. 3–49.

14. With the exception of P. P. Griskiavicus in Lithuania, the names of the forty first secretaries can be found in Grey Hodnett and Val Ogareff, *Leaders of the Soviet Republics, 1957–1972: A Guide to Posts and Occupants* (Canberra: Australian National Universities Press, 1973).

15. Many of these secretaries are identified by nationality in *Deputaty Verkhovnago Soveta SSSR* (Moscow: Izdatel'stvo "Izvestiia Sovetov Deputatov Trudiashchikhsia SSSR," 1970). See also Borys Lewytzkyj and Kurt Müller, *Sowjetische Kurzbiographien* (Hannover: Verlag für Literatur und Zeitgeshehen, 1964).

16. A. Pravdin, "Inside the CPSU Central Committee," *Survey*, 20 (Autumn 1974), 101.

17. Abdurakhman Avtorkhanov, *The Communist Party Apparatus* (Chicago: Henry Regnery Co., 1966), p. 187.

18. Bilinsky, "Rulers and the Ruled," p. 21.

19. In the 1960s Armenia and Estonia, like the Ukraine and White Russia, had native first and second secretaries. The Estonian first secretary, I. G. Kebin, is said to be so assimilated that he speaks Russian with an Estonian accent but Estonian with a very strong Russian accent, which in itself could explain why for so many years another native Estonian (L. N. Lentsman) was permitted to hold the generally more important position of second secretary. Both men spent the interwar years in the Soviet Union

and belong to what has been called the "Moscovite faction" of the Estonian Party. An explanation for the Armenian anomaly is less apparent. See Bialer, "How Russians Rule Russia," p. 50; Bilinsky, "Rulers and the Ruled," p. 21.

20. Bilinsky, "Rulers and the Ruled," pp. 21, 25.

21. Alex Inkeles, "Soviet Nationality Policy in Perspective," in Abraham Brumberg, ed., *Russia under Khrushchev* (New York: Praeger, 1962), pp. 316–317. Lenin once remarked that "the Russified non-Russian always likes to exaggerate when it comes to 100 percent Russian attitudes." (Document cited in Bertram D. Wolfe, *Khrushchev and Stalin's Ghost* [New York: Praeger, 1957], p. 272.)

22. See Brzezinski and Huntington, *Political Power*, pp. 132–133; *Pravda*, April 9, 1966, p. 2; April 10, 1971, p. 1; December 19, 1972, p. 1; April 28, 1973, p. 1; March 6, 1976, p. 1.

23. According to Brezhnev, voting at sessions of the Politburo is an infrequent occurrence. If there is no consensus, a small group or committee of members is selected to resolve the disputed issue. See the summary of Brezhnev's session with American newsmen, in the *New York Times*, June 15, 1973, p. 3. On those rare occasions when voting takes place, the principle of majority rule is followed. Candidate members of the Politburo apparently do not have the right to vote. (See T. H. Rigby and L. G. Churchward, *Policy-Making in the USSR, 1953–1961: Two Views* [Melbourne: Lansdowne Press, 1962], pp. 7, 10.)

24. Michel Tatu, *Power in the Kremlin: From Khrushchev to Kosygin*, trans. Helen Katel (New York: Viking Press, 1970), pp. 197–198.

25. See reports by I. V. Kapitonov to the Twenty-Third, Twenty-Fourth, and Twenty-Fifth Party Congresses, in *Pravda*, April 1, 1966, p. 6; April 3, 1971, p. 4; February 28, 1976, p. 4. A case for the importance of the five obkoms (Moscow, Leningrad, Rostov, Gorky, and Sverdlovsk) is built in some detail by Peter Frank, "Constructing a Classified Ranking of CPSU Provincial Committees," *British Journal of Political Science*, 4 (April, 1974), 227, 229.

26. Merle Fainsod, *How Russia Is Ruled*, rev. ed. (Cambridge, Mass.: Harvard University Press, 1963), p. 169; Wolfgang Leonhard, *The Kremlin since Stalin*, trans. Elizabeth Wiskemann and Marian Jackson (New York: Greenwood, 1962), p. 235.

27. See "O razvitii konstitutsii SSSR v svete reshenii XXI s'ezda KPSS," *Sovetskoe gosudarstvo i pravo*, September 1959, p. 114, for a discussion of the extra-constitutional power enjoyed by the USSR Council of Ministers.

28. See the *New York Times*, June 25, 1974, p. 15; June 9, 1975, p. 2.

29. Robert Conquest, *Russia after Khrushchev* (New York: Praeger, 1965), p. 23; idem, *Power and Policy in the USSR: The Study of Soviet Dynastics* (New York: St. Martin's Press, 1961), p. 27.

30. Fainsod, *How Russia Is Ruled*, p. 165.·

31. See Rush, *Political Succession*, pp. 33–34; Leonard Schapiro, *The*

*Communist Party of the Soviet Union* (New York: Random House, 1959), p. 260.

32. See Schapiro, *Communist Party*, p. 287, n. 4; Leon Trotsky, *Stalin's Frame-Up System and the Moscow Trials* (New York: Pioneer Publishers, 1950), p. 14.

33. Lenin's preference for Trotsky is discussed in Rush, *Political Succession*, pp. 17–18; Leon Trotsky, *My Life* (New York: Grosset and Dunlap, 1960), pp. 478–480; Isaac Deutscher, *The Prophet Unarmed* (New York: Oxford University Press, 1959), pp. 35–37, 68–69. The full text of Lenin's political testament, in which Trotsky is described as "the most able man in the present central committee" *(samii sposobnii chelovek v nastoiashchem Ts.K.)*, can be found in the *New York Times*, October 18, 1926, p. 5, and in Wolfe, *Khrushchev*, pp. 262–263.

34. Deutscher, *Prophet Unarmed*, pp. 92–94.

35. *Dvenadtsatyi s'ezd rossiiskoi kommunisticheskoi partii (bol'shevikov)* (Moscow: Izdatelstvo "Krasnaia Nov", 1923), p. 577. Lenin's views on the nationality problem were set forth in a series of notes written in December 1922. See Wolfe, *Khrushchev*, pp. 271–276, for the complete text of these notes.

36. Leon Trotsky, *The Living Thoughts of Karl Marx* (New York: Fawcett Publications, 1963), p. 163.

37. Richard B. Day, *Leon Trotsky and the Politics of Economic Isolation* (London: Cambridge University Press, 1973), p. 77.

38. See Conquest, *Power and Policy*, p. 27; Conquest, *Russia after Khrushchev*, p. 105; Brzezinski and Huntington, *Political Power*, pp. 193, 230, 267.

39. Conquest, *Power and Policy*, p. 27.

40. The connection between de-Stalinization and the development of Soviet society is apparent from a Soviet response to Chinese criticism, printed in the *New York Times*, July 15, 1963, p. 13. The argument that Malenkov had reservations about de-Stalinization is rejected by at least one well-known scholar who bases his interpretation of Malenkov's position on an enigmatic statement by Khrushchev in retirement that Malenkov "possibly" gave him personal support for delivery of the Secret Speech. *(Khrushchev Remembers,* trans. Strobe Talbott [Boston: Little, Brown, 1970], p. 350.) More relevant, perhaps, is the statement by Marshal Zhukov a year after the Twentieth Party Congress that Malenkov was among those Soviet leaders who "stubbornly opposed the measures taken by the Party for eliminating the consequences of the cult of the individual leader, particularly the unmasking and calling to account of those bearing primary responsibility for violations of legality in the past." *(Pravda,* July 15, 1957, p. 3.)

41. Schapiro, *Communist Party*, p. 403.

42. See Conquest, *Russia after Khrushchev*, p. 111.

43. Conquest, *Power and Policy*, pp. 260–262, 333.

44. Zbigniew K. Brzezinski, *The Permanent Purge: Politics in Soviet Totalitarianism* (Cambridge, Mass.: Harvard University Press, 1956), p. 76;

Brzezinski and Huntington, *Political Power*, p. 335; John Erickson, *The Soviet High Command: A Military-Political History 1918–1941* (New York: St. Martin's Press, 1962), pp. 505–506.

45. Conquest, *Russia after Khrushchev*, p. 201.

46. *Pravda*, December 16, 1958, p. 2; December 20, 1958, p. 1. See also Rigby and Churchward, *Policy-Making*, p. 21, n. 10.

47. *Pravda*, December 10, 1963, p. 1.

48. Interview with Harrison E. Salisbury, referred to in the *New York Times*, October 3, 1967, p. 18.

49. See *The Anti-Stalin Campaign and International Communism: A Selection of Documents* (New York: Columbia University Press, 1956), pp. 12, 14, 47, 50, 52.

50. See Sidney I. Ploss, ed., *The Soviet Political Process: Aims, Techniques, and Examples of Analysis* (Waltham, Mass.: Ginn and Co., 1971), p. 125, for an elaboration of the view that Soviet politics are conducted in an atmosphere of conspiracy.

51. Palmiro Togliatti, in *The Anti-Stalin Campaign*, p. 104.

52. During the years of Khrushchev's dominance, 1958–1964, Party control over a fourth important power cluster, the secret police, had been reasserted through the leadership of Alexsandr Shelepin (1958–1961) and V. Ye. Semichastny (1961–1967). Before their appointments to the KGB apparatus both men had served as First Secretary of the Komsomol, climaxing more than a decade of apprenticeship in that organization, and both men had been in charge of the Central Committee Department of Party Organs shortly before they were selected to head the KGB. Semichastny's promotion to full membership in the Central Committee following Khrushchev's ouster in 1964 suggests that the KGB is indeed under Party control, even during periods of severe political stress.

53. See *Izvestia*, November 20, 1962, p. 2; B. Vladimirov and V. Nakoriakov, "Blizhe k liudiam, k proizvodstvu," *Kommunist*, September 1964, p. 82.

54. Meyer, *Soviet Political System*, p. 216. The Soviet press soon called Khrushchev to task, arguing that there is nothing more harmful to the economy than "uninterrupted reorganizations." (*Izvestia*, November 19, 1964, p. 1.)

55. See *Trud*, May 16, 1963, p. 2; *Pravda*, February 6, 1965, p. 2.

56. See John A. Armstrong, "Party Bifurcation and Elite Interests," *Soviet Studies*, 17 (April 1966), 422, 426, for a discussion of the resentments harbored by a majority of the old obkom first secretaries.

57. Meyer, *Soviet Political System*, pp. 259–260.

58. See Fainsod, *How Russia Is Ruled*, p. 396.

59. David T. Cattell, "Leningrad: Case Study of Soviet Local Government," *Western Political Quarterly*, 17 (June 1964), 197.

60. See *Izvestia*, September 5, 1964, p. 3.

61. S. Buravlev and G. Kliushin, "Partkom i apparat sovnarkhoza," *Partiinaia zhizn*, September 1964, pp. 37–38.

62. See the *New York Times,* October 23, 1965, p. 13.

63. It has been argued in the *Worker* that the immediate precipitant of Khrushchev's ouster from power was a memorandum urging a division of agriculture into seventeen administrative regions, a reorganization that would have been consistent with the 1961 party program. See the *New York Times,* November 1, 1964, p. 4; Jan F. Triska, ed., *Soviet Communism: Programs and Rules* (San Francisco: Chandler, 1962), p. 81.

64. See Leonard Schapiro, *The Government and Politics of the Soviet Union* (New York: Random House, 1965), p. 130; Brzezinski and Huntington, *Political Power,* p. 346.

65. Paul M. Cocks, "The Purge of Marshal Zhukov," *Slavic Review,* 22 (September 1963), 491.

66. See Thomas W. Wolfe, "Political Primacy vs. Professional Elan," *Problems of Communism,* 13 (May–June 1964), 46.

67. Matthew P. Gallagher, "Military Manpower: A Case Study," *Problems of Communism,* 13 (May–June 1964), 54.

68. Roman Kolkowicz, "The Military," in H. Gordon Skilling and Franklyn Griffiths, eds., *Interest Groups in Soviet Politics* (Princeton: Princeton University Press, 1971), pp. 158, 161; Gallagher, "Military Manpower," p. 57.

69. See Rush, *Political Succession,* pp. 106–107.

70. See Linden, *Khrushchev,* pp. 106–107.

71. With the substitution of "American" for "Russian," Soviet marshals would surely have accepted the Senate testimony given by General Curtis E. LeMay in opposition to a nuclear test ban: "Fear of the unknown is played up by cartoons, propaganda, half-truths and misinformation as to the effects of fallout. I do not wish to imply that fallout cannot be a hazard; however, with proper precautions, such as those taken by the AEC, the hazard is minimized. A good public information program could allay most of the present concern. It is clear that effects from fallout are far less dangerous to our people, and the people of the free world, than the risks of Russian predominance in the nuclear weapons field. Unless we are willing to undertake our testing program enthusiastically, and to expend the necessary effort and resources to insure a positive U.S. superiority in all of the critical nuclear areas, the Soviets stand to gain a clear margin of nuclear superiority vis-à-vis the United States. In the current world environment, preserving peace means maintaining preponderant military power. To maintain a favorable balance of military power we must have nuclear superiority. To do this I firmly believe we must continue our nuclear weapon development programs and be able to conduct nuclear testing as required." *Hearings before the Preparedness Investigating Subcommittee of the Committee on Armed Services United States Senate Eighty-Eighth Congress First Session,* I (Washington, D.C., U.S. Government Printing Office, 1964), p. 356.

72. Gallagher, "Military Manpower," pp. 57–61.

73. See Kolkowicz, "Military," p. 166.

74. Khrushchev's handling of foreign policy matters (for example,

the Cuban Missile Crisis and Sino-Soviet relations) no doubt also undercut his position in the Politburo, although it is likely that the decision to remove Khrushchev from office rested primarily on his record of failures in the domestic sphere.

75. Some authorities argue that Kirilenko would become nothing more than a "caretaker" in view of his age (three months older than Brezhnev). There is no precedent in the Soviet Union, however, for such a development. Furthermore, there are numerous instances in recent history of great longevity for both individuals and cabinets whose initial role was seen in "caretaker" terms.

76. *Pravda*, June 12, 1974, p. 3; June 8, 1974, p. 2.

77. Ibid., June 15, 1974, p. 2; June 8, 1974, p. 3; June 12, 1974, p. 3.

78. In the late 1960s Polyansky clashed openly with Brezhnev over the need for additional funds in the development of agriculture. (See Sidney I. Ploss, "Politics in the Kremlin," *Problems of Communism*, 19 [May–June 1970], 7–8.)

79. *Pravda*, June 4, 1974, p. 2.

80. See Linden, *Krushchev*, pp. 194–195, 199.

81. *Pravda*, June 13, 1974, p. 2.

82. Hodnett, "Succession Contingencies," p. 10. As first secretary of the Moscow gorkom, Grishin may also have had a hand in breaking up the unofficial Moscow art exhibition in the fall of 1974.

83. There is some evidence to suggest that an effort was made as early as 1965 to replace Kosygin with Ustinov as prime minister. See Hodnett, "Succession Contingencies," pp. 8, 10.

84. In the early 1970s the present duumvirate went on record as favoring the expansion of the "B" or consumer goods sector of the economy more rapidly than the "A" or heavy industry sector. See the reports by Brezhnev and Kosygin to the Twenty-Fourth Party Congress, in *Pravda*, March 31, 1971, p. 5; April 7, 1971, p. 3. As regards achieved as contrasted with planned goals, however, only in 1968, 1970, and 1971 has the "B" sector of the economy grown more rapidly than the "A" sector. The "A" sector has been restored, moreover, in words as well as deeds to its pedestal by the Five Year Plan for 1976–1980. It is perhaps not coincidental that this step backward, at least from the point of view of the consumer, was accompanied by the elevation of Ustinov from candidate membership to full membership in the Politburo at the Twenty-Fifth Party Congress.

| Year | Planned Rate of Growth | | Actual Rate of Growth | |
|------|------|------|------|------|
| | "A" | "B" | "A" | "B" |
| 1965 | 8.2% | 7.7% | 8.7% | 8.5% |
| 1966 | 6.9 | 6.0 | 9.0 | 7.0 |
| 1967 | 7.5 | 6.6 | 10.2 | 9.0 |
| 1968 | 7.9 | 8.6 | 8.0 | 8.3 |

| Year | Planned Rate fo Growth "A" | "B" | Actual Rate of Growth "A" | "B" |
|------|------|------|------|------|
| 1969 | 7.2 | 7.5 | 7.0 | 6.9 |
| 1970 | 6.1 | 6.8 | 8.2 | 8.5 |
| 1971 | — | 7.4 | 7.7 | 7.9 |
| 1972 | 6.8 | 7.1 | 6.8 | 6.0 |
| 1973 | 6.3 | 4.5 | 8.2 | 5.9 |
| 1974 | 6.6 | 7.5 | 8.3 | 7.2 |
| 1975 | 7.0 | 6.0 | 7.9 | 6.5 |

The figure for Planned Rate of Growth, "A" sector, was not given by N. K. Baibakov, chairman of Gosplan, although he referred to 'priority growth" for the "B" sector of the economy.

85. Carl J. Friedrich, *The Philosophy of Hegel* (New York: Random House, 1953), p. 227.

7    PARTY "SATURATION" IN THE SOVIET UNION
     *Jerry F. Hough*

1. Austin Ranney, *The Governing of Men,* rev. ed. (New York: Holt, Rinehart, and Winston 1966), p. 358. For other references, see T. H. Rigby, *Communist Party Membership in the USSR, 1917–1967* (Princeton: Princeton University Press, 1968), p. 412, n. 1.

2. For the same argument, see Rigby, *Communist Party Membership,* p. 412.

3. T. B. Bottomore, *Elites and Society* (New York: Basic Books, 1964), p. 8.

4. George K. Schueller, "The Politburo," in Harold D. Lasswell and Daniel Lerner, eds., *World Revolutionary Elites* (Cambridge, Mass.: MIT Press, 1965), pp. 97–178.

5. Alfred G. Meyer, *The Soviet Political System* (New York: Random House, 1965), p. 136.

6. This concept is developed in Rigby, *Communist Party Membership.* See also Zbigniew Brzezinski and Samuel P. Huntington, *Political Power USA/USSR* (New York: Viking Press, 1964), p. 100; Mervyn Matthews, *Class and Society in Soviet Russia* (London: Allen Lane, Penguin Press, 1972), pp. 217–225.

7. For 1973 Party membership, see *Partiinaia zhizn,* no. 14 (July 1973), p. 10; for 1973 population, see *Narodnoe khoziaistvo SSSR v 1972 g.* (Moscow: Statistika, 1973), p. 34.

8. See, for example, Ranney, *Governing of Men,* p. 358. Philip S. Gillette, "Models and Analogies" (letter), *Problems of Communism,* vol. 21, no. 6 (November–December 1972), p. 90.

9. This approach is used, for example, in Rigby, *Communist Party Membership*, p. 449. The age distribution of the population for 1973 is found in *Narodnoe khoziaistvo SSSR v 1972 g.*, p. 34. Since the age groupings in the census do not correspond to the groupings required for the analysis of Party membership, extrapolations were required both here and in later analyses of saturation by age group. It was simply assumed, for example, that in the 15–19 age group listed in the census, two-fifths were aged 18 and 19. The result is inexact because of irregularities in the birth rates from year to year, but the errors should not be serious for our purposes.

10. *Pravda*, March 31, 1971, p. 9.

11. The biographies of the deputies, including their year of birth and of Party admission, can be found in the volumes of *Deputaty Verkhovnogo Soveta* published by the Izvestia Publishing House (Moscow) shortly after the 1958, 1962, 1966, and 1970 elections to the Supreme Soviet. By my count, 742 deputies joined the Party after 1946, and they form the basis for my calculations.

12. *Partiinaia zhizn,* no. 14 (July 1973), p. 19; *Narodnoe khozyaistvo v 1972 g.*, p. 34.

13. *Partiinaia zhizn,* no. 14 (July 1973), p. 18.

14. *Narodnoe khoziaistvo v 1972 g.*, p. 34.

15. *Partiinaia zhizn,* no. 14 (July 1973), p. 14.

16. *Itogi vsesoiuznoi perepisi naseleniia 1970 goda* (Moscow: Statistika, 1972), III, 6–7.

17. The urban-rural distribution of Party membership is rarely discussed, but a recent book reports the number of Communists "who work in rural districts": 1959, 3,510,613 (42.6 percent of the total); 1961, 3,809,470 (41.1 percent); 1966, 4,694,984 (38.0 percent); 1971, 5,409,905 (37.6 percent). (V. I. Strukov, compiler, *Kommunisticheskaia partiia Sovetskogo Soiuza, Nagliadnoe posobie po partiinomu stroitelstvu* [Moscow: Politizdat, 1973], p. 126.) These figures go well beyond the estimates made by T. H. Rigby (*Communist Party Membership*, pp. 486–491), and the 1947 statistics cited by Strukov (2,449,983) run higher than the 1,714,000 rural Communists that *Bolshevik* reported at the time. (Quoted ibid., p. 488.) Part of the problem may be the difference between working and living in rural areas, but the major problem is whether to count Communists in small rural towns as urban or rural—and at what size of town or village to draw the borderline.

18. *Partiinaia zhizn,* no. 14 (July 1973), p. 16; *Narodnoe khoziaistvo v 1972 g.*, p. 38.

19. Calculated from *Itogi vsesoiuznoi perepisi naselenniia 1970 goda*, III, 6–7.

20. In 1970 only 28.9 percent of the men in the 20–24 age group were married, but this figure rose to 77.2 percent in the 25–29 group. (Ibid., II, 263.)

21. Rigby, *Communist Party Membership*, p. 491.

22. See, for example, Darrell P. Hammer, "The Dilemma of Party Growth," *Problems of Communism*, vol. 20, no. 4 (July–August 1970), pp. 16–21.

23. *Spravochnik partiinogo rabotnita,* 6th ed. (Moscow: Politizdat, 1966), pp. 383–386.

24. *Partiinaia zhizn,* no. 14 (July 1973), p. 12.

25. The number of registered voters was 140,000,000 in 1963 and 146,075,945 in 1967, and the calculation assumes 143,000,000 in 1965. (*Pravda*, March 7, 1963, p. 1; March 21, 1963, p. 1; March 26, 1967, p. 1. I could not easily find 1965 statistics on this point.) There were said to be 156,507,828 registered voters in 1973, (ibid., June 23, 1973, p. 1), but there must have been an undercount in that election. 161,724,222 persons were registered for the 1974 national election—a figure that implies a proper registration of some 159 million the year before. I have adopted the 159 million figure, partly because it falls more in line with what would have been expected from census. (If one took the official 1973 registration, the rise in the adult population would be 9.4 percent.) For the 1974 registration figures, see *Izvestia,* June 19, 1974, p. 1.

26. *Itogi vsesoiuznoi perepisi naseleniia 1970 goda,* II, 12–13.

27. Ibid., II, 12–13.

28. Ibid., VI, 172.

29. *Narodnoe khoziaistvo v 1964 g.,* (Moscow: Statistika, 1964), p. 33; *Narodnoe khoziaistvo v 1972 g.,* p. 38.

30. See, for example, *Pravda,* July 4, 1973, p. 2.

31. The documentation on participation statistics and a longer argument on the question of the influence of Soviet participation can be found in Jerry F. Hough, "Political Participation in the Khrushchev and Brezhnev Periods," *Soviet Studies,* 27 (January 1976), pp. 3–20.

32. Zbigniew Brzezinski and Samuel P. Huntington, *Political Power: USA/USSR* (New York: Viking Press, 1964), p. 93.

8   THE SCIENTIFIC–TECHNICAL REVOLUTION AND THE
    SOVIET ADMINISTRATIVE DEBATE
    *Robert F. Miller*

1. Merle Fainsod and Lincoln Gordon, *Government and the American Economy,* rev. ed. (New York: W. W. Norton, 1948), p. xi.

2. H. H. Gerth and C. Wright Mills, eds., *From Max Weber: Essays in Sociology* (New York: Oxford University Press, 1958), ch. 8.

3. Jerry F. Hough has definitively analyzed this relationship at the provincial level in terms of a prefectoral model in *The Soviet Prefects: The Local Party Organs in Industrial Decision-Making* (Cambridge, Mass.: Harvard University Press, 1969); see especially chs. 3–7.

4. Iu. A. Tikhomirov, ed., *Sluzhashchii Sovetskogo gosudarstvennogo apparata* (Moscow, 1970), p. 95; V. Lisitsyn and G. Popov, "Razvivat len-

inskuiu nauku upravleniia sotsialisticheskoi ekonomiki," *Kommunist,* no. 1 (January 1970), p. 64.

5. See, for example, V. I. Lenin, *State and Revolution* (New York: International Publishers, 1932), especially, pp. 42–44; Lenin, "Uderzhat li bolsheviki gosudarstvennuiu vlast?" in *Polnoe sobranie sochinenii,* 34 (Moscow, 1962), especially 311–312.

6. Jeremy R. Azrael, *Managerial Power and Soviet Politics* (Cambridge, Mass.: Harvard University Press, 1966), ch. 3.

7. V. I. Lenin, "Luchshe menshe, da luchshe," in *Polnoe sobranie,* vol. 45, p. 390.

8. Fainsod observed that the situation that so alarmed Lenin in Moscow was even worse in the provinces. (Merle Fainsod, *How Russia Is Ruled,* rev. ed. [Cambridge, Mass.: Harvard University Press, 1963], p. 92.)

9. V. I. Lenin, "Kak nam reorganizovat Rabkrin," in *Polnoe sobranie,* vol. 45, p. 384.

10. Ibid., p. 387.

11. Leonard Schapiro, *The Communist Party of the Soviet Union* (New York: Random House), pp. 272–273.

12. That Lenin was not entirely realistic in his expectations is evident in his assertion that financial savings from organizational reforms would constitute a substantial contribution to the financing of industrial development. ("Luchshe menshe, da luchshe," p. 405.)

13. Paul Cocks, "The Rationalization of Party Control," in Chalmers Johnson, ed., *Change in Communist Systems* (Stanford, Calif.: Stanford University Press, 1970), pp. 157–159, 163.

14. For example, the analysis of construction problems at Dneprostroi carried out by RKI in mid-1929 was thoroughly professional and would probably have been considered extremely useful in another political climate. (D. A. Chugaev, ed., *Materialy po istorii SSSR,* no. 8, *Dokumenty po istorii sovetskogo obshchestva* [Moscow: Academy of Sciences, 1959], pp. 175–202.)

15. Azrael, *Managerial Power,* pp. 90–104. See also the speech in May 1931 by V. V. Kuibyshev, then chairman of Gosplan and a member of the Politburo, rejecting the idea that only experts can be entrusted with economic planning. (V. V. Kuibyshev, *Izbrannye proizvedeniia* [Moscow, 1958], pp. 270–271.)

16. Bruce Franklin, ed., *The Essential Stalin: Major Theoretical Writings, 1905–52* (Garden City, N.Y.: Anchor Books, Doubleday and Co., 1972), p. 377.

17. Azrael, *Managerial Power,* pp. 104–106.

18. Robert F. Miller, "The New Science of Administration in the USSR," *Administrative Science Quarterly,* 18 (September 1971), 250–251.

19. V. A. Vlasov, *Sovetskii gosudarstvennyi apparat (osnovnye printsipy organizatsii i deiatelnosti)* (Moscow, 1951), p. 193.

20. This useful concept was coined by Victor A. Thompson and is defined and applied in his *Modern Organization* (New York: Alfred A. Knopf, 1961); see especially ch. 2.

21. For discussions of the effects of these reorganizations on industrial management see Hough, *Soviet Prefects,* ch. 8; and Azrael, *Managerial Power,* pp. 136–147; for the effects in agriculture see Robert F. Miller, *One Hundred Thousand Tractors: The MTS and the Development of Controls in Soviet Agriculture,* (Cambridge, Mass.: Harvard University Press, 1970), chs. 12, 15; and "Continuity and Change in Soviet Agricultural Administration Since Stalin," in James R. Miller, ed., *The Soviet Rural Community* (Urbana, Ill.: University of Illinois Press, 1971), ch. 3.

22. Cocks, "Rationalization of Party Control," pp. 170–178.

23. My interpretation here differs considerably from that of Azreal, *Managerial Power,* p. 145, who views the sequence of reorganizations from 1957 almost exclusively in political terms.

24. B. Vladimirov and V. Nakoriakov, "Blizhe k liudiam, k proizvodstvu," *Kommunist,* no. 13 (September 1965), p. 88.

25. For a discussion of Khrushchev's attack on the economists see Richard W. Judy, "The Economists," in H. Gordon Skilling and Franklyn Griffiths, eds., *Interest Groups in Soviet Politics,* (Princeton, N.J.: Princeton University Press, 1971), pp. 225–227.

26. See, for example, Ts. A. Iampolskaia, "Major Characteristics of Public Organizations in the USSR in the Contemporary Period," trans. in *Soviet Law and Government,* vol. 1, no. 2 (Fall 1962), pp. 32–39; Iampolskaia, "The Development of the Structural and Organizational Forms of Governmental Administration," trans. in ibid., vol. 3, no. 3 (Winter 1964–1965), pp. 43–51. For an early suggestion of the use of modern techniques and training in scientific administration see L. Kachalina, "Problemy nauchnoi organizatsii upravlencheskogo truda," *Kommunist,* no. 15 (October 1964), pp. 42–46.

27. See, for example, A. Butenko, "The Soviet State of the Entire People," trans. in *Soviet Law and Government,* vol. 2, no. 3 (Winter 1963–1964), pp. 3–13. Cocks, "Rationalization of Party Control," notes that some of these early elaborations of Khrushchev's concept of the "state of the entire people" were later repudiated as premature (p. 177). This reaction in 1967 corresponded to the conservative counterattack on administrative theory that I have noted in the essay.

28. Decree of the November 1964 Plenum of the Central Committee of the CPSU, "Ob obedinenii promyshlennykh i selskikh oblastnykh, kraevykh partiinykh organizatsii," *KPSS v rezoliutsiiakh,* vol. 8 (Moscow, 1972), pp. 495–496; Decree of the September 1965 Plenum of the Central Committee of the CPSU, "ob uluchshenii upravleniia promyshlennostiu, sovershenstvovanii planirovaniia i usilenii ekonomicheskogo stimulirovaniia, promyshlennogo proizvodstva," ibid., pp. 516–522.

29. V. G. Afanasev, "Nauchnoe rukovodstvo sotsialnymi protsessami," *Kommunist,* no. 12 (August 1965), pp. 58–73.

30. I should point out, incidentally, that I am not primarily concerned here with the so-called Scientific Organization of Labor (NOT) movement, which has undergone a great revival in the post-Khrushchev

period. This movement is concerned mainly with rationalization of industrial processes at the plant level and is very much in the Taylorist tradition of the 1920s. Indeed, one of the activities of the movement has been to reprint works from the twenties by Soviet elaborators of Taylorism, for example, A. K. Gastev and P. M. Kershentsev (see Miller, "New Science," p. 250). Cocks has discussed this revival at length in a recent work ("Rationalization of Party Control," pp. 179–188). The administrative application of NOT principles (Scientific Organization of Administrative Work—NOUT) is of greater significance for this essay, but NOUT, too, is more concerned with the "nuts-and-bolts" aspects of management.

31. Ibid., p. 60.

32. For an interesting discussion of the theory of open systems as applied to social organization see Walter Buckley, *Sociology and Modern Systems* (Englewood Cliffs, N.J.: Prentice-Hall, 1967).

33. I have discussed Bogdanov's theories briefly in Miller, "New Science," pp. 249–250.

34. V. I. Lenin, *Materialism and Empirio-Criticism* (Moscow: Foreign Languages Publishing House, n.d.), pp. 336–345.

35. "Obzor otklikov na materialy k teme 'Nauchnoe rukovodstvo sotsialnymi protesessami,'" *Kommunist,* no. 17 (November 1965), p. 62.

36. Afanasev, "Nauchnoe rukovodstvo," p. 69.

37. "Obzor otklikov," p. 67.

38. See, for example, the formulations in Afanasev's latest book, *Nauchno-tekhnicheskaia revoliutsiia, upravlenie, obrazovanie* (Moscow, 1972), pp. 37–39, 182–183. A. K. Belykh gives a slightly different formulation in "Obzor otklikov," p. 62.

39. For example, the criticism of the "narrow cybernetic approach" to social administration by A. G. Sorokin, "Obzor otklikov," p. 62.

40. V. A. Iadov, "Obzor otklikov," p. 63.

41. Afanasev, "Nauchno rukovodstvo," p. 62.

42. Ibid.

43. For example, I. A. Maizel, "Obzor otklikov," p. 63.

44. D. M. Gvishiani, "K voprosu ob izuchenii zarubezhnogo opyta organizatsii upravleniia: Kritika burzhuaznoi teorii," in *Sorevnovanie dvukh sistem, sbornik* (Moscow, 1963).

45. For a full-length discussion of the subjective factor and its current applications to the theory of social control see B. A. Chagin, *Subektivnyi-faktor: struktura i zakonomernosti* (Moscow, 1968), especially chs. 1 and 3.

46. Ibid., p. 70.

47. Afanasev, "Nauchnoe rukovodstvo" p. 70.

48. "Sovershenstvovat stil i metody khoziaistvennogo rukovodstva," lead editorial, *Kommunist,* no. 11 (July 1972), p. 10.

49. D. Lubsanov, *Iz opyta konkretno-sotsiologicheskikh issledovanii* (Ulan-Ude, 1968).

50. For a general discussion of the content of these studies see Miller, "New Science," pp. 251–253.

51. A. Rumiantsev, "Ekonomicheskaia nauka i upravlenie narodnym khoziaistvom," *Kommunist*, no. 1 (January 1966), p. 45. An example of the rather favorable reappraisal of Bogdanov see E. A. Fomin, "Nekotorye voprosy issledovaniia organizatsii," *Chelovek i obschestvo*, no. 2 (Leningrad, 1967), p. 14. Even Afanasev had some surprisingly charitable criticisms of Bogdanov in his *Nauchnoe upravlenie obshchestvom (opyt sistemnogo issledovaniia)* (Moscow, 1968), 223–228.

52. V. G. Afanasev, "Stroitelstvo kommunizma—nauchno upravliaemyi protsess," *Kommunist*, no. 14 (September 1967), p. 74.

53. "O merakh po dalneishemu razvitiiu obshchestvennykh nauk i povysheniiu ikh roli v kommunisticheskom stroitelstve," *Kommunist*, no. 13 (September 1967), p. 5.

54. G. Glezerman, "Istoricheskii materializm i problemy sotsialnykh issledovanii," *Kommunist*, no. 4 (March 1970), pp. 83–84.

55. N. Sviridov, "Partiinaia zabota o vospitanii nauchno-tekhnicheskoi intelligentsii," *Kommunist*, no. 18 (December 1968), p. 39; Ia. Kronrod, "Ob ekonomicheskikh printsipakh i zakonomernostiakh sotsializma," ibid., no. 11 (July 1969), pp. 23–24.

56. V. A. Iadov, "O sootnoshenii teoreticheskogo i empiricheskogo podkhodov k konkretnomu sotsiologicheskomu issledovaniiu," in B. A. Shtoff, ed., *Problemy metodologii sotsial'nogo issledovaniia* (Leningrad, 1970), pp. 13–15.

57. L. I. Brezhnev, "Otchetnyi doklad Tsentralnogo Komiteta KPSS XXIV Sezdu Kommunisticheskoi partii Sovetskogo Soiuza," *Kommunist,* no. 5 (March 1971), p. 44.

58. Ibid., pp. 53–54.

59. "Nasushchnye zadachi ekonomicheskoi nauki," lead editorial, *Kommunist*, no. 11 (July 1971), p. 15.

60. M. Suslov, "Obshchestvennye nauki—boevoe oruzhie partii v stroitelstve kommunizma," *Kommunist*, no. 1 (January 1972), pp. 22–23, 27.

61. G. Glezerman, V. Kelle, and N. Pilipenko, "Istoricheskii materializm—teoriia i metod nauchnogo poznaniia i revoliutsionnogo deistviia," *Kommunist*, no. 4 (March 1971), p. 70.

62. Sviridov, "Partiinaia," pp. 44–45.

63. Lisitsyn and Popov, p. 64.

64. Decree of the Central Committee, CPSU, "O merakh po uluchsheniiu podgotovki partiinykh i sovetskikh kadrov v Vysshei partiinoi shkole pri Ts K KPSS," *Kommunist*, no. 16 (November 1972), p. 3.

65. See, for example, V. Akhundov, "Sovetskii khoziaistvennik," *Kommunist*, no. 17 (November 1965), pp. 29–31; Tikhomirov, *Sluzhashchii*, pp. 254–255; Afanasev, *Nauchno-tekhnicheskaia revoliutsiia*, pp. 415–416.

66. Tikhmirov, *Sluzhashchii*, pp. 246–249; Afanasev, *Nauchno-tekhnicheskaia revoliutsiia*.

67. Tikhmirov, *Sluzhashchii*, pp. 65–66.

68. Afanasev, *Nauchno-tekhnicheskaia revoliutsiia*, pp. 189–190, 414.

69. Ibid., pp. 410–411.

70. D. Gvishiani, "O sovremennykh burzhuaznykh teoriiakh uprav-leniia," *Kommunist,* no. 12 (August 1970), pp. 119–121.
71. Andrei Amalrik, *Will the Soviet Union Survive until 1984?* (New York: Harper & Row, 1970), pp. 14–28.
72. Afanasev, *Nauchno-tekhnicheskaia revoliutsiia,* p. 380.

9    THE POLICY PROCESS AND BUREAUCRATIC POLITICS
*Paul Cocks*

1. See Henry S. Rowen, "Bargaining and Analysis in Government," in Louis C. Gawthrop, ed., *The Administrative Process and Democratic Theory* (Boston: Houghton Mifflin, 1970), pp. 31–37. For a general discussion, see the excellent commentary by Gawthrop in this fine collection of essays.
2. See Herbert Kaufman, "Administrative Decentralization and Po-litical Power," in Dwight Waldo, ed., *Public Administration in a Time of Turbulence* (New York: Chandler Publications, 1971), pp. 1–18.
3. See particularly the articles by Jerry F. Hough, "The Bureaucratic Model and the Nature of the Soviet System," *Journal of Comparative Administration,* 5 (August 1973), 134–167, and "The Soviet System: Petrifica-tion or Pluralism?" *Problems of Communism,* 21 (March–April 1972), 25–45.
4. An eloquent argument advocating the use of a systems approach is made by Franklyn Griffiths, "A Tendency Analysis of Soviet Policy-Making," in H. Gordon Skilling and Franklyn Griffiths, eds., *Interest Groups in Soviet Politics* (Princeton: Princeton University Press, 1971), pp. 335–377.
5. Donald V. Schwartz, "Recent Adaptations of Systems Theory to Ad-ministrative Theory," *Journal of Comparative Administration,* 5 (August 1973), 233–264. See also Dzherman M. Gvishiani, *Organization and Manage-ment: A Sociological Analysis of Western Theories* (Moscow: Progress Pub-lishers, 1972); Iu. V. Katasanov and E. A. Chizhov, "Sistema PPB v federal-nom pravitelstve," *S Sh A,* 1 (1972), 46–53; I. G. Kurakov, "Upravlenie i nauchno-tekhnicheskaia revoliutsiia," *Voprosy filosofii,* 3 (1970), B. G. Yudin, "Novye elementy v tekhnologii kapitalisticheskogo upravleniia," *Voprosy filosofii,* 1 (1973), 83–95; M. M. Kreisberg, *S Sh A: Systemnyi podkhod v upravlenii i praktika promyshlennykh korporatsii* (Moscow: Nauka, 1974); I. V. Blauberg and E. G. Yudin, *Stanovlenie i sushchnost sistemnogo pod-khoda* (Moscow: Nauka, 1973); B. Z. Milner, ed., *S Sh A: Sovremennye metody upravleniia* (Moscow: Nauka, 1971).
6. Merle Fainsod, "Khrushchevism in Retrospect," *Problems of Com-munism,* 14 (1965), 8.
7. For the seminal articles on these divergent positions, see Zbigniew Brzezinski, "The Soviet Political System: Transformation or Degeneration?" *Problems of Communism,* 15 (1966), and Hough, "Soviet System."
8. Hough, "Soviet System," p. 25.
9. H. Gordon Skilling, "Interest Groups and Communist Politics: An Introduction," in Skilling and Griffiths, *Interest Groups,* p. 8.
10. Ibid., p. 15.

11. Hough, "Bureaucratic Model," pp. 147–148.

12. This apt term is T. H. Rigby's. See his "The De-concentration of Power in the USSR, 1953–1964," in John D. B. Miller and T. H. Rigby, eds., *The Disintegrating Monolith: Pluralist Trends in the Communist World* (Canberra: Australian National University, 1965), pp. 17–45.

13. Jeremy R. Azrael, "Decision-Making in the USSR," in Richard Cornell, ed., *The Soviet Political System: A Book of Readings* (Englewood Cliffs, N.J.: Prentice-Hall, 1970), p. 214. See also the discussion by Darrell P. Hammer, *USSR: The Politics of Oligarchy* (Hinsdale, Ill.: Holt, Rinehart and Winston, 1974), pp. 226–227.

14. Hough, "Soviet System," pp. 27–29.

15. Hammer, *Politics of Oligarchy*, pp. 223–256.

16. Robert V. Daniels, "Soviet Politics Since Khrushchev," in John W. Strong, ed., *The Soviet Union under Brezhnev and Kosygin* (New York: Van Nostrand Reinhold, 1971), pp. 22–23.

17. Skilling, "Interest Groups and Communist Politics," p. 17.

18. Hough, "Soviet System," p. 28.

19. Ibid., p. 29; see Skilling, "Interest Groups and Communist Politics," p. 15, and his "Groups in Soviet Politics: Some Hypotheses," pp. 19–20. See also Joel J. Schwartz and William R. Keech, "Group Influence and the Policy Process in the Soviet Union," *American Political Science Review*, 62 (September 1968), 840–851; Philip D. Stewart, "Soviet Interest Groups and the Policy Process: The Repeal of Production Education," *World Politics*, 22 (October 1969), 29–50.

20. Hough, "Soviet System," p. 29, and "Bureaucratic Model," p. 152.

21. Merle Fainsod, *How Russia Is Ruled* rev. ed. (Cambridge, Mass.: Harvard University Press, 1963), p. 386.

22. Hough, "Bureaucratic Model," p. 152, and "Soviet System," pp. 34–35.

23. See Skilling, "Interest Groups and Communist Politics," pp. 8–9, and "Groups in Soviet Politics," pp. 19–20; Sidney I. Ploss, "Interest Groups," in Allen Kassof, ed., *Prospects for Soviet Society* (New York: Praeger, 1968), pp. 76–103, and his larger study, *Conflict and Decision-Making in Soviet Russia* (Princeton: Princeton University Press, 1965); Carl A. Linden, *Khrushchev and the Soviet Leadership* (Baltimore: Johns Hopkins University Press, 1966).

24. Hough, "Soviet System," p. 28.

25. Hammer, *Politics of Oligarchy*, p. 286.

26. Skilling, "Interest Groups and Communist Politics," p. 9.

27. Azrael, "Decision-Making in the USSR," pp. 219–220.

28. Hammer, *Politics of Oligarchy*, pp. 283–286.

29. Ploss, "Interest Groups," p. 95. See also the discussion by Henry W. Morton, "The Structure of Decision-Making in the USSR," in Peter H. Juviler and Henry W. Morton, eds., *Soviet Policy-Making: Studies of Communism in Transition* (New York: Praeger, 1967), pp. 9–12.

30. See his perceptive essay, "The Change to Change in Communist

Systems: Modernization, Post-Modernization, and Soviet Politics," in Henry
W. Morton and Rudolf L. Tokes, eds., *Soviet Politics and Society in the
1970's* (New York: Free Press, 1974), p. 390.

31. Hough, "Soviet System," p. 28.

32. Ibid., p. 29. See also his "Bureaucratic Model," pp. 162–163.

33. Jerry F. Hough, "The Party Apparatchiki," in Skilling and Griffiths, *Interest Groups*, p. 68. These ideas are developed by Hough in greater
depth in *The Soviet Prefects: The Local Party Organs in Industrial Decision-
Making* (Cambridge, Mass.: Harvard University Press, 1969).

34. Hough, "Soviet System," p. 29.

35. Again Hough is the most explicit in his use of this decision-making
model, but many of the basic assumptions of the incremental-bargaining
approach pervade much of the recent work by Sovietologists applying group
theory in their analyses.

36. See the discussion by Allen Schick, "Systems Politics and Systems
Budgeting," in Fremont J. Lyden and Ernest G. Miller, eds., *Planning-Programming-Budgeting: A Systems Approach to Management,* 2nd ed. (Chicago: Rand McNally, 1972), pp. 78–101. The classic works on this approach
are Aaron Wildavsky, *The Politics of the Budgetary Process* (Boston: Little,
Brown, 1964), and Charles E. Lindblom, "The Science of Muddling
Through," in *Public Administration Review*, 19 (Spring 1959), 79–88, and
Lindblom's larger study, *The Intelligence of Democracy* (New York: Macmillan, 1965).

37. Griffiths, "Tendency Analysis," p. 335.

38. Skilling, "Groups in Soviet Politics," p. 23.

39. Andrew C. Janos, "Group Politics in Communist Society: A Sec-
ond Look at the Pluralistic Model," in Samuel P. Huntington and Clement
H. Moore, eds., *Authoritarian Politics in Modern Society: The Dynamics of
Established One-Party Systems* (New York: Basic Books, 1970), pp. 437–450.

40. Griffiths, "Tendency Analysis," p. 336.

41. Ibid., p. 335.

42. Skilling, "Groups in Soviet Politics," p. 36.

43. Nor is power as fixed and tangible a thing—something to have
and to hold—as this view sometimes depicts it. The dynamic and relational
attributes of power are not addressed. The notion that leaders are not so
much "powerholders" as "powerhandlers," who use and wield power in the
pursuit of other goals, values, and interests, is also not taken into account.
This is surprising since such views on power are much more appropriate for
a political model emphasizing bargaining relationships.

44. A notable exception to this omission is Philip Stewart, who has
shown the role of groups to resist and frustrate the implementation of
policies. See his fine essay "Soviet Interest Groups and the Policy Process."
Hammer also notes the importance of "authority leakage" and says that this
phenomenon is much more significant in the Soviet Union than is generally
realized. (See *Politics of Oligarchy,* p. 230.)

45. Michael D. Reagan, ed., *The Administration of Public Policy*

(Glenview, Ill.: Scott, Foresman, 1969), p. 16. Harold Seidman also notes that organizational arrangements are not neutral. "Organization is one way of expressing national commitment, influencing program direction, and re-ordering priorities." A particular organizational structure tends to give some interests and perspectives more effective access to those with decision-making authority. See his *Politics, Position, and Power: The Dynamics of Federal Organization* (New York: Oxford University Press, 1970), pp. 13–14.

46. Rowen, "Bargaining and Analysis in Government," p. 32.

47. See the excellent discussion by Alf Edeen, "The Administrative Intelligentsia," in Cornell, *Soviet Political System*, pp. 294–305. See also Alen Abouchar, "Inefficiency and Reform in the Soviet Economy," and Roger A. Clarke, "Dr. Abouchar and Levels of Inefficiency," in *Soviet Studies*, 25 (1973), 66–76 and 77–87, respectively.

48. Griffiths, "Tendency Analysis," p. 351.

49. In his essay Griffiths tries to look at and explain the policy process from this perspective, emphasizing what he calls "system-dominant conflict of tendencies of articulation."

50. See Roger E. Kanet, "The Communist Party of the Soviet Union and Soviet Politics: Recent Western Interpretations," paper delivered at the 1974 Annual Meeting of the American Political Science Association, August 29–September 2, 1974.

51. Yehezkel Dror, "Muddling Through—'Science' or Inertia?" *Public Administration Review*, 24 (1965), 154–155.

52. See, for example, his comments reported in *Pravda* on April 14, April 22, and June 13, 1970, as well as his comments on March 31, 1971, at the Twenty-Fourth Party Congress. Since 1971 this theme constantly punctuates his speeches.

53. See Gertrude Schroeder, "Recent Developments in Soviet Planning and Incentives," in Joint Economic Committee, U.S. Congress, Ninety-Third Congress, first session, *Soviet Economic Prospects for the Seventies* (Washington, D.C., 1973), pp. 11–38. For an excellent discussion of recent trends in modernizing technical aspects of the policy process, see Erik P. Hoffmann, "Soviet Metapolicy: Information Processing in the Communist Party of the Soviet Union," *Journal of Comparative Administration*, 5 (August 1973), 200–232, and "Soviet Information Processing: Recent Theory and Practice," *Soviet Union*, 2 (1975), 22–49.

54. As Rowen says, "We should not just assume that good technical or economic decisions will be made or even taken into account by a system operating primarily in a partisan mutual adjustment mode." See "Bargaining and Analysis in Government," pp. 34–35.

55. See William M. Capron, "The Impact of Analysis on Bargaining in Government," in Gawthrop, *Administrative Process*, pp. 364–365. Similar arguments are found in James R. Schlesinger, "Systems Analysis and the Political Process," ibid., pp. 336–353.

56. See the discussion by B. P. Rassokhin and M. P. Ring, "Pravo i vnedrenie dostizhenii nauki i tekhniki," *Sovetskoe gosudarstvo i pravo*, 3 (1973), 59–60. With a systems approach toward planning, financing, and

management, one Soviet authority writes, "The new will not have to 'fight its way up' from below, proving its right to exist . . . all shoots of the new will be visible from above and can always be given timely assistance." (G. Pospelov, "The Systems Approach," *Izvestia*, March 21, 1974.)

57. See the discussion by Schick, "Systems Politics and Systems Budgeting."

58. Rowen, "Bargaining and Analysis in Government," p. 32.

59. See Brezhnev's own comments at the Twenty-Fourth Party Congress, his speech in December 1972 on the occasion of the Fiftieth Anniversary of the USSR, and at the December 1973 plenum of the Central Committee. The latter can be found in L. I. Brezhnev, *Ob osnovnykh voprosakh ekonomicheskoi politiki KPSS na sovremennom etape: Rechi i doklady* (Moscow: Politizdat, 1975), II, 355–358. It is interesting to note that the Krasnoyarsk region, the center of a number of vast and complex projects for the development of natural resources, has been particularly singled out by the Soviet press for its success in applying the systems approach. Moreover, it was none other than the former First Secretary of this region, V. I. Dolgikh, whom Brezhnev brought into the Central Party Secretariat in December 1972 and placed in charge of heavy industry. On the need for the systems approach, consult Pospelov, "Systems Approach"; V. Afanasev, "Improve the Machinery of Socialist Economic Management," *Pravda*, January 11, 1974; G. M. Dobrov et al., *Programmno-tselevoi metod upravleniia v nauke* (Moscow, 1974); M. Ya. Lemeshev and A. I. Panchenko, *Kompleksnye programmy v planirovanii narodnogo khoziaistva* (Moscow: Ekonomika, 1973); A. V. Bachurin, *Planovo-Ekonomicheskie metody upravleniia* (Moscow: Ekonomika, 1973); Yu. Tikhomirov, "Paths for the Optimization of Decisions," *Pravda*, March 9, 1974.

60. Gvishiani, *Organization and Management*, p. 172.

61. He first made this statement in June 1970 (see *Pravda*, June 13, 1970).

62. M. I. Piskotin, "The Functions of the Socialist State and the Administrative Apparat," *Sovetskoe gosudarstvo i pravo*, 10 (1973), 3–11. See also "Nauchnye osnovy khoziaistvovaniia: problemy, poiski perspektivy," *Kommunist*, 13 (1972), 88.

63. See the excellent discussion by Robert W. Campbell, "Management Spillovers from Soviet Space and Military Programmes," *Soviet Studies*, 23 (1972), 586–607.

64. Pospelov, "Systems Approach," V. Afanasev, "Ways of Improving Management," *Pravda*, March 3, 1973.

65. Raymond Hutchings, "Soviet Technological Policy," in *Soviet Economic Prospects for the Seventies*, p. 76.

66. Gvishiani, *Organization and Management*, pp. 140, 142.

67. *Ekonomicheskaia gazeta*, 2 (January 1974), 13–14.

68. L. Blyakhman in *Neva*, 1 (January 1973), in *CDSP*, vol. 25, p. 6.

69. O. Deineko, "From the Enterprise to the Ministry," *Pravda*, April 17, 1973.

70. For a fine treatment of PPBS in the U.S., see the essays by Allen

Schick, "The Road to PPB: The Stages of Budget Reform," and "Systems Politics and Systems Budgeting," in Lyden and Miller, *Planning-Programming-Budgeting*, pp. 15–40, 78–101.

71. As one Western analyst notes in writing about the resistance on the part of ministerial officials to the formation of industrial associations and R & D complexes, "Here we see how a bureaucracy which has been set up to support a system becomes (within certain limits) an independent force, one which in the interests of self-preservation is able to offer serious resistance to the leadership's measures intended to modernize this system." (Allan Kroncher, "Associations: Old Problems with a New Look," Radio Liberty Report, December 4, 1973.)

72. Afanasev, "Improve the Machinery"; A. Tolkachev, "The Plan and Discipline," *Pravda*, March 22, 1974.

73. Schroeder, "Recent Developments," p. 12.

74. It is true that the amount of bonuses given for introducing new technology steadily rose after 1965. In 1969, 34 percent more money in bonuses of this kind was paid to industry than in 1966. However, their share of the total sum of money paid in bonuses actually declined during these years. (See *Pravda*, December 3, 1970.) The reforms failed to accelerate technological innovation appreciably, which caused Brezhnev to call for new, more stringent measures at the Twenty-Fourth Party Congress. "We must create conditions that will compel enterprises to produce the latest types of output, literally to chase after scientific and technical innovations and not to shy away from them, figuratively speaking, as the devil shuns incense," stressed the General Secretary (ibid., March 31, 1971). For general discussion of the weaknesses of the reforms, see Gertrude Schroeder, "Soviet Technology: System vs. Progress," *Problems of Communism*, 19 (1970), 19–29; A. M. Rumiantsev, "Voprosy nauchnotekhnicheskogo progressa," *Voprosy ekonomiki*, 1 (1971), 12.

75. *Ekonomicheskaia gazeta*, 43 (1970), 5–6; Bachurin, *Planovo-Ekonomicheskie metody upravleniia*, pp. 57–71; K. I. Taksir, "Integratsiia nauki i proizvodstva pri sotsializme," *Znanie (novoe v zhizni, nauke, tekhnike: seriia ekonomika)*, 10 (1975).

76. Fainsod gives an excellent discussion of this in *How Russia Is Ruled*, pp. 386–420.

77. Edeen, "Administrative Intelligentsia," p. 305.

78. The elevation of G. V. Romanov, the First Secretary of Leningrad Province, to alternate membership in the Politburo in May 1973 and to full membership at the Twenty-Fifth Party Congress may be seen in this light to some extent. The Leningrad region has been in the forefront of the *obedinenie* movement to form science-production associations. While it is too early to tell, the growth of large R & D complexes and industrial associations will probably, on balance, enhance the influence of Party officials vis-à-vis ministerial functionaries both within the associations and complexes as well as in the particular areas where they are clustered.

79. See V. Shcherbitsky, "Partiinye organizatsii i sovershenstvovanie

upravleniia ekonomikoi," *Kommunist*, 6 (1973); V. Degtiarev, "Partiinye organizatsii i nauchno-tekhnicheskii progress," ibid., 14 (1972). It may be noted that the theme of enhanced Party supervision over the implementation of technical progress figured much more prominently at the republic Party conferences which met a month before the Twenty-Fifth Party Congress than at the national Party Congress in February, 1976.

80. John P. Hardt, "West Siberia: The Quest for Energy," *Problems of Communism*, 22 (1973), 30.

81. Ibid., p. 32. See also N. Baibakov, "Socialist Planning and Soviet Economic Development," *Social Sciences* (Moscow), 1 (1972), 17–32; N. Fedorenko, "Optimal Functioning of the Soviet Economy," ibid., pp. 34–45.

82. Hardt, "West Siberia," p. 25.

83. Campbell, "Management Spillovers," p. 589.

84. Rumiantsev, "Voprosy nauchno-tekhnicheskogo progressa," p. 6.

85. D. M. Gvishiani, "The Scientific and Technological Revolution and Scientific Problems," *Social Sciences*, 1 (1972), 52. Emphasis added.

86. L. Blyakhman, "Associations Link Science and Industry," *Pravda*, December 1, 1971.

87. A. Bachurin, "The Industrial Association and Technical Progress," *Ekonomicheskaia gazeta*, 43 (1970), 5–6.

88. See the discussion by Ronald Amann, "The Soviet Research and Development System: The Pressures of Academic Tradition and Rapid Industrialization," *Minerva*, 8 (1970). He notes that direct government intervention in speeding and supervising technological advance has been limited, for the most part, to high priority defense fields. Enforcement of priorities and concentration of resources by the central authorities was undertaken only intermittently (see pp. 221–222, 225). The All-Union Scientific and Technical Information Center under the USSR State Committee for Science and Technology has been responsible only since 1968 for registering and recording all research projects. The state registration of experimental design did not begin until 1973 (*Pravda*, April 5, 1972).

89. See E. Zaleski, J. P. Kozlowski, H. Wienert, R. W. Davies, M. J. Berry, and R. Amann, *Science Policy in the USSR* (Paris: Organization for Economic Cooperation and Development, 1969), p. 80.

90. Gvishiani, *Organization and Management*, pp. 125–126.

91. See I. V. Bestuzhev-Lada, "Forecasting as One Category of Approach to Problems of the Future," in A. M. Rumiantsev and I. V. Bestuzhev-Lada, *Problemy obshchei i sotsialnoi prognostiki* [Problems of general and social prognosis], no. 1, 1968, in Joint Publications Research Service no. 48537 (August 1, 1967), pp. 3–17.

92. Gvishiani, *Organization and Management*, p. 126.

93. See I. V. Gromeka and V. S. Vasilev, "Otsenka posledstvii vnedreniia novoi tekhniki," *S Sh A*, 12 (1972), 103–112.

94. Premier Kosygin lectured the central planning body on this score in September 1972 (*Planovoe khoziaistvo*, 11 [1972]). Since then others have also taken Gosplan to task over this issue. See the editorial in *Kommunist*,

3 (1973), 3–13; Afanasev, "Improve the Machinery," *Pravda*, January 11, 1974.

95. "Management by objectives" is my translation of the Russian term *tselevoe upravlenie*. It should be recalled that planning is predominantly on an institutional basis while the research and development process spills over this institutional framework. In addition, Soviet planning is also highly structured and entrenched along branch lines while research and development projects are essentially interbranch in nature. Finally, financing is predominantly organized on an input basis by item of expenditure. Funding tends to be based largely on structure and staff rather than on productivity, demonstrated need, or research priority. As one Soviet authority stresses, "We must finance not only organizations, enterprises, and associations but also goals and tasks, or projects and programs." Again the emphasis is to shift away from inputs to outputs and results, to link funding more closely to performance. (See Pospelov, "Systems Approach.")

96. Amann, "Soviet Research and Development System," pp. 218–219.

97. Zaleski et al., *Science Policy in the USSR*, pp. 92–93.

98. See F. Amirdzhaniants, V. Disson, L. Maksimov, "Sovershenstvovanie metodov i pokazatelei planirovaniia razvitiia nauki i tekhniki," *Planovoe khoziaistvo*, 11 (1973), 44–45, and G. Efimov, "Nauchno-tekhnicheskii progress: organizatsiia i upravlenie," *Kommunist*, 10 (1973), 94–95. In addition to the integrated programs for introducing new technology that were included in the 1973 plan, similar comprehensive programs were also elaborated at that time to raise the technical standards of various industrial branches. See L. Gatovskii, "O kompleksnom upravlenii effektivnostiu novoi tekhniki," ibid., 14 (1973), 60–73. A key problem has been the fragmentation of the planning system with separate plans for protection, capital investment, material-technical supplies, and construction.

99. One is reminded of a similar discrepancy that existed in the U.S. before the advent of PPBS. The main impetus for PPB, Schick explains, came from the new decisional technologies associated with economic and systems analysis, not from public administration or political science. Thus, the government-wide introduction of PPBS occurred at a time when the pluralists' bargaining model had reached its academic apogee, about one year after the publication of major works by Lindblom and Wildavsky. Interestingly, at a time when Western scholars, like Hough and Skilling, are applying the incremental-bargaining model more and more widely to the Soviet policy process, PPBS-type techniques are becoming more and more widespread in the Soviet Union and being pushed by political decision-makers in the Kremlin.

100. See Francis E. Rourke, *Bureaucracy, Politics, and Public Policy* (Boston: Little, Brown, 1969), pp. 105–106.

101. See Schwartz, "Recent Soviet Adaptations of Systems Theory to Administrative Theory," pp. 242–247.

102. I discuss this theme more fully in "Retooling the Directed Society: Administrative Modernization and Developed Socialism," to appear in

Jan F. Triska and Paul M. Cocks, eds., *Political Development in Eastern Europe* (forthcoming from Praeger Special Studies).

103. See his article, "Hopes and Illusions: The Scientific and Technological Revolution and Management," *Novy mir*, 7 (1972).

104. Shcherbitsky, "Partiinye organizatsii i sovershenstvovanie upravleniia ekonomikoi," p. 33.

105. *Pravda*, March 31, 1971. Emphasis added.

106. Ibid., May 11, 1973.

107. Keith Pavitt, "Technology, International Competition, and Economic Growth: Some Lessons and Perspectives," *World Politics*, 25 (1973), 198.

## 10   THE VIRGIN LANDS SINCE KHRUSHCHEV
### Richard M. Mills

I am indebted to Fordham University for the Faculty Fellowship which supported the research for this study, to the Harvard University Russian Research Center for facilitating the final stages of the research, and to the editors of this volume for their valuable suggestions.

1. See W. A. Douglas Jackson, "The Virgin and Idle Lands of Western Siberia and Northern Kazakhstan," *Geographical Review*, 46 (1956), pp. 1–19; Frank Durgin, "The Virgin Lands Programme," *Soviet Studies*, 13 (January 1962), pp. 255–280; Carl Zoerb, "The Virgin Lands Territory: Plans, Performance, Prospects," in Roy D. Laird and Edward L. Crowley, eds., *Soviet Agriculture: The Permanent Crisis* (New York: Praeger, 1965), pp. 29–44; Keith Bush's "Commentary" on Zoerb's article, ibid., pp. 44–51; J. W. Cleary, "The Virgin Lands," *Survey*, 56 (July 1965), pp. 95–105; Lazar Volin, *A Century of Russian Agriculture: From Alexander II to Khrushchev* (Cambridge, Mass.: Harvard University Press, 1970), pp. 484–496.

2. Separate calculations for these oblasts are necessary because in the three most widely cited Soviet sources for both gross grain production and state grain purchase statistics the figures given for the Kazakh virgin lands are actually those for the entire Kazakh Republic. Compare *Selskoe khoziaistvo SSSR* (Moscow: Gosstatizdat, 1960), pp. 226–227, and *Narodnoe khoziaistvo SSSR v 1960 g.* (Moscow, 1961), pp. 440–441, with pp. 418–419 of the latter volume and also with *Selskoe khoziaistvo SSSR: statisticheskii sbornik* (Moscow: Statistika, 1971), pp. 158–159.

3. Kazakhstan produced 21.5 million tons of grain in 1969, 22.2 million in 1970, 21.0 million in 1971 and a minimum (according to a preliminary announcement) of 28 million in 1972. Average annual production in Kazakhstan in the 1955–1968 period had been 16.5 million tons. No statistics are yet available for individual oblasts in recent years (excepting 1972), but it can safely be estimated that about two-thirds of the grain was produced by the six oblasts in question. See also note 8 below.

4. See the *New York Times*, February 23, 1964; Robert Conquest, *Russia after Khrushchev* (New York: Praeger, 1965), pp. 91–92.

5. Zoerb, "Virgin Lands Territory," p. 34. In 1963 the yield was 2.8 quintals per hectare.

6. S. B. Baishev and F. K. Mikhailov, eds., *10 let osvoeniia tseliny* (Alma-Ata: Nauka, 1964), p. 129. Of the total 245.8 million rubles were lost in the sale of grain, and 383.8 million in the sale of cattle products, all because purchase prices were too low. The rest were intra-farm losses. Some farms were regularly profitable, some regularly unprofitable. While most grain farms' profitability fluctuated depending upon the size of the harvest each year, profitability was ordinarily undermined by the substantial depreciation allowances paid on the large quantity of underutilized equipment. See *Kazakhstanskaia pravda* February 5, 1966, report on VASKHNIL session. Hereafter *KP*.

7. See N. S. Khrushchev, *Stroitelstvo kommunizma v SSSR i razvitie selskogo khoziaistva*, 8 vols. (Moscow, 1962–1964), I, 85–100, for the text.

8. S. B. Braishev, ed., *Materialno-tekhnicheskaia baza kommunizma i yee ekonomicheskie problemy v Kazakhstane* (Alma-Ata: Nauka, 1966), p. 146. The statistics on grain purchases reflect more accurately the real contribution of the virgin lands than do the ones on grain production. The latter are normally inflated by about 15 percent because they measure grain that has not been cleaned or dried.

9. Cleary, "Virgin Lands," has treated these questions in detail. Owing to improved equipment and better farming practices, wind erosion and the resultant dustbowls have since been minimized, though not entirely eliminated. In Pavlodar oblast, the worst affected in the early 1960s, wind erosion damage was held to 1 percent in 1968 when very strong winds raged. Of the total 33,000 hectares affected about 4,000 were reported as seriously harmed. (V. M. Slobodin, *Ekonomika tselinnogo zemledeliia* [Alma-Ata: Kolos, 1970], p. 100,)

10. The proceedings are in I. I. Siniagin et al., eds., *Problemy selskogo khoziaistva severnogo Kazakhstana i stepnykh raionov zapadnoi Sibiri* (Moscow, 1966). The recommendations on grain farming are on pp. 550–554.

11. Werner Hahn has analyzed some of the politics of these personnel changes in *The Politics of Soviet Agriculture, 1960–1970* (Baltimore: Johns Hopkins University Press, 1972), pp. 7–161.

12. *Plenum Tsentralnogo kommiteta Kommunisticheskoi partii Sovetskogo Soiuza 24–26 marta 1965 g.* (Moscow, 1965), p. 104.

13. See *Current Digest of the Soviet Press*, 17 (April 14, 1965), 5, for Brezhnev and *KP*, April 8, 1965, for Kunaev. Owing to the new leaders' habit of releasing little information about their internal decision-making processes it is impossible to determine when and how the decision was made to retain the virgin lands but modify Khrushchev's administrative procedures there. One of the five choices listed had to be made, and the one chosen was merely announced after it had been made. These circumstances marked a radical departure from practice in the Khrushchev era which made it possible to know a good deal more about how the virgin lands policy was originally formulated. (See Richard M. Mills, "The Formation of the Virgin Lands Policy," *Slavic Review*, 29 [March 1970], 58–69.)

14. Zoerb, "Virgin Lands Territory," p. 40. *Ekonomika selskogo khoziaistva,* no. 5 (1970), p. 65.

15. There is very little information on this matter. One state farm director gave the cost of working one hectare of *fallow* tilled with a regular plow (2.47 rubles) and tilled with a specialized plow (2.23 rubles) as opposed to one hectare of *unfallowed* land tilled in the preceding fall with a regular plow (1.94 rubles) and tilled in the preceding fall with a specialized plow (1.77 rubles.) *KP,* March 25, 1966, D. Masalkin. A decree in *KP,* July 15, 1967, gives details on the failure to work the fallows.

16. Those highly dubious claims have been analyzed in Bush, "Commentary," and Volin, *Russian Agriculture,* pp. 493–96. Relative profit and loss must be weighed against the grain's value in the light of the commitment to self-sufficiency, a political consideration that loomed large for the leadership up to 1972.

17. *Ekonomika selskogo khoziaistva,* no. 3 (1971), p. 69.

18. N. Kurchina, First Secretary of the Tselinograd obkom, discusses these shortages in *Pravda,* December 24, 1973.

19. As a result of the Komsomol recruiting drive starting in 1954, by October 1961 about 700,000 persons had been sent to *all* virgin lands areas. (*Voprosy istorii,* no. 8 [1962], p. 6.) Some of these recruits were sent to the new lands untrained, others received specialized technical training before being dispatched, and other persons were assigned to the virgin lands via *orgnabor.* The available statistics on the recruitment, assignment, and abandonment of the virgin lands by the recruits can only be described as chaotic. In sum, one can say that if the recruiting campaign was successful in providing untrained personnel, it was more of a failure in providing permanent personnel. The incidence of personnel turnover was very high among the Komsomol recruits because of harsh working and living conditions.

20. M. A. Govar et al., eds., *Voprosy ekonomiki i organizatsii selskogo khoziaistva Tselinnogo kraia* (Alma-Ata: Krainar, 1965), pp. 169–170. This source unfortunately gives no precise dates for the information respecting the variation in the number of persons employed.

21. Bashev, *Materialno tekhnicheskaia,* p. 166.

22. P. M. Pakhmurnyi, ed., *Kommunisticheskaia partiia v borbe za osvoenie tselinnykh zemel v Kazakhstane* (Alma-Ata: Kazakhstan, 1969), p. 419. *KP,* January 17, 1969, decree. *KP,* August 13, 1972, agricultural report. The statistic for the combine park is calculated from *Narodnoe khoziaistvo Kazakhstana v 1968,* pp. 173–174. The total tractor park in the virgin lands oblasts in 1968 was 94.6 thousand in physical units. (Ibid.)

23. *KP,* January 17, 1969. The decree published here announcing the training program gave no data on the numbers to be trained although it hinted that the program would be large. The 1969 effort was most likely a failure in view of the sizeable new program initiated in the following year.

24. *KP,* April 17, 1969, Kunaev's speech. The low purchase prices simultaneously made it possible for the farms to experience financial losses, while the state reaped a profit, so to speak, from the ultimate sale of grain products to the consumers.

25. Slobodin, *Ekonomika,* pp. 138–150, discusses the negative aspects of the virgin lands' state farms' not receiving for some years the same benefits accruing to the collective farms from the purchase price increases of 1965 for grain produced over the planned amount.

26. *Pravda,* February 8, 1969.

27. Calculated from data in *Narodnoe khoziaistvo Kazakhstana v 1968,* p. 116, and *Narodnoe khoziaistvo SSSR v 1968* (Moscow; Statistika, 1969), p. 351.

28. Calculated from the same two sources, pp. 133 and 371, respectively.

29. Siniagin et al., *Problemy,* p. 173.

30. *Ekonomika selskogo khoziaistva,* no. 5 (1970), p. 63.

31. *KP,* July 19, 1970.

32. Extracts from the decree initiating the program are in *Pravda,* April 3, 1974.

33. A preliminary account of these projections is in the *New York Times,* May 1, 1976.

## 11 SOCIALISM AND MODERNITY
*Gail Warshofsky Lapidus*

1. This perspective finds its most comprehensive and suggestive formulation in Richard Lowenthal, "Development vs. Utopia in Communist Policy," in Chalmers Johnson, ed., *Change in Communist Systems* (Stanford: Stanford University Press, 1970). Lowenthal argues that "in classical Communist ideology, the task of modernization played no central role," and that it was only the failure of revolutionary movements in advanced industrial societies which compelled the new Soviet regime, and later the victorious Communist parties of other underdeveloped countries, to attempt politically forced modernization (p. 39). This view gives insufficient weight to the interventionist thrust of Leninism from its very origins, as well as to the way in which Leninism involves the identification of socialism with modern organizational forms in economic and political life.

2. The span of time covered by this essay reflects the fact that by the mid-1930s the structure and ethos of the Soviet educational system had assumed a form that would persist for several decades. While important aspects of this system were called into question during the ascendancy of Khrushchev, his reforms were largely reversed by his successors. Although there is considerable current discussion of the need to adapt the Soviet educational system to the new requirements of the age of scientific-technological revolution, recent changes have been too modest to alter the fundamental patterns established under Stalin.

3. V. I. Lenin, *Lenin o narodnom obrazovanii* (Moscow, 1957), pp. 354–355.

4. V. I. Lenin, *O vospitanii i obrazovanii* (Moscow: Gosudarstvennoe izdatelstvo politicheskoi literatury, 1963), pp. 337–349.

5. *KPSS v resoliutsiyakh i resheniyakh syezdov, konferentsii i plenumov TsK*, 7th ed., vol. I (Moscow: Gosudarstvennoe izdatelstvo politicheskoi literatury, 1954) p. 419. The 1903 program is found on pp. 37–43.

6. This movement joined two somewhat distinct theoretical strands, one deriving from the rationalism of the Enlightenment tradition of secular public education and the other, a Tolstoyan impulse toward a liberating and child-centered education greatly influenced by the ideas of Rousseau and Pestalozzi. For an illuminating treatment of this intellectual tradition see Frederick Lilge, "Lenin and the Politics of Education," *Slavic Review*, vol. 27, no. 2 (June 1968), pp. 230–257. See also Patrick L. Alston, *Education and the State in Tsarist Russia*, (Stanford: Stanford University Press, 1969); Nicholas Hans, *The Russian Tradition in Education* (London: Routledge and Kegan Paul, 1963), and his *History of Russian Educational Policy, 1701–1917* (New York: Russell and Russell, 1964). The proposals of a number of organizations concerned with public education in the decade before the revolution are reviewed in Joan Pennar, Ivan Bakalo, and George Bereday, *Modernization and Diversity in Soviet Education*, (New York: Praeger, 1971), pp. 11–26.

7. Nadezhda Krupskaya, *Memories of Lenin* (New York, n.d.), p. 3.

8. This view is expressed most fully in "Our Revolution," written in January 1923; see V. I. Lenin, *Collected Works*, vol. 33 (Moscow: Progress Publishers, 1966), pp. 476–479.

9. Marx's ideal is expressed most vividly in a passage in *Capital* which contrasts the narrowly specialized and repetitive labor of the contemporary worker with the activities of a fully developed man fit for a variety of labors and able to face any change in the productive process (Modern Library edition, I, 534).

10. For a fascinating treatment of the industrial and mechanistic imagery of revolutionary ideology, of the influence of the American model, and of the view of socialist man as "Russian Americans," see Rene Fülöp-Muller, *The Mind and Face of Bolshevism* (New York: Harper and Row, 1965).

11. For an excellent treatment of conflicting priorities in higher education in the immediate post-Revolutionary period see James McClelland, "Bolshevik Approaches to Higher Education, 1917–1921," *Slavic Review*, vol. 30, no. 4 (December 1971), pp. 818–831. A comprehensive discussion of early Soviet cultural policy is presented in Sheila Fitzpatrick, *The Commissariat of Enlightenment: Soviet Organization of Education and the Arts under Lunacharsky* (Cambridge: Cambridge University Press, 1970); and in "The 'Soft' Line on Culture and Its Enemies: Soviet Cultural Policy, 1922–1927," *Slavic Review*, vol. 33, no. 2 (June 1974).

12. A more elaborate treatment of the relationship of cultural revolution and educational policy in the Soviet Union will be found in my forthcoming study, "Educational Strategies and Cultural Revolution," in Sheila Fitzpatrick, ed., *Cultural Revolution in the USSR: 1928–1933* (Bloomington: University of Indiana Press). For a comparative perspective see Richard

Fagen, *The Transformation of Political Culture in Cuba* (Stanford: Stanford University Press, 1969); Theodore Hsi-en Chen, *The Maoist Educational Revolution* (New York: Praeger, 1974).

13. The relevant decrees are gathered in *Direktivy VKP (B) i postanovleniia sovetskogo pravitelstva o narodnom obrazovanii, 1917–1947*, 2 vols., ed. N. I. Boldyrev (Moscow, 1947).

14. A. V. Lunacharsky, *O narodnom obrazovanii* (Moscow: Izdatelstvo Akademii pedagogicheskikh nauk, 1958), p. 523.

15. Nicholas Hans and Sergius Hessen, *Educational Policy in Soviet Russia* (London: King and Son, 1930), p. 232.

16. Ibid.

17. The decline in the proportion of educational expenditures covered by the budget of the central government is depicted in *Narodnoe prosveshchenie*, the Narkompros yearbook, for 1928–29. While in 1917 educational expenditures were shared equally between the state budget and local communities, the share of the latter rose to over 70 percent of the total by 1927–28.

18. The number of primary schools in the USSR declined from 114,235 in 1920–21 to 87,559 in 1922–1923, and the number of pupils from 9,211,351 to 6,808,157. At the secondary level the number of schools declined from 4,163 to 2,478. The number of students reached a low of 520,252 in 1921–1922 and began to rise the following year. (Hans and Hessen, *Educational Policy*, p. 232.)

19. *Narodnoe prosveshchenie v RSFSR k 1927–1928: Otchet NKP za 1926–1927 uchebnyi god* (Moscow, 1928), pp. 94–102, 108–109; *Narodnoe prosveshchenie v RSFSR k 1929–1930: Otchet NKP za 1928–1929 uchebnyi god* (Moscow, 1930), p. 25. For a thoughtful treatment of the politics of proletarianization see James McClelland, "Proletarianizing the Student Body: The Soviet Experience during the New Economic Policy" (unpublished paper).

20. Fitzpatrick, *Commissariat of Enlightenment*, p. 220.

21. For a review of early Soviet policy toward the bourgeois specialists see Jeremy Azrael, *Managerial Power and Soviet Politics* (Cambridge, Mass.: Harvard University Press, 1966); Kendall Bailes, "The Politics of Technology: Stalin and Technocratic Thinking among Soviet Engineers," *American Historical Review*, vol. 79, no. 2 (April 1974).

22. Fitzpatrick, *Commissariat of Enlightenment*, pp. 256–290.

23. *Narodnoe prosveshchenie, 1927–1928*, p. 45.

24. *Narodnoe prosveshchenie, 1928–1929*, p. 44.

25. *Kulturnoe stroitelstvo 1929*, diagram 8.

26. Ibid.

27. David Lane, "The Impact of Revolution: The Case of Selection of Students for Higher Education in Soviet Russia, 1917–1928," *Sociology*, vol. 7, no. 2 (May 1973), p. 247. Lane cites the results of a 1923 survey of the educational aspirations of 2,000 peasants. Nevertheless, even that survey revealed a high level of aspiration among the respondents for primary education.

28. Cited in Hans and Hessen, *Educational Policy,* p. 208.

29. *Narodnoe prosveshchenie, 1927–1928,* p. 47. The proportion of women at university level was actually unchanged from 1915. The distribution of women among different specialties was uneven, ranging from 58 percent of the total in medicine and in pedagogy to 16 percent in industrial-technical specialties. (Ibid., p. 107.)

30. *Narodnoe prosveshchenie, 1928–1929.*

31. Yet is would be a mistake to conclude, as do most conventional treatments, that Soviet efforts at proletarianization were a failure. While it is true that the proportion of workers in higher educational institutions failed to rise sufficiently to satisfy the hopes of Narkompros, or its more radical critics, it is nonetheless likely that the proportion of workers was significantly larger than it would have been in the absence of preferential policies. Comparisons with the prewar period are extremely problematic because of the use of different socioeconomic categories by Tsarist statisticians. Between 1924 and 1928, correcting for inflated statistics, the proportion of worker students actually increased more rapidly in relation to the proportion of workers in the population at large than did the nonmanual category. Increases in both these categories occurred at the expense of peasant representation. For a careful analysis of these trends, and the conclusion that from an international comparative perspective the Soviet Union by 1928 had achieved an unprecedented level of proletarian access to higher education, see McClelland, "Proletarianizing the Student Body."

32. The Proletkultists were the best organized manifestation of cultural radicalism, and Bukharin their most influential supporter within the Party leadership in the early post-Revolutionary period.

33. Lenin, *O vospitanii i obrazovanii,* pp. 434–435.

34. Shulgin's views are explored at greater length in my "Educational Strategies and Cultural Revolution." His basic orientation is set forth in *Osnovnye voprosy sotsialnogo vospitaniia* (Moscow, 1926) and in *V borbe marksistkuiu pedagogiku* (with M. V. Krupenina) (Moscow, 1929).

35. Cited in Fitzpatrick, *Commissariat of Enlightenment,* p. 215.

36. Ibid., p. 218.

37. Nicholas DeWitt, *Education and Professional Employment in the USSR* (Washington, D.C.: National Science Foundation, 1961), p. 80.

38. Hans and Hessen, *Educational Policy,* p. 24. A perspective from inside is offered by N. Ogynov, *The Diary of a Communist Schoolboy,* as well as his *Diary of a Communist Undergraduate* (Westport: Hyperion, 1973).

39. Nadezhda Krupskaya, *Pedagogicheskie sochineniia v desiati tomav,* (Moscow, 1959) VII, 12.

40. Hans and Hessen, *Educational Policy,* p. 18. This preamble is omitted from the official compilation of decrees published in 1947 with the note that it contained serious ideological errors: *Direktivy VKP,* p. 120.

41. See, for example, his speech to the Third Komsomol Congress, cited in R. Fisher, *Pattern for Soviet Youth* (New York: Columbia University Press, 1963), p. 307.

42. Lunacharsky, *O narodnom obrazovanii*, pp. 403–405.

43. Cited in Fitzpatrick, *Cultural Revolution*.

44. A detailed account of the purge of Smolensk State University is given in Merle Fainsod, *Smolensk under Soviet Rule* (Cambridge, Mass.: Harvard University Press, 1958), ch. 18.

45. Dewitt, *Education and Professional Employment*, p. 655.

46. F. F. Korolev, *Narodnoe khoziaistvo i narodnoe obrazovanie v SSSR* (Moscow, 1961) p. 24.

47. The new orientation can be dated from the decree of September 5, 1931; *Direktivy VKP*, p. 151.

48. For a discussion of the changes in psychological theory underlying the reorientation of educational methods see Raymond Bauer, *The New Man in Soviet Psychology* (Cambridge, Mass.: Harvard University Press, 1959).

49. Holland Hunter, "The Overambitious First Soviet Five-Year Plan," *Slavic Review,* vol. 32, no. 2 (June 1973); Moshe Lewin, *Russian Peasants and Soviet Power: A Study of Collectivization* (Evanston, Ill.: Northwestern University Press, 1968); Roy Medvedev, *Let History Judge: The Origins and Consequences of Stalinism* (New York: Random House, 1971). Recent Soviet studies of Stalin's educational policy are also extremely critical of its effects on the teaching of both the natural and the social sciences. See, for example, V. V. Ukraintsev, *KPSS—organizator revoliutsionnogo preobrazovaniya vysshay sholy* (Moscow, 1963), p. 49.

12    VALUES AND ASPIRATIONS OF SOVIET YOUTH
*Ruth W. Mouly*

1. *Literaturnaia gazeta,* April 28, 1972, p. 10.

2. In evaluating these characteristics, the author has drawn on interviews with graduate students who have spent from two months to five years studying in the Soviet Union, the written accounts of scholars who have had recent contacts with Soviet youth, articles from the Soviet press and her own experiences and observations on several trips to the USSR.

3. S. Ikonnikova and V. Lisovsky, *Youth in Our Time* (Moscow: Novosti Press Publishing House, 1969), p. 78.

4. Quoted in Ernest Simmons, "The New 'New Soviet Man,'" in C. Faust and W. Lerner, eds., *The Soviet World in Flux*. (Atlanta: Southern Regional Education Board, 1967), p. 28.

5. Ibid.

6. Joel Schwartz, *Soviet Fathers versus Soviet Sons: Is There a Conflict of Generations?* (Pittsburgh: University of Pittsburgh Press, 1966), p. 5.

7. Colette Shulman, *We the Russians* (New York: Praeger, 1971), p. 72.

8. Interview with Caroline Crooks, a student at the University of Leningrad in 1969.

9. Robert Kaiser, *Russia, the People and the Power* (New York: Atheneum, 1976), p. 36.

10. Hedrick Smith, *The Russians* (New York: New York Times Book Co., 1976), p. 173.

11. Schwartz, *Soviet Fathers*, p. 6.

12. *Uchitelskaia gazeta*, July 22, 1972.

13. Allen Kassof, *The Soviet Youth Program, Regimentation and Rebellion* (Cambridge, Mass.: Harvard University Press, 1965), p. 160.

14. Smith, *Russians*, p. 189.

15. Quoted from the *Sun Telegram*, London, by *Atlas*, September 1971, p. 31.

16. Shulman, *We the Russians*, p. 57.

17. Alexander Garbovsky, "A New Kind of Involvement," *UNESCO Courier*, April 1969, p. 29.

18. Ikonnikova and Lisovsky, *Youth in Our Time*, pp. 75–76.

19. Ibid., p. 76.

20. N. Vikrov, Metal Worker, *Komsomolskaia pravda*, December 21, 1965.

21. *Izvestia*, February 6, 1973.

22. *Izvestia*, April 10, 1973.

23. Kassof, *Soviet Youth Program*, p. 149.

24. Zev Katz, "Sociology in the Soviet Union," in *Problems of Communism*, 20, (May–June 1971), 35.

25. Ikonnikova and Lisovsky, *Youth in Our Time*, p. 78.

26. Katz, "Sociology," p. 35.

27. Stanislav Sergeyev, "Collective Portrait of a Tenth Grade Class," *Soviet Life*, (October 1973, p. 22.

28. L. M. Archangelskii and Iu. Petrov, "Life Plans and Ideals of Soviet Youth," *Soviet Review*, Spring 1968, pp. 33–34.

29. Ibid., p. 34.

30. William Taubman, *The View from Lenin Hills* (New York: Coward, 1967), p. 47.

31. Kassof, *Soviet Youth Program*, pp. 145–46, 148.

32. Walter Conner, *Deviance in Soviet Society* (New York: Columbia University Press, 1972), p. 351.

33. Martin Chancey, "Russian Students," *Yale Review*, Spring 1972, p. 351.

34. Joel Schwartz, "The Elusive 'New Soviet Man,'" *Problems of Communism*, 22 (September–October 1973), 45.

35. Ibid.

36. *Literaturnaia gazeta*, July 26, 1966.

37. Schwartz, *Soviet Fathers versus Soviet Sons*, p. 4.

38. Schwartz, "The Elusive 'New Soviet Man,'" p. 43.

39. *Pravda*, March 10, 1962.

40. Quoted in Merle Fainsod, "Soviet Youth and the Problem of the Generations," *Proceedings of the American Philosophical Society* (October 1964), p. 435.

41. *Moskovski Komsomolets*, July 10, 1963.

42. Schwartz, *Soviet Fathers versus Soviet Sons*, p. 7.

43. E. Simmons, "New Soviet Man," p. 28.

44. N. S. Mansurov, "Research on Problems of Youth in the USSR," *Sovetskaia pedagogica*, 1968, p. 12.

45. Quoted in Schwartz, *Soviet Fathers versus Soviet Sons*, p. 8.

46. Ibid.

47. W. Taubman, *Lenin Hills*, p. 178.

48. *Chyrvonaya zmena*, Minsk, April 4, 1962.

49. Schwartz, *Soviet Fathers versus Soviet Sons*, p. 11.

50. Fainsod, "Soviet Youth," p. 430.

51. Peter Reddaway, *Uncensored Russia* (New York: American Heritage, 1972), p. 32.

52. Smith, *Russians*, p. 187.

53. Ibid., p. 193.

54. Taubman, *Lenin Hills*, p. 192.

55. Ibid., p. 188.

56. Chancey, "Russian Students," p. 363.

57. Ibid.

58. Ibid., p. 353.

59. Taubman, *Lenin Hills*, p. 59.

60. Ibid., p. 248.

61. Kaiser, *Russia*, p. 37.

13  MODERNIZATION, GENERATIONS, AND THE UZBEK SOVIET INTELLIGENTSIA
*Donald S. Carlisle*

1. Merle Fainsod, *Smolensk under Soviet Rule* (Cambridge, Mass.: Harvard University Press, 1958), p. 454.

2. Ibid., p. 453.

3. For information on F. Khodzhaev and A. Ikramov, see *Kritika*, vol. 8, nos. 2 and 3 (1971–1972).

4. Joseph Stalin, *Marxism and the National and Colonial Question* (New York: International Publishers, n.d.), pp. 176–177.

5. See *Pravda Vostoka*, June 18, 1937, p. 1.

6. See People's Commissariat of Justice of the USSR, *Report of Court Proceedings in the Case of the Anti-Soviet "Bloc of Rights and Trotskyites,"* Verbatim Report, Moscow, 1938, especially pp. 743–748.

7. Ibid., especially pp. 754–758.

8. A slowdown in the turnover rate is evident from the fact that of 1940 Uzbek Central Committee full members, only 54.7 percent had not been members or candidate members in 1938. Russians had played and continued to play a crucial role in the Uzbek SSR. The following table shows the percentage of Russians and natives among the full members of the Central Committee of the Uzbek Party during the 1930s:

|            | 1939 | 1934 | 1937 | 1938 | 1940 |
|------------|------|------|------|------|------|
| Russians   | 45   | 52   | 46   | 56   | 51   |
| Natives    | 55   | 48   | 54   | 43   | 49   |

In 1934 of the nineteen (twelve members and seven candidate members) on the Bureau of the Central Committee, fourteen (eight members and six candidate members) were natives. Of the eleven total members on the Bureau in June 1937, eight were natives. In 1938 of the eleven on the Bureau, only five were natives. As of March 1940, of the eleven Bureau members six were natives. In addition, two of the Bureau's five candidate members were Uzbeks.

9. Usman Yusupov died on May 7, 1966. His obituary appeared in *Pravda Vostoka,* May 9, 1966.

10. For Abdurakhmanov's biography see *Uzbek Sovet Entiklopediysi,* I (Tashkent, 1972), 36.

11. Abdurakhmanov died on October 3, 1975. See *Pravda Vostoka,* October 4, 1975, p. 2.

12. Fainsod, *Smolensk under Soviet Rule,* p. 92.

13. Egon Erwin Kish, *Changing Asia* (New York: Alfred A. Knopf, 1935), pp. 36–38. The original volume was published in German in 1932.

14. *Kommunisticheskaya partiya Uzbekistana v tsifrakh, (sbornik statisticheskikh materialov, 1924–64)* [The Communist party of Uzbekistan in figures, a collection of statistical materials, 1924–1964] (Tashkent, 1964), p. 36.

15. Gosplana SSR, *Kulturnoe stroitelstvo SSSR v tsifrakh ot VI k VII Sezdu Sovetov (1930–1934)* [Cultural construction, the USSR in figures from the VI to the VII Congress of Soviets (1930–1934)] (Moscow, 1935).

16. Ibid.

17. Ibid., p. 60.

18. Ibid.

19. The Uzbek press attacked "Europeans" for their treatment of natives and stressed the ill will created when a Moselm found in his pocket "pig fat, sausage, (when) he is called 'a fool,' 'an ass,' 'a savage,' 'an Asiatic,' etc. etc." (*Pravda Vostoka,* October 12, 1931, p. 2.) Also see the issues for September 22, 1932, p. 2; June 8, 1933, p. 3; August 28, 1933, p. 2; October 9, 1933, p. 2.

20. No longer was Great Russian chauvinism singled out as the "greatest danger" on the nationality question as at the Sixteenth Party Congress in 1930. In his report to the Congress, Stalin reintroduced local nationalism as an equally great danger, depending on the local circumstances.

21. M. Vakhabov, *Formirovinie Uzbekskoi sotsialisticheskoi natsii* [The formation of the Uzbek socialist nation], (Tashkent, 1961), p. 483.

22. M. Gulyamova, *Iz istorii Uzbekskoi sovetskoi intelligentsii* (1933–1937) [From the history of the Uzbek soviet intelligentsia (1933–1937)], (Tashkent, 1962), p. 74.

23. Cited in Z. Brzezinski, *The Permanent Purge* (Cambridge, Mass.: Harvard University Press, 1956), p. 38.

24. Merle Fainsod, *How Russia Is Ruled*, rev. ed. (Cambridge: Harvard University Press, 1963), p. 249.

25. *Bolshaia Sovetskaia Ensiklopedia* [Great Soviet Encyclopedia], vol. 18 (Moscow, 1953), p. 270.

26. For the period from the end of 1936 until January 1, 1939, the Uzbek party admitted a total of only 5,195 to candidate status. In the first four months of 1939, 10,972 were admitted as candidates. *Pravda Vostoka,* May 17, 1939, p. 1.

27. *Kommunisticheskaia partiia Uzbekistana v tsifrakh* [The Communist party of Uzbekistan in figures], pp. 73, 77.

28. Ibid., pp. 67, 71.

29. Ibid. The focus on youth resulted even in the recruitment of those below the age of twenty. In 1939, 863 who were under twenty were admitted.

30. Ibid., pp. 68, 72.

31. In the Uzbek SSR in January 1941 there were 20,200 "specialists with higher education." Within this group there were only 2,900 Uzbeks. However among those with a tekhnikum training, it is likely that there were many more natives. See A. K. Valiev, *Formirovanie i razvitie sovetskoi natsionalnoi intelligentsii v Srednei Azii* [The formation and development of the Soviet national intelligentsia in Central Asia], (Tashkent, 1966), pp. 122–123.

32. Fainsod, *Smolensk under Soviet Rule*, p. 452.

33. *Pravda Vostoka*, February 6, 1976, p. 1.

34. R. Pipes, "Muslims of Soviet Central Asia: Trends and Prospects, Part II," *Middle East Journal*, no. 3 (1955), p. 301.

35. A recent article suggests that moment may not be in the too distant future. Under topics such as "De-Russification," "Resurrection of the Pre-Revolutionary Past" and the "Quest for Autonomy under Soviet Rule," the author makes a strong case for an emergent national restiveness in Uzbekistan. See James Critchlow, "Signs of Emerging Nationalism in Moslem Soviet Republics," in Norton T. Dodge, ed., *Soviets in Asia* (Mechanicsville, Maine: Cremona Foundation, 1972), pp. 18–27.

36. However, in late April 1969 submerged ethnic tension surfaced when a riot took place in Tashkent outside the Paskhator football stadium. The Tashkent disturbance continued into early May 1969, and involved fighting between Uzbeks and Russians. One source reported the events as follows: "In mid-May there were large-scale national disturbances in a number of places in Uzbekistan. They took the form of spontaneous meetings and rallies, under the slogan 'Russians get out of Uzbekistan!' The

disturbances assumed such a violent character that troops were brought into Tashkent. About one hundred and fifty arrests were made in Tashkent and other towns. The majority were allowed to go free, but about thirty people were given fifteen days in prison for 'petty hooliganism.' According to unconfirmed rumors, one of those kept under arrest was Rashidova, daughter of the First Secretary of the Central Committee of the Communist Party of Uzbekistan, and another, the son of one of the deputy chairmen of the Uzbek Council of Ministers." (P. Reddaway, ed., *Uncensored Russia, Protest and Dissent in the Soviet Union* (New York: Cowles, 1972), pp. 402–403.)

37. Fainsod, *How Russia Is Ruled,* p. 128.

## 14    MODERNIZATION AND NATIONAL POLICY IN SOVIET CENTRAL ASIA
*Gregory J. Massell*

1. See Samuel P. Huntington, *Political Order in Changing Societies* (New Haven: Yale University Press 1968), pp. 335–336, 402, 8, 137.

2. I have dealt with some Soviet developmental strategies and problems in Central Asia in *The Surrogate Proletariat: Moslem Women and Revolutionary Strategies in Soviet Central Asia, 1919–1929* (Princeton: Princeton University Press, 1974). For some other recent studies of Soviet Central Asia by Western scholars (from a variety of perspectives), see ibid, pp. 3–4, n. 1.

3. For a very helpful discussion of some aspects of this issue, see Henry Riecken, "Social Science and Contemporary Social Problems," *Items* (Social Science Research Council), 23 (March 1969), 1–6.

4. I have considered this issue in some detail in *Surrogate Proletariat,* especially pp. 55–89, 185–191, 390–411.

5. See *Pravda,* December 15, 1965, reporting on a conference of social scientists of Central Asian academies of science in Alma-Ata.

6. Some of the arguments used in this analytical framework develop (albeit from a different perspective) notions incorporated in my paper "Human Rights and Ethnic Tensions in Soviet Central Asia," read at the Conference on Human Rights in the USSR, Columbia University, May 1972.

7. See Massell, *Surrogate Proletariat,* pp. 58ff.

8. See Barrington Moore, *Terror and Progress—USSR* (Cambridge, Mass.: Harvard University Press, 1954), p. 200.

9. See Merle Fainsod, *How Russia Is Ruled* (Cambridge, Mass.: Harvard University Press, 1953), p. 496; cf. the revised edition (1963), chapters 11 and 17, where the emphases differ.

10. Although their perspectives differ, they appear to be essentially congruent on this issue. See H. Eckstein, "Authority Patterns and Governmental Performance: A Theoretical Framework," mimeographed (Center of International Studies, Princeton University, 1968), pp. 20ff; A. Etzioni, *The Active Society: A Theory of Societal and Political Processes* (New York: Free Press, 1968), ch. 21.

11. Etzioni, *Active Society,* p. 639.

12. See George Fisher, *The Soviet System and Modern Society* (New York: Atherton Press, 1968), especially pp. 1–18, 135–153.

13. For a discussion of congruence and consonance in authority relations, see Eckstein, *Authority Patterns,* and his "A Theory of Stable Democracy," mimeographed (Center of International Studies, Princeton University, 1961).

14. Cyril Black, in A. Kassof, ed., *Prospects for Soviet Society* (New York: Praeger, 1968), p. 52 (emphasis added). Cf. Vernon Aspaturian's parallel argument in ibid., pp. 143–198.

15. Cf. R. Pipes, "The Solution of the Nationality Problem," *Studies on the Soviet Union,* 6 (1967), 35–47.

16. The latter involve, of course, the need to recruit or propitiate nationalist allies and potential revolutionary converts abroad.

17. See R. Pipes, *The Formation of the Soviet Union* (Cambridge, Mass.: Harvard University Press, 1954), pp. 49, 295–297, and chs. I, II, IV, VI; "The Forces of Nationalism," *Problems of Communism,* 13 (January–February 1964), 1–6.

18. Immanuel Wallerstein, "The Two Modes of Ethnic Consciousness: Soviet Central Asia in Transition?" in E. Allworth, ed., *The Nationality Question in Soviet Central Asia* (New York: Praeger, 1973), p. 168 (emphasis added).

19. Some of these circumstances are discussed in the sections that follow, especially those pertaining to the problems of modernization and the functions of heretical models.

20. See, for example, E. Goldhagen, ed., *Ethnic Minorities in the Soviet Union* (New York: Praeger, 1968); R. Conquest, *Soviet Nationalities Policy in Practice* (New York: Praeger, 1967).

21. See Allworth, "Regeneration in Central Asia," in Allworth, *Nationality Question,* pp. 3–18, especially p. 15.

22. Ibid. See also Robert Barrett, "Convergence and the Nationality Literature of Central Asia," in Allworth, *Nationality Question,* pp. 19–34.

23. See Allworth, *Nationality Question,* especially the essays by Anna Procyk ("The Search for a Heritage," pp. 123–133); Eden Naby ("Tajik and Uzbek Nationality Identity," pp. 110–120); and Barry Rosen ("An Awareness of Traditional Tajik Identity," pp. 61–72).

24. See Allworth, *Nationality Question,* especially the essays by Procyk, Naby, and Barrett.

25. See Barrett's essay in Allworth, *Nationality Question.* Cf. A. Bennigsen et al., *Islam in the Soviet Union* (New York: Praeger, 1967), pp. 208–230; H. Achminow, "Social Conflicts in Soviet Central Asia," *Studies on the Soviet Union,* 7 (1968), 79–98; G. Hodnett, "The Debate over Soviet Federalism, *Soviet Studies,* 18 (April 1967), 458ff.

26. For some fragmentary indications of this trend, see Allworth, *Nationality Question,* especially the essays by John Hanselman ("Leadership and Nationality," pp. 100–109); Mobin Shorish ("Who shall be educated," pp. 86–98); and Barry Rosen (pp. 61–72).

27. See Bennigsen et al., *Islam in the Soviet Union*, pp. 195, 222–230.

28. See, for example, Mobin Shorish, "Who Shall Be Educated," in Allworth, *Nationality Question*, pp. 86–99.

29. See, for example, R. S. Clem, "The Impact of Demographic and Socioeconomic Forces upon the Nationality Question in Soviet Central Asia," in Allworth, *Nationality Question*, pp. 35–44. Cf. D. Carlisle's observations in *Problems of Communism*, 16 (September–October 1967), 134; V. Conolly, *Beyond the Urals* (London: Oxford University Press, 1967), pp. 356–358.

30. See Fainsod, *How Russia Is Ruled*, p. 495.

31. For a discussion of the function of heretical models in Central Asia, albeit in a different context, see Massell, *Surrogate Proletariat*, especially pp. 249–251.

32. R. D. Hansen, "Regional Integration," *World Politics*, 21 (January 1969), 270.

33. Needless to say, such a consideration is admittedly based, even more than in other cases we have discussed, on inference and fragmentary evidence rather than on hard data (no one has access to the latter, perhaps not even Moscow).

34. There may be new additions to the list of outside challenges in the coming decades when, flushed with oil-money and eager to resurrect the glory of past empires, some of the renascent Moslem powers along Russia's southern frontiers may seek to influence the spiritual and political evolution of their coreligionists and kinsmen in Soviet Central Asia.

35. It is a suggestive datum that recent Soviet discussions of the objective need to "encourage" greater native migration to Central Asian cities have been marked by ambiguity as well as ambivalence. On the one hand, Central Asians are now viewed as, by and large, inexplicably "immobile"—somehow uninterested in moving to their own cities in large numbers. On the other hand, their proposed urbanization is envisioned in the context of building *new* cities to handle the hoped-for native influx, or of enlarging small provincial (hence largely native) towns. The local migration process, if at all encouraged, would apparently exclude the movement of natives into the region's large urban centers, where Europeans, for the most part, already constitute an absolute majority. See V. Perevedentsev, "Step Out of the Village . . . ," *Komsomolskaia Pravda*, January 28, 1976, p. 2, trans. in *The Current Digest of the Soviet Press*, vol. XXVIII, no. 4, February 25, 1976.

36. Of course, this pressure may be relieved to some extent through the expansion of arable or otherwise usable land (through irrigation, for example), which has indeed been Moscow's policy so far. But a heavy emphasis on this policy alone—one that is inherently limited, in any case, by the relative scarcity of suitable land—would further accentuate the Central Asians' growing concentration in rural milieus. By the same token, it would also help to preserve local customs and traditions in the rural hinterland, clearly vitiating long-term Soviet revolutionary initiatives. In fact, the preser-

vation of local traditional patterns could only reinforce two long-term ethnocentric and communocentric tendencies in the region: the Central Asians' very low rates of intermarriage with European nationalities, and their relatively high identification with their ancestral languages as their primary means of communication.

37. For some recent important indications of Soviet concern about the rise of a "surplus" population in Central Asia, and about the imperatives and problems of "removing" this surplus elsewhere, see V. Perevedentsev, "Step Out of the Village . . . " For an interesting discussion of the implications of the last of these options—involving dispersal—see Immanuel Wallerstein, in Allworth, *Nationality Question*, especially pp. 173–175. Cf. John Armstrong's notion of an "internal proletariat" in Goldhagen, *Ethnic Minorities in the Soviet Union*, especially the discussion beginning on p. 7.

38. These are, of course, but a few of the imaginable options. Some other possibilities could be readily deduced, but they would be even more problematic than the ones already mentioned, and thus even less likely to be found acceptable. For example—to cite but one obvious constraining option—Moscow might consider encouraging or enforcing systematic birth control among Moslems (whose birthrate is now the highest in the USSR) without applying the same policy to Europeans, including Slavs. Needless to say, such selective control of human reproduction would inevitably invite charges of ethnic genocide, and is likely to fan precisely those fires of suspicion and resentment Moscow has been trying to dampen for over fifty years.

15    PEACEFUL COEXISTENCE
*Paul Marantz*

1. V. I. Lenin, *Collected Works*, 4th ed., 45 vols. (Moscow: Progress, 1960–1970), XXX, 365; XXXII, 317; XXXIII, 385, 387; XLII, 195–196; *Christian Science Monitor*, December 17, 1919, p. 1.

2. Lenin, *Collected Works*, XXX, 365.

3. Ibid., XXXIII, 387.

4. V. I. Lenin, *Sochineniia*, 4th ed., 45 vols. (Moscow, 1941–1967), XXXII, 295–296. In Lenin, *Collected Works*, XXXII, 317, there is a slightly different translation of this sentence.

5. It is interesting to note that not even once did Lenin, the supposed originator of the current doctrine of peaceful coexistence, even use the official phrase for peaceful coexistence, *mirnoe sosuschestvovanie*. Instead he used a different phrase, *mirnoe sozhitel'stvo*, which can be translated as "peaceful coexistence," but which literally means "peaceful cohabitation" (from the word *zhitel'stvo* meaning "dwelling").

6. For valuable discussions of the early roots of the doctrine of coexistence, see Dale Terence Lahey, "Soviet Ideological Development of Coexistence: 1917–1927," *Canadian Slavonic Papers*, VI (1964), 80–94; Franklyn

Griffiths, "Origins of Peaceful Coexistence: A Historical Note," *Survey*, no. 50 (January 1964), pp. 195–201.

7. L. Trotsky, *Sochineniia* (Moscow: Gosudarstvennoe Izdatelstvo, n.d.), vol. III, part ii, p. 163.

8. Ibid., p. 165.

9. Ibid. Also see ibid., p. 326.

10. J. V. Stalin, *Works*, 13 vols. (Moscow: Foreign Languages Publishing House, 1952–1955), V, 157. Also see ibid., p. 18, 23, 37, 59, 158, 193.

11. S. Studenikina, ed., *Istoriia Sovetskoi Konstitutsii* (Moscow, 1957), pp. 459, 460. As late as his speech to the Fourteenth Party Congress in December 1925, Stalin was still referring to the "co-existence and fraternal co-operation" of the peoples of the Soviet Union. (Stalin, *Works*, VII, 299.)

12. Stalin, *Works*, VII, 268. Also see ibid., pp. 293–295.

13. Lahey, "Ideological Development," pp. 90–93.

14. Kathryn W. Davis, *The Soviets at Geneva* (Geneva: Librairie Kundig, 1934), p. 202.

15. Stalin, *Works*, X, 295 (emphasis in the original).

16. Duclos' accusations against Browder are excerpted in Robert V. Daniels, ed., *A Documentary History of Communism*, 2 vols. (New York: Random House, 1960), II, 139–142.

17. J. V. Stalin, *Sochineniia*, 3 vols. (Stanford: Hoover Institution Press, 1967), I, 128; III, 104, 305–306.

18. *The Current Digest of the Soviet Press*, vol. I, no. 52 (1950), pp. 3–6.

19. Ibid., vol. II, no. 13 (1950), pp. 15–16.

20. Ibid., no. 17 (1950), pp. 12–15.

21. Ibid., vol. I, no. 52 (1950), p. 3.

22. Marshall Shulman's *Stalin's Foreign Policy Reappraised* (New York: Atheneum, 1965) has sometimes been misinterpreted on this point. He clearly does not argue that peaceful coexistence meant the same to Stalin and Khrushchev. Although Shulman stresses the importance of continuity in Soviet foreign policy, he is also aware of the very limited meaning given to peaceful coexistence under Stalin: "The concept of peaceful coexistence has always had a variety of meanings, both before and after Stalin. In the sense in which it was used at the Nineteenth Congress, it implied no conciliation with the West, no prospect of settlements, no soft words for the Western leaders" (p. 252).

23. Elliot R. Goodman, *The Soviet Design for a World State* (New York: Columbia University Press, 1960), p. 185; Henry A. Kissinger, *The Troubled Partnership* (New York: McGraw-Hill, 1965), p. 192; Wladyslaw W. Kulski, *Peaceful Co-existence* (Chicago: Regnery, 1959), pp. 127–137.

24. *Current Digest of the Soviet Press*, vol. V, no. 30 (1953), pp. 3–12; VI, no. 11 (1954), pp. 6–8.

25. Further evidence is provided by Malenkov's speech of March 15, 1953. In this speech he adopted a moderate and conciliatory tone. He declared: "At the present time there is no disputed or unresolved question

that cannot be settled peacefully by mutual agreement of the interested countries. This applies to our relations with all states, including the United States of America." Yet this speech contains no mention of peaceful coexistence. Ibid., vol. V, no. 8 (1953), p. 5.

26. The following sources were used: for 1950–1964, *The Current Digest of the Soviet Press*; for 1926–1949, *Pravda*; and for 1918–1925, Harold D. Lasswell et al., *The Language of Politics* (New York: G. W. Stewart, 1949), pp. 253–257. It appears that for some reason no May Day slogans were issued in 1921 and 1923. (Lasswell, *Language of Politics*, p. 243.)

27. A compilation of all the books published during a given year is contained in *Ezhegodnik Knigi SSSR* published regularly since the second half of 1941. The author consulted the volumes covering the years 1945–1960 (Moscow, 1946–1962). A week by week breakdown is available for the entire period since 1917 in *Knizhnaia Letopis*. Some of the periods of highest probability (for example, 1927) were examined, but since more than one thousand separate weekly lists are involved for the period 1917–1940, an exhaustive search could not be made. In all the primary and secondary source material examined, the author has not encountered a single reference to a book on peaceful coexistence published in the Soviet Union before 1955.

28. N. S. Khrushchev, *Report of the Central Committee of the Soviet Union to the 20th Party Congress* (Moscow: Foreign Languages Publishing House, 1956), p. 38.

29. Ibid., p. 35.

30. Ibid., p. 40.

31. Ibid., pp. 24, 25.

32. Ibid., pp. 40–41.

33. Philip E. Mosely, "The Meanings of Coexistence," *Foreign Affairs*, 41 (October 1962), 36–46; Sir William Hayter, "The Meaning of Coexistence," *Survey*, no. 50 (January 1964), pp. 23–29; Gustav A. Wetter, "The Soviet Concept of Coexistence," *Soviet Survey*, no. 30 (October–December 1959), pp. 19–34. A notable exception is Robert C. Tucker's pioneering study, "Dialetics of Coexistence," in *The Soviet Political Mind* (New York: Norton, 1963), pp. 201–222.

34. Khrushchev's revision of Marxist-Leninist doctrine is examined in detail in my Ph.D. dissertation, "The Soviet Union and the Western World: A Study in Doctrinal Change, 1917–1964" (Harvard University, 1971).

35. *The Current Digest of the Soviet Press*, vol. IX, no. 24 (1957), p. 6.

36. The text of the resolution is reprinted in Robert Conquest, *Power and Policy in the USSR* (New York: Harper and Row, 1967), pp. 458–463. Also see "Leninskii kurs na mirnoe sosushchestvovanie," *Kommunist*, no. 11 (1957), pp. 3–11; "For a Leninist Peace Policy," *International Affairs*, no. 7 (1957), pp. 5–10; B. Leontev, "O mirnom sosushchestvovanii stran s razlichnymi sotsialnymi sistemami," *V Pomoshch Politicheskomu Samoobrazovaniiu*, no. 7 (1957), pp. 50–59.

37. For example, see *The Current Digest of the Soviet Press*, vol. XIV, no. 45 (1962), p. 7, and XV, no. 21 (1963), p. 5.

38. Khrushchev, *Report to the Central Committee*, p. 46. Also see Khrushchev's statement to the Twenty-Second Party Congress in *The Current Digest of the Soviet Press*, vol. XIII, no. 41 (1961), p. 7.

39. V. Golikov, "Vazhnyi printsip leninskoi vneshnei politiki," *Kommunist*, no. 18 (1965), pp. 98–99; V. Popov, "Vneshnaia politika SSSR," *Voprosy Istorii*, no. 10 (1966), p. 157; V. Yegorov, *Mirnoe Sosushchestvovanie i Revoliutsionnyi Protsess* (Moscow: Izdatelstvo "Mezhdunarodnye Otnosheniia," 1971), pp. 160–167.

40. See Brezhnev's speech of November 6, 1964, in *The Current Digest of the Soviet Press*, vol. XVI, no. 43 (1964), p. 8. Similar formulations are to be found in Brezhnev's reports to the Twenty-Third and Twenty-Fourth Party Congresses. (Ibid., XVIII, no. 21 [1966], p. 34; XXIII, no. 12 [1971], p. 4.) Changes in the official attitude toward peaceful coexistence are graphically reflected in the different editions of the *Diplomaticheskii Slovar* (Diplomatic Dictionary). The 1948–1950 edition has not even a single entry for "peaceful coexistence." In the next edition (1960–1964) it receives more than six columns. In the post-Khrushchev revision, peaceful coexistence is still treated as quite important, but it is accorded less space, fewer than four columns.

41. The text of this declaration is contained in *The Current Digest of the Soviet Press*, vol. XXIV, no. 22 (1972), pp. 22–23.

42. A good example is G. Arbatov's authoritative article in *Kommunist*, no. 3 (1973), translated in *The Current Digest of the Soviet Press*, vol. XXV, no. 14 (1973), pp. 1–8. For an extensive compilation of Soviet statements on peaceful coexistence from both the pre- and post-1964 periods, see Foy D. Kohler et al., *Soviet Strategy for the Seventies* (Miami: University of Miami, 1973).

43. This aspect of Khrushchev's foreign policy is treated in Adam B. Ulam, *Expansion and Coexistence*, 2nd ed. (New York: Praeger, 1974), ch. 11; Vernon V. Aspaturian, "Foreign Policy Perspectives in the Sixties," in Alexander Dallin and Thomas B. Larson, eds., *Soviet Politics since Khrushchev* (Englewood Cliffs, N.J.: Prentice-Hall, 1968), pp. 129–162.

44. In March 1972 Brezhnev somewhat surprisingly said that it might be possible to accede to a Chinese proposal that relations between the two countries be based on the principle of peaceful coexistence. It would appear that he made this statement not with any intention of broadening the scope of peaceful coexistence, but for the very different purpose of emphasizing just how far China had distanced itself from the Socialist camp. (*The Current Digest of the Soviet Press*, vol. XXIV, no. 12 [1972], p. 8.) Brezhnev reiterated this position in his speech to the Twenty-Fifth Party Congress. (*Pravda*, February 25, 1976, p. 2.)

16    GLOBAL POWER RELATIONSHIPS IN THE SEVENTIES
*Robert H. Donaldson*

1. See, for example, Michel Tatu, "The Great Power Triangle: Washington-Moscow-Peking," *Atlantic Review*, no. 3 (December 1970); Zbigniew Brzezinski, "The New Triangle," *Newsweek*, June 28, 1971.

2. President Nixon expressed his views in a speech in Kansas City on July 6, 1971. For a critique of the alleged Nixon-Kissinger vision of a pentagonal "balance of power" world, see Stanley Hoffmann, "Weighing the Balance of Power," *Foreign Affairs*, 50 (July 1972), 618–643.

3. See Hoffmann's article cited above, and his *Gulliver's Troubles, or the Setting of American Foreign Policy* (New York: McGraw-Hill, 1968), ch. 2.

4. Vernon V. Aspaturian, "The Soviet Military-Industrial Complex—Does It Exist?" *Journal of International Affairs*, 26 (1972), 1–28. See also Alexander Dallin, "Soviet Foreign Policy and Domestic Politics: A Framework for Analysis," *Journal of International Affairs*, 23 (1969), 250–265.

5. For an excellent analysis of the Soviet world view before 1968, see William Zimmerman, *Soviet Perspectives on International Relations 1956–1967* (Princeton: Princeton University Press, 1969).

6. A. Sovetov, "The Leninist Policy of Peace and the Future of Mankind," *International Affairs* (Moscow), July 1972, pp. 3–10.

7. See V. M. Berezhkov, "Soviet-U.S. Relations and the Modern World," *SShA: Ekonomika, politika, ideologia*, September 1973, pp. 3–14; Anatoly Gromyko and A. Kokoshkin, "U.S. Foreign Policy Strategy in the Seventies," *International Affairs*, September 1973, pp. 87–96.

8. May 1972, pp. 63–66.

9. Gromyko and Kokoshkin, "U.S. Foreign Policy Strategy," pp. 87–96.

10. Berezhkov, "Soviet-U.S. Relations," pp. 3–14; Georgii Arbatov, "Soviet-U.S. Relations at a New Stage," *Pravda*, July 22, 1973, pp. 4–5.

11. Gromyko and Kokoshkin, "U.S. Foreign Policy Strategy," pp. 87–96.

12. Leonid Zamyatin and Valentin Zorin, on Moscow Television, August 10, 1974, in *Foreign Broadcast Information Service: Soviet Union*, August 12, 1974.

13. *Pravda*, August 10, 1974.

14. Arbatov, "Soviet-U.S. Relations," pp. 4–5.

15. "Soviet-American Summit Talks," *SShA: Ekonomika, politika, ideologia*, August 1973, p. 3.

16. *Pravda*, June 30, 1973, p. 1.

17. Arbatov, "Soviet-U.S. Relations," pp. 4–5.

18. Georgii Arbatov, "On Soviet-American Relations," *Kommunist*, no. 3 (1973), pp. 101–113.

19. See *Pravda*, August 22, 1973, and *Kommunist*, no. 14 (1973), pp. 3–23.

20. Vikentii Matveyev, "Positive Changes," *Izvestiia*, April 19, 1973, p. 2.

21. *Pravda*, November 30, 1973.

22. "The Strength of a Policy of Realism," *Izvestiia*, June 22, 1972, pp. 3–4, in *Current Digest of the Soviet Press* (hereafter *CDSP*), 24 (1972), 4–6. (Emphasis added.)

23. Thomas W. Wolfe, "Soviet Approaches to SALT," *Problems of*

*Communism,* 19 (September–October 1970), 1–10. See also his *Soviet Interests in SALT: Political, Economic, Bureaucratic and Strategic Contributions and Impediments to Arms Control,* RAND Monograph P-4702 (Santa Monica, Calif.: Rand, 1971).

24. "Agreements of Historic Importance," *International Affairs,* August 1972, pp. 14–20.

25. "Soviet Foreign Policy: Steadfast and Consistent," *New Times,* no. 18 (1972), p. 20.

26. "The Real Forces of International Development," *Pravda,* June 15, 1972, pp. 4–5.

27. *Pravda,* June 15, 1974.

28. *Pravda,* July 12, 1973.

29. *Krasnaya zvezda,* July 9, 1974.

30. *Pravda,* February 23, 1974.

31. Georgii Arbatov, "The Impasses of the Policy of Force," *Problemy mira i sotsializma,* February 1974, pp. 41–47.

32. *Nedelya,* no. 46 (1974), p. 14.

33. N. A. Milshtein and L. S. Semeyko, "The Problem of the Inadmissability of a Nuclear Conflict (New Approaches in the United States)," *SShA: Ekonomika, politika, ideologia,* November 1974, pp. 2–13.

34. *Pravda,* November 25, 1974.

35. *Izvestia,* November 25, 1974.

36. *Izvestia,* June 21, 1972, pp. 1, 3.

37. "Vital Tasks of Ideological Work," *Pravda,* July 8, 1972, p. 1.

38. *Pravda,* June 5, 1974.

39. *Pravda,* October 18, 1974.

40. *Pravda,* August 7, 1973.

41. *New Times,* no. 39, 1974.

42. M. Ukraintsev, "Asia and the Peking Empire-Builders," *New Times,* no. 23 (1970), p. 14.

43. *Pravda,* March 21, 1972, p. 3.

44. *Pravda,* October 7, 1974.

45. D. Vostokov, "The Foreign Policy of the People's Republic of China since the 9th Congress of the CPC," *International Affairs,* January 1972, pp. 23–25.

46. O. Ivanov, "With Whom, against Whom: A Look at Certain Modifications of Peking Policy," *New Times,* no. 35 (1972), pp. 4–5.

47. Tatu, "Great Power Triangle," December 1970.

48. Brzezinski, "New Triangle," June 28, 1971.

49. V. P. Lukin, "American-Chinese Relations: Concept and Reality," *SShA: Ekonomika, politika, ideologia,* February 1973, pp. 12–23, in *CDSP,* 25, no. 2 (1973), p. 5.

50. Ibid., p. 7.

51. Some of what follows is drawn from my book, *Soviet Policy toward India: Ideology and Strategy* (Cambridge, Mass.: Harvard University Press, 1974), pp. 218–241.

52. *Izvestia*, May 29, 1969, p. 3.

53. L. I. Brezhnev, *For a Greater Unity of Communists, for a Fresh Upsurge of the Anti-Imperialist Struggle* (Moscow, 1969), p. 53.

54. See Peter Howard, "A System of Collective Security," *Mizan*, 11 (1969), 201.

55. " 'System of Collective Security in Asia'—Soviet Revisionism's Tattered Flag for an Anti-China Military Alliance," *Peking Review*, no. 27 (1969), pp. 22–23, 32–33.

56. G. Dudin and A. Usvatov, "Soviet-Indian Treaty in Action," *New Times*, no. 39 (1971), pp. 10–11.

57. *Pravda*, March 21, 1972, p. 3.

58. *Pravda*, June 21, 1972, p. 4. See also two articles by V. Pavlovsky: "Collective Security: The Way to Peace in Asia," *International Affairs*, July 1972, pp. 23–27, and "Asia: Regional Cooperation and Collective Security," *New Times*, no. 30 (1972), pp. 18–20.

59. Viktor Mayevsky, *Pravda*, June 21, 1972, p. 4.

60. Ivanov, "With Whom, against Whom," no. 35 (1972), pp. 4–5. See also V. Pavlov, "Europe in Peking's Plans," *International Affairs*, March 1972, pp. 15–17, and I. Aleksandrov, "On Certain Tactical Features of the Peking Leadership's Current Policy," *Pravda*, September 5, 1972, pp. 4–5.

61. For the statement of principles in the Asian case, see Brezhnev's speech above. In the European case, see N. I. Lebedev, "Exchange of Opinion," *International Affairs*, May 1972, pp. 67–68.

62. "Integrity and Effectiveness of Soviet Foreign Policy," *Pravda*, June 9, 1972, pp. 4–5, in *CDSP*, 24 (1972), p. 3.

63. Vikenti Matveyev, "European Security and NATO," *International Affairs*, February–March 1970, pp. 91–92.

64. E. Novoseltsev, "Europe Twenty-Five Years Later," *International Affairs*, July 1970, pp. 21–22. (Emphasis in original.)

65. *Pravda*, September 26, 1973.

## 17 SOVIET POLITICS
### Zbigniew Brzezinski

1. On this see A. M. Kleimola, "The Duty to Denounce in Muscovite Russia," *Slavic Review*, December 1972, especially pp. 777–779.

2. On use of the census, see Karl A. Wittfogel, "Russia and the East: A Comparison and Contrast," *Slavic Review*, December 1963, especially pp. 638–640.

3. E. H. Carr, *Socialism in One Country*, vol. 1 (Baltimore: Penguin Books, 1970), p. 25.

4. This emerged extremely well from I. Deutscher's *The Prophet Unarmed* (London: Oxford University Press, 1959).

5. Jerry F. Hough, "The Soviet System: Petrification or Pluralism?" *Problems of Communism*, 21 (March–April 1972).

6. Roy Medvedev, *On Socialist Democracy* (New York: Alfred A.

Knopf, 1975), pp. 67–68. Medvedev develops in his book a much more detailed analysis of the outlook of various oppositionist groups and concludes with a lengthy statement of the desirable evolution towards socialist democracy in the Soviet Union.

7. Ibid., p. 107.

8. For an earlier attempt to discuss it, see my *Between Two Ages,* ch. 4, in which different futures for the Soviet system are discussed. For a perceptive critique, including of my own views, see William Taubman, in Henry W. Morton and Rudolf W. Tokes, eds., *Soviet Politics and Society in the 1970's* (New York: Free Press, 1974), ch. 10, "The Change to Change in Communist Systems: Modernization, Postmodernization, and Soviet Politics."

9. I am sympathetic to the arguments developed by Joseph Ben-David, "How to Organize Research in the Social Sciences," in *Daedalus* (Spring 1973).

10. Vladimir Shubkin, " 'Bank Grez' i Balans Sudeb," *Literaturnaia Gazeta*, no. 2 (January 8, 1975), p. 11.

11. Medvedev, *On Socialist Democracy,* p. 90.

# Contributors

ZBIGNIEW BRZEZINSKI is Director of the Research Institute on International Change and Herbert Lehman Professor of Government at Columbia University. His books include *The Soviet Bloc* and *Between Two Ages.*

DONALD S. CARLISLE, Associate Professor of Political Science at Boston College and an Associate at Harvard's Russian Research Center, is the author of the Uzbek section in Zev Katz et al., editors, *Handbook of Major Soviet Nationalities.*

PAUL COCKS is a Research Fellow at the Hoover Institution and Lecturer in Political Science at Stanford University. He is the author of a study on the scientific-technical revolution and Soviet politics and coeditor of *Political Development in Eastern Europe.*

ROBERT V. DANIELS is Professor of History at the University of Vermont. His books include *The Conscience of the Revolution* and *Red October.*

ROBERT H. DONALDSON, Associate Professor of Political Science and Associate Dean of the College of Arts and Science at Vanderbilt University, is the author of *Soviet Policy toward India: Ideology and Strategy.*

TERESA RAKOWSKA-HARMSTONE is Professor of Political Science at Carleton University in Ottawa. She is the author of *Russia and Nationalism in Central Asia: The Case of Tadzhikistan* and coeditor of *Communist States in Disarray.*

NANCY WHITTIER HEER is Dean of the College and Professor of Government at Wheaton College, Norton, Massachusetts. She is the author of *Politics and History in the Soviet Union* and coeditor of *Windows on the Russian Past: Essays on Recent Soviet Historiography.*

JOHN H. HODGSON, Professor of Political Science at Syracuse University, is the author of *Communism in Finland: A History and Interpretation* and *Den rode eminensen O. W. Kuusinens politiska biografi.*

JERRY F. HOUGH, Professor of Political Science at Duke University, is the author of *The Soviet Prefects: The Local Party Organs in Industrial Decision-making* and *The Soviet Union and Social Science Theory.*

GAIL WARSHOFSKY LAPIDUS is Lecturer in the Department of Political Science and Research Associate at the Institute of International Studies of the University of California, Berkeley. Her publications include, "Political Mobilization, Participation and Leadership: Women in Soviet Politics" in *Comparative Politics,* and *Women in Soviet Society: Equality Development and Social Change.*

PAUL MARANTZ is Assistant Professor of Political Science at the University of British Columbia. He has contributed articles to *International Studies Quarterly, Western Political Quarterly, Soviet Union* and *International Perspectives.*

GREGORY J. MASSELL, Professor of Political Science and Chairman, Russian Area Studies Graduate Program, Hunter College, City University of New York, is the author of *The Surrogate Proletariat: Moslem Women and Revolutionary Strategies in Soviet Central Asia, 1919–1929* and a contributor to *Politics and Society: Studies in Comparative Political Sociology,* edited by Eric A. Nordlinger.

ROBERT F. MILLER is Senior Fellow at the Research School of Social Sciences of the Australian National University, Canberra. He is the author of *One Hundred Thousand Tractors: The MTS and the Development of Controls in Soviet Agriculture* and coauthor of *Political and Administrative Aspects of the Scientific and Technical Revolution in the USSR.*

RICHARD M. MILLS, Associate Professor of Political Science at Fordham University, is the author of "One Theory in Search of Reality: The Development of United States Studies in the Soviet Union," and "The Formation of the Virgin Lands Policy."

RUTH MOULY is an employment interviewer in the Bureau of Employment Security of the Commonwealth of Pennsylvania. She has contributed essays to *We Propose: A Modern Congress* and *Soviet Society: A Book of Readings.*

DINA SPECHLER is Lecturer in Political Science at Tel Aviv University. Her publications include "The Russians" in Zev Katz et al., editors, *Handbook of Major Soviet Nationalities,* and "The Human Cost of US–Soviet Trade" in *Worldview.*

ADAM B. ULAM is Professor of Government and an Associate at the Russian Research Center at Harvard University. His publications include *Ideologies and Illusions: Revolutionary Thought from Herzen to Solzhenitsyn* and *The New Face of Soviet Totalitarianism.*

# Index

# RUSSIAN RESEARCH CENTER STUDIES

*Out of print.

†Publications of the Harvard Project on the Soviet Social System.